Persuasive Communication

Persuasive Communication

FOURTH EDITION

Erwin P. Bettinghaus
Michigan State University

Michael J. Cody
University of Southern California

Holt, Rinehart and Winston, Inc.
New York   Chicago   San Francisco   Philadelphia
Montreal   Toronto   London   Sydney   Tokyo

Library of Congress Cataloging-in-Publication Data

Bettinghaus, Erwin Paul.
  Persuasive communication.
  Bibliography: p.
  Includes index.
  1. Persuasion (Psychology) I. Cody, Michael J.
II. Title.
BF637.P4B4   1987   303.3′4   86-25643
ISBN 0-03-063359-1

Printed in the United States of America.
       8   9   0   016   9   8   7   6   5   4   3

Preface

This is the fourth edition of *Persuasive Communication*. More than twenty years have passed since the first edition of *Persuasive Communication* was published in 1966, and the field has grown so fast that a single author simply can no longer handle all of the relevant areas adequately. Mike Cody has joined forces with Erv Bettinghaus on this fourth edition, and rather than searching desperately for those relatively few pieces of research that were available in 1966, the central task in preparing the fourth edition of *Persuasive Communication* became one of cutting, refining, and updating materials in order to keep the manuscript a reasonable size and still present the reader with a text that covers the major topics relevant to the field of persuasive communication today. Colleen Keough has contributed an important new chapter on negotiation for this edition.

It is hoped that this book will be of value to students enrolled in courses in persuasive speaking, in management communication, and in personal influence. Because it tries to examine the use of persuasion in contemporary situations, *Persuasive Communication* should also interest people who are concerned with public relations, labor-management problems, advertising directed toward social issues, and social action programs.

The authors have greatly benefited from the careful readings and suggestions made by a number of their colleagues. Peter Marston read the entire manuscript and was centrally important in reducing the size of the manuscript to a manageable size. Pat Cesarz put the entire manuscript on a word processor and patiently made all of the corrections that were needed. Chapters were read and criticized by Judee Burgoon, University of Arizona, Bill Donohue, Michigan State University, John Greene, Purdue University, Sandi Smith, Purdue University, Curtis Austin, Florida State University, Al Louden, Wake Forest University, Patricia Riley, University of Southern California, and several hundred undergraduates at U.S.C. We also wish to thank the following reviewers: Terrance L. Albrecht, University of Washington; Edward M. Bodaken, University of Southern California; Jesse Delia, University of Illinois; Kassian A. Kovalcheck, Vanderbilt University; John T. Marlier, Northeastern University; David Paine, University of Texas at Austin; Susan L. Sharpe, University of Wyoming; Don Sieker, New Hampshire College; Glenn Smith, University of Central Arkansas; and Ted Smith, University of Virginia-Charlottesville.

Finally, a special thanks must go to Cay and Peggy, who read some of the chapters and tolerated the whole effort with good humor and patience.

EPB
MJC

East Lansing, Michigan
Los Angeles, California

Contents

CHAPTER EIGHT

Structuring Messages and Appeals

CHAPTER NINE

Using Communication Channels Effectively

CHAPTER TEN

Persuasion in Interpersonal Relationships

CHAPTER ELEVEN

Bargaining As Persuasion

CHAPTER TWELVE

Persuasion in Small-Group and Legal Settings

Persuasive Communication

CHAPTER ONE

Persuasion and Communication

"Take me to the movies." "Abortion is murder. Vote against using our taxes for abortions." "If you vote for me for sheriff, I'll make sure that the criminals are behind bars and not roaming the streets." "All of the best scientists agree that smoking causes lung cancer. The sooner you quit, the better." "You can't take this medicine only when you feel like it. You have to take it two times a day, *every* day."

These are messages—messages sent from one person, or a group of persons, to another person or group of persons. Each message asks that you *do* something. You are asked to vote, take medicine, stop smoking, or do something you hadn't planned on doing. We call such messages *persuasive messages*, and their use in our society is the substance of this book.

Persuasion is an important part of the daily life of every human being. What we eat, what we wear, whom we listen to, what music we prefer, what church we go to, and whom we will vote for are all affected by persuasive communication. In fact, persuasion is used so frequently and is so pervasive in our daily lives that we often fail to recognize when we are using persuasive communication or when we are exposed to it.

There are many reasons why one should study, and become proficient in, the art and science of persuasion. We all want to be successful, to be recognized and promoted, to sell more goods or services, and so on. Beyond all of these concrete reasons, however, rests one fundamental benefit for why you need to become an expert in persuasion: In the last 40 years our population has grown, the interdependence among citizens has deepened, and our society has developed a keen sense of each individual's rights. As a consequence, persuasion has become one of the *few* socially acceptable methods of social control. In contrast to South Africa or Russia, groups, organizations, and governmental agencies in our society can no longer disenfranchise whole groups of people, they can no longer restrict people from membership on the basis of sex, creed, or religion, they cannot segregate people, they cannot coerce people into doing things, and they cannot incarcerate people without sufficient legal cause and the use of correct procedures. To influence others, people must exchange information, accurately transmit their messages and intentions, and identify and understand how other people are attempting to influence them.

To be effective in society today, a person needs to know as much as possible about the persuasion process. How are attitudes formed and changed? What types of receivers are most susceptible to fear appeals, emotional appeals, or reward appeals? When is it important to be an expert, a celebrity, a physically-attractive speaker, or a "likeable" one? How do you use language in order to be persuasive? How do you use nonverbal communication in order to be persuasive? What should you do to be effective in bargaining? On a jury? In an organization? Each of these questions will be addressed in this book, along with many other topics. First, however, we need to define what we mean by "persuasion."

Communication and persuasion

People *want* to communicate. Any time an innovation promising better communication comes along, millions of people rush to buy it. While television was the growth industry of the last 25 years, the personal computer promises to be the product of the next 25 years. The personal computer not only allows the individual to draw upon information contained in large data banks all over the world, it also allows people to communicate in ways never before available. Individuals as well as corporations spend billions of dollars each year in order to enhance their communication capabilities—to improve listening skills, the effectiveness of the company spokesperson, patients' compliance to medical recommendations, the comprehensibility of legal instructions/communications, and so on.

Many attempts have been made to define human communication. At the simplest level communication exists whenever one person transmits a message that is received by another individual and is acted upon by that individual. When a teacher walks into a room and says "Hello!" to a student who looks up and smiles, the teacher is engaging in a simple form of communication. He is acting as a *source* of communication, using symbols or stimuli that have shared meanings for individuals, as a *message* to be delivered or passed along some *channel*, to someone who is a *receiver* of communication.

These four elements—source, message, channel, and receiver—are present in every communication situation. As situations become more and more complicated, the basic elements remain, although we may have more than one source, more than one receiver, many messages spread out over time, and several different channels being used. As communication situations become increasingly complex, the models we must derive to explain those situations also become more complex. Such elaborations have been provided by Berlo,[1] Gerbner,[2] Schramm,[3] Westley and McLean,[4] and Shannon and Weaver.[5]

Persuasion always involves communication. To illustrate the difference between "a communication situation" and "a *persuasive* communication situation," let us contrast two situations: The first is the one we used above, where a teacher walks into a room, and says "Hello" to a student. For the second situation, imagine that same teacher walking into a room and saying, "Will you go to the library for me?" The student in the first situation looks up and smiles. In the second, the student looks up and says, "Of course. What do you need from the library?" In both situations, there is a source of communication and a receiver of communication. In both situations, there is a message being transmitted, and the use of an oral channel to transmit the message. In both situations, the receiver makes a response to the message. The major difference lies in the intent of the source. The first situation is one in which the source does not expect any specific reaction from the receiver. The second, however, is one in which the source hopes that the receiver will respond in a particular way to the message. The *intent* of the source was to influence the behavior of the receiver in a specified manner.

There is general agreement that the variable of *intent* is what distinguishes persuasive communication from other communication situations. *The Random House Dictionary* says that persuasion implies ". . . influencing someone's thoughts or actions."[6] Andersen says that "Persuasion is a communication process in which the communicator seeks to elicit a desired response."[7] Scheidel, in writing about persuasive speaking, says that it is ". . . that activity in which speaker and listener are conjoined and in which the speaker consciously attempts to influence the behavior of the listener by transmitting audible and visible symbolic cues."[8] Bostrom defines persuasion as ". . . communicative behavior that has as its purpose the changing, modification, or shaping of the responses (attitudes or behavior) of the receivers."[9] Each of these definitions emphasizes that persuasion involves a conscious effort at influencing the thoughts or actions of a receiver. Any message might have an effect on the behavior of any recipient of the message, whether the effect was intended or not. For example, you might overhear someone saying to another, "That movie is one of the best I've ever seen. It is an absolute must." Although the message was not intended for you, you might well decide to see the movie as a result of hearing the remark. We do not wish to label such situations as persuasive situations, although many of the elements of such situations are similar to persuasive situations. The argument has sometimes been made that since the effects of persuasive communication are frequently impossible to distinguish from outcomes of other communication situations, the insistence on *intent* as a necessary condition of persuasion makes little sense. We argue that it is necessary to preserve intent because we wish to include an ethics of persuasion as an essential part of the process. Obviously, if persuasion cannot be distinguished from any accidental communication situation, it is difficult to urge speakers and writers to some standard of ethical behavior in the message they create.

This book, therefore, is concerned with those situations in which people deliberately produce messages designed to elicit specific behavior or influence specific attitudes on the part of a receiver or group of receivers. As a minimal condition, to be labeled as persuasive, a communication situation must involve a *conscious attempt by one individual to change the attitudes, beliefs, or behavior of another individual or group of individuals through the transmission of some message.*

Studying persuasive communication

One of the most natural tendencies that people have is to view communication only from their own perspectives. If we are acting as a source of communication, and attempting to persuade someone else to do something, we normally do not think about what the other person is thinking about, or what the other person is getting ready to say to us. Similarly, if we are listening to a commercial on television, we do not usually ask ourselves anything about the motives or possible reactions of the source of the commercial. We tend to look at persuasion as a one-way process, and we seldom take the other person into account. Until very recently, most scholars and communication researchers also tended to study persuasion as a one-way process, occurring at a single moment in time. The research model that has most frequently been studied imagines that a receiver's attitudes have been determined. Then the receiver is exposed to a persuasive message; and after the message has been sent, the receiver's attitudes are measured again. If there is some change in attitude in favor of the message, we say that persuasion was successful. In similar fashion, experiments are designed that expose receivers to messages asking them to take some specific action. After the message is sent, the experimenter waits for a period of time, and then checks to see whether the receivers actually did what the message asked them to do. Again, the message is judged to be successful if some significant proportion of the audience actually voted for the candidate, attended the movie, or bought the product. This concept of persuasion as an essentially one-way process pervaded most of the experimental literature in the field until very recently.

The concept is no longer adequate. If we are to understand persuasive communication, we must extend our research and knowledge beyond this simple model. Persuasion must be viewed as an interactive process. At the same time a source is sending a message, the source is being influenced by the actions of the receiver for whom the message is intended. Messages are not sent in vacuums, although much of our research is conducted as if all possible effects were due to very simple causes. Both source and receiver are typically influenced by each other, as well as by activities that take place long before the message is actually sent. The realities are that sources and receivers are interchangeable, that when a source is trying to persuade you to her point of view, the source is also trying to understand your point of view, and is exposed to your message.

The interactional view requires that we study both Speaker A and Speaker B since the two speakers influence each other—nonverbally as well as verbally. Thus, interactive instances of persuasive communication occur when a lawyer adjusts her arguments when perceiving that the jury members are scowling, when one family member uses a hostile tactic to influence another family member, who reciprocates by also using a hostile tactic, or when management counters a bargaining move by a union. Let us look at how an interactive persuasive situation might differ from some experimental models developed and used in the past.

Suppose you wanted to look at a persuasive context relevant to many people in real life—what can you say to a police officer that would improve your odds of not getting a speeding ticket? You work out a list of arguments a driver may use,[10] and you want to know why drivers use the statements they do and if some of the statements lead to less ticketing. In a traditional, one-way model, one's emphasis is on the speaker, and we judge whether or not the speaker is successful if a significant proportion of the receivers believe the speaker and, in this example, let the speaker go with just a warning—not a ticket. You collect data concerning what the speaker says and how the receiver reacts, and you find out that some of the statements, as expected, lead to fewer ticketings than other statements. However, you notice that a number of drivers employed statements such as "No way. No way would I drive 83 mph—especially at night," or "You're wrong. Let me see your radar," or "I'll see you in court." Since you thought that drivers would generally be respectful to the police, you are surprised by how frequently people argued with the police. *Why* would they do so?

You decide to adopt an interactive model, believing that how the police ask people to account for why they are speeding influences what the drivers say. You thus find a number of patterns, including examples such as:

"The officer approached and, as asked, I gave him my license. He looked absolutely *disgusted* (with me). He said: 'Lady, that was a school zone back there. There were kids—Didn't you see the flashing light?' I said: 'Oh, I'm sorry—terribly sorry. I just didn't see it. We came through that alley and the kids and I were talking. I just didn't notice it. I would have slowed down. I'm usually more careful than that. . . .'

"The officer said: 'Ma'am, is there some reason why you were exceeding the speed limit?' I said: 'Well, yes, sir. I am in a hurry to get to X. I've been driving since 6 a.m. and the construction back in Y slowed me down. I'm all alone and I didn't want to be this far away from X when it was so dark. . . .'

"The officer said: 'Son, we clocked you going 80 mph. Step back here please.' I said: 'What???? You're kidding. *Me* drive 80? No way. . . .' "

Your analysis indeed indicates that how the officer interacts with the driver influences the type of argument made to the officer. In the first example, the officer's disgust (yet use of open-ended questions) led the driver to be more *apologetic*; the officer in the second example asked for *reasons*, and the driver gave more reasons; and in the last example, the officer was more aggressive and the driver felt falsely accused of the particular offense, and thus denied driving 80 mph. There are, then, a number of contexts where adopting an interactive perspective may provide us with a more complete analysis of persuasion, and a more thorough understanding of behavior.

Basic factors in persuasion

A selection of the major factors that might account for persuasive changes is difficult. In any given situation, seemingly trivial factors may play a decisive role. Studies conducted by Gerald Miller[11] on the use of video-tape in the courtroom illustrate the importance of such factors. In one situation, the experimenters were testing whether a woman claiming a back injury was persuasive with a simulated jury under a number of different circumstances. In one of the experimental situations, however, a jury member noticed that the woman was wearing high heels. The jury member convinced the rest of the panel that the woman had to be lying, because someone with a serious back injury would not be able to wear high heels. The audience change was thus due not to the actual message that had been sent, but to a factor that appeared to be completely unrelated to the experimental condition. Obviously, it is im-

possible to take account of all such minor factors in persuasive communication.

Further, different receivers are affected differently by the same persuasive message. Thus, an examination of the differences between receivers is in order. Some may be demographic in nature, such as differences in age, sex, education, race, or occupation. A second set of factors may be psychological in nature and include such influences as motivation to respond, cognitive balance, and various personality factors.

Of central importance to our analysis is the fact that differences between sources affect persuasion. Study after study has demonstrated that when two different sources send exactly the same message, receivers do not respond in identical fashion to the two sources. Thus we shall be looking at source credibility, social power, societal role, relationship to the receiver, and various demographic characteristics as factors in persuasion.

When people are exposed to messages, they are most likely to be affected by the topic or content of the message, but it is also important to examine the effects of systematic variation in the appeals or arguments used, the organizational structure of the message, the language characteristics embodied in the message, and the stylistic design of the message.

Early persuasive communication research looked closely at the "channels" used to transmit messages. Was it better to be in a face-to-face situation with a receiver, or would telephone or radio serve just as well? Differences in the channel used to carry a persuasive message are important, and we shall review the research literature in that area.

A final variable in persuasion is the nature of the situation in which it occurs. If you want to convince someone to donate to the United Fund, is it better to meet the person privately, or over lunch with a number of other people present? Obviously, there can be an almost infinite number of kinds of situations within which communication *can* take place. Only a few such variations have been carefully studied. Included are situations where persuasion occurs in the presence of a group of individuals, where the setting is either familiar or unfamiliar to the receiver, where the situation is pleasant or unpleasant, and settings involving formal organizations such as a corporation, the courtroom, or the city council.

Basic factors in persuasion thus include:

1. similarities and differences between sources and receivers,
2. variations in the content of messages,
3. variations in message organization or style,
4. differences in the channels used to conduct persuasion,
5. differences in the nature of the situation in which persuasion takes place.

Each of these factors can be expected to produce differential responses on the part of receivers, and should trigger different kinds of messages on the part of sources. It is the extremely large number of possible outcomes that makes persuasion both so difficult and so interesting.

The effects of persuasion

Persuasion is linked to changes in attitudes, beliefs, or behavior. In the examples used thus far, the inference might be drawn that the effects of a persuasive message are always immediately observable. Such a conclusion is seldom justified in real life. Imagine listening to a speaker who advocated raising taxes in order to build an addition to the local high school. Before the speech, a listener might declare flatly, "No more taxes. I am tired of all these people coming here and asking for more money." The speech is dynamic, and the speaker has taken great care to point out how each member of the community will benefit from the proposed new addition. After the speech, our listener says, "I'm still opposed to more taxes, but that speaker was really great."

The speaker did not succeed in getting our listener's vote with that one speech, but do we want to say that the speech had *no* effect? Certainly *something* happened to the listener as a result of listening to the speech. The effect or outcome was not precisely what was intended, but further speeches might lead our listener to eventually vote for the proposed school addition. Changes in a receiver's attitudes or behavior frequently take place in small, incremental steps, and may be difficult to assess at any particular point in time. It is inaccurate to attempt to make final judgments about the effects of persuasive messages in terms of immediately observable behavior. There are very likely to be both short-run effects as well as long-run effects to any message.

To understand persuasion, we must also understand what is meant by "attitude." We will examine the concept of attitude closely in the next section, but we need a general understanding in order to look at the kinds of changes we can expect in persuasive communication. Rosenberg and Hovland[12] suggest that *attitudes* can be defined as general predispositions to response. In persuasive communication situations, attitudes are seen as predispositions toward three kinds of changes in behavior: (1) changes in *cognition*, (2) changes in *affect*, or (3) changes in *behavior*. Figure 1.1 is an adaptation of the model developed generally by Rosenberg and Hovland and illustrates the role that attitudes play in a persuasive communication situation.

Cognitions include the concepts we have, the beliefs we hold about various objects, the values we place on objects, and the perceptions we have of the world around us. Typically, changes in cognitions can be identified by the verbal statements that people make after being exposed to a persuasive message. For example, imagine that you are asked before a speech what you think about changing the legal drinking age in your state. You state that you are completely opposed to any change in the laws about the legal drinking age. Then you listen to a speaker talk about the possible advantages of raising the age limit to 21. After the speech, you are again asked what you think. If you reply that the speaker has not changed your mind, the conclusion would be that your cogni-

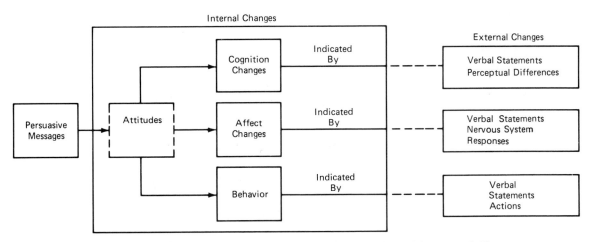

Figure 1.1. The Relationship of Attitude to Internal Change and to Observable External Change

tions had not changed, and we would say so on the basis of your verbal statements. If, on the other hand, you now say that there is merit in raising the age limit, we would conclude that a cognitive change had taken place. The change would be indicated by the change in your verbal statements.

Cognitive changes can also be indicated by changes in perceptions, that is, the way in which individuals see the world around them. Such indicators of change can be illustrated by a simple example. Imagine looking at a picture containing some "hidden objects." You look intently at the picture but fail to spot any of the objects. Then a friend says, "Look at the upper left-hand corner next to the tree trunk." You do so and find a hidden tennis racket. The chances are very good that when you look at the picture again, the tennis racket will seem to almost leap out of it. Your perceptions have been changed as a result of the message telling you where to look.

Perception changes are not limited to such simple examples as tennis rackets hidden in pictures. A man may drive through a New York slum and see some people as dirty, ragged, drunken derelicts. After he listens to a speech from a social worker in that area, he may begin to see the same people as sober and dressed in clean, worn clothing.

Affect changes are harder to describe. These are changes in our emotional states. Most people cannot tell us exactly how they feel, but when an experience is responsible for producing an emotional change, they know that the change has occurred. Affect changes are changes in mood, in emotions, and they may be indicated by laughing, crying, shivers running up and down the spine, and similar bodily events. In some cases, the psychologist working in the laboratory can show changes resulting from the presentation of messages through the use of instruments for detecting changes in heart rate, blood pressure, galvanic skin response, and sweating. Outside the laboratory, such instruments are not available, and we usually depend on verbal statements from receivers about emotional changes and the extent to which a particular persuasive message produced the change.

Regardless of the difficulties in indexing affect changes, there is ample evidence that these changes can result from persuasive communication. Examples may be noted when someone exclaims, "I cried at the ending of that movie," or "His speaking sent shivers up and down my spine," or "That book really discourages me." Fund raisers for charitable organizations frequently send persuasive messages attempting to make listeners or viewers feel sorry for the victims that the charity has been set up to help. For years, the Easter Seal campaign has been based on a poster showing a crippled child. The obvious intent of the campaign is to produce a sympathetic reaction on the part of receivers that will then be translated into writing a check for the campaign.

Finally, *behavior* changes resulting from persuasion must be discussed. In one sense, *any* observable change in behavior, including changes in the nervous system and verbal statements, could be called behavior changes since the individual is doing something, but it is helpful to distinguish between cognitive changes, emotional changes, and other types of overt, easily observable behavior. Getting an individual to agree, cognitively, that racial segregation is bad is far easier than getting that same individual to agree to stand on a street corner and hand out leaflets about racial segregation. Behavior changes, then, are changes in overt, physical actions that may result from attending to a particular persuasive message.

Behavior changes may become the focus of a persuasive communication situation. Helping clean up a river, marching against the construction of a nuclear power plant, buying nonpolluting soaps, voting for additional school taxes, or joining a march on the board of trustees to protest sexism in faculty hiring are all examples of behavior changes that might be desired by persuasive communicators. Changes in behavior are best assessed by direct observations of the receiver, but in some situations, results may be able to be assessed by the verbal statements made by the receiver.

Cognitive, affective, and behavioral changes are not easily separated into three distinct and mutually exclusive categories. In almost any situation involving persuasive communication, combinations of effects will be noted. A man may listen to a speech that argues for a constitutional amendment to give voters the right to vote on all tax increases. Following the speech, the man signs a petition to place the amendment on the ballot, and also tells a friend how the speech changed his mind about taxes. He clearly exhibited a behavior change, but his comments also indexed a cognitive change. You can be emotionally stirred by a speech, and also make a contribution to charity. Or you can be emotionally stirred by a speech, but never make a contribution because of financial inadequacy. You can be exposed to a television commercial, laugh at the commercial, but pass up the product when you see it on a store shelf a few days later. Or you can pass up the product the first time you see it, then talk to a neighbor who did buy the product, and buy it on the neighbor's recommendation. The combinations of cognitive changes, affect changes, and overt behaviors that can occur as a result of persuasion is complex. The careful communicator is going to carefully plan a strategy before entering into a persuasive situation.

Attitudes and beliefs

Figure 1.1 suggests that all of the effects of persuasion stem from changes in *attitude*. Before a communicator can expect a receiver to change a behavior, or to change cognitions, the model proposes that there has to be some corresponding change in an attitude. We have already provided a general definition of the term "attitude." At this point, however, we need a clearer understanding of the term "attitude" as well as the related term "belief." We shall be using both of these concepts frequently, as all of our current models and theories about persuasive communication rest on an understanding of belief and attitude change and on the way in which these concepts are related to observable responses.

Attitudes are an individual's likes and dislikes, while *beliefs* express the relationships we see between two or more events, or people, or the relationships between events and characteristics of those events. Thus, I can express an attitude by saying "I like Ford cars," and can express a belief by saying "I believe Ford cars are very durable." Note that my statements are only *expressions* of the underlying attitude or belief. Both attitudes and beliefs are nonobservable, cognitive states. No one has ever seen, heard, tasted, touched, or smelled an attitude or belief. Attitudes and beliefs are conceptual bridges between what an individual *does* and the cognitive processes that lead him to do it.

Although we cannot directly observe an attitude or a belief, we can find out about it. This is done by *making inferences* from the observable behavior of an individual to what we think the person's internal state might be. One man hits another in a bar, and we infer that negative feelings are being displayed. Two people walk up to one another, smile, and shake hands, and the observer infers that positive attitudes are being displayed. In many cases, we make inferences about an individual's attitudes and beliefs from the verbal statements that are made. Attitudes are indexed in statements such as "I like Clint Eastwood," "That movie is excellent." Beliefs relate things, and might be inferred from statements like "College students today are too money oriented," "Taxes are far too high," and "All students must have a general education." In each of these statements, it is not the attitude or belief that is being observed. The existence of an attitude or belief is being inferred from the verbal statement or from the overt behavior.

Attitudes and beliefs, then, reflect psychological processes. Attitudes are described in terms of the favorability or unfavorability of the evaluation made by an individual of an object, person, or event. Beliefs measure the relationships that individuals "see" in their environment.

It should now be obvious why the behavioral scientist is interested in attitudes and beliefs. The scientist postulates a positive relationship between attitudes and beliefs and cognitions, affect, and behavior. If you hold a highly favorable attitude toward General Motors, a commercial designed to sell Buicks ought to have more impact on you than if you have a neutral or negative attitude toward General Motors. If I hold a highly favor-

able attitude toward you, I am more likely to seek your company, would be more willing to spend time talking to you, and would be more likely to listen to your persuasive messages. If the positive relationship we postulate actually exists, attitudes can serve as a predictor of how likely an audience is to take some action as a result of a persuasive message, or how much resistance they are likely to demonstrate. The relationship between attitudes and beliefs and the behavior a person exhibits is positive, but there is no one-to-one correspondence. Merely possessing a favorable attitude is not a sufficient guarantee that a particular kind of behavior will result. For example, imagine that a person holds extremely unfavorable attitudes toward minority groups, and particularly toward blacks and Jews. If we give the person a paper and pencil test to assess attitudes toward these groups, we may find that the individual consistently indicates prejudice toward members of these minority groups. If we were to take the attitude test as a firm indicator of the individual's actual behavior, we would have to predict that the individual would behave negatively toward both groups. However, it is unlikely that such an individual *will* exhibit overt, physical hostility when meeting a black person on the street, at a cocktail party, or at a business function. People are concerned, and restrained, by the legal system, by fear of reprisals, by the possible responses from others, and so on. In another example, we may have a negative attitude toward a behavior, but engage in it because of our beliefs. Most of us dislike going to the dentist, but most of our beliefs about medical practices, about what we should do for ourselves as mature persons, and so on, keeps us going back to the dentist twice a year. Thus, there are times when *beliefs* and *norms* lead us to behave in particular ways.

If attitudes and beliefs cannot be seen, if they can only be inferred from observable behavior, why talk about them at all? Why not talk only about what can be directly observed, that is, verbal statements or overt actions? One reason why we retain these conceptual bridges lies with the nature of the research that has been performed by behavioral scientists interested in persuasion. Imagine that you make a speech to a group of people in which you advocate that they vote against a proposed new shopping mall. After listening to you, the audience goes home. How can you find out whether any of these people were persuaded by the speech? You can't actually follow people into the voting booth and watch them mark their ballots. You might follow some of the audience around town and see whether they made any statements opposing the mall, but in most situations, following people is frowned on in our society. Some indication of success is obtained when the actual vote is taken, but that is normally a bit too late. If you knew ahead of time that you hadn't convinced a lot of the audience, you could plan for further persuasive efforts in the attempt to defeat the new mall. The difficulties and the expense of attempting to make direct observations are apparent.

On the other hand, you could have the audience answer a short questionnaire about their attitudes and beliefs regarding the mall project just after the speech. The answers given would provide at least some indication of the way in which the audience members were likely to vote. There are certainly going to be many times when it is difficult, if not impossible, to obtain attitude measures in the attempt to gain some indication of the success of a persuasive message. But scholars have developed many ways of making estimates of attitude change in persuasive communication situations. We shall discuss a number of the methods available to the persuasive communicator in this volume.

Judging the effects of persuasion

Ultimately, persuasive communication must be judged in terms of its effect on the participants. Was it successful? Did it fail to achieve its goal? What if only part of a speaker's goals are realized? Do we conclude that persuasion was successful, or unsuccessful? How long do we wait before we attempt to judge the success of a persuasive message? Norman Thomas, who ran several times for the presidency of the United States on the Socialist ticket, never won. In fact, he never really came close to winning. Yet the United States has adopted as policy a number of the ideas that he advocated. Should we call his persuasive campaign a total failure? Or should we give him at least some praise for the eventual adoption of some of his major ideas? It is not easy to determine just what constitutes success or failure in persuasion, and a more careful examination of the effects of persuasion is needed.

One measure of the effects of persuasion is obtained by assessing the correspondence between the intentions of the source and subsequent behavior of the receiver. When an editorial asks its readers to change their attitude toward an increase in millage for improvement of the local school district, and later questionnaires indicate that there has been no change in attitude, the editorial would seem to have been a failure. When a mayor asks the people of a community to vote for him, and he wins the election, his campaign would seem to have been a success.

Using this criterion of the degree of correspondence between the stated intentions of the source and an assessment of the subsequent behavior of a receiver would seem to be a simple matter. Unfortunately, it is not. Many times, persuasive messages will fail in their immediate intent, but will have long-range impact. The National Association for the Advancement of Colored People was formed in the first years of this century. From its inception the NAACP advocated better treatment for black citizens. They long concentrated their efforts on the system of segregated schools in the South. For years, their words seemed to fall on deaf ears, if one judges their efforts by the number of schools that were desegregated. Was the organization a failure? Certainly not, if you judge the results by events occurring since 1954 when their efforts helped lead to the Supreme Court decision declaring segregated school systems unconstitutional.

A second criterion for judging the success of a

persuasive message is the *degree* of change that is secured. Sales messages are one of the best examples we can use to illustrate this situation. Jane Jones is demonstrating a new food processor in the local department store. A crowd of 25 people is watching as she demonstrates the appliance, and tries to sell it to the audience. Her chances of getting all 25 members of the audience to buy a machine are obviously very small. How many machines does she have to sell before the message can be considered effective? To more than half the people? Less than half? Only one? If no one rushes up to buy one of the processors, do we consider Jane a failure? Should we fire her? The difficulties in making an immediate assessment are obvious. Some members of the audience might go home, think about the demonstration, talk to their friends and neighbors, and finally buy a processor two months later. If the store had fired Jane in the meantime, most of us would agree that an injustice had been done.

Persuasion must be judged in terms of gradations of success. One end of the scale may represent no change at all in any of the participants along any of the dimensions we have discussed. At the other end of the scale, we would find that all of the participants in the situation have changed in ways that reflect their mutual desires to find common ground on which decisions and actions are possible. Most outcomes of persuasive communication fall between these two extremes.

A third criterion that can be used to measure the success of a persuasive campaign is the nature of the opposition to the campaign. We expect that persuasion is going to be more successful if there is no organized opposition. In the United States, there has been a strong campaign opposing the Supreme Court's decision allowing abortion. If one examined only the persuasive messages that oppose abortion, one might expect that most Americans would be demanding the abolishment of all abortions in the country. The campaign conducted by those opposed to abortion is intense and anti-abortion messages are presented in many different media. Attitude studies conducted through national polls suggest, however, that

there has been relatively little change in the basic attitudes of most Americans toward abortion. People who opposed abortion before the Supreme Court decision by-and-large still oppose it. People who favored legalizing abortion still favor it. What has happened? Those opposed to legalizing abortion are not conducting their campaign in a vacuum. There is just as powerful a group of individuals who argue for freedom of choice in matters of abortion as there are people who oppose freedom of choice. The end result is that there is little visible public change in this area. People hold their beliefs more and more strongly, but few are converted. Both sides are trying to attract the uncommitted to their position. The presence or absence of opposition will have significant influence on the success or failure of persuasion.

The final criterion we must use in judging the success or failure of persuasion is the level of difficulty of the task. Advocating a tax reduction is easier than advocating tax increases. In many districts in the South, a Democratic candidate may have an easier time in winning an election than a Republican. If you are advocating strong efforts to control crime, your task may be easy, since few people are in favor of increased crime. However, if you are in favor of an increase in the state income tax in order to finance increased welfare payments, you are likely to have a very difficult time. The persuasive speaker who advocates stronger measures to control crime may have an easy time and will feel that the audience is with him. That same speaker may be totally rejected when he advocates an increase in the income tax to pay for new prisons. In the one case, we might label the speaker a success. In the other, we might label the same person a failure.

Changing firmly fixed attitudes is more difficult than changing attitudes that are weakly held. The difficulty level of the communicator's task can be assessed by comparing the initial position of a receiver on a particular topic to the position desired by the communicator. If the change in attitude desired is large, successful persuasion will be more difficult to achieve than if the source wants the receiver to change only a small amount from a currently held position. Imagine two persuasive communicators, one delivering a message to a receiver with very firm attitudes, and the other delivering a message to a receiver with only weakly held attitudes toward a topic. If both communicators are successful in obtaining attitude change, we might wish to say that the first communicator was more successful than the second because the task was more difficult to accomplish.

Four criteria must be considered in judging the effects of persuasive communication. Situations can be assessed in terms of the *nature of the correspondence* between the intentions of the participants, the *degree of correspondence* between the intentions of the source and the subsequent behavior of the receiver, the *nature of the opposition* to be expected to the communicator's position, and the *difficulty level* of the task being engaged in.

The ethics of persuasion

Persuasion is a field for scientific research, a field similar to those disciplines that study political behavior, mental illness, or juvenile delinquency. Few object to the psychologist who is interested in trying to cure the psychotic, the criminologist working at the prevention of crime, or the historian trying to understand the causes of war. Many people, however, have objected to the study and practice of persuasion. The term itself seems to suggest the manipulation of others, whether by physical force, or by the force of words playing on the emotions. This concern about the power of persuasive communication arose early in recorded history, and philosophers from Aristotle to David Hume to John Stuart Mill have addressed some of the philosophical problems arising from the recognition that persuasion can be a very powerful tool.

The most serious charge against the use of persuasion comes from those who argue for "openness" in the communicative relationships between people. This position can be recognized in a number of identifiable phrases. Proponents will say: "Just give them the facts," "Don't tell me what to do, let me make up my own mind," or "I'm a person, not something to be manipulated." The argument is intriguing, because it appears to recognize the power that persuasion can have in changing behavior, and at the same time argues against the use of that power in favor of a position that states that individuals should make their own decisions. This argument against persuasion is essentially an ethical argument, and it deserves exploration before we attempt to specify an ethical position of our own.

First, we should note that the proponents of such a position are engaged in persuasion when they attempt to get others to adopt their own position. We would not want to say that such persuasion is bad, but it does seem ironic that the very people who argue against persuasion are dependent upon its use to get their position adopted.

A second major reason we argue against a total "openness" position is that we feel strongly that to refuse to persuade is to abdicate one's responsibility to society.[13] If you think something needs doing in the community, do you not have the responsibility to attempt to persuade others to your point of view? Those who say, "Just give them the facts, and let them make up their own mind," deny that responsibility. A more ethical approach would be one that argued the responsibility of every individual to examine data, draw conclusions, and then use persuasion as the tool for obtaining a consensus within the society.

In advancing these arguments against the openness position as an extreme position, we do not mean to deny it entirely. We believe firmly that more honesty, more trust in each other, more use of data, and greater faith in the value of each human being are goals that are not antithetical to the use of persuasion.

The charges against persuasion are difficult to answer simply. We shall attempt to do so by fashioning a series of related questions, and answering them.

1. Can persuasion be used for evil ends? Of

course it can, but so can medicine, law, banking, or accounting. No one would argue that we should close all medical schools because they have the potential of being used wrongly. A more rational suggestion is that we keep the medical school, and place some restrictions on the way in which people practice medicine. With regard to persuasion, our society has argued the same way. The advertiser is allowed to attempt to persuade people to buy his product, but we make him legally responsible for the safety of the product.

2. When we teach about persuasion, do we put power over others in the hands of those we teach? Yes, we do, but we do also when we teach a child how to write, teach a college student how to take a blood sample, or teach a soldier how to use a bayonet. Everyone who goes to school to learn how to be a farmer, banker, doctor, engineer, salesman, lawyer, plumber, or auto mechanic has acquired information that will help in controlling the lives of others. Knowledge is always powerful, but its power to control depends on the exclusivity with which it is held. If only a few knew how to persuade others, persuasion would be a very powerful weapon indeed. When everyone knows how to use persuasion effectively, and knows how to evaluate the persuasive messages that are received, persuasion becomes far more a tool, and less a weapon.

3. Does the use of persuasion lead to manipulation, and thus does it make people into objects? Persuasion is an attempt to control one's environment and people are an important part of that environment. If you mean by "manipulation" the changing of the behavior of others through conscious attempts to change their behavior, persuasion does result in manipulation. Having said that, we might examine the original question a bit more closely. The use of the word "manipulation" has come to have a very negative meaning. If we substituted the word "education" or "socialization" or "rehabilitation" for the term manipulation, no one would worry about the association of persuasion with any of the three concepts. Yet each of them can be defined as conscious attempts to change the behavior of others. Society regards

education, socialization, and rehabilitation as positive in nature. We all attempt to control the environment around us. We wouldn't be living organisms if we didn't, and persuasion is but one way we use to fit ourselves within our society.

4. Can we protect people against persuasion? Our answer here has to be: not completely. Unless we bar all communication between people, human beings are always going to attempt to persuade others and are always going to be subject to persuasion by others. Societies can pass laws forbidding certain types of persuasion, as we have done in putting limitations on advertising. We do not, for example, allow manufacturers to make claims for their products that cannot be substantiated. Such laws or limitations on persuasion can cover only a very small number of possible communication situations. We believe firmly that a better solution to the use of unethical communication is to teach all people to use persuasion effectively, and to recognize and evaluate persuasion when it is directed to them. The more information the people in a society have about persuasion and persuasive techniques, the more likely it is that people can increase their resistance to would-be hucksters. If we could be sure that all members in a society were adequately educated, there would be little need for laws or rules governing the use of advertising persuasion.

We started this section with the question as to whether we should teach, study, and write about persuasion. The answer we have arrived at is yes, but our conclusion comes only after considering the alternatives to the effective use of persuasive communication by all members of a society. There are alternatives, and mankind has tried and keeps trying almost all of them. The Red Brigade engages in terrorism in Italy, because they claim that peaceful discussions haven't worked. The army in a Latin American country objects to the slow pace of reforms, so it revolts and throws out one government to install another. A group of citizens in the United States objects to materials in a textbook, and threatens the school board with recall if the objectionable materials are not removed. An individual citizen objects to an editorial in the local newspaper, and calls the editor threatening to shoot the editor if there is no apology. The alternatives to persuasion include bribes, tortures, murder, and warfare. In the short run, at least, the alternatives are just as effective, and perhaps more effective at shaping human behavior than persuasion. We hope that no one wishes to argue that any of these alternatives are a more desirable method for shaping a society than persuasion, even though they might be more effective.

Responsibilities

The remainder of this book views persuasion from the standpoint of a behavioral scientist. As such, it presents practical suggestions to the potential speaker, writer, reader, and listener. Such knowledge implies certain responsibilities that sources and receivers have to themselves, to other people, and to society. A few of these responsibilities are outlined below:

1. Develop a personal set of ethical standards of conduct to help guide your own behavior. We are not advocates for any particular moral code or any specific set of ethical standards. We do believe that as authors, teachers, citizens, and scholars, we do have a personal set of ethical standards. By the time you finish this book, you should be able to identify those standards that we possess, and be able to evaluate them in terms of your own standards. Most people do have standards, although we do not always attempt to set them out in a systematic fashion. We believe that when you engage in persuasive communication it should always be consistent with the set of ethical and moral standards you have developed.

2. Know all you can about persuasion. You do not normally attempt to use an electric drill without finding out where the switch is and what the drill can do. Persuasion is also a tool, and you ought to know what the effects are likely to be if you use this tool.

3. Establish for yourself some criteria for making decisions. Decision making is an important

part of the persuasive process, and you ought to understand the ways in which decisions are made. Persuasion is used in communicating decisions about a topic. If the decision you make is a poor one, your persuasive efforts may or may not be successful, but most probably, the long-range effects are not likely to be desirable.

We all act as both source and receiver of persuasive messages. Most of our formal education, however, has gone toward training us to be better sources of communication, while the fact remains that we act as receivers of communication far more than we are able to act as sources of communication. We listen to the radio, read the newspaper, listen to other people, and view the television set many more hours a day than we spend in actually putting out messages. Here are some suggestions to help you predict the effects of particular persuasive messages:

1. Know what your own biases are. We cannot know exactly how we will react to each persuasive message we face, but we can make ourselves aware of some of the types of arguments to which we react favorably or unfavorably. Some people, for example, may react positively to the argument that a product is "built to last." They may tend to forget other aspects of the product, and concentrate only on its durability. Other people listening to or viewing a persuasive message may be more receptive to a claim that a product is "easy-cleaning," or "beautiful."

2. Know your source. You are exposed to newspapers, magazines, television, radio, neighbors, friends, and relatives. It is impossible for you to become an expert on all the problems that face you. You will have to depend on the credibility of the people with whom you communicate.

3. Become a collector of information. As you listen to the messages available to you, your predispositions toward listening to one message and refusing to listen to another message may make it difficult for you to make final decisions based on all the available information. If, however, you collect information from all kinds of sources, and of all degrees of reliability, you can include this information in your decision-making process. Peo-

ple are going to receive information differently, but perhaps they should fight against the tendency to limit what they listen to and read.

Nations, cultures, and societies have evolved over the centuries through the measures they take to control the behavior of individuals within the society. A country can allow great diversity to exist within its borders, but there must be some situations in which all members of the society behave in the same way. A simple example is driving a car. A country cannot allow some people to drive on the left side of the road, and some on the right. In order to secure conformity, societies develop educational campaigns, methods of child socialization, and the use of laws. Most such efforts grow out of the specific values that a society places upon the acts and customs of individuals. For example, in Sicily, the man who murders his wife's lover may receive a term of three years in jail, while the man who robs a train may receive a life sentence. Different values have led to different laws and customs.

Not every society has the same values, and there is no culture, nation, or society that cannot be improved, nor any that is not constantly changing. It will become obvious that we are in favor of using persuasion as a method of social change within our society. Persuasion, however, is not the only tool a free society needs in order to grow, to prosper, and to change. Compromise, mediation, arbitration, compliance, socialization, education, law, and customs are other valuable tools that a society must possess and develop. In order to aid in the development of persuasive communication as a major tool in our society, we believe that there are steps that should be taken:

1. Protect persuasion by law and by custom. As a nation, we pride ourself on freedom of speech, and it can be argued that we need not protect one form of communication more than is already provided for in our Constitution and by our laws. That protection, however, is always fragile and sometimes uncertain. There are always groups of people who would nibble away at the protections we have given to free speech, and a continual recognition of the value of persuasion

to the operation of a democratic society is in order.

2. Encourage the acquisition of knowledge. Many people object to persuasion on the grounds that successful persuasion frequently uses emotional appeals. It does so successfully only when people have no other basis for judgment. In an age of specialization, we have developed more and more knowledge as a society, but the amount of knowledge that is available to any one individual has become increasingly limited. This has the effect of preventing the average citizen from fully participating in the decisions required in the society. In the agrarian society of 100 years ago, each citizen had much in common with all other citizens. Deciding where a road should be placed could be done by pooling the common knowledge of all the people within the area to be served by the road. Today, batteries of engineers, city planners, computers, and construction companies are required, and the input of the people in the area seems less and less needed.

There are no complete solutions to the problem of knowledge acquisition. It is a problem that has always plagued societies wishing to operate in a democratic fashion. It becomes a more serious problem in our increasingly technological society. As individuals, we are highly interdependent, and we must be able to meaningfully delegate the responsibilities for many decisions to others, just as others will delegate some responsibilities to us. Even if we are willing to give decision-making power to others, we argue strongly that all members of a society must have a knowledge base if the society is to be successful.

3. Learn how to teach rationality. In later chapters, we will examine evidence that shows that people do not behave rationally or logically in many communication situations. The evidence seems overwhelming that we are not born as either logical or rational, but perhaps ways of teaching rational decision making can be found.

4. Keep an open society. Before World War II, the Japanese government wished to convince its citizens that Japan was being discriminated against by the Western Powers. The government

succeeded to an amazing degree in uniting its population. Scientists suggested that one possible reason for the success was that the people were asked to turn in all short wave radios for the war effort. Being an island nation, the populace was effectively shut off from the possibility of any contradictory messages being received. This example points to the necessity for any society to remain open. When all points of view can be expressed, when all available information can be assessed by a citizenry, the probability increases that rational decisions can be made.

Our country has always vacillated between the pressures to keep an open society and those to close the society. We pass open meeting laws, and the Freedom of Information Act. But as soon as we pass such laws, others within the society argue that people do not need to know so much, that we may weaken ourselves by disclosing too much information. We must very positively affirm openness in society. We think it is required for rational decision making, and for the successful operation of persuasive communication.

5. Develop and protect the mass media within society. The population of the United States is growing, and will continue to grow for many years. The larger the population, the harder it is to communicate with all citizens of the country. Yet as the population grows, it will become more and more necessary that all citizens have the kinds of information needed for rational decision making. The mass media can be used primarily for entertainment, or they can be of major assistance in education and transmission of information. In this society, we have come down harder on the side of entertainment than on the side of education, and this is regrettable. If we are to keep our society an open one, we must increase the ability of the mass media to reach all of the population with news, information, discussions, debate, and arguments about the affairs of the nation.

These are some of the responsibilities that we see for all of us if we are to be able to use persuasion effectively—responsibilities for sources of communication, for receivers of persuasion, and for our society as a whole.

Summary

Persuasion is a form of human interaction. It takes place when one individual desires some particular response from one or more other individuals and deliberately sets out to secure that response through the use of communication. It also takes place when two or more individuals agree to communication cooperatively in an attempt to reach a consensus on which decisions and actions can be based. Persuasion has always been a tool used by societies to secure social changes, but we argue here that it has the potentiality of becoming the major tool for solving problems and arriving at a consensus for the pluralistic society in which we live.

In this chapter, we have defined persuasion, and placed it within a communication framework. We have noted some of the major factors that help determine the success or failure of persuasive communication situations. The nature of the anticipated effects on a receiver exposed to persuasion was discussed, and methods for judging those effects were noted. Finally, some suggestions for an ethics of persuasion and the responsibilities of communicators within our society were outlined.

Footnotes

1. D. K. Berlo, *The Process of Communication* (New York: Holt, Rinehart and Winston, 1960), pp. 40–72.
2. G. Gerbner, "The Interaction Model: Perception and Communication," in J. Ball and F. Byrnes, eds., *Research, Principles and Practices in Visual Communication* (E. Lansing, Mich: National Project in Agricultural Communication, 1960), pp. 4–15.
3. E. Schramm, "How Communication Works," in W. Schramm, ed., *The Process and Effects of Mass Communication* (Urbana, Ill.: University of Illinois Press, 1954), pp. 3–26.

4. B. H. Westley and M. S. McLean, Jr., "A Conceptual Model for Communication Research," *Journalism Quarterly,* vol. 34 (1957), pp. 31–38.

5. C. Shannon and W. Weaver, *The Mathematical Theory of Communication* (Urbana, Ill.: University of Illinois Press, 1949), pp. 4–6.

6. *The Random House Dictionary of the English Language* (New York: Random House, 1967), s.v. "persuasion."

7. K. Andersen, *Persuasion Theory and Practice* (Boston: Allyn & Bacon, 1971), p. 6.

8. T. Scheidel, *Persuasive Speaking* (Glenview, Ill.: Scott Foresman, 1967), p. 1.

9. R. Bostrom, *Persuasion* (Englewood Cliffs, N.J.: Prentice-Hall, 1983), p. 11.

10. See M. J. Cody and M. L. McLaughlin, "Models for the Sequential Construction of Account Episodes," in R. Street and J. N. Cappella, eds., *The Sequential Nature of Social Interaction* (London: Edward Arnold, 1985), pp. 50–69.

11. G. R. Miller, Michigan State University, personal communication, 1978.

12. M. J. Rosenberg and C. I. Hovland, "Cognitive, Affective, and Behavioral Components of Attitudes," in C. I. Hovland and M. J. Rosenberg, eds., *Attitude Organization and Change* (New Haven, Conn.: Yale University Press, 1960), pp. 1–14.

13. This responsibility is discussed in detail in H. W. Simmons, *Persuasion: Understanding, Practice, and Analysis* (Reading, Mass.: Addison-Wesley, 1976), pp. 35–38.

CHAPTER TWO

Developing Attitudes and Beliefs

The model of persuasion we have advanced postulates that changes in attitudes and beliefs are necessary before changes in emotions, cognitions, and behavior can occur. The fact that we emphasize *changes* in attitudes and beliefs suggests that all of the parties to persuasive communication situations have a set of attitudes or a series of beliefs even before they are exposed to persuasive messages. How do people obtain the attitudes they have? What kinds of beliefs do people have? Can we improve our understanding of persuasion by finding out how attitudes and beliefs are developed? This chapter looks carefully at these questions, and concludes that both learning and cognitive processes are directly related to the development of attitudes and beliefs.

Attitudes are the feelings of liking and disliking we have for things in the world around us. Thus

you may like dogs, chocolate cake, the Republican Party, and your mother. In similar fashion, you may dislike snakes, dormitory food, and your high-school principal, and you may be neutral toward tennis matches, labor unions, and foreign cars.

Some attitudes are held with deep intensity. We may be attracted to a girl friend, a boyfriend, or a spouse with such intensity that all else pales by comparison. We will do anything to be with these people, and would believe anything they say. At the other end of the spectrum, we may dislike spiders so much that we get physically ill at the very sight of a spider. Other attitudes are held more lightly. We may enjoy seeing Angela Lansbury on television, but it doesn't ruin our day if we happen to miss a particular show.

A single experience is all it takes for attitudes to

begin to form, but we would expect those attitudes to be weakly held unless the experience was a very powerful one. A child bitten at an early age by a large dog might need only one such experience to develop highly negative attitudes toward dogs, but most of the attitudes we hold intensely have been formed after *many* experiences. Attitudes are formed not only as the result of direct encounters with the world around us, but also through the indirect impressions we receive from others talking or writing about events. Once we have formed our basic set of attitudes, we use the attitudes as a kind of filter that determines how new attitudes are going to be formed. This set of attitudes we call a *frame of reference*, and it helps govern our behavior.

The development of a set of reference frames is based on both genetic and environmental factors. Certain genetic characteristics that influence the development of an individual's attitudes and eventual reference frames include eyesight, hearing, height, basic intelligence level, and energy level.

Despite the presence of genetic factors, environmental factors play the major role in the development of attitudes. Children are engaged in gathering information about the world from the minute they are born. They receive information about the world from their parents, brothers and sisters, aunts and uncles, friends, neighbors, and teachers. They are given information about their community, their church, and their country. A child learns to avoid the neighborhood bully, and to be attracted to a nice kid down the block. Each time the child has an experience, interacts with the world, or learns something, the frame of reference is further developed.

The information we gather is not perceived as a "blooming, buzzing, confusion." Our brain operates in such a way that the information we receive is placed into structures of related information. We develop structures about nature, people, education, churches, and governments. By the time we are adults, these structures have become extremely complex. Reference frames are not composed of simple attitudes alone. The *beliefs* we hold are also part of the reference frames we have.

Following Rokeach,[1] we view beliefs as simple propositions or statements that can be preceded by the phrase, "I believe that. . . ." Many people believe that the world is round, that world population control is necessary, that students should not cheat on exams, and that man will someday reach the stars. Whenever individuals profess to see some relationship between two events or objects or people, or between some event and a characteristic of the event, we say that they hold a *belief*. As in our attitudes, there seems to be considerable variety in our beliefs. The belief that the world is round is a different type of belief from the belief that man will reach the stars. How can we distinguish between these two beliefs?

We can distinguish between beliefs in two ways. First, we can attempt to see whether different beliefs can be classified with respect to what they tell us about the world around us. Thus, the belief that the world is round is a *descriptive* belief statement. It makes a statement about the world, and could be examined as to its truth or falsity. The belief that your university is a wonderful place to learn is an *evaluative* belief. It says something about what one thinks is good or bad. And the belief that students should not cheat on exams is a *prescriptive* belief. It makes a statement about what we think should happen, or about what we think people should do.

A second way of classifying beliefs is in terms of how difficult a belief would be to change through the use of a persuasive message. For example, we can think of no arguments or evidence that would make us change our minds about the belief in a round world, yet an individual source who knows mathematics and physics might be able to put together an argument that would make us modify our belief that man *will* someday reach the stars to a belief that it is *improbable* that man will ever reach the stars. The first belief, however, is so firmly a portion of one's belief structure, was acquired so early in life, and is taken so much for granted that nothing is going to disturb it. Both Rokeach[2] and Bem[3] suggest that one of the organizing features of beliefs is a "central-peripheral" dimension.

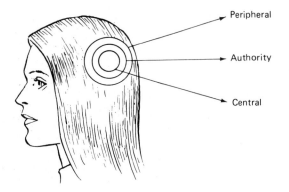

Peripheral

Authority

Central

Figure 2.1. Belief System

Figure 2.1 illustrates this view of an individual's belief structure. Highly *central* beliefs, such as: "The world is round," "Water is heavier than air," and "I believe what my eyes see," form the core of any individual's belief structure. We acquire our most central or "primitive" beliefs very early in life. Furthermore, we continue to strengthen these beliefs as we go through life, and continuously validate them from our experiences.

Rokeach suggests that there are two types of central beliefs. For one type, there is complete agreement within the society that the belief is correct. The belief that "rocks fall to the ground when dropped" is an example of a primitive belief that everyone within a society would agree upon. The other type of highly central belief is illustrated by expressions such as "I believe in God," "Black cats bring bad luck," and "I am basically a nice person." These are beliefs that are held very strongly by individuals, but there may not be consensus among members of a society as to the validity of these beliefs.

A second layer of beliefs illustrated in Figure 2.1 is comprised of those connected with *authority*. Children learn that they can trust some individuals and not others. They learn to place faith in what their parents and teachers tell them. They learn that the president of the United States ought to be believed, but that Russian and Chinese leaders are less trustworthy. Our beliefs about authorities lead us to categorize others either as *positive* or *negative* authorities. We place faith in the state-

ments of positive authorities, and tend to disbelieve what negative authorities tell us.

Our beliefs about authority are firmly held. They do shift slowly over time, but for an adult, changing such beliefs is difficult. Authority beliefs are less firmly held than central beliefs, but they help govern to whom we will listen, and whom we will respect.

Finally, we can talk about *peripheral* beliefs. Beliefs such as: "Harvard is the best university in the United States" or "Steak is best when it is cooked rare" are examples of peripheral beliefs. Peripheral beliefs can be divided into two categories. *Some of our peripheral beliefs are derived from central, more primitive beliefs.* Thus, the individual who holds that abortion is wrong may have arrived at that belief from a more central belief that all human life is sacred. On the other hand, many peripheral beliefs do not seem to be based directly on more central beliefs. They seem to arise from an immediate set of experiences. The belief that CBS has the best news programs may be simply a matter of taste, and not based on any other beliefs.

The frames of reference we construct are composed of the attitudes and beliefs we have. Because each of us has different sets of experiences, each of us has frames of reference at least slightly different from the frames of every other person. If there were absolutely no predictability in the way reference frames are developed and organized, the persuasive communicator would have a very difficult time in finding appropriate messages. Attitudes and beliefs do not develop in completely random fashion, however, and the reference frames that are eventually formed from our attitudes and beliefs can also be used to make predictions about the effects of persuasion. Beliefs are formed along a central-peripheral set of dimensions, and this organization allows us to make predictions about the probable effects of persuasive messages.

First, *the more central the belief, the more resistant individuals will be to changes in the belief*. If your persuasive goal demands that the receiver change a central belief, it is very unlikely that success will come easily or come at all. The difficulty of changing a primitive belief through persuasion is greatly magnified if the belief is one that has consensus within the society. Imagine trying to get someone to change a belief that "the world is round." Changing a central belief that does *not* have consensus within the society is also difficult, but perhaps not impossible. However, central beliefs are so deeply ingrained into our reference frames that little can be done to change them. Perhaps better advice to the persuasive communicator is that these central beliefs can frequently be used as supporting arguments in messages advocating change in other beliefs. Wars have been justified many times by the argument that "God wants it."

Beliefs based on authority are also resistant to change, but not to the extent that central beliefs are. The individual who believes through long experience that "policemen are always trustworthy" may have that belief weakened if an example of "police brutality" is witnessed.

Peripheral beliefs are subject to change. Individuals can change their beliefs about hair styles, about the importance or lack of importance of environmental pollution, about abortion reform, about increased taxes, and about the quality of universities. These beliefs are constantly undergoing shifts and changes as a result of the persuasive messages that are encountered by the receiver. It is with the peripheral belief system that the persuasive communicator will have the best success.

The second major implication of our analysis of belief structures is that *those beliefs that are derived from central beliefs are more resistant to change than those beliefs that exist only as peripheral beliefs*. We have suggested that many peripheral beliefs are derived from more primitive beliefs. In a study conducted in 1953, Bettinghaus found that students tended to believe that the president of the United States was a most trustworthy figure, regardless of who was president.[4] When the president was quoted as favoring compulsory arbitration of labor disputes to one audience, there was more attitude change than when a well-known labor leader was quoted as favoring compulsory arbitration. Rokeach[5] found that primitive-based beliefs are more resistant than beliefs based on

authority, and authority-based beliefs are in turn more resistant than those entirely peripheral in nature.

This principle holds another implication for persuasion. When a belief held by an individual rests on a more central belief, it may be necessary to change the more central belief before it is possible to change the peripheral belief. Abortion reform is a good example. In order to change the stand of an individual who is opposed to legalized abortion, it may be necessary to change the individual's attitude toward the value placed on human life. Thus, a message directed only toward the peripheral belief may not succeed unless it is accompanied by messages directed toward the more central beliefs that are the foundation of the receiver's beliefs.

The third implication for persuasion to be drawn from our analysis is that *the more central the belief that is changed, the more widespread will be the changes in the remainder of the individual's belief structure*. The central beliefs we hold are connected to many peripheral beliefs. If I believe in God, I may also believe in the Bible as an authority, in ministers as mediators between God and myself, in tax exemption for churches, in the desirability of using public funds for church-supported schools, and in the legality of prayer in the public schools. Each of these beliefs may have been *derived* from the central belief in God. Further, as I develop a well-articulated frame of reference, I see many distinctions between more and more religious beliefs—the importance of various sacraments, papal authority, issues pertaining to heaven, and so on. Now, what might happen if the individual should change the belief about the existence of God? Imagine that something traumatic happens to the individual, a sudden death of a wife or child. If that event results in the individual's changing a central belief, we might expect the individual to also change the peripheral beliefs that derive from the primitive belief.

This third principle suggests that the persuasive communicator may find that a desired change will also produce unexpected changes in other beliefs. It is frequently impossible to predict whether this secondary change will be favorable or unfavorable to the communicator's cause. The communicator who is able to effect a change in a receiver's beliefs about the value of compulsory government health insurance may find that the receiver has also changed beliefs about the role of physicians in the health-care system.

Individuals do not simply discard the frames of reference they have acquired but usually adapt those frames to new information so that sweeping persuasive changes are difficult to obtain. Consider racial prejudice. If an individual believes that members of a particular minority group are dirty, lazy, stupid, and troublesome, meeting someone from that reference group who is not dirty, lazy, stupid, and troublesome will not result in drastic changes of the original frame of reference. The new information will be assimilated into the original frame, but the belief pattern might now be: "Members of that minority group are dirty, lazy, stupid, and troublesome, except for Joe Jones, who is almost like me." Many encounters with many Joes are necessary to produce basic changes in the frame of reference used to evaluate messages about a given minority group.

The difficulties that are encountered in persuasive situations can be partially assessed by looking at the nature of the relationship between a reference frame and a message containing new information. Several situations are possible:

1. If the individual's frame of reference is extensive and relatively complete, new information that is contrary to that frame will produce few noticeable changes in behavior. In fact, it may seem as though the material is not being perceived at all. In such a situation, the persuasive communicator either has to be able to bring a new frame of reference into play or has to continue communicating until enough information has been added to force changes in the receiver's attitude structure.

2. If a frame of reference is extensive and relatively complete, new information that is not contrary to the frame serves to strengthen the frame. For example, if a man is a firm believer in safety measures to protect lives in the home and factory, he is also likely to be an individual who will be easily persuaded that seat belts save lives.

3. If an individual's frame of reference is sketchy and still incomplete, new information contrary to the frame serves further to increase the level of uncertainty that the individual holds toward the reference frame. The new information may not result in the abandonment of an incomplete frame, but may make the application of the frame as a decision-making tool in future situations less likely.

4. If a frame of reference is sketchy and incomplete, new information that is not contrary to the frame serves to decrease uncertainty. The frame of reference, when completed by new information, will become a major decision-making tool for the receiver. For example, most people in the United States have developed a reference frame that suggests that they are against pollution. These reference frames, however, are not well developed. People do not have specific technical information about the subject. When they encounter a speaker who tells them how many pollutants they breathe in every minute, that information may serve to strengthen their reference frame so that they view further information about pollution with heightened awareness.

Individuals do not view life through a single reference frame. Each of us has developed many different reference frames, covering different subjects and parts of our environment. What mechanisms govern the way in which a reference frame will be developed? There are some psychological principles that help govern the development and utilization of different reference frames. Frames of reference are developed through *learning*. Once frames of reference are formed, however, there is a tendency for individuals to try to see *consistencies* between beliefs. Generally speaking, we do not like to hold two beliefs that contradict each other (for example, "I smoke over a pack of cigarettes a day" and "Smoking causes cancer and killed my grandfather"), and we are motivated to *reduce inconsistencies*.

Learning

Most people have a common understanding of what is meant by the term "learning." Everyone agrees that children have to *learn* how to read a book, ride a bicycle, and drive a car. This common-sense definition can be extended to a general definition of learning as *the process by which some aspect of human behavior is acquired or changed through an individual's encounter with events in the environment*.

Over the years that scholars have been interested in the process of learning, many elaborate theories of learning have been developed and tested. We cannot in this volume discuss any of the major theories in detail. Rather, we shall attempt to isolate and discuss those ideas that seem most applicable to persuasive communication.

Basic to all theories of learning is the assumption that there is an explainable or predictable relationship between *stimuli* and *responses*. A "stimulus" can be defined as any event that can be perceived by the organism. Thus, in a persuasive communication situation, the message serves as a stimulus. The source serves as another stimulus, as does the physical setting for the situation. A "response" can be defined as anything that the receiver does as a result of perceiving a stimulus. Thus the original category scheme we defined in Chapter 1 (changes in affect, cognition, and behavior) covers the kinds of responses in which we might be interested.

The persuasive communicator normally wants to elicit a specific response from a receiver or group of receivers. The communicator can present a message and then wait passively until a receiver makes an appropriate response. Or the source can present a message under such conditions as to lead the receiver to an appropriate response. These two different approaches have been termed *instrumental* learning and *conditioned* learning.

1. In *instrumental-* (also referred to as "operant") learning situations, a stimulus is presented to an organism, and when the correct or desired response has been made, some reinforcement or reward is given in order to either fix or strengthen the response. In instrumental-learning situations, the theory suggests that if the organism makes several incorrect responses that are not rewarded and then makes a correct response that is rewarded, the probability is increased that the person will repeat the correct response if the same stimulus is presented.

Instrumental learning works because people want to maximize rewards and minimize punishments. If rewards are *contingent* upon a person's successfully selecting the correct behavior, and if the rewards are indeed valued by the individual, then rewards strengthen the individual's tendency to engage in the behavior. We have all used instrumental learning on others, and have had instrumental learning used on us. For example, suppose a fund-raising agency sends several letters urging that an individual donate money to some charity. If the individual eventually does send a contribution, the fund raisers immediately send a letter of thanks, and perhaps a small token of appreciation such as a pin or a ball-point pen. This is an example of instrumental learning, and the follow-up letter and gift are designed to be the *reinforcing* agent.

Considerable research evidence indicates that we can *verbally* shape the attitudes of others. Since the 1950s, studies have found that experimenters can influence the frequency by which a person engaged in a behavior by conditioning the behavior with positive verbal statements (for example, "good"). The study by Insko[6] is an excellent example of this approach. The study was conducted at the University of Hawaii, where there is an annual Aloha Week Festival. Students were called and interviewed about their attitudes toward establishing a second, springtime, Aloha Festival. Generally speaking, most students should have mixed feelings about the second festival, since on one hand, it would disrupt university operation, and distract from the traditional festival. On the other hand, a second festival would be fun. Students were telephoned and were read 14 statements concerning pros and cons about the springtime festival and were asked to indicate the extent to which they agreed or disagreed with the statements. During this interview phase, whenever half of the students made a statement favoring the Aloha Week Festival, the interviewer would reward them by saying "good;" the other half of the students were rewarded with "good" whenever they expressed an attitude toward the festival that was unfavorable. After reading the statements, the interviewer thanked the students and hung up.

If verbal reinforcement can shape one's attitudes, then you'd expect that the first half of the students would be more in favor of Aloha Week after the interview, while the second half would be less in favor of it. This expectation was exactly what Insko found. A week or so after the telephone survey, Insko distributed a "Local Issues Questionnaire" and one of the items just happened to be about a springtime Aloha Week Festival. Even a week after being interviewed, students who had been rewarded for making positive statements about the festival indicated more positive attitudes than students who were rewarded for expressing antifestival sentiments.

Why does verbal reinforcement work, and when does it work best? According to Insko and Cialdini[7] a verbal reward does several things. First, a verbal reward communicates to the student the interviewer's attitude. This communication represents the *information* conveyed by reinforcement—that "good" informs the student of the interviewer's point of view and allows for agreement or conformity to exist. Second, a verbal reward communicates approval and liking for the student. According to this second outcome, the more often an interviewer says "good," the better the interviewer-student *rapport* becomes. Insko and Cialdini argued that verbal responses, thus, have an impact on two psychological variables: *amount of information* and *rapport*. They felt that both these variables are important in learning.[8]

Influencing behavior through reinforcements and verbal rewards is a pervasive way in which learning occurs in our society. We learn the alphabet, table manners, saying please and thank you, how to keep friends and not to make enemies, and much, much more by attending to rewards and by avoiding punishments.

2. In *classical conditioning* learning situations, a stimulus that has already been tied by the organism to a rewarding (or punishing) response is presented to the organism along with an unfamiliar stimulus. After a number of trials, the new stimulus should elicit the same response as the original stimulus. This is the famous "Pavlov's dog" situation, where it was established that the presentation of food elicits salivation from the dog. Figure 2.2 diagrams the classical conditioning situation. In this situation, a slice of meat is referred to as an *unconditioned* stimulus and the salivation is the *unconditioned* response (panel (a), Figure 2.2). These are called *unconditioned* because the meat-salivation relationship occurs natu-

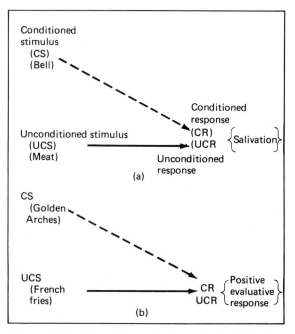

Figure 2.2. Illustration of Classical Conditioning. Panel (a) illustrates conditioning of a dog's response to a ringing bell. Panel (b) illustrates the classical conditioning of a favorable attitude toward "Golden Arches," through a person's love for French fries.

rally in the world without any conditioning. In the Pavlov studies, a bell (or light) does not produce, naturally, salivation in a dog. However, if a bell is *paired* with the presentation of the meat consistently over time, then a dog will learn to salivate when the bell is rung. Similarly, some of us enjoy tasty French fries and salivate at the thought of French fries. If the act of eating French fries is consistently paired with a pair of "Golden Arches," then the positive feeling of eating French fries carries over to our liking for the "Golden Arches." The reader should keep in mind that in *instrumental learning* the individual received a reward *after* selecting an appropriate behavior, while in *classical conditioning* one behavior (bell ringing) is *simultaneously paired* with another event or behavior (that is, presenting meat to the dog).

As in the case of instrumental learning, considerable research evidence supports the operation of classical conditioning. For example, many studies have paired offensive odors with nonsense syllables, Turkish letters, and so on (stimuli on which we have neutral attitudes), or with names of people. After consistently pairing the two, students tend to dislike the name, or the Turkish character, or whatever. In fact, one study paired either the name of "George" or the name of "Ed" to 16 unpleasant adjectives over the course of a study.[9] Later, the students walked down the hall of the psychology building and reported to a "second study" that allegedly involved group discussion. This second experiment was rigged so that group discussants were called "Ed" and "George." The students who had just been exposed to negative adjectives and the name "George" behaved in a manner friendlier toward "Ed" than toward "George," while the students who were conditioned to dislike the name "Ed" behaved in a manner friendlier toward "George" than toward "Ed." Classical conditioning, then, can influence our attitudes and our behaviors.

Conditioning principles are also frequently used by persuasive communicators. The advertiser knows that men are attracted to pictures of pretty girls, and that children like toys. So the advertiser presents a picture of his or her product being shown by a pretty girl, or shows a breakfast food that has a small toy in the box on a children's television show. The assumption is that the product will be seen as tied to a stimulus that is already rewarding to the receiver, and the sale of the item will thus be enhanced. Many perfume commercials, designer-jeans commercials, and magazine lay-out ads for clothes employ the classic "sex appeal" so that the product is paired with a stimulating male or female.

In sum, learning theories are concerned with the connections between responses and specifiable stimuli. Some theories are concerned with an analysis of response probabilities and pay minimal attention to the cognitive state of the individual organism making the response. Such theories have been labeled stimulus-response (S-R) learning theories. Other theorists insist that any analysis of response probabilities must be based on an analysis of the internal state of the individual organism, as well as on an analysis of the stimuli and responses present in a given situation. Such theories have been called stimulus-organism-response (S-O-R) theories. The theoretical orientation of this book leans toward the latter type of theories, and our presentation owes much to the early work of Clark Hull[10] and Charles Osgood.[11]

Before discussing general principles of learning, we should note that the two types of learning discussed here represent the major ways in which individuals learn attitudes and develop behaviors. They do not represent *all* the ways in which we might develop attitudes or beliefs. "Observational learning" means that we learn a behavior by merely observing others, while "vicarious learning" means that we observe others engage in a behavior and observe them get rewards for engaging in the behavior (for example, when J. R. Ewing engages in successful deceit and is rewarded with more money and benefits, children may tend to believe that deceit has advantages). Chances are, many teenagers get ideas about flirting and courtship from modeling older brothers and sisters (or from the movies they watch) or they may see how a new dance is done by observing others. In each of these examples, the receivers may "learn" a claim, or fantasize about some event (doing the dance successfully and gaining esteem), and these perceptual changes and belief changes are obviously important products of a number of persuasion attempts.

Some general principles of learning

Individuals differ in the ways in which they learn any given response, and differ in the ways in which they perceive any given stimulus. One person may perceive a stimulus and quickly assimilate it into an already existing frame of reference. Another person may not assimilate it as rapidly, and the stimulus will need to be repeated several times before it is firmly built into a frame of reference. Thus the persuasive communicator must be aware that the probability of a particular response being learned, and thus becoming part of an individual's frame of reference, will vary widely among the audience members. Six principles help explain some of the different responses made by receivers exposed to exactly the same message.

1. Individuals differ in their ability to respond. This principle implies that when two people receive the same message, their responses may be different simply because they differ in their ability to respond. Imagine a message urging people to take a wonderful ten-day vacation to England. Even though many people may wish to take the trip, it is likely that only a few would have the money.

2. Individuals differ in their readiness to respond. Some people cannot operate at full efficiency early in the morning. Others have a period immediately after lunch or dinner when they are not very attentive to any messages. Imagine two men sitting in the living room watching a television advertisement for a new car. One person has a four-year-old car, while the other man

bought a new car just three months ago. The readiness principle would predict that, other things being equal, the individual with a four-year-old car is readier to respond favorably to the advertisement than the man with the almost new automobile.

When is an individual likely to be ready to respond to any particular message? Here are some questions that may help in determining the optimum time to present a message. (1) Is the receiver paying attention? (2) Are the physical surroundings such that they will not detract from the communicator's message? (3) Has there been any attempt at "preteaching"? The term "preteaching" refers to the messages that may be sent ahead of time to give the receiver the necessary background for an understanding of the source's message. (4) Did we make the message easy to *comprehend* for a receiver? People will always differ in their readiness to respond, but if we can answer "yes" to these questions, we make the task of the persuasive communicator just a bit easier.

3. Individuals differ in their motivation to respond. There are a number of *motives* or *drives* that help determine the nature of the response made to messages. Some of these drives are *biologically* determined, such as hunger, thirst, pain avoidance, and sex. Other motives are *learned*, such as preservation of health, loyalty to country, duty, or competition. Learning is facilitated when the receiver is made to feel that a message is appealing to a particular motive. One person, for example, who has acquired a strong motive to compete may be attracted by a message promising that the receiver can be "first" in some skill, activity, or event. For other receivers, an appeal to loyalty, or friendship, or cooperation may prove to be a stronger motive.

4. Reinforcement is helpful in establishing response. This is the principle of reward and punishment that has already been discussed in describing instrumental learning. The little girl who is given a cookie after tying her shoes correctly is more likely to tie them correctly in the future. The reinforcement principles cannot be stressed too strongly. Many scientists believe that learning is *never* fixed or completed until some reinforcement has been given.

People do not all react to the same reward. For one individual, praise given after completion of a desired response is sufficient to ensure future repetition of the behavior. For another, a direct monetary reward may be necessary. Some people are motivated to avoid fear, others to gain economically, and still others to gain esteem. Many problems of the persuasive speaker today include linking the appropriate reward to the appropriate audience. Individuals also differ in the number of times they need reinforcement in order to continue to maintain a desired response. For some, every two or three times may be sufficient; for others, every 20 times may be enough. The frequency with which reinforcement is offered will remain one of the crucial decisions that must be made.

Reinforcement may be either positive or negative. A positive reinforcement is anything that increases the probability of a desired response when it is added to the learning situation. A negative reinforcement is anything that increases the probability of a desired response when it is removed from the learning situation. In laboratory situations, it is easy to provide both positive and negative reinforcers. In real-life situations, negative rewards are more difficult to apply. The teacher can praise the student who learns the correct lesson, but what kind of things can the teacher remove from the situation as a negative reward? What can one do to the person who refuses to vote for needed school taxes? Finding a negative reinforcer for this situation is difficult. Both positive and negative reinforcements have an effect on learning, but positive reinforcement seems to produce better results than negative reinforcement in most of the persuasive communication situations that have been studied. (See also Chapter 13.)[12]

5. In learning, active participation is better than passive participation. This principle is useful whether you are engaged in a traditional persuasive campaign, or are engaged in mutual persuasive attempts with another individual. Billy Graham does not merely *ask* people to make a "decision for Christ." He asks people to rise from their seats and go to the front of the room. The active participation of an individual in the learning process facilitates the response desired.

Many contemporary campaigns, worthy of great support, have failed because the participants in persuasion were given nothing specific to do. We argue with a friend, "Pollution is bad. We must all reduce pollution." We say, "Abortions are necessary if we are to control population growth." Then we stop communicating, assuming that because we have made a short speech, we have done our job. The message, however, may not have been assimilated into a frame of reference, nor even responded to, because we failed to tell the receiver exactly what *he* or *she* could do to stop pollution, or achieve abortion reform. This principle seems obvious if you think about trying to teach a child to ride a bicycle, ice-skate, or play golf.

6. Meaningful responses are learned more easily than meaningless ones. This is another principle that seems obvious, but examples exist to show that communicators sometimes forget to make their demands meaningful to the receiver. In 1966, Medicare became part of the American scene. Originally, everyone over the age of 65 who signed up for the program by March 31, 1966, was to be covered under the program. Those who did not sign up by that time would have to wait more than two years. Many people signed up, but many others did not. The main emphasis in the messages sent out by the government was that people sign up by a particular date. Relatively little attention was given in the many messages to telling receivers just *what* Medicare would do for them. For many receivers, this was probably a meaningless message. Eventually, the deadline had to be extended, and the officials concerned began directing attention to the reasons why people should sign up, thus finally tying Medicare to the original message. Learning is better accomplished when the material to be learned is meaningful to the receiver.

The principles discussed above are related to the initial development of frames of reference, as well as to the initial learning of a particular response. The persuasive communicator, however, is also interested in the long-range effects of messages. Joe Salesman wants Mr. Smith to buy the product the first time in order to try it. But Joe isn't a very good salesman if he stops with messages advocating a single purchase. Joe Salesman should be interested in responses becoming *habitual* for the receiver, and frames of reference becoming strengthened so that they are consistently used by the receiver. For Joe Salesman to be completely successful, Mr. Smith should reach for the same brand of shampoo every time. Habits are developed over a period of time, with repeated stimuli being presented, and the correct responses being rewarded.

Six principles concerning the development of habits

If 10 percent of the U.S. population habitually buy the same toothpaste (that is, they develop "brand loyalty") hundreds of thousands of dollars can be made. Hence, the study of habits is important. Here are six principles concerning the development of habits.

1. As the number of rewarded repetitions of the response increases, the probability that the response will be made increases. Many persuasive messages and campaigns have immediate and apparently successful effects. People *do* become stirred up about crime in their community. People *do* call on their city officials for better pollution controls. As time passes, however, the response to repeated messages lessens and eventually disappears or becomes attached to another stimulus. Either *extinction* of the original stimulus-response relationship has taken place because the individual no longer finds it satisfying, or a *transfer* of the response from one stimulus to another has occurred. Rather constant vigilance is needed to avoid extinction or transfer effects.

2. The time interval between response and reward must be kept short for effective building of habit patterns. When there is a long delay between the time a desired response is made to a particular stimulus and the time the receiver perceives the reinforcement to the response, the probability that the response will be repeated is lowered. If the time interval is long, other responses will have occurred more recently, and the reinforcement is likely to be transferred to a more recent stimulus.

3. Habit formation is facilitated when stimuli are presented in isolation. The persuasive communicator who has to compete for space in the newspaper or has to sandwich the message in between many other messages on the radio will have a more difficult time in securing desirable responses than if able to present the message in the absence of other messages. We are all faced every day with many, many competing messages. The television set, the demands of parents, wives, husbands, roommates, employers, and the radio blaring in the next room, all compete for our attention. The chance of any persuasive message getting through is very low. If all of us could present our persuasive messages when there was nothing else competing for the receiver's attention, our task would be easy. Since that is seldom possible, we must strive to eliminate as many sources of competing messages as possible, or make our message stand out above all others.

4. The complexity of the response desired affects the ease of habit formation. It is much harder to obtain a change in attitude in favor of a complex set of zoning regulations than a change in favor of a bill to place a sign at the edge of the city welcoming strangers. Many tasks can be broken down into smaller units, and an entire program of change may slowly be implemented. The first phase, when assimilated, helps strengthen the frame of reference so that the second step will be received more favorably, and that step in turn facilitates the third step. Joe Salesman, then, might well be advised to design his messages in such a way that the first message merely tries to attract interest in the product, the second asks that the receiver adopt a favorable attitude toward the product, the third attempts to persuade the receiver to come into the store, the next message argues for a first purchase of the product, and the final set of messages is designed to make the buyer want to buy the product again and again. When the response desired by a persuasive communicator is very complex, even receivers who respond favorably to the message will form habits far more slowly and with less stability than those individuals who respond to messages advocating simpler responses. Complex intentions on the part of the communicator are best broken down into simpler parts to facilitate the formation of reference frames, and the eventual formation of habitual responses.

5. Individuals tend to generalize the responses they make.

Generalization is a common phenomenon in learning situations. It can be illustrated easily by an example from animal learning. Imagine that a cat has been trained to come for food when a certain bell is rung. It is very likely that a bell slightly higher or slightly lower in tone will also produce the same response in the cat, but a bell that is much higher or lower will not produce the response. This is *stimulus generalization*, the making of the same response to slightly different stimuli. *Response generalization* is an analogous phenomenon in which slightly different responses are made to the same stimuli.

This principle explains many of the effects seen in persuasive communication. For example many of the large multinational corporations have established a single trademark. Corporations such as ITT, TransAmerica, and CitiBank have spent hundreds of thousands of dollars attempting to identify and then publicize an appropriate trademark to be attached to all of their products. The intent is that favorable responses about one product will be transferred to any other product bearing the same label.

It is fortunate that we do generalize. If generalization did not occur, the speaker could elicit learned responses from a receiver only when exactly the same message was repeated. This is seldom possible. There is significant evidence that generalization effects can be strengthened or weakened by reinforcement. To establish a class of responses to the same stimulus (response generalization), the source must provide reinforcement for all of the responses that fit the intent of the communicator. To establish a single response to a class of stimuli (stimulus generalization), the source must ensure that the single response is reinforced whenever it is made to any of the desired stimuli and that it is not reinforced for any other stimulus. Our brief description of this problem may make it sound simple. In fact, finding and applying appropriate reinforcements in any generalization situation is a difficult task for any advertiser or for any persuasive communicator.

Through selective reinforcement relatively wide ranges of either stimulus or response generalization can be made. Furthermore, through selective reinforcement the receiver can be made to respond to only a single, very narrow range of stimuli. This phenomenon is called *discrimination*, and again, it has an important place in persuasive communication. The advertiser who has to sell a particular brand of soap product is a good example. Grocery store shelves are lined with many soap products, all claiming to perform much the same function. The advertiser's task in such a situation is to ensure that the buyer is reinforced not only for buying soap but also for buying one particular brand of soap. Sometimes the advertiser offers special prices. At other times coupons may be offered, but the attempts are to force the buyer to discriminate between products.

6. Providing information about receiver performance leads to improved performance.

This principle is particularly important to the interactive view of persuasion that we have discussed. The acquisition of language and the

individual to develop intrinsic re-
to an ability to use information about
nce to correct the performance for sub-
esentations. Thus, if one can systemati-
rm receivers about the quality of the re-
being made, the information can be used
ove future responses.

viding the receiver with information about
of responses not only helps improve the re-
er's responses, it also helps strengthen the
ne of reference. For example, several months
o, an ecologist made a speech about pollution.
le gained considerable support from his audience. They were "with him." Then he offered to
take them on a walk through the city, where they
were to show him what they had learned about
pollution. As they walked, he asked people to help
him identify some of the sources of environmental
pollution in the area. They did so, and then he
asked them to walk back over the same route with
him. This time, he pointed out all the conditions
they had missed. It was a dramatic performance,
and when their own performance was corrected,
the audience members were able to sharpen their
appreciation of the problems he had originally
pointed out. Rewards are important to successful
learning, but human response can be improved if
the individual can be told how to improve.

So far in this chapter we have argued that people have to acquire a frame of reference that will
let them attend to the message before persuasion
can be successful. The development of a reference
frame depends upon the acquisition and assimilation of information. This is largely controlled by
the process of learning. Once a reference frame
has been developed, it can only be changed by the
learning of new materials that force the person to
make behavior changes. We admit, however, that
our examination of the role of learning in persuasion is far from complete. We have mentioned
only those principles that seem to have high relevance to persuasion. Furthermore, learning theories are not the only theories for explaining human behavior. Many theorists criticize learning
theories for what they see as a very simplistic stimulus-response model. Critics argue that learning

theories do not take into account psychological
mechanisms within the individual that may *not*
require reinforcement. In fact, we shall now examine a class of theories that suggests that people
sometimes respond in ways that seem to be
against their best interests. Regardless of the criticism to which learning theories have been exposed, all behavioral scientists agree that the role
of reinforcement in determining responses to new
situations and new people is extremely important.

Cognitive consistency

One of the major charges against classical learning
theories is that they fail to recognize the importance of the mediation activities the mind engages
in between the time a stimulus is perceived and a
response is given. There is a whole class of theories referred to as "cognitive" theories that see the
mind as a vital mechanism that organizes the messages it receives into meaningful wholes. Cognitive theories argue that the brain does not simply
respond to those stimuli that are reinforced while
rejecting those stimuli that are not reinforced. Instead, the argument is made that the mind is constantly at work organizing the stimuli that are perceived into patterns.

Some of the most important cognitive theories
have been termed "consistency theories." A person does not perceive the world as a series of
completely unrelated stimuli. When a new event is
recorded by the individual, the stimulus is processed within existing frames of reference. The
trend of this processing is toward *minimizing the
internal inconsistencies* among the items that form
the frame of reference. Furthermore, the fact that
we tend to form consistent reference frames
means that our responses—emotions, cognitions,
and actions—also tend to be consistent. Because
the pressure toward consistency seems to be important in shaping our reference frames as well as
our responses, some elaboration of consistency
theories as they apply to persuasive communica-

tion will be helpful to communicators and receivers.

Consistency theories were first propounded in the early 1940s, although the roots for such theories undoubtedly go back much further.[13] Since World War II, the various cognitive consistency theories have provided one of the most fruitful areas of study within communication and the behavioral sciences.

The term "cognitive consistency" is used in this book to cover a number of specific theories that we have tried to apply to different types of persuasive communication situations. Although the various consistency theories have unique aspects, all the theories are based on the common premise that inconsistency is somehow unpleasant or painful or distasteful, and that the tensions created by this unpleasant state will lead to attempts to reduce the tensions. Festinger refers to consonance and dissonance,[14] Osgood to congruity and incongruity,[15] Abelson and Rosenberg to consistency,[16] and Heider to balance and imbalance.[17] The psychological mechanism that is being studied appears to be much the same for all these researchers.[18] We have, therefore, chosen to label the general psychological mechanism as *cognitive consistency*, while recognizing that there are differences between each theory.

The research literature on cognitive consistency theory is very extensive and would fill several volumes the size of this one. Rather than attempt to review the entire body of research literature, we have chosen to present examples of the major theories as they may be used to illustrate persuasive communication.

Issues in cognitive consistency

While we will talk about consistency theories in several additional chapters of this book, we will discuss two topics here: (1) balance and (2) the theory of cognitive dissonance

1. What is balance? When we say we have a theory of "cognitive consistency" we are saying we have a theory about "cognitions" that deals

with the "consistency" of those cognitions. "Cognitions" are all the beliefs you might have, as discussed above. These various cognitions can be related to one another in a number of ways. First, two beliefs may simply be unrelated to one another: "The price of snowshoes in Nome went up 25 percent since last year" and "Bus 25 will take you downtown." Second, two beliefs can be consonant or compatible or positively related to one another: "Inflation remained high last year" and "The price of snowshoes went up 25 percent." Finally, two cognitions can be incompatible or contradictory: "USC will win the Rose Bowl" and "Ohio State will win the Rose Bowl." We dislike inconsistency and contradiction among our beliefs, and we are often motivated to resolve discrepancies when we experience them.

The simplest version of a cognitive consistency theory relevant to persuasion is balance theory.[19] In this perspective three cognitive elements are called a cognitive structure, where elements can have a positive or negative relationship with one another. Various combinations of these structures are in Figure 2.3; where "P" means *person*, "O" means *other*, and "X" means the topic or issue that person and other view, discuss, and so on. The three elements in the structure can form one of two kinds of relationships: *balanced* or *imbalanced*. By "balance" we mean that the elements are in a harmonious relationship with one another, where we see the relationships among elements as pleasant, desirable, stable, and expected, and where we do not feel any pressure to change any

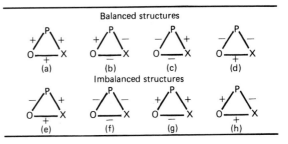

Figure 2.3. Balanced and Imbalanced Cognitive Structures

of the elements in order to make them fit together.

All of the structures on the top row of Figure 2.3 are balanced, and all of the structures in the second row are imbalanced. Structure (a) is balanced—Peter (P) likes Olaf (O), Olaf likes modern art (X), and Peter likes modern art. All the elements are harmonious to one another—Peter likes the people who like the same things he likes. Structure (b) is also balanced: Peter likes Olaf and both Peter and Olaf find Punk Rock (X) to be offensive. Structure (c) is also balanced—Peter does not like Olaf, Olaf does not like the Republican Party, and Peter does. Such a relationship is harmonious—Peter thinks that people he dislikes dislike the things he likes. Finally, in (d), Peter dislikes Olaf, Peter doesn't like opera, but Olaf does like opera—people I hate like the things I dislike.

Structures e, f, g, and h are imbalanced and we feel some tension toward making them balanced. In (e), Peter doesn't like Olaf, but both Peter and Olaf enjoy modern art. Peter would feel a little out of sorts with this arrangement because he anticipates liking people who like the things he likes, and does not anticipate that his enemies would get pleasure from the same things he gets pleasure from. The more intensely Peter hates Olaf, the more likely Peter would be disturbed by the relationships among elements in (e). To make the structure balanced, Peter can change his attitude toward modern art or change his attitude toward Olaf. Which? One of the most important rules of making structures balanced is that *the less important element is usually the one which is changed*. If Peter truly hated Olaf, he would tend to lose some of his liking for modern art.

In the last paragraph we noted two ways in which a structure could be made balanced— changing the P-X relationship or changing the P-O relationship. Certainly, there are other ways to make a structure balanced. In fact, Heider[20] noted a range of ways in which balance can be achieved. In one study, students were given the following scenario, and were asked for their reactions: "Bob thinks Jim is very stupid and a first-class bore. One day Bob reads some poetry he likes so well that he takes the trouble to track down the author in order to shake his hand. He finds that Jim wrote the poems." Heider noted that 46 percent of the students felt that Bob would upgrade his opinion of Jim; another 29 percent felt that Bob would feel less enthusiastic about the poetry. Still, 19 percent felt that they wouldn't resolve the imbalance, but noted that some tension would be felt. Five percent of the students even questioned Jim's authorship of the poetry, and 2 percent felt that Bob would make a concession—thinking that Jim wrote some good lines and some bad lines. As these numbers indicate, the two *major* ways of making a structure balanced is to change one of the elements.

The remainder of the structures are also imbalanced. In (f) Peter dislikes Olaf and also dislikes opera and Olaf also dislikes opera—Peter finds himself in the peculiar situation of sharing the same attitude (disliking opera) with his enemies. In (g), Peter likes Olaf and Peter likes the Detroit Lions, but Olaf dislikes the Lions; while in (h) Peter likes Olaf, Olaf likes the Lions, and Peter does not.

Considerable research has focused on our reactions to balanced and imbalanced structures; we find balanced ones to be more pleasant, harmonious, and memorable and we perceive them to be more stable than imbalanced ones. Further, there is considerable evidence that we prefer the structure where all elements are positive—structure (a) in Figure 2.3 is rated highest in preference. This preference for positive relationships between all elements is used by advertisers on a routine basis. That is, advertisers find spokespersons for their products that we like, thus making the P-O relationship positive (that is, put yourself in the structure as P). Then, these spokespersons extol the positive virtues of a particular product (X), thus creating a positive O-X relationship. What is *your* attitude toward X if balance theory is correct, and the P-O relationship is positive and O-X relationship is positive? A brief look at television commercials or a look through some magazine layouts will indicate the existence of a preponderance of positive P-O and O-X links—J. R. Ewing loves his underwear, Arnold Palmer is ecstatic over his motor oil, and Jack Klugman is enthusiastic about his copier service. Since we have a preference for balance and for positive relationships, we should develop positive attitudes toward these products.

The second implication of balance theory for persuasion deals with dyadic communication—since one possible option is for Peter to try to persuade Olaf to like the Lions. Newcomb[21] developed a model of balance that was very similar to Heider's where communication was one of the means by which an individual can reduce strain caused by imbalanced structures. Suppose Peter and Olaf were discussing who they would vote for in a presidential campaign, and the structure (a) in Figure 2.3 represented the state of affairs. Little *persuasion* would occur because Peter and Olaf like each other and both agreed about voting. However, we would see one probable effect their communication would have—communication between the two will probably strengthen the resistance of both individuals to outside communicators who may transmit messages to them about voting for the opponent. Their resistance would increase because both have received new information (that is, social support) that is consistent with an already existing belief structure. However, in a number of situations (such as g and h), we find that Peter can try to persuade Olaf to change his mind toward the topic on hand in order to make the structures balanced. We have much to say about how Peter might go about this dyadic or face-to-face persuasion in Chapters 10, 11, and 12.

2. The theory of cognitive dissonance and attention to competing messages.
Every year millions of Americans are faced with the task of purchasing a new automobile, buying a house, voting for political candidates, deciding whether to vote for increased school taxes, or simply evaluating the editorials they read in the newspaper. In each of these situations, several different messages are likely to be available to the individual. The Ford Motor Company sends a message extolling

the virtues of a Ford; General Motors argues for a Chevrolet; and Volkswagen tells you that the only way to go is with a Rabbit. The incumbent state senator tells you that he should be reelected, while his opponent tells you that the incumbent ought to be turned out of office. One editorial tells us that our community needs more business and fewer people trying to obstruct the growth of business, while the competing paper argues for a moratorium on new business until the community has solved its sewage problem.

If the persuasive communicator could know which messages were more likely to be attended to, it would make the task much easier. Consistency theory reasons that changes in the frame of reference and changes in responses should be in line with making cognitive structures more consistent. In the case of competing messages, works by Festinger,[22] Brehm and Cohen,[23] and McGuire[24] specify some of the factors that might control this situation. The problem can be illustrated by looking at the process of buying a car.

Elizabeth Dawson has just graduated from college and has been hired by a large chemical company to work in their public relations office. Elizabeth has moved to the city where she is to begin work, and soon realizes that she must have a car. The plant is located far from any housing, and she can see that recreation on weekends will depend on being able to get away from the city. So Elizabeth begins looking for an automobile.

It is at this point that the problem of competing messages beings to emerge. Several questions are of interest to the persuasive communicator in this situation. To which messages is Elizabeth most likely to listen? What factors are likely to guide Elizabeth in making a choice of automobile? After Elizabeth has made a choice and purchased one of the competing models, how is she likely to behave toward other messages regarding automobiles? Our theory allows us to make predictions about each of these questions.

Perhaps the biggest decision that Elizabeth faces will be one of price. As a newly-hired graduate, it is not likely that she will be able to afford an extremely expensive car, so the chances are that she will rule out automobiles that are in the upper price brackets. Our theory says that she will stop paying much attention to messages about Cadillacs and Lincolns. Even after Elizabeth has decided on the price range she *can* afford, however, there are still likely to be several different makes and models that fall within that price range. For each model there will be a lot of persuasive literature and many different advertisements to which she will be exposed. In addition, Elizabeth faces a barrage of competing information from salesmen and the comments of friends and relatives. These

---

BOX 2.1
THE THEORY OF COGNITIVE DISSONANCE

According to the theory of cognitive dissonance, cognitions can have a relevant or irrelevant relationship. Relevant relations are of two types: *dissonant* and *consonant*. According to Festinger, "two elements are in a dissonant relation if, considering these two alone, the obverse of one element would follow from the other (p. 13). Suppose, for example, Mike believed "I am not a racist." However, at a party Mike told a racist joke. The two cognitions are incompatible with one another, and Mike experiences a state of dissonance. In this example in the text, Elizabeth Dawson believes, "I make good decisions." If this is true, then the element "I made the wrong choice when I bought the Edsel" would be undesirable since it would be dissonant to the first one. Hence, Elizabeth would be motivated to avoid the second belief. In postdecision dissonance, dissonance is aroused when (a) the decision is important to the person, (b) the decision means giving up relatively attractive features of the unchosen object, and (c) the objects one selected from had dissimilar attributes. This latter criterion needs clarification. If Elizabeth Dawson had to select between two street cars, she would experience a certain amount of dissonance. However, if Elizabeth had to select from a street car and a four-wheel-drive vehicle she would experience more dissonance since what she can do with one car cannot be done with the other.

Festinger suggested a number of ways in which people can reduce dissonance. First, people can try to revoke the decision. Second, they can increase their liking for the selected object (you start liking your new car even more, and you *selectively expose* yourself to information supportive of the decision), or, similarly, decrease your liking for the car you didn't buy. Third, you can increase the "cognitive overlap" between the two cars (you tell yourself that, now that you've thought about it, the two cars are pretty similar after all, so making the decision was not important). Finally, you can add consonant elements to change the ratio of dissonant to consonant ones.

There are a number of contexts where we experience dissonance, and dissonance theory's predictions apply to these contexts. For one, there is very solid evidence that indicates that we experience dissonance if we make a decision (of our own free will) and the topic of the decision involves some aspect of our *self-concept*.

SEE: L. Festinger, *A Theory of Cognitive Dissonance* (Stanford: Stanford University Press, 1957).

conflicting claims and messages provide, according to Festinger, a *dissonant* situation for the receiver. Dissonance theory states that Elizabeth will, in this situation where she is "just looking," be willing to look at many different kinds of literature, view all the television advertisements, and pay attention to anyone that has something to say about automobiles. Elizabeth is in an *information gathering* phase, and if our theory is correct, she will be willing to gather information from all the sources she can.

After talking to many people, and reading all the literature she can get, Elizabeth is going to have to make a decision, and order her car. That decision is going to be made in light of the evidence she has collected, and her feelings about the people who acted as sources of information. If there is an individual in whom she has great trust, it is very likely that the recommendations of that person will be very influential. This is in line with the importance of authority beliefs that we discussed earlier. At any rate, the eventual decision Elizabeth makes is going to be one consistent with her own frames of reference and the messages she has been exposed to.

Finally, the discussions are over, and Elizabeth signs an order for a new automobile. She has made a *choice*, and in so doing, she has finally lowered the tensions that arose because she was faced with competing information. What is her behavior going to be now that the decision has been made? Dissonance theory suggests that now she will be quite selective in the materials she reads about automobiles. She will not read or listen to messages about the cars she did not choose, unless the messages point out faults in the cars she could have chosen, but did not. The theory also suggests that Elizabeth will continue to be receptive to information about the automobile she did choose, but only *positive* information. Information that might indicate that she made a bad choice will not be received or sought out.

We have used our short example to show that dissonance theory purports to be able to predict the communication behaviors of individuals before a choice is to be made, to help in predicting what choice will be made, and to tell us what communication behaviors the individual will engage in after a choice has been made. Our example merely illustrates a number of factors that are of importance to persuasive communication, and that can be extended beyond the car-buying example.

First, an individual is placed in a dissonant situation whenever faced with a choice in which the elements are perceived to be an *inverse relationship* to one another. Smoking is a good example. Smoking is pleasurable, but smoking may also cause lung cancer. If people do not know that smoking may cause lung cancer, they may continue to choose to smoke with no psychological tension. The frames of reference such people hold about smoking are relatively simple, and there are no conflicting elements within those frames. What happens to such individuals when a report comes out that makes it clear that smoking *is* related to an increased risk of lung cancer? Our theory says that when people become aware of such discrepant information, dissonance results, and there will be attempts to reduce it. There are different ways to reduce dissonance in this situation, and we may expect that different people will use different methods. Some may decide to quit smoking, an act that does reduce dissonance. Others may decide that the pleasures of smoking outweigh the dangers of lung cancer, and that decision also reduces dissonance. Still others may decide that the risk of lung cancer is fairly large, but that the danger of gaining weight and increasing the risk of a heart attack is even larger, and thus it is still better to smoke. Again, dissonance is reduced. Note that an outsider may not at all agree with the mental gymnastics used by many of the people in our example, but each of the ways we have cited in which dissonance may be reduced is perfectly compatible with individual frames of reference. If nothing else, the example should tell a persuasive communicator that it may not be enough to just "give people the facts." The communicator may have to steer the receiver in the direction desired by the source.

Second, the *magnitude* of the dissonance that is

present will be a function of the importance of the elements or stimuli that are involved, the intensity with which attitudes are held toward the elements, and the number of elements involved. For example, Mr. Mason enjoys two television programs, both of which are programmed into the same time slot. Mr. Mason is in a dissonant relationship in this situation, but it is not really an important decision for him to make, so the amount of dissonance he will experience should be relatively small. One would imagine that the persuasive communicator would have an easy time persuading him to watch one show as opposed to the other. On the other hand, imagine the cognitive tensions arising in Mr. Rivers when he realizes the conflict he has over a job offer from a major firm. During his college years, Mr. Rivers worked long and hard on campus to achieve a cleanup of the river running through campus. His interest in ecology and a clean environment is very high. Just before accepting the job, he finds that his prospective company has been cited by the federal government as a major polluter. In this situation, we expect the magnitude of the dissonance that Mr. Rivers will experience to be extremely high. Mr. Rivers knows that he needs a job, but the past four years have been spent in building a frame of reference in conflict with the type of job he now finds himself considering.

How can Mr. Rivers reduce the dissonance that he is experiencing? He could, of course, turn down the job. That would reduce dissonance, but if jobs are very hard to find in his field, turning down the job is not going to reduce dissonance. A more likely course of action would be to accept the job, and tell himself that he will be able to work to change the company's practices and image. That does reduce dissonance, but it does so only as long as the individual feels that he is making progress. A similar kind of situation is found when a person P (Peter) has a friend, person O (Olaf), who drinks, smokes, and gambles, or does anything else that Peter disapproves of. Peter may justify his actions by the belief that he can change his friend "for the better." His dissonance level may be high, and we expect his actions to be extreme (if Olaf is a very close friend), producing a large change in Peter's frames of reference. In general, when the magnitude of the dissonance is very high, the probability of sweeping changes in the person's frame of reference is also high, *if* the individual is to succeed in reducing the dissonance. When dissonance is low, persuasion is more likely to be successful, because it may take only minimal information to change the situation, and thus reduce dissonance.

A third factor of importance to persuasion is the relationship between *choice* and a consequence of choice, *commitment*. Commitment to the various elements of a situation is an important requisite for the occurrence of significant dissonance. An individual can hold conflicting frames of reference, but if there is no public commitment to any of the frames, there is little dissonance produced when the inconsistency is pointed out. If, however, such conflicting reference frames are held, and a person is publicly committed to one of the frames, great dissonance may result. Thus the magnitude of the dissonance and the consequent expected attitude change increase as the degree of inconsistency between reference frames and public commitment increases.

The importance of such commitment can be seen in our educational system all across the United States. Many people in the northern tier of states applauded the Supreme Court decision of 1954 that called for an end to segregated schools. The news was full of state governors and legislators who announced that they were completely in favor of the decision, and veiled comments were made about those southerners who came out in opposition to the Court's decision. That attitude prevailed throughout much of the 1960s and early 1970s. Today, however, courts have moved beyond the early stage, and have called for an end to *de facto* segregation in many large northern cities. Most such plans call for the massive use of busing. The same individuals who welcomed the original Supreme Court decision now find themselves in a highly dissonant situation. They may *not* be in favor of having children bussed. They may be in favor of neighborhood schools. In the past, they could be generally in favor of integration and also in favor of neighborhood schools. In city after city, however, people are being forced to make a choice between integration and neighborhood schools. The dissonance produced in attempting to make that choice is threatening to tear our society apart. Our theory tells us that the amount of dissonance produced would be less if people had not earlier committed themselves to public support of integration.

A final factor relating to dissonance may be termed *exposure* to inconsistency. All of us hold some conflicting frames of reference, some conflicting attitudes and beliefs. We continue to hold them until the inconsistency is made known to us. When that inconsistency is made known to us, we can predict that there will be pressures in the direction of greater consistency. Rokeach[25] has demonstrated that this can occur. He obtained attitude and value ratings from a number of students about the topics of "equal rights" and "civil rights demonstrations." Then he went back to the students and showed them that most students ranked "freedom" first and "equality" sixth. At the same time, he showed the students that low rankings were given to "equality" by those students who said they were unsympathetic to civil rights demonstrations. Following this demonstration, the students were given a statement about the rating task they had originally done. They were told that they and their friends who had participated in the experiment seemed to be interested in their own freedom, but that they were obviously not interested in freedom for others. The students were then thanked for their help, and asked to think about the implications of the various rankings.

Three weeks later, the students were tested again. The results were generally what we would expect from a cognitive consistency theory framework. Students who had ranked both "equality" and "freedom" high showed little attitude change. Students who had ranked both concepts equally low also showed little change. Students who ranked "equality" high and "freedom" low, however, showed a significant shift of attitude by ranking their attitude about civil rights demonstrations higher. Rokeach tested again after a three-to-five-month period, and found that there

had been even more of a shift toward balancing the two sets of attitudes. This experiment suggests that the persuasive communicator can sometimes change attitudes in the desired direction by simply exposing the inconsistencies between two frames of reference and allowing the receiver's cognitive consistency mechanisms to work at closing the gap.

People do seek to reduce the amount of dissonance they experience when faced with competing messages. One of the consequences of an open society, such as ours, is that there are many competing messages on many topics. Our research frequently uncovers situations in which a persuasive message seems to result in attitude change, but when a later check is made, the individuals have moved back to their original positions. This may be due to competing messages that result in later changes in attitude. Successful persuasion cannot stop with a single, apparently successful message. When a persuasive communicator succeeds in getting a receiver to make a choice favorable to the communicator's position, the next step is getting the receiver to continue to support that choice. Just as Joe Salesman needs to send messages to keep people coming back to the store, the source that has succeeded in getting the receiver to adopt a position that was dissonantly held can aid in fixing the decision more firmly for the individual by "postdecision communication." Such messages offer receivers even more reasons why their choices were good ones. The automobile company that Elizabeth chose invariably makes use of this technique after the new car is delivered. Elizabeth will get a letter congratulating her on picking the particular car she did, will list the features that made her choice a wise one. One might think that Elizabeth would not be interested in automobile literature after just buying a new car, but our theory suggests that she *will* be interested in any materials that tend to confirm the choice she made.

The general base for all consistency theories is the idea that whenever an individual is placed in an unbalanced situation, there will be tension, and attempts made to reduce the tension. All consistency theories can be classified as drive-reduction theories of behavior. The force for changes in behavior is inconsistency, a force providing powerful motivation to reduce tensions. Attempts at tension reduction will result in changes in the individual's reference frames, and thus in changes in the responses the individual makes to persuasive communication.

One final note ought to be added before we end our discussion of consistency theories and their application to persuasion. At the beginning of our discussion, we suggested that not all social scientists agreed on the importance of consistency as a psychological mechanism. This area of disagreement deserves further mention. Consistency theories have been opposed on methodological grounds by Chapanis and Chapanis[26] and Lott.[27] Further, some theorists argue that we seek the novel, the unpredictable, and the complex. This approach, presented by writers such as Berlyne[28] and Fowler,[29] argues that while it might be true that there is a tendency to balance the information we receive, it is also true that there is a tendency to seek the unexpected, look for the novel, and enjoy the complex. They suggest that a desire to seek the "novel" is not compatible with the desire to keep reference frames stable and to balance the information we receive. McGuire[30] argues that the two theories, while apparently somewhat contradictory, may both be true. We may seek the novel or the new, for example, as a way of balancing a reference frame that is causing tension. We may use the novel as a way of justifying beliefs that educated men and women ought to be open to new ideas. Perhaps the best conclusion is that there is no serious threat to the importance of balance theories as a predictor of human behavior from novelty theories.

Summary

Human beings are constantly receiving information about the world around them. Our senses convey a steady stream of bits and pieces of information that allows us to decide whether we will put on a raincoat in the morning, cross the street to a store, vote for a tax increase, or execute any other behavior in our daily lives. The bits of information we receive do not come into sensory channels in random fashion. From the time we are born until the time we die, our mind is in the process of fashioning a set of complex frames of reference. These frames help determine what we will attend to, what we will come to believe in, whom we will like and dislike, and how we will respond to the messages to which we are exposed.

The frames of reference we develop help determine how we will behave in persuasive communication situations. Our reference frames are composed of attitudes and beliefs, and successful persuasion is linked to changes in attitudes and beliefs. Regardless of the type of persuasion in which we are interested, two major areas are of significance to us. We must understand the ways human beings learn and acquire new information. If persuasion is to be successful, the individuals participating may have to acquire new information before they can change existing attitudes, opinions, emotions, or actions. Similarly, various theories of cognitive consistency seem applicable to persuasion. Individuals tend to try to achieve consistency in the way they respond to messages and to other people. The attempts we make to achieve consistency are important indicators of the potential outcomes of any persuasive communication situation.

Footnotes

1. M. Rokeach, *The Open and Closed Mind* (New York: Basic Books, 1960).

2. M. Rokeach, *Beliefs, Attitudes and Values* (San Francisco: Jossey-Bass, 1968).

3. D. Bem, *Beliefs, Attitudes and Human Affairs* (Belmont, Calif.: Brooks/Cole, 1970).

4. E. Bettinghaus, "The Relative Effect of the Use of Testimony in a Persuasive Speech upon the Attitudes of Listeners" (M.A. thesis, Bradley University, 1953).

5. Rokeach, *Beliefs, Attitudes and Values,* pp. 22–61.

6. C. A. Insko, "Verbal Reinforcement of Atti-

tude," *Journal of Personality and Social Psychology,* vol. 2 (1965), pp. 621–623.

7. C. A. Insko and R. B. Cialdini, "A Test of Three Interpretations of Attitudinal Verbal Reinforcement," *Journal of Personality and Social Psychology,* vol. 12 (1969), pp. 333–341.

8. For a readable discussion of Insko and Cialdini's "two-factor model of verbal reinforcement," see R. E. Petty and J. T. Cacioppo, *Attitudes and Persuasion: Classic and Contemporary Approaches* (Dubuque, Iowa: Wm. C. Brown, 1981).

9. L. Berkowitz and K. A. Knurek, "Label-mediated Hostility Generalization," *Journal of Personality and Social Psychology,* vol. 13 (1969), pp. 200–206.

10. C. L. Hull, *A Behavior System: An Introduction to Behavior Theory Concerning the Individual Organism* (New Haven, Conn.: Yale University Press, 1951).

11. C. E. Osgood, *Methods and Theory in Experimental Psychology* (New York: Oxford University Press, 1953), pp. 299–599.

12. E. R. Hilgard, *Theories of Learning* (New York: Appleton-Century-Crofts, 1956), pp. 485–488.

13. For discussion of early work on consistency theories, see W. McGuire, "The Current Status of Cognitive Consistency Theories," in S. Feldman, ed., *Cognitive Consistency* (New York: Academic Press, 1966), pp. 2–4.

14. L. Festinger, *A Theory of Cognitive Dissonance* (Stanford: Stanford University Press, 1957).

15. C. E. Osgood, P. Tannenbaum, and G. Suci, *The Measurement of Meaning* (Urbana, Ill.: The University of Illinois Press, 1957), pp. 189–216. See also C. E. Osgood and P. Tannenbaum, "The Principle of Congruity in the Prediction of Attitude Change," *Psychological Review,* vol. 62 (1955), pp. 42–55.

16. R. P. Abelson and M. J. Rosenberg, "Symbolic Psycho-Logic: A Model of Attitudinal Cognition," *Behavioral Science,* vol. 3 (1958), pp. 1–13.

17. F. Heider, "Attitudes and Cognitive Organization," *Journal of Psychology,* vol. 21 (1946), pp. 107–112. See also F. Heider, *The Psychology of Interpersonal Relations* (New York: Wiley, 1958).

18. See, for example, N. P. Chapanis and A. Chapanis, "Cognitive Dissonance: Five Years Later," *Psychological Bulletin,* vol. 61 (1964), pp. 1–22; D. O. Sears and R. P. Abelson, "Attitudes and Opinions," *Annual Review of Psychology,* vol. 20 (1969), pp. 253–288; and R. B. Zajonc, "Cognitive Theories in Social Psychology," in G. Lindzey and E. Aronson, eds., *The Handbook of Social Psychology,* 2nd ed., vol. 1 (Reading, Pa.: Addison-Wesley, 1968), pp. 320–441.

19. F. Heider, "Attitudes and Cognitive Organization," *Journal of Psychology,* vol. 21 (1946), pp. 107–112; F. Heider, *The Psychology of Interpersonal Relations* (New York: Wiley, 1958).

20. Heider, *The Psychology of Interpersonal Relations;* see also: C. A. Insko, *Theories of Attitude Change* (New York: Appleton-Century-Crofts, 1967).

21. T. M. Newcomb, "An Approach to the Study of Communicative Acts," *Psychological Review,* vol. 60 (1963), pp. 393–404.

22. Festinger, *A Theory of Cognitive Dissonance.*

23. J. W. Brehm and A. R. Cohen, *Explorations in Cognitive Dissonance* (New York: Wiley, 1962).

24. W. McGuire, "Cognitive Consistency and Attitude Change," *Journal of Abnormal and Social Psychology,* vol. 60 (1960), pp. 345–353.

25. M. Rokeach and G. Rothman, "The Principles of Belief Congruence and the Congruity Principle as Models of Cognitive Interaction," *Psychological Review,* vol. 72 (1965), pp. 128–142; see also: M. Rokeach, *The Nature of Human Values* (New York: Free Press, 1973).

26. Chapanis and Chapanis, "Cognitive Dissonance: Five Years Later," pp. 1–22.

27. B. Lott, "Secondary Reinforcement and Effort: Comment on Aronson's 'The Effect of Effort on the Attractiveness of Rewarded and Unrewarded Stimuli,' " *Journal of Abnormal and Social Psychology,* vol. 67 (1963), pp. 520–522.

28. D. E. Berlyne, *Conflict, Arousal and Curiosity* (New York: McGraw Hill, 1965).

29. H. Fowler, *Curiosity and Exploratory Behavior* (New York, Macmillan, 1965).

30. McGuire, "The Current Status of Cognitive Consistency Theories," pp. 35–38.

CHAPTER THREE

Successful Persuasion: Predicting Individual Response

If you prepare a persuasive message, and then direct it toward a number of receivers, it is likely that the results will show that some people are dramatically affected by the message, others are affected to a lesser degree, and some people do not seem to be at all affected. Even if you have attempted to ascertain carefully what the original attitude level of the audience is, and have determined that everyone receiving the message does have the ability to respond, you can expect differences in the way people behave. What causes people to respond to a message in different ways?

Communication scholars and other behavioral scientists have been interested in questions about individual response to messages for some time. After all, being able to make even *some* predictions about the ways in which people are likely to respond to a message would be of tremendous help

to a source. Just think of some of the many situations in which the ability to predict would be of use. Will my boyfriend or girlfriend respond favorably to an invitation to a concert? What will my communication instructor do if I ask him to postpone the midterm examination? What will my boss do if I ask her for a raise?

Making such predictions is admittedly difficult. None of the theories we are going to discuss below is foolproof in any sense of the word, but each of them approaches the interpersonal persuasive situation from a slightly different point of view, and each of them has proven to be a useful way of making predictions about human behavior.

First, we shall discuss *personality theory*. Second, we shall discuss how a person's level of *involvement* in a topic affects the process of persuasion.

Finally, we shall introduce *attribution theory* and *exchange theory*. In the next chapter we shall examine approaches that help in making predictions about larger audiences.

Personality theory

This is the age of Psychological Man. Everybody seems to be interested in psychology. Newspapers carry columns about human behavior, popular songs try to interpret our behavior, and a number of popular magazines are devoted to the analysis of human behavior. Business and government spend large sums training their personnel in management methods based on psychology. In view of this emphasis, it is not surprising to find studies indicating that psychological differences between individuals may be important in determining the effects of persuasive messages.

A large unabridged dictionary contains approximately 18,000 words to help differentiate between people. That huge number is an example of the importance we place on being able to catalog each person as an individual. Some of these words refer to physical differences between individuals, words such as tall, bald, heavy, young, and well dressed. Others refer to an individual's affective orientation toward some person, such as interested, attentive, angry, fearful, sad, loving, and jealous. Finally, some refer to firmly structured, persisting, cognitively oriented differences in the ways in which people face the world. We call these structured differences "personality," and use the structures to make predictions about behavior. Personality structures include such cognitive organizations as need achievement, dogmatism, egotism, rigidity, and anxiety. This section examines personality traits and their relation to communication.

One may wonder why it is helpful to consider personality as a variable after just having discussed the nature of belief systems. After all, personality structures are belief structures. They form part of the reference frames that we all develop. Personal-

ity structures, however, are organizations of beliefs and attitudes that become pervasive for the individual, and thus tend to affect the way in which the individual will behave in many kinds of situations.

The average person uses personality terms many times a day, and uses them rather casually. Everyone has heard statements similar to the following: "Joe you've got to have an open mind on this subject," or "Don't you think Sam is a bit aggressive, you know, too pushy?" A little thought shows why the psychologist tends to be disturbed by such relatively casual use of technical terms. Determining personality is necessarily done through a process of *inference* by which conclusions about an individual's probable orientations toward people, objects, and events are drawn from observable behavior. One of the major problems in defining personality characteristics is the necessity to decide what *kinds* of behavior ought to be observed in order to make an assessment of personality.[1]

The most widely used approach for assessing personality utilizes *personality inventories*. These tests consist of a number of statements about which an individual indicates attitudes or feelings. Examples of the type of statements that might be found in a personality inventory include:

a. Certain religious sects whose beliefs do not permit them to salute the flag should be forced to conform to such patriotic action, or else the sects should be abolished.

b. A large-scale system of sterilization would be one way of breeding out criminals and other undesirable elements in our society and so raise its general standards and living conditions.

c. We are spending too much money for the pampering of criminals and the insane, and for the education of inherently incapable people.[2]

These are examples from an older test used to measure ethnocentrism. Today, we would use updated examples, but the principle is the same. The response to any one statement is relatively meaningless, but when an individual's entire set of responses are compared to the responses of a large number of others, meaningful comparisons can be made. We will look at some of the studies that have attempted to isolate the relationships between personality traits and persuasion. We cannot cover all the studies that have been done, but we can focus on those areas that seem to have the most applicability to the persuasive communicator. Further, in later chapters we look at how our personalities affect the way we try to influence others.

Self-esteem

One of the most pervasive aspects of personality is the way in which people look at themselves. A person displaying *high self-esteem* will typically appear to be confident, optimistic, and competent. The person will display few feelings of inadequacy, will not feel socially inhibited, and will not exhibit a high degree of anxiety. People with high self-esteem face the world with good impressions of themselves. In contrast, individuals with *low self-esteem* will admit to being anxious in decision-making situations, will tend to be pessimistic, may not appear to be competent, and may testify that they do not feel confident in social situations. Such individuals are always consulting others before making decisions, or taking a position on a topic.

Most of the available research tends to support this hypothesis. DiVesta[3] suggests that when individuals are threatened with a loss of self-esteem, they tend to prefer their own judgments to those of others. Janis,[4] in some early research, suggested that adjustment factors such as feelings of social inadequacy, inhibition, and depression, all indications of low self-esteem, are related to high persuasibility. Additional support for this general relationship has been found by researchers who demonstrated that increasing a person's level of esteem makes him or her more resistant to persuasion.[5]

There is considerable evidence to indicate that self-esteem is not only related to persuasibility,

but to the comprehension of messages and to susceptibility to certain *types of appeals* as well. First, if receivers are truly low in self-esteem, they may not only have doubts about their own judgment on the topic, but they may also have more difficulty attending to a message. In a classic study by Nisbett and Gordon,[6] the experimenters gave students messages about medical topics ("Some Harmful Effects of Chest X-rays" or "Some Dangerous Effects of Excessive Tooth Brushing"). Nisbett and Gordon measured the students' levels of self-esteem and manipulated the ease with which the message was constructed. These researchers found that when the message was simple, students with *moderate* self-esteem were persuaded *more* than those with low or high self-esteem. When the message was complex, students with *high* self-esteem were persuaded *more* than students with either moderate or low self-esteem. To some extent, those with low self-esteem may have been *overwhelmed* by the messages concerning possible health problems and, thus, became inactive, a notion subsequently tested by research by Leventhal and his colleagues.[7]

In some of their research on "fear appeals" (see Chapter 8), Leventhal and his colleagues wanted to induce people to stop smoking and to get chest X-rays. Some receivers were exposed to "low-fear appeals," others to "moderate-fear" and others to "high-fear appeals." The latter saw a repulsive color film of an operation for lung cancer. Leventhal found that persons with *high* self-esteem were the ones *most* likely to be moved by *high* fear. Why? Because if you had high self-esteem then you would like yourself, you would want to maintain your health and continue being high in self-esteem, and great fear motivates you to treat yourself well. On the other hand, those with low self-esteem were *least* likely to take immediate action when confronted with a highly frightening message. However, and as Aronson[8] notes, *after a delay* the receiver with low self-esteem behaved very much like the one with high self-esteem.

How can these research results be explained? Simply! Those with low self-esteem lack confidence in themselves and probably spend a good deal of time thinking about problems (more so than those with high self-esteem). Hence, when a high fear message is received, the person with low esteem must first cope with the problem of having more things to think and worry about than his or her counterpart with high self-esteem. As Aronson[9] noted, "A high-fear communication overwhelms them and makes them feel like crawling into bed and pulling the covers up over their heads. Low or moderate fear is something that they can more easily deal with at the moment they experience it. But, if given time—that is, if it's not essential that they act immediately—they will be more likely to act if the message truly scared the hell out of them."

The results of the studies of Leventhal and his colleagues are highly compatible with the types of reference frames developed by persons with high and low self-esteem. On one hand, those with high self-esteem have more confidence and see fewer problems in the world; they desire to maintain high self-esteem and, thus, are susceptible to appeals that tell them how they can maintain a positive self-image. On the other hand, persons with low self-esteem already have a number of worries and doubts, and will take action to reduce fear after they have had time to process the new set of problems the new message has given them. Persons with low self-esteem, then, are sensitive to immediate pressures and are motivated to respond to these pressures.

From these studies, we can conclude that, first, as a general rule, people with low self-esteem can be expected to be persuaded more easily than people with high self-esteem. However, this is only a general rule, since receivers at different levels of self-esteem are susceptible to different appeals and attend to different aspects of messages. Second, persons with low self-esteem are more likely to become "overloaded" from a high-fear appeal, thus experiencing less attitude change *immediately* after the persuasion.

Self-esteem is an important variable, because it is one of which some estimates can be made by simply observing receivers as they work and inter-act with others. Individuals with low self-esteem behave less confidently than others. They ask for advice more than the individual with high self-esteem. They seem to worry more about what they are doing. Such individuals are more likely to be susceptible to persuasive messages.

Intelligence

Many readers probably think that less intelligent receivers are more easily persuaded than more intelligent receivers. However, there is no *consistent* relationship between intelligence and susceptibility. Some studies have found that the better educated and brighter receivers are more persuaded because they attend more, comprehend more, and remember more than the less educated.[10] Other studies found no relationship between intelligence and persuasibility.[11] How can such results be explained? According to McGuire,[12] receiver factors such as intelligence may have different effects on different processes involved in persuasion. His explanation, also discussed at the bottom of Box 3.1, is simple. To be persuaded, receivers need to attend to a message, comprehend what is being said, and remember (that is, retain) information. Finally, a person has to yield to the conclusion (for example, "Buy Savings Bonds"). McGuire argues that the more intelligent receivers can attend, comprehend, and remember more than less intelligent ones—thus, the more intelligent receiver will be more easily persuaded. On the other hand, intelligent persons are also more analytical, critical, mentally active, and self-assured; thus, they would be better at counterarguing a message and would be *less* persuaded.

If McGuire's explanation is correct, then it follows that less intelligent receivers would be less persuaded if a message were complex and they had a difficult time comprehending it. Further, intelligent receivers would be persuaded by messages containing supportive, complex messages and would be less persuaded by simple and unsupported messages. Such a notion was tested by Eagly and Warren,[13] who had students listen to

---

BOX 3.1
THE MESSAGE LEARNING APPROACH TO
PERSUASION AND PERSONALITY DIFFERENCES

Is personality linked to persuasion in the sense that different types of persons are gullible, or susceptible, or are simply easy to influence? Actually, the relationship between personality and persuasibility is not a simple one. One of the classic and traditional approaches to persuasion is called the "Message Learning" approach. This approach was employed by Carl Hovland and his colleagues at Yale during and immediately after World War II. Hovland and his colleagues argued that persuasion occurs after a person has learned the *content* of the message (hence, "message learning"). They felt that a persuasive message was one that raised a question in the mind of the receiver, offered an answer to the question, and provided incentives for adopting the advocated position. They suggest that *four* underlying processes were involved in successful persuasion. First, the receiver must *attend* the message. Second, the receiver must *comprehend* what is being said. Third, the receiver must *yield* to the message content; that is, the receiver decides to vote Republican, to try Cocoa Cookie cereal, and so on. Finally, there must be some probability that the person will *retain* information from the message.

Example: Advertisers want to find ways in which to get a six year old's attention. Hence, they use ringing bells, jingles, slogans, and variations in volume and in the narrator's voice qualities so that their commercial will be noticed even though it is embedded among many others on Saturday mornings. Further, the advertisement must be made so that the six year old can comprehend it; thus certain words are selected over others, and there may be a high degree of repetition. Next, the child decides she would like to try the cereal because it looks and sounds good, and all the children on the commercial appear to have so much fun eating it. Finally, since the advertisement was constructed in such a way as to get the child to remember the product, she remembers the product and her desire for it, and when she goes shopping with her parents, she begs for it.

How do personality differences fit into all of this? There are personality measures related to at least two of these four processes. Specifically, higher intelligence in receivers is related to increased *comprehension*. However, more intelligent individuals are also more likely to resist *yielding*. In another example, highly anxious individuals are more likely to yield (up to a point); however, if they are too anxious or our messages make them too anxious, then they stop attending to and comprehending the message. What can be concluded? Direct links between personality and susceptibility do not exist. One has to look at how personality type is related to these processes, and look at the types of messages or appeals to which different personality types might be susceptible.

two six-minute, tape-recorded messages, one on penicillin use and the other on brushing one's teeth. The messages argued that we use too much penicillin and that we brush our teeth too frequently. The messages were constructed so that they either contained five supportive persuasive arguments, or contained no supportive arguments. Eagly and Warren found that people of higher intelligence were more persuaded when arguments were included and were less persuaded when supportive arguments were omitted. Further, the students who scored higher on verbal skills (which was used to measure intelligence) learned more than less intelligent receivers. The implication of McGuire's results is that if you attempted to persuade an audience of intelligent receivers you should try to present as much evidence and support as possible, especially if the evidence is strong and convincing. Later, in Chapter 8 ("Structuring Messages and Appeals"), we will add further that a two-sided message is preferable for more intelligent audiences, as opposed to a one-sided message.

Anxiety

One of the factors making up a personality structure is the degree of *anxiety* exhibited in various situations. Anxiety may be displayed by feelings of tension, apprehension, uncertainty, or panic in everyday encounters with situations and events. We are *not* concerned here with that level of anxiety that becomes so severe that it is an indicator of emotional disturbance. We *are* concerned with the types of tension that all of us experience when meeting new situations, or making important decisions. The research suggests that people who experience relatively high anxiety levels about decisions are less susceptible to persuasion. Nunnally and Bobren[14] have shown that persons with high anxiety tend to show low interest in persuasive messages regardless of the message form. Since persuasion has to depend on initial attention to the message, this study supports the hypothesis. Janis and Feshbach[15] and Haefner[16] worked with strong and weak fear appeals in a

series of messages and showed that when strong fear appeals are used and the receivers are highly anxious, less persuasion occurs. When weak fear appeals are used, the difference between people high and low in anxiety tends to disappear, but there is still some indication of *defensive reactions* to the message.

What can be said about persuasion and completely normal levels of anxiety? Anxiety seems to exhibit a curvilinear relationship to persuasion. That is, if we feel completely free from anxiety, what motivates us to attend to a message, process it, and yield? On the other hand, if extremely high levels of anxiety occur, then we may feel so anxious, self-conscious, and uncertain that we may be overwhelmed by the message, fail to comprehend it, and not be persuaded. Thus, McGuire[17] argued that frightening a person (with the content of the message) will *increase resistance* to persuasion if the person was initially anxious about the topic, and that frightening a person would lead to *increases in persuasion if the person was initially low in anxiety*. Also, comprehension levels work differently when one attempts to manipulate complex and simple messages. That is, Millman[18] found that complex messages, which require considerable cognitive processing, result in *less* attitude change if they are accompanied by high fear because the receiver must contend with both the processing of a large amount of material as well as cope with the anxiety.

Petty and Cacioppo[19] conclude that three conditions must be met if anxiety arousal or fear arousal is going to be effective. (See also Chapter 8.) First, a message should provide *strong arguments* for the possibility that the receiver will suffer some extremely negative consequence unless some action is taken (for example, update one's tetanus shot, get a chest X-ray, or stop smoking). Second, the argument must be made that the possible negative consequences are *very likely* to occur if the recommendations are not followed. Third, the persuasive message must provide *strong assurances* that if the receiver adopts specific recommendations, he or she can effectively eliminate the negative consequences. This latter point is important in several ways. First, people who are already anxious about an issue, for example, their health, may take action if they know *specifically* what they can do. For instance, if the persuasive message included a map to the Health Center, explained what documents a student would need, informed the student of the hours the center was open, informed the student of the fees, and so on, then the persuasive message gave specific methods for reducing anxiety, and people would know what to do in order to eliminate feelings of anxiety. On the other hand, if a message did not tell the receiver specific ways to reduce anxiety, then an anxious person would feel "residual emotional feelings" after hearing the message and simply remain anxious without taking preventative action. In fact, one classic study on fear or anxiety arousal found that inducing worry and anxiety in receivers but failing to tell them specific ways to reduce the anxiety resulted in increased susceptibility to counterpropaganda.[20]

Where do you see some of these research results put into practice? On the one hand, authorities feel that there are some young persons who do not feel much anxiety about poor driving habits and accidents. Hence, a hefty dose of anxiety aimed at making this group more conscious of driving habits is given in high school. Similarly, venereal disease may seem a bit distant to some new Army recruits, so they also receive an anxiety-arousing message. Generally young people are not believed to have given much thought to cigarette smoking, driving while drinking, using drugs, and accepting rides from strangers, and so a moderate to high anxiety-arousing message is given to them in schools to reinforce their intentions not to do these things when they get older. On the other hand, there are certain contexts where the receiver may be expected to be initially anxious about the topic. Commercials telling us (adults) to go to the dentist emphasize keeping a beautiful smile—if the advertisements emphasized pain, people wouldn't go. Older Americans are already worried about financial stability and high medical bills. Advertisements aimed at them do not in-

crease their already high anxiety—the advertisements instruct the elderly on how they can pay 46 cents a day, safely and conveniently, to increase medical coverage; the ads emphasize *specific recommendations on how to reduce worry and enjoy life.* Finally, a number of commercials today advertise clinics for the treatment of alcoholism. The majority of these advertisements do not attempt to make the potential patient *more* anxious, but to point out how easy it is, in terms of time and money, to go to the clinic. By increasing the receiver's level of anxiety (and embarrassment at claiming he or she has a drinking problem) receivers would be put off. The messages are more successful if they can communicate to the receiver that other people have this problem, that the treatment is successful and less costly than the diseases, that other people support the decision, and that time and money are not problems in getting treatment.

Dogmatism

Milton Rokeach and his associates introduced a personality characteristic they refer to as "open-mindedness."[21] They use the terms "closed-minded" and "dogmatic" as synonymous, and they suggest that these terms refer to the ways in which individuals tend to approach people, ideas, beliefs, and messages. Dogmatism has been shown to be a pervasive personality trait affecting many aspects of an individual's behavior. Our discussion of the open and closed mind emphasizes the centrality of belief to show the importance of this personality trait to the understanding of persuasive communication.

An open-minded individual, one who is not highly dogmatic, tends to be able to bring various belief structures together for purposes of comparison. There is little discrepancy in the beliefs held by such an individual. The individual will tend to have an optimistic outlook about the way in which the world is put together, will not hold that authorities are absolute determiners of policies, will not believe that decisions made today will hold forever, and will tend to view information along a very broad time perspective. The open-minded individual does not compartmentalize beliefs. Open-minded people are more willing to be exposed to controversial materials and are also more willing to express themselves about material that might be contrary to their own attitudes.

In contrast to open-minded people, closed-minded or dogmatic individuals tend to compartmentalize the beliefs they hold, and to be very reluctant to compare various beliefs. Dogmatic people are more likely to be pessimistic about the future of the world, more inclined to believe in the absolute correctness of authorities, and inclined to reject messages from people that are not in agreement with the authorities in which the dogmatic person believes. The closed-minded person is inclined to take a very narrow view of the world's problems.

A number of studies have related dogmatism to persuasibility. One major characteristic of the highly dogmatic individual is a heavy dependence on authority as a source of personal attitudes and beliefs. If an authority the dogmatic individual believes in supports a particular position, the dogmatic individual tends to believe that position as well. In a study by Bettinghaus, Steinfatt, and Miller,[22] receivers were asked to judge the logical validity of syllogisms. Some syllogisms had been presented as coming from a source valued positively by the receiver, and some were attributed to negative sources. The results showed that the highly dogmatic subjects made more errors when the syllogisms were attributed to a negative source than to a positive source. The result did not hold true for the individuals classified as "low dogmatic." The more open-minded individuals tended to evaluate the messages on their own merits, rather than on the recommendations of trusted authorities. In another study, Powell showed that closed-minded individuals had difficulties in separating the ideas presented in a message from the authorities who supported or rejected the ideas.[23]

The implication of these studies for persuasion

is clear. People who are highly dogmatic can be expected to be more persuasible in those situations where the ideas presented are supported by authorities in whom the individual places trust, and less persuasible in situations linked to authorities in whom little trust is placed. People who are not highly dogmatic are less likely to have a belief in an authority linked to a belief in an idea. Such open-minded individuals are better able to evaluate the ideas in a message apart from the sources of those ideas or the supporters of those ideas.[24]

Dogmatism has further implications for persuasion. The evidence suggests that the open-minded individual is able to relate new ideas to existing reference frames and is able to more easily make adjustments in those frames (that is, open-minded receivers are more creative). Thus a persuasive message that suggests changes away from the status quo, or argues for sweeping changes in the social order, ought to be more successful with receivers who are open-minded than with those who are closed-minded. The highly dogmatic person holds beliefs very closely, and is unwilling to allow changes in those beliefs. The highly dogmatic person is unwilling to entertain messages that point out conflicts in belief structures. For example, it is inconsistent to believe that smoking causes lung cancer and to still continue to smoke. We ought to expect more attitude change from a message pointing out this discrepancy and urging people to stop smoking when it is presented to open-minded receivers than to closed-minded receivers. Closed-minded receivers hold beliefs in a compartmentalized fashion, and are unwilling to bring inconsistent beliefs together to reconcile them.

Receivers cannot be divided into two separate groups, dogmatic and nondogmatic. Most people have varying degrees of dogmatism, and only a few fall at the extreme ends of the dogmatism scale. Nevertheless, many people can separate their friends into those who tend to be open-minded individuals and those who lean more toward a closed-minded position. Attaining some knowledge of this personality characteristic will help in predicting how an individual is likely to react to new ideas that might be suggested, to the use of evidence in a message, and to the use of supporting materials. Note that we have *not* concluded that dogmatism is generally or systematically related to increased or decreased persuasiveness. Instead, if one has to convince a very dogmatic person, such as Archie Bunker on reruns of *All in the Family*, one must keep in mind that the receiver will not necessarily be persuaded by logic or evidence, or by new ideas. Rather, this type of person can be influenced by appealing to his or her authority figures and to traditional values, and by keeping in mind that he or she has a rigid belief system that does not tolerate much inconsistency.

Authoritarianism

For 35 years, psychologists have been conducting research on individuals who possess in varying degrees what has been termed the "authoritarian personality." The emphasis in this work has been on the reaction of certain personality types to situations involving racial and religious minorities. Many persuasive communication situations also involve attempts to reduce prejudice, involve the use of sources representing minorities, or are directed toward members of minority groups. Thus, the work originally presented by Adorno and his colleagues in *The Authoritarian Personality*[25] seems applicable to the general study of persuasive communication.

Basically, people possessing an authoritarian personality tend to be highly reliant on the moral authority of their own reference group, tend to adhere fairly rigidly to middle-class values, and become preoccupied with the relative power and status of other people and with their own power and status. Such people tend to make absolute judgments regarding the values they hold, and to see the world in black and white. They are not easily swayed by messages that might seem to contradict the beliefs they have or the authorities they rely on, despite the judgments of others that

the message is rational and logical. Furthermore, the highly authoritarian personality tends to identify with individuals in the groups that appear to have power. The authoritarian personality tends to have the same beliefs as the leaders of those groups, and may reject and act prejudiced and hostile toward individuals in other groups.

An analysis of individuals who seem to have highly authoritarian personalities would suggest that their reaction to persuasion will depend on their reactions to factors other than the merits of the ideas presented. Rohrer and Sheriff,[26] for example, examined the reactions of individuals to messages about blacks. They report that while individuals who are not high on the authoritarian scales tended to be persuaded by the ideas in the messages they read, the subjects who were high authoritarians tended to be persuaded by the authorities presented in the messages. This was true for the high authoritarians regardless of whether the message they read was problack or antiblack. The controlling factor in this study seemed to be the dependence of the high authoritarian on the infallibility of the authority figures cited in the messages. The high authoritarian, then, seems to be highly reliant on the authority dimension of the belief structure, and links beliefs about authorities to peripheral beliefs.

Harvey and Beverly[27] point to one of the possible reasons for the differences in attitude change typically found in high and low authoritarians. In their study, they found that high authoritarians changed in the direction of the position advocated by a high-status source to a significantly greater degree than did low authoritarians, but that the high authoritarians could not reproduce the points made in the speech with the same degree of accuracy as could the low authoritarians. Again, the reported attitude change seemed to be the result of the perceived status and power of the source, rather than the strength of the message itself. Similar results have been reported by Paul[28] and Weiss[29] on the basis of their studies of authoritarianism and attitude change.

Our description of the closed-minded personality and the authoritarian personality suggests that there is undoubtedly some overlap between the two kinds of constructs. The correlations, however, are not complete, and many researchers feel that we are dealing with two different personality factors. Studies of the authoritarian personality were originally directed toward explaining racial and religious prejudice. The authors of *The Authoritarian Personality* suggest that prejudice can be explained, in part, as a reaction against an "outgroup." For high authoritarians, belief and trust is placed only in members of the groups to which they belong. Other groups are rejected, and rejected in such ways that negative actions are taken against members of the out-groups.

Merely possessing a highly authoritarian personality does not necessarily mean that a person will be more persuasible. Authoritarianism seems to be linked only to the use of authorities, and is not necessarily related to persuasion in all situations. Understanding authoritarianism as a personality factor and using those particular kinds of messages that emphasize the endorsement of trusted authorities ought to result in more successful persuasion.

One area using the authoritarian personality scale is research on juries. Authoritarian jurors seem to believe that if the state or the prosecutor charges that the defendant is guilty, then he or she probably is guilty. More specifically, research indicates that authoritarians require less evidence to convict someone (especially in murder cases), and give harsher sentences than low authoritarians.[30] There also is evidence that authoritarians reinforce each other during jury deliberations by becoming even harsher when they realize that other authoritarian jurors also prefer harsh sentences (that is, groups of authoritarians give harsher sentences than juries with a mix of low and high authoritarians). This jury bias is *reversed*, however, if the defendant is an authority (police officer) or if the defendant claims to have "followed orders."[31] Obviously, one question of interest to lawyers is what can be done to reduce such biases. According to Kaplan and Miller,[32] lawyers should impress on jury members that evidence presented in a trial is extremely reliable.

The need for achievement

David McClelland and his associates[33] have been working for 30 years to clarify a personality variable they refer to as an individual's "need for achievement" or "n-achievement." McClelland measures n-achievement by having individuals write short essays about pictures of individuals working and talking with other people. The essays are scored for the number of "achievement" themes in the subject's description of the situation.[34] The replies an individual makes indicate his rank on the n-achievement scale.

McClelland's work has been extended in many different directions. He has related this variable to economic success in underdeveloped countries, to the question of whether n-achievement can be trained into an individual, and to the relationship between a child's need for achievement and the parents' achievement need. More recently, Atkinson and his colleagues[35] have examined the role of need for achievement in organizations. Persons with a high need for achievement typically seek out more challenging jobs, desire to accept responsibility for decision making, and want to receive feedback (so they can improve their performances). Steers and Spencer[36] found that persons with a need for achievement performed better when their jobs were rich in responsibility, variety, feedback, and autonomy, while people low in need for achievement did not improve in performance as job richness increased.

Individuals who possess a high need for achievement in our society tend to be entrepreneurs, always trying to improve themselves, and trying to do so by their own personal efforts. Such individuals are seemingly driven to greater efficiency, attempting to solve problems and pit themselves against any challenge that might be placed in their path. Yet people with a high n-achievement are *not* gamblers; they seem to want to solve the problems they encounter with methods that take risks into account. On the other hand, individuals who score relatively low on this variable are more artistically sensitive; they will take more risks and they lead a less worried life. Lower socioeconomic-class families tend to produce more individuals who score low on n-achievement, but so do individuals from the upper classes. High n-achievement is a characteristic of middle-class parents and middle-class children. This does not mean that other individuals will not exhibit high n-achievement, but the trait is found more frequently among the middle class.

The relationship between the n-achievement variable and persuasibility seems to lie in the nature of the *topics* chosen for persuasion and the appeals used in the message. We might expect that message topics that seem to promise, in *specific* terms, how the receiver can advance in personal status, economic condition, or power would have a special appeal for the receiver scoring high in n-achievement. On the other hand, we might expect that topics that imagined the receiver giving up something for the benefit of society might not be as successful with the person who is very high in n-achievement. When the persuasive communicator uses a set of appeals that challenges the receiver to action, appeals to the receiver's ability to use personal effort, or offers the possibility of personal gain at moderate risk, the appeals ought to be successful with receivers who are characterized by having a high need for achievement.

Involvement

So far we have discussed personality variables that can be measured via questionnaires or projective tests. In this section of the chapter we will discuss two issues dealing with the person's *level of involvement* with the topic of persuasion, and we will discuss how involvement influences how we process the persuasive message, and how we are influenced by the message. Our two topics deal with *issue involvement* and *ego involvement*.

1. Issue involvement. The word "involvement" means different things to different people.

Generally speaking, *ego involvement* implies that a person is so involved in a particular issue or cause that his or her self-concept ("ego") is highly interrelated to the issue or cause; thus, ego-involved issues are ones that are *central* to the person's beliefs. *Issue involvement* often means, however, that the topic of persuasion is relevant to the person, or affects his or her future. We are issue involved on hundreds of topics (for example, Will our college tuition go up again? Will the price of gasoline go up again?) but we are probably ego involved on relatively few issues. Thus, three "levels" of involvement will be noted: topics on which one is uninvolved (including issues that are irrelevant), topics on which one is issue involved, and, at a higher level of intensity, issues on which one is ego involved.

In the last ten years, considerable work has focused on the differences between high and low issue involvement. In fact, a major hypothesis called *cognitive response analysis* has been developed, and advocates of this hypothesis argue that a good deal of persuasion stems from active mental processes.[37] The central thesis is that the more involved we are in a topic, the more actively we attend and process the message, the evidence, and the advocated conclusion. Recall, in Box 3.1, that a "message-learning approach" argued that people are persuaded if they attend to the message, comprehend the message, retain information, and yield. While there is no doubt that these processes take place, we'd have to admit that the approach characterizes the receiver as being fairly *passive*— the receiver is characterized as *only* learning the content of the message. Clearly, however, receivers often involve themselves actively with messages and pay greater attention to message content as they decode them.

When we say that highly-involved persons employ thoughtful strategies that rely on message content, we mean that they respond *cognitively* to the message—when listening to a message and while processing that message, they *generate* or *elaborate* their own arguments. Receivers generate *supporting arguments* that were not part of the message when they think of additional reasons in favor of the proposition; they generate *counterarguments* when they think of arguments contrary to the proposition that were not included in the message; and, finally, they can generate *neutral* thoughts if some ideas came to them while they listened to the message that actually had no impact on accepting or rejecting the proposition. The more we are involved with a topic, the greater our cognitive response to it—as a Russian diplomat generates a large number of counterarguments while he listens to a speech being given by an American diplomat. Further, according to Petty and Cacioppo[38] we are persuaded when we list many supporting arguments and list few counterarguments. Such a relationship is not surprising, since it indicates that the more *actively* a person responds to a message, the greater its impact. According to this approach, simply learning the content of a message has little bearing on being persuaded—what *we* as receivers *do* with the message is more important. Let's look at a few examples of how involvement affects cognitive responses and persuasion.

Petty and Cacioppo[39] had college students listen to a speech dealing with the possibility of changing the visitation hours in dormitories. Some students heard a message that advocated that the visitation hours should be changed at a university different than their own (this was the "low-involvement" message, since the issue has little impact on the receiver); other students heard that the change was proposed for their own university ("high involvement"). Further, some of the messages advocated that the dormitory policy should be made more *lenient* ("proattitudinal") while some messages argued against leniency ("counterattitudinal"). (Petty and Cacioppo assumed that the average college student would be in favor of leniency and against increased restrictions.) Thus, there were four versions of the speech: high-involvement proattitudinal, high-involvement counterattitudinal, low-involvement proattitudinal, and low-involvement counterattitudinal.

What would you expect to find, in terms of cognitive responses? If the cognitive response approach is correct, people should be more actively responding when they were involved, and should increase agreement with a message if they were *both* involved and they found the position acceptable (the message argued for increased leniency). Decreased agreement would be obtained if they were involved and they found the message unacceptable (decreased leniency). These expectations were exactly what Petty and Cacioppo found. First, the students who were highly involved generated more favorable thoughts and fewer counterarguments to the message that advocated leniency (as opposed to stricter visitation hours). Second, *uninvolved* receivers did not differ in how much they responded to the counterattitudinal and proattitudinal messages (that is, uninvolved receivers are less motivated to process messages). Third, students changed their attitudes most when they were involved and heard the proattitudinal message, while highly involved students exhibited decreased agreement with the message that argued for reduced leniency. Clearly, high involvement increases the extent to which one responds to messages.

Petty, Cacioppo, and Schumann[40] similarly demonstrated that involvement was important when people responded to advertisements. Petty, Cacioppo, and Schumann constructed booklets containing advertising stimuli, and had students evaluate the booklets. Embedded in the booklets were different versions of an advertisement of "Edge disposable razors." Half the advertisements contained a "celebrity endorsement": "Professional Athletes Agree: Until you try new Edge disposable razors you'll never know what a really close shave is." The other half of the endorsements included an "average citizen endorsement" ("Bakersfield, California, Agrees . . ."). Further, half the advertisements contained *quality arguments*; the razors were claimed to have been "scientifically designed," with five outstanding features: "new advanced honing method creates unsurpassed sharpness," "special chemically formulated coating eliminates nicks and cuts and prevents rusting," and so on. The other half of the advertisements contained weak arguments, claiming that the razor was "designed for beauty," "floats in water with a minimum of rust," and so on. Finally, half of the students who read and evaluated the booklets were led to believe that the razor was being introduced into their city as part of the test market (high involvement), while the other students were led to believe that the product was being tested elsewhere and was not going to be introduced into their market in the near future (low involvement). This study found that less-involved students liked the product more when endorsed by celebrities than by the average citizen, and that quality of argument had little impact on their attitudes. On the other hand, quality of argument had a major impact on attitudes when individuals were involved, but type of endorsement was irrelevant to the attitudes of involved receivers.

The results of the above studies indicate that uninvolved individuals are less motivated to attend to a message and, thus, can be influenced by such manipulations as celebrity endorsement. On the other hand, it is unlikely that involved receivers would be influenced unless strong supporting evidence is supplied. How can one persuade an involved person? Generally, the better-quality arguments that are presented, the greater the impact on involved receivers. In Petty and Cacioppo,[41] messages were manipulated so that they contained either three arguments or nine arguments supporting the claim that the university should implement a comprehensive test for seniors. The messages either included strong or weak arguments.[42] Further, high involvement was manipulated by arguing that the testing process would start next year; low involvement, in ten years. This study found that uninvolved students were in favor of the testing program if they heard nine arguments in support of it; quality of arguments had no impact. That is, uninvolved persons didn't concern themselves with the quality of the arguments, but operated under a very simple rule: *the more arguments, the better the program must be.* However, involved students were only persuaded by quality of arguments—the sheer number of arguments was unimportant.

In sum, when the topic of persuasion is not relevant to us, we are often persuaded by rather simple rules—do what the celebrity says (without thinking); do what the physically attractive speaker says; do what the expert says; if there seem to be a lot of arguments, then it must be right. However, persuading the involved receiver takes greater effort and one must supply evidence, supporting data, statistics, and so on.

2. Ego involvement. Imagine the following incident: You have to give a persuasive speech in your speech class, and you decide to pick a topic you believe to be safe. You give a speech in which you argue that the state should not change the current drinking age. After all, you argue, 18 year olds are old enough to be drafted, they pay taxes, and they should be allowed to become full-fledged members of society. Thus, they should be allowed to drink alcohol. You conclude, in fact, that alcoholic beverages should continue to be available in limited quantities to 18–21 year olds—"this is America, and they have their rights too." Since the class includes many college-age students, you thought you selected a safe topic. However, almost immediately at the end of your speech a person stands up to announce that she is co-chairperson of the local chapter of M.A.D.D. (Mothers Against Drunk Driving), and she states that her daughter was hit by a drunk teenage driver five years ago; she further discloses that she has led sign-carrying protesters through the grounds at the state capitol, that she has personally lobbied with the governor, and that she helped to establish two chapters of M.A.D.D. in her part of the state. Finally, she turns to announce that she vehemently disagrees with "everything" you just said. She asserts that when it comes to alcoholic beverages, too many youths are immature, alcoholism is a disease that takes years of coping with, and nobody can take a reasonable or rational course of action even after just one drink.

Needless to say, you are not particularly pleased about this occurrence. After all, you felt you were arguing a fairly neutral position. Chances are, the person from the class was *ego involved* in this particular issue.

Sherif, Sherif, and Nebergall's[43] theory of ego involvement is a classic theory of attitude change. (The theory is also called "social judgment theory" or "assimilation-contrast theory.") According to this theory, a person's attitude on a topic can be measured by using a *reference scale*. This scale (Figure 3.1) includes a representative set of statements concerning attitudes on a topic, where the statements can be ordered from extremely favorable ones to extremely unfavorable ones.

A. Since alcohol is the curse of mankind, the sale and use of alcohol, including light beer, should be completely abolished.
B. Since alcohol is the main cause of corruption in public life, lawlessness, and immoral acts, its sale and use should be prohibited.
C. Since it is hard to stop at a reasonable moderation point in the use of alcohol, it is safer to discourage its use.
D. Alcohol should not be sold or used except as a remedy for snake bites, cramps, colds, fainting, and other aches and pains.
E. The arguments in favor and against the sale and use of alcohol are nearly equal.
F. The sale of alcohol should be so regulated that it is available in limited quantities for special occasions.
G. The sale and use of alcohol should be permitted with proper state controls, so that the revenue from taxation may be used for the betterment of schools, highways, and other state institutions.
H. Since prohibition is a major cause of corruption in public life, lawlessness, immoral acts, and juvenile delinquency, the sale and use of alcohol should be legalized.
I. It has become evident that man cannot get along without alcohol; therefore, there should be no restriction whatsoever on its sale and use.

Figure 3.1. Example of Reference Scale Used in Research on Ego Involvement

SOURCE: C. I. Hovland, O. J. Harvey, and M. Sherif, "Assimilation and Contrast Effects in Reactions to Communication and Attitude Change," *Journal of Abnormal and Social Psychology,* vol. 55 (1957), pp. 244–252.

Respondents are asked to place an "X" through statements they find unacceptable, to put a circle around statements they find acceptable, and to underline the one statement that best reflects their own attitude. The first step identifies the *latitude of rejection*, and the second step identifies the *latitude of acceptance*.[44] (If any statements are left blank, they are referred to as the latitude of noncommitment.)

The theory holds that the latitudes of rejection and acceptance tell us a good deal about the receiver. First, if a person had an extremely wide latitude of rejection (say, rejecting all statements C to I in Figure 3.1) and had a narrow latitude of acceptance (only statement A was included as an acceptable position), then we call the person ego involved. This person finds all counterattitudinal positions unacceptable, also finds neutrality unacceptable and feels that only a limited selection of statements can be tolerated. Such people feel strongly about the topic, have set ideas about the topic, and are closed-minded when it comes to new ideas on the matter. In fact, the anti-alcohol student in your speech class may very well have an attitude just as we described. On the other hand, a person who rejects only statements H and I and finds statements A to E acceptable is less ego involved, more open to discussion, and is easier to persuade.

Second, according to this theory a person's own position represents an anchor or a reference point that the person uses when perceiving all statements and messages he or she receives on the topic. In fact, this theory argues that when we compare messages we receive to the reference point, we distort the placement of the messages in systematic ways. For example, a person is said to *assimilate* a message by *perceiving it closer to their anchor than is actually the case. Contrast* effects occur when a person perceives a message as *further from their anchor than is the case.* Generally speaking, the more ego involved a person becomes, the greater the likelihood that assimilation and/or contrast effects will occur.

There are two major ways that this theory is useful to persuaders. First, there is considerable evidence that politicians purposefully employ ambiguity in their messages so that they appear to be attractive to more of the electorate. That is, politicians who are liked, generally speaking, can try to maintain an ambiguous, middle-of-the-road campaign so that more and more potential voters will assimilate their positions. Granberg,[45] in fact, lists several specific examples of the operation of the principle of ambiguity:

1. When Bill Brock, the . . . Republican national chairman, ran for the Senate in 1970, his billboards read, "Bill Brock believes." His speeches were about as informative, and before long, he was being attacked for running an empty, issue-less campaign. So he promised he would spell out his message more fully before election day. And he kept that promise. With three weeks left in the campaign, the billboards blossomed with a new slogan: "Bill Brock Believes What We Believe."[46]

2. Carter and Ford are hardly charismatic figures, but experience has taught politicians that it is unwise to sharpen the issues too much. Nixon said almost nothing in 1972 and got a landslide from McGovern, who tried to be specific; so did Stevenson and Goldwater— they got clobbered, too. Our system puts a premium on ambiguity.[47]

The second implication of this theory is that it is extremely difficult to persuade the ego-involved person. As Sereno and Bodaken[48] noted, one needs to prompt the ego-involved person to engage in a good deal of attitudinal restructuring in order for persuasion to occur. The persuader needs to, first, get the involved person to reduce his/her latitude of rejection and to expand his/her latitude of noncommitment. Second, the person needs to expand his or her latitude of acceptance. No single message can achieve all of these changes, which is not surprising if one considers how it is that the ego-involved person became ego involved. According to Miller[49] a minimum of four variables serve as the cause of ego involvement: (a) the issue is perceived to be *important*, and as having important consequences; (b) the individual has *social support* in that he or she knows of others, or has joined groups, where there exists similarity and support for the atti-

tudes; (c) the person has *practiced* or *rehearsed* beliefs and supporting arguments for his/her position on the topic; and (d) the person is *committed* to the cause in the sense that he or she has distributed literature, walked pickets, and let the public know where he or she stands on the issue.

In sum, we have made a distinction between the uninvolved, the issue-involved, and the ego-involved receiver. The uninvolved receiver is often persuaded by rather simple rules: follow what the celebrity, the beautiful person, or the expert says, and agree with what the sheer *volume* of arguments seems to say. On the other hand, both the issue-involved and the ego-involved receiver are more likely to be persuaded by good arguments, and by multiple sources sending them the good arguments. Further, it may require multiple messages over time to persuade the ego-involved receiver.

An introduction to attribution theory and to social exchange theory

Personality variables and one's level of involvement are only two approaches to the study of an individual's response. We will briefly overview two additional theories that deal with an individual's response. Both of these theories are extremely important, and we will refer to these theories many times in later chapters.

Attribution theory

Attribution theory is a cognitive theory concerned with how we go about perceiving the *causes* of behavior. There are several varieties of attribution theories, and these are reviewed by Seibold and Spitzberg, and by Shaver.[50] Our concern here is with two questions: (1) How do we go about perceiving the cause of other people's behavior, and (2) How does this process influence the outcome of persuasion situations? The reader should keep in mind a fundamental concern of attribution theory: *Attribution theory* argues that *any* time we observe the behavior of others, we will attempt to *attribute* that behavior to *personal* factors or to *situational* factors. Let's start with an example.

Suppose you go to every football game. On your left, a fellow is friendly with the group around him and the group never has become drunk or rowdy. Then, after midterms and during the Notre Dame game he and his friends drink excessively. You probably will think that they were celebrating some occasion. You would make a *situational* (also called "external") attribution—the situation causes the behavior, the cause of the behavior was "external" to the individual. On your right, however, a fellow has come to every game in the same inebriated state, regardless of the status of his friends. You are likely to make a *personal* (or "internal") attribution—he loves beer, *he* is the *cause* of his behavior. The types of attributions we make for the causes of behavior obviously influence the tactics we use to influence others, as we shall see later. A more fundamental question in attribution theory deals with *how we go about making internal or external attributions*.

Kelley[51] suggests that there are three factors we take into consideration when we make attributions of causality: *distinctiveness, consistency,* and *consensus*. Distinctiveness generally refers to whether or not a person's behavior is distinctly different in one situation or task from others. For example, if a worker performs well on all tasks but poorly on one, then we are likely to make a dispositional judgment—the one machine is too difficult for the worker. Or, we say that a particular statistics class is too difficult for the particular student. On the other hand, low distinctiveness means that the worker had trouble on all machines (or that the student had trouble with *all* math classes), and we would make the internal attribution (the worker is inept, the student is not competent with numbers). In our example of the drinking student, the more different situations in which you saw the student drinking, the more likely you are to say that he is the cause of his behavior—he is a beer lover.

Consistency refers to the extent to which the worker's behavior is the same over time. Low consistency means that the worker has performed well on the one particular machine in the past; hence, difficulty with the machine today cannot be attributed to a fault of the worker—the machine is out of order. Similarly, it is difficult for us to believe that a student is incompetent in math when she received A's in math in high school, yet now is doing poorly in analytic geometry in college. Chances are, we'd look for a number of possible causes for her performance—such as the type of instruction, the time of day, or other types of pressures she may be feeling. Low consistency leads to external attributions. High consistency means that the worker has consistently had difficulty running a particular machine over time. In our football example, we are more likely to believe the student loves beer if we see the student drink beer consistently over time (which, of course, is the internal attribution).

Consensus deals with the perception of how all of the workers perform with the machine. High consensus means that all the workers have a difficult time operating a particular machine, and we are less likely to believe that one worker who had a difficult time operating the machine was inept (internal attribution). Similarly, if the student drank beer with a large group of other people who drank beer (high consensus) then we are more inclined to say that they are all celebrating—not that the one person is a beer lover. In this framework, then, we are inclined to make an internal attribution when distinctiveness is low, consistency is high, and consensus is low; or when the student drinks beer in many different situations, drinks beer consistently over time, and drinks beer when no one else is drinking beer.

The types of attributions we make about the causes of another's behavior are fundamental to the outcome of a number of persuasive situations. First, the attributional processes are important in terms of interpersonal influence. For example, if a worker's poor performance is attributed to internal causes by his or her supervisor, then the supervisor is much more likely to use punitive tactics on the worker than if the supervisor had made an external attribution. A second area in which attribution theory is relevant to persuasion is in terms of how people make *attributions* about a speaker based on his or her speech patterns, hesitation behaviors, conversational style, and so on. Studies on this topic are cited in many of the chapters that follow. A third major area of relevance to persuasion is the area of communicator effects. An example of this will be helpful.

Some theorists of attribution processes[52] argue that persuasion depends, in part, on the receiver's analysis of why a communicator is arguing the particular position he or she is advocating. Typically, receivers know something about the internal and external pressures that influence or constrain the speaker's behavior, and receivers are regarded as attempting actively to determine the credibility or believability of the message. According to attribution theorists, part of our decision regarding the validity of a message is determined by the situational and personal attributions made about the persuasion event. For example, all receivers expect that Ralph Nader will speak against pollution. Thus, the receivers know Nader's position (some would say he is biased), and they would know that he will feel pressure to argue against pollution. Hence, when receivers try to estimate the objective validity of the arguments, evidence, and conclusions of Nader's speech, they can discount it.

According to the attribution theorists, messages not constrained by the situation or by the communicator may not represent the truth, so they are not persuasive.[53] Instead, if Nader went to the Sierra Club and argued that General Motors was doing as good a job as one might expect, the receivers may feel that he is speaking more objectively. Another example: If President Reagan argued in favor of improved relations with the Russians, many people would be persuaded—the president's typical and expected line of argument is that the Russians can not be trusted. Hence, if the president argues for improved relations it may be the case that he (as an expert) has compelling reasons for changing his

mind. On the other hand, if we heard the president argue this position *during* the 1984 campaign, we can make the claim that he is simply arguing the way he is because of the campaign, not because of any true change. Since the situational explanation suggests a lack of objective validity (politicians say all sorts of things during campaigns) we are not influenced. However, if the president argued his position *after* the campaign, we would find the argument very persuasive.

Another version of attribution theory that is relevant to persuasion is called "self-perception theory." This theory, advanced by Bem,[54] argues that *we* (as receivers) come to know our own beliefs and attitudes according to the same type of processes noted above. That is, we *infer* the cause of our own behavior from the attributions we make about our reactions to environmental factors. Suppose you walked across the campus and before you entered the commons you spied a beautiful person of the opposite sex at a table. On the table was a large sign that listed 12 reasons why you should be against animal research, and as you walk by, the attractive person asks if you'd sign the petition. You sign it. As you walk on a friend comes over and says, "Gee, I didn't know you were against animal research." Actually, you've never given animal research much thought. "Why did I sign that petition?" you (briefly) ask yourself. Was it because of the 12 convincing reasons? No, in fact you don't really remember reading them and can't even remember what they were. Was it simply because you liked the good-looking female (male), and you'd like her (him) to like you? If the answer to this question is yes, then you (as the actor) perceived your behavior to be *externally* caused. The third option is to say to yourself, "Why, yes, I am against animal research—didn't I just sign a petition stating so?" If the student made this last attribution as the true reason for why he/she signed the petition, then he/she self-perceived the cause of the behavior as internally caused—*I am in favor of this cause.* Now, from a persuader's point of view, the difference between the external attribution and the internal attribution made in this situation is critically important. Suppose you wanted to ask these students to donate money or time to your cause? If the student made the external attribution, then there is no commitment to the cause and the student is not likely to donate much money or time (except, of course, if the request was to spend time with, or give money to, the beautiful opposite-sexed volunteer). On the other hand, if the student made the internal attribution that he or she was against animal research, then the probability that he or she will donate time or money is increased. There exists 20 years of research on how we might use self-perception theory in order to get individuals to comply with requests of this nature (see Chapter 10, "Persuasion in Interpersonal Influence").

Social exchange theory

Both personality theory and attribution theory can be described as essentially "one-way" theories. *Social exchange theory* is different, because it is based on the belief that one can best understand the behavior of people by considering the behavior of *both* source and receiver. What makes exchange theory different from other social paradigms is that it considers human behavior to be like money, goods, and services. Behavior can be offered for exchange, and the vendor and the buyer both take into account the "cost" of the behavior and the "reward" associated with the behavior. Just as learning theory assumes that the amount of the reward offered is directly related to the probability that a response will be made, social exchange theory assumes that the strength of the reward is responsible for the way in which the individual will behave. Learning theory assumes that difficult behavior will be learned less easily than easy behavior, and in similar fashion, social exchange theory assumes that behavior with high cost will occur less frequently than behavior with low cost.

There are, as with attribution theory, several versions of social exchange theory. All of the versions agree that much of our behavior is guided by our perceptions of costs and rewards. In fact, the following principle has been called many things, such as the "basic hedonic" principle or the "minimax principle," and represents the heart of social exchange theory: *People desire to maximize rewards and minimize costs.* While there are exceptions to this general principle, our typical behavior is directed toward maximizing rewards while avoiding costs. Costs include money, the loss of benefits and rewards (as when your parents took away privileges when punishing you when you were younger), losses to one's esteem, and so on. Rewards, of course, include money, material objects, increased status, prestige, recognition and increased liking, love, and other intangibles.

We will have much more to say about social exchange theory, costs, and rewards in later chapters in this book. Here, we'd like to point out several general concerns the persuader should consider when trying to persuade others. Social exchange theory offers us the opportunity to make suggestions to the source about situations involving persuasive communication.

1. Make an analysis of the costs versus the benefits for any persuasive message you might send. This is really seldom done by persuasive communicators. They tend to look only at potential rewards if successful, and seldom assess costs of making an exchange, or make an analysis of the potential disadvantages.

2. Make an analysis ahead of time of the costs versus the benefits for the receiver to whom the message is directed. Again, we think about the potential rewards to the receiver, but seldom attempt to estimate the costs. If we did, we might sometimes find that there are no circumstances under which it would be possible for the receiver to answer "yes" to our message.

3. Make sure that your message specifies the reasons why it should be accepted. Many persuasive messages simply propose that the receiver take some action. The source hopes that the perceived reward is implicit in the message. Perception is selective, however, and it is frequently the case that the rewards the source

sees so clearly in analyzing the task are misperceived or not seen at all by the receiver.

4. Be sure to consider the future effects of persuasion on both yourself and your receiver. We may make an analysis of a particular situation, and decide to proceed with our message. If, however, we had made an analysis of the potential effects of a receiver's behavior on our future behavior, we might not have decided to take the initial plunge.

Social exchange theory, then, is an attempt to understand the behavior of people in interactional situations. The theory assumes that people will act in accordance with economic principles, making decisions based on an analysis of the perceived costs and perceived benefits. We must note that the word "perceived" is an important one. Social exchange theory does not claim that everyone will behave in exactly the same way when confronted by the same situation. One person may perceive the costs differently from another. One person may be willing to take large risks, while another attempts only to maintain a current position. Social exchange theory provides another tool to both source and receiver in approaching the persuasive communication situation, a tool that allows understanding and prediction of persuasion.

Summary

There are many different types of persuasive communication situations. Some of the most important are those situations involving interpersonal communication, where a communicator is talking to one or a very few people. Predicting the nature of the attitudes and beliefs that the receiver holds in that situation is extremely important to the communicator. In this chapter we examined several theories designed to make it easier to make an accurate assessment.

Personality theory is based on the assumption that when our belief structures become relatively fixed, we may be able to identify the structures in terms of various personality characteristics. These personality categories can help the communicator in making predictions about the ways in which people are likely to react in a persuasive situation. Further, we have looked at the role played by the receiver's level of involvement in the topic both in terms of how the receiver cognitively responds to the message and in terms of changing attitudes.

Attribution theory is based on the premise that all of us make attributions as to the causes of behavior when we observe the behavior of those around us. The theory suggests that we tend to attribute behavior to either personal or situational factors. The communicator who can make a careful assessment of the attributions from which receivers will operate. can improve understanding and prediction.

Finally, we discussed social exchange theory, an approach to studying human behavior that concentrates on the analysis of the costs and benefits that sources and receivers can expect from engaging in communication. Suggestions to help the source improve the ability to predict behavior point to the usefulness of exchange theory.

Footnotes

1. N. L. Munn, *Psychology: Fundamentals of Human Adjustment*, 3rd ed. (Boston: Houghton Mifflin, 1956), pp. 170–184.

2. T. W. Adorno, E. Frenkel-Brunswick, D. J. Levinson, and R. N. Sanford, *The Authoritarian Personality* (New York: Harper & Row, 1950).

3. F. J. DiVesta and J. C. Merwin, "The Effects of Need-Oriented Communications on Attitude Change," *Journal of Abnormal and Social Psychology*, vol. 60 (1960), pp. 80–85.

4. I. L. Janis, "Personality Correlates of Susceptibility to Persuasion," *Journal of Personality*, vol. 22 (1954), pp. 504–518.

5. G. R. Miller and M. Burgoon, *New Techniques of Persuasion* (New York: Harper & Row, 1973), pp. 21–23.

6. R. E. Nisbett and A. Gordon, "Self-Esteem and Susceptibility to Social Influence," *Journal of Personality and Social Psychology*, vol. 5 (1967), pp. 268–279.

7. See H. Leventhal, "Findings and Theory in the Study of Fear Communications," in L. Berkowitz, ed., *Advances in Experimental Social Psychology*, vol. 5 (New York: Academic, 1970), pp. 119–186.

8. E. Aronson, *The Social Animal*, 3rd ed. (San Francisco: W. H. Freeman, 1980).

9. Aronson, *The Social Animal*, p. 76.

10. I. L. Janis and D. Rife, "Persuasibility and Emotional Disorder," in I. L. Janis and C. I. Hovland, eds., *Personality and Persuasibility* (New Haven, Conn.: Yale University Press, 1959), pp. 121–37; C. I. Hovland, A. A. Lumsdaine, and F. D. Sheffield, *Experiments on Mass Communications* (Princeton, N.J.: Princeton University Press, 1949).

11. L. Wheeless, "The Effects of Comprehension Loss on Persuasion," *Speech Monographs*, vol. 39 (1971), pp. 327–330.

12. W. J. McGuire, "Personality and Attitude Change: An Information-Processing Theory," in A. G. Greenwald, T. C. Brock, and T. M. Ostrom, eds., *Psychological Foundations of Attitudes* (New York: Academic, 1968), pp. 171–196.

13. A. H. Eagly and R. Warren, "Intelligence, Comprehension and Opinion Change," *Journal of Personality*, vol. 44 (1976), pp. 226–242.

14. J. C. Nunnally and H. M. Bobren, "Variables Governing the Willingness to Receive Communications on Mental Health," *Journal of Personality*, vol. 27 (1959), pp. 275–290.

15. I. L. Janis and F. Feshbach, "Effects of Fear-Arousing Communications," *Journal of Abnormal and Social Psychology*, vol. 49 (1954), pp. 211–218.

16. D. P. Haefner, "Some Effects of Guilt-Arousing and Fear-Arousing Persuasive Communications on Opinion Change" (Ph.D. dissertation, University of Rochester, 1956).

17. W. J. McGuire, "The Nature of Attitudes and Attitude Change," in G. Lindzey and E. Aronson, eds., *The Handbook of Social Psychology*, vol. 3 (Reading, Mass.: Addison-Wesley, 1969), pp. 136–314.

18. S. Millman, The Relationship between Anxiety, Learning, and Opinion Change, unpublished doctoral dissertation, cited in McGuire, "The Nature of Attitudes."

19. R. E. Petty and J. T. Cacioppo, *Attitudes and Persuasion: Classic and Contemporary Approaches* (Dubuque, Iowa: Wm. C. Brown, 1981).

20. I. L. Janis and S. Feshback, "Effects of Fear-Arousing Communications," *Journal of Abnormal and Social Psychology*, vol. 48 (1953), pp. 78–92.

21. M. Rokeach, *The Open and Closed Mind* (New York: Basic Books, 1962).

22. E. P. Bettinghaus, T. Steinfatt, and G. Miller, "Source Evaluation, Syllogistic Content, and Judgments of Logical Validity by High- and Low-Dogmatic Persons," *Journal of Personality and Social Psychology*, vol. 16, no. 2 (1970), pp. 238–244.

23. F. A. Powell, "Open- and Closed-Mindedness and the Ability to Differentiate Source and Message," *Journal of Abnormal and Social Psychology*, vol. 65 (1962), pp. 61–64.

24. R. Vacchiano, P. Strauss, and L. Hockman, "The Open and Closed Mind: A Review of Dogmatism," *Psychological Bulletin*, vol. 71, No. 4 (1969), p. 261.

25. T. W. Adorno, E. Frenkel-Brunswick, D. J. Levinson, and R. N. Sanford, *The Authoritarian Personality* (New York: Harper & Row, 1950).

26. J. H. Rohrer and M. Sherif, *Social Psychology at the Crossroads* (New York: Harper & Row, 1951).

27. O. J. Harvey and G. D. Beverly, "Some Personality Correlates of Concept Change through Role Playing," *Journal of Abnormal and Social Psychology*, vol. 63 (1961), pp. 125–130.

28. I. H. Paul, "Impressions of Personality, Authoritarianism, and the *Fait Accompli* Effect," *Journal of Abnormal and Social Psychology*, vol. 53 (1956), pp. 338–344.

29. W. Weiss, "Emotional Arousal and Attitude Change," *Psychological Review*, vol. 6 (1960), pp. 267–280.

30. R. Bray and A. Noble, "Authoritarianism

and Decisions of Mock Juries: Evidence of Jury Bias and Group Polarization," *Journal of Personality and Social Psychology*, vol. 36 (1978), pp. 1424–1430; V. P. Hans and N. Vidmar, "Jury Selection," in N. L. Kerr and R. M. Bray, eds., *The Psychology of the Courtroom* (New York: Academic, 1982), pp. 39–82.

31. V. L. Hamilton, "Obedience and Responsibility: A Jury Simulation," *Journal of Personality and Social Psychology*, vol. 36 (1978), pp. 126–146; Hans and Vidmar, "Jury Selection."

32. M. F. Kaplan and L. E. Miller, "Reducing the Effects of Juror Bias," *Journal of Personality and Social Psychology*, vol. 36 (1978), pp. 1443–1455; M. F. Kaplan, "Cognitive Processes in the Individual Juror," in N. L. Kerr and R. M. Bray, eds., *The Psychology of the Courtroom* (New York: Academic, 1982), pp. 197–220.

33. D. C. McClelland, A. W. Atkinson, R. W. Clark, and E. L. Lowell, *The Achievement Motive* (New York: Appleton-Century-Crofts, 1953); D. C. McClelland, *The Achieving Society* (Princeton, N.J.: D. Van Nostrand, 1961).

34. T. G. Harris, "Achieving Man: A Conversation with David C. McClelland," *Psychology Today*, vol. 4. no. 8 (January 1971), p. 36.

35. See J. W. Atkinson, *Motives in Fantasy, Action and Society* (Princeton, N.J.: Van Nostrand, 1958). See also J. D. Andrews, "The Achievement Motive and Advancement in Two Types of Organizations," *Journal of Personality and Social Psychology*, vol. 6 (1967), pp. 163-168; R. M. Steers, "Effects of Need for Achievement on the Job Performance-Job Attitude Relationship," *Journal of Applied Psychology*, vol. 60, (1975), pp. 678–682; R. M. Steers, "Task-Goal Attributes, N Achievement, and Supervisory Performance," *Organizational Behavior and Human Performance*, vol. 13 (1975), pp. 392–403.

36. R. M. Steers and D. G. Spencer, "The Role of Achievement Motivation in Job Design," *Journal of Applied Psychology*, vol. 62 (1977), pp. 472–479. Quote from page 476.

37. Petty and Cacioppo, *Attitudes and Persuasion;* R. E. Petty, T. M. Ostrom, and T. C. Brock, eds., *Cognitive Response in Persuasion* (Hillsdale, N.J.: Erlbaum, 1981).

38. Petty and Cacioppo, *Attitudes and Persuasion.*

39. R. E. Petty and J. T. Cacioppo, "Issue Involvement Can Increase or Decrease Persuasion by Enhancing Message-Relevant Cognitive Responses," *Journal of Personality and Social Psychology*, vol. 37 (1979), pp. 1915–1926.

40. R. E. Petty, J. T. Cacioppo, and D. Schumann, "Central and Peripheral Routes to Advertising Effectiveness: The Moderating Role of Involvement," *Journal of Consumer Research*, vol. 10 (1983), pp. 135–146.

41. R. E. Petty and J. T. Cacioppo, "The Effects of Involvement and Responses to Argument Quantity and Quality: Central and Peripheral Routes to Persuasion," *Journal of Personality and Social Psychology*, vol. 46 (1984), pp. 69–81.

42. For example, on the topic of implementing comprehensive tests for seniors, the following represents *strong* arguments: (a) Prestigious universities have comprehensive exams to maintain academic excellence; (b) institution of the exams has led to a reversal in the declining scores on standardized achievement tests at other universities; (c) graduate and professional schools shows a preference for undergraduates who have passed a comprehensive exam; (d) average starting salaries are higher for graduates of schools with the exams; (e) schools with the exams attract larger and more well-known corporations to recruit students for jobs; (f) the quality of undergraduate teaching has improved for schools with the exams; (g) university alumni would increase financial support if the exams were instituted, allowing a tuition increase to be avoided; and (h) the (fictitious) National Accrediting Board of Higher Education would give the university its highest rating if the exams were instituted.

The *weak* version of these messages also contained eight arguments but relied more on quotations and opinions than on statistics and data to support the following arguments: (a) Adopting the exams would allow the university to be at the forefront of a national trend; (b) graduate students have complained that since they have to take comprehensives, undergraduates should take them also; (c) by not administering the exams, a tradition dating back to the ancient Greeks was being violated; (d) parents had written to administrators in support of the plan; (e) the exams would increase student fear and anxiety enough to promote more studying; (f) the exams would help cut costs by eliminating the necessity for other tests that varied with instructor; (g) the exams would allow students to compare their performance with that of students at other schools; and (h) job prospects might be improved.

The *very weak* version of these messages relied exclusively on personal opinion and personal examples. The following arguments were presented: (a) Most of the author's friends supported the proposal; (b) the author's major adviser took a comprehensive exam and now had a prestigious academic position; (c) whatever benefit the exams had for graduate students would also accrue to undergraduates; (d) requiring graduate students but not undergraduates to take the exams was analogous to racial discrimination; (e) the risk of failing the exam was a challenge most students would welcome; (f) the difficulty of the exam would prepare one for later competitions in life; (g) the Educational Testing Service would not market the exams unless they had great educational value; and (h) if the exams were instituted, Northeastern would become the American Oxford.

The source of these essays is R. E. Petty, S. Harkins, and K. Williams, "The Effects of Group Diffusion of Cognitive Effort on Attitudes: An Information-Processing View," *Journal of Personality and Social Psychology*, vol. 38 (1980), pp. 81–92. However, all studies employing the topic of comprehensive tests for seniors have used arguments like the ones listed above.

43. C. W. Sherif, M. Sherif, and R. Nebergall, *Attitude and Attitude Change: The Social Judgment-Involvement Approach* (Philadelphia: Saunders, 1965).
44. See C. Hovland, O. J. Harvey, and M. Sherif, "Assimilation and Contrast Effects in Reaction to Communication and Attitude Change," *Journal of Abnormal and Social Psychology*, vol. 55 (1957), pp. 242–252.
45. D. Granberg, "Social Judgment Theory," in

M. Burgoon, ed., *Communication Yearbook 6* (Beverly Hills: Sage, 1982), pp. 304–329.
46. D. Broder, "Brock and Good Choice," *Columbia Daily Tribune*, February 2, 1977, p. 6; cited in Granberg.
47. TRB, "Gracious Interval," *The New Republic*, November 13, 1976, pp. 56–57.
48. K. K. Sereno and E. M. Bodaken, "Ego-Involvement and Attitude Change: Toward a Reconceptualization of Persuasive Effect," *Speech Monographs*, vol. 39 (1972), pp. 151–158.
49. N. Miller, "Involvement and Dogmatism as Inhibitors of Attitude Change," *Journal of Experimental Social Psychology*, vol. 1 (1965), pp. 121–132. In the text we say that the four variables represent a minimum of possible causes because Norman Miller's manipulation of these four only partially caused increased involvement to be measured.
50. D. R. Seibold and B. H. Spitzberg, "Attribution Theory and Research: Review and Implication for Communication," in B. Dervin and M. J. Voigt, eds., *Progress in Communication Sciences*, vol. 3 (Norwood, N.J.: Ablex, 1982), pp. 85–126; L. G. Shaver, *An Introduction to Attribution Process* (Cambridge, Mass.: Winthrop, 1975).
51. H. H. Kelley, "Attribution Theory in Social Psychology," in D. Levine, ed., *Nebraska Symposium on Motivation,* vol. 15 (Lincoln, Neb.: University of Nebraska Press, 1967), pp. 192–238.
52. See S. T. Fiske and S. E. Taylor, *Social Cognition* (Reading, Mass.: Addison-Wesley, 1984); A. H. Eagly, S. Chaiken, and W. Wood, "An Attribution Analysis in Persuasion," in J. H. Harvey, W. J. Ickes, and R. F. Kidd, eds., *New Directions in Attribution Research*, vol. 3 (Hillsdale, N.J.: Erlbaum, 1981), pp. 37–62.
53. S. T. Fiske and S. E. Taylor, *Social Cognition* (Reading, Mass.: Addison-Wesley, 1984), p. 344.
54. D. J. Bem, "Self Perception: An Alternative Interpretation of Cognitive Dissonance Phenomena," *Psychological Review,* vol. 74 (1967), pp. 183–200; D. J. Bem, "Self-Perception Theory," in L. Berkowitz, ed., *Advances in Experimental Social Psychology*, vol. 6 (New York: Academic, 1972), pp. 2–62.

CHAPTER FOUR

Successful Persuasion: Group Influences

Every four years, the United States holds a presidential election. The major political parties select candidates to run for the office of president and vice-president of the United States. During the political conventions, and during the subsequent political campaigns, newspapers, magazines, radio commentators, and television news pundits spend many hours trying to predict which candidates are likely to win the election. There are, of course, millions of voters in the United States, and it is simply impossible to ask each and every person how they are likely to vote. What does the political analyst do to improve the chances of making a correct prediction? How can the opinion polling organization ask only a few people how they are going to vote, and then proceed to make statements about the nation as a whole?

The political analyst and the opinion polling expert base their predictions on a single assumption: *People who are alike in some way tend to vote alike.* A newspaper story will state that "Candidate Jones will have a definite appeal to Jewish voters," or a television commentator will say that "Candidate Doe is meeting with the Hispanic leadership in Miami." In every election we hear references to the "women's vote," the "black vote," and the "labor vote." These statements and references are all based on the assumption that people who belong to a particular ethnic, religious, racial, or socioeconomic group are likely to be responsive to persuasive messages that are perceived to appeal to that group. This chapter investigates the assumption that there is a relationship between persuasion and those characteristics that individuals possess as a result of their membership in particular groups.

Perhaps the first question we should ask is whether there is any basis *at all* for assuming that people who are members of some group might behave in ways similar to other members of the group. Many scholars believe that there is such a basis. It stems from the belief that the attitudes that people possess are in part determined by the experiences they have had. If you were raised as a strong Roman Catholic for the first 20 years of your life, if all the members of your family were Roman Catholics, and if you went to Catholic parochial schools, it is very likely that the attitudes and beliefs you possess are going to be similar to those of other people raised as you were. If a persuasive speaker can find out what attitudes are held generally by Roman Catholics, the speaker can direct a message to you with some confidence that you will respond favorably to it. We have already discussed the development of attitudes and beliefs, and the role they play in persuasive situations. Over a period of years, people develop a set of reference frames that help govern the way in which they will eventually respond to persuasive messages. Whether a receiver is in an interpersonal, face-to-face situation, or whether the receiver is simply one of many people who are the intended receivers of a message, knowing something about the receiver's reference frames will assist in message preparation. How can we make estimates about people when we do not know them personally? How can we predict responses when we cannot ask all members of a prospective audience about their behavior?

The development of reference frames is influenced by the *groups of people with whom an individual associates*. The people we associate with are constantly sending us messages, and we react to those messages. If you are a college student living in a dormitory on campus, the likelihood is that you will be receiving and acting upon many messages sent by fellow students. You cannot help but be influenced by these messages, and you will most likely become more like your fellow students than like your high school classmates who did not go to college and are working on a production line in a factory. When you as a college student receive messages from any source, you are likely to respond to those messages with behavior colored by reference frames developed as a result of your association with other college students. The influence that groups have on the development of attitudes and beliefs is important information for the persuasive communicator.

Reference groups

People belong to many different groups, and they possess attitudes and beliefs about a variety of topics. Some of those topics are relevant to some of the groups we belong to, while others are relevant to other groups. If a person behaves in such a manner that her behavior is similar to other members of one of the groups to which she belong, we say that she has made use of a *reference group*. The term "reference group" is used to describe any group to which people relate their attitudes and beliefs.

Reference groups serve two major functions. One function is to help determine appropriate behavior for an individual by setting group standards or norms of behavior. The second function of reference groups is to serve as a standard or checkpoint for making decisions about persuasive messages.

Kelley suggests that the use of a reference group as a standard or checkpoint is really a "comparison function." He says, "A group functions as a comparison reference group for an individual to the extent that the behavior, attitudes, circumstances, or other characteristics of its members represent standards or comparison points which he uses in making judgments and evaluations."[1]

One way of looking at reference groups is to divide them into *membership* and *nonmembership* groups. That is, they can be groups of which the individual is actually a member, such as a fraternity, the Junior Chamber of Commerce, the local Methodist Church, or the American Legion. They can also be groups of which the individual is not a member, but that serve as a standard that is used in making decisions. The college student who does not belong to a fraternity may use what he knows or thinks he knows about fraternities in making judgments about certain issues. A second way of distinguishing between reference groups is described by Newcomb when he refers to *positive* and *negative* reference groups.[2] In terms of persuasive communication, a positive reference group is a group toward which an individual aspires. A message opposing socialized medicine might be viewed favorably by someone who wants to become a physician, since the receiver may feel that physicians do not tend to view socialized medicine favorably. A negative reference group is one the individual opposes. To use the same example in reverse, an individual who believes that "all doctors charge too much" might oppose a message arguing against socialized medicine, taking the position: "If doctors are against it, I'm for it."

Our interest in reference groups is based both on pragmatic grounds (what *works* in persuasion) and on theoretical grounds. Leon Festinger[3] proposed a *theory of social comparisons* that suggests that people have a basic need to compare themselves to others so that they might evaluate their own competencies and attitudes. It is common for people to compare test scores, SAT results, rules of behavior established by parents, college football records, and other areas where comparison might help people arrive at an attitude or behavior. According to work on social comparison processes, we compare ourselves to a reference group similar to ourselves in some relevant or important way.[4] Typically, we compare ourselves to people who are similar to ourselves in terms of age and sex. Suls, Gastorf, and Lawhon,[5] for example, administered a creativity test to high school students and, when returning the scores, gave the students a selection of different group averages so that the high school students can compare scores. The overwhelming choice was to compare one's score first to the same-sex-same-age group, followed by the same-age-different-sex group. That is, a female high school student first compared her score to other high school females, and then compared her score to other high school males. Few of the students in this study compared their scores to high school freshman or to college students.

Age and gender are not the only characteristics on which people will make comparisons. Wheeler, Koestner, and Driver[6] placed college students in a laboratory context where they would receive training in reasoning tasks before they took an "analogical reasoning abilities test." Some students received no practice rounds, others received 10 practice rounds, and others received 20 practice rounds. When given their scores later, students were allowed to compare their scores with other students and were given a choice of another student's test score for comparison. Students selected to compare their scores with another student who had the same number of practice trials. Of course, if you wanted to know whether you were doing well or poorly, you'd want to compare yourself to another student who had the same ability to practice as you. You get little feedback by comparing yourself to a student who had no practice. Miller[7] conducted a study where female college students completed a reasoning test and were allowed to select scores from one of several groups for the sake of comparison. Miller found that women compared their scores to that of similarly attractive women, even though attractiveness was *unrelated* to scores on the reasoning test. We apparently find it natural to compare ourselves to others based on similarities in age, sex, practice or training, level of attractiveness—and possibly a host of other variables.

We should note in passing that a person might have more than one reference group for any particular skill or ability. Suppose a male runs routinely with a particular group of peers. On a day-by-day basis he will compare how fast he runs the mile relative to this particular group who are all approximately the same age and who all started jogging at the same time. However, suppose this particular male hoped to run one day in the citywide marathon. He might establish a second "reference point" of marathon runners—a group to which he does not yet belong but to which he hopes to belong one day. On any given week, then, he might apply one of the two standards as a means for assessing his relative speed as a runner. Most of us, however, probably have one group to which we compare our relative abilities, skills, and so on.

Festinger extends his theory of social comparisons beyond a comparison of competencies, abilities, or skills to the area of attitudes. We may be uncertain about our attitudes on many topics, especially for those attitudes we hold that are complex or ones for which there is very little objective justification: Should I vote in favor of or against Proposition 51? Does a particular fashion look good on me? For these and similar areas, we may turn to people we know in order to compare our information and attitudes with theirs. After hearing a presidential debate, many friends ask their friends, neighbors, relatives, and coworkers about their reactions. Only then do we come to a firm position of our own.

Not surprisingly, we are influenced by the outcome of the social comparison process: When we compare our attitudes to that of a positive reference group and notice a difference we feel the need to reduce the discrepancy by changing our attitudes, by attempting to influence the group's position, or by rejecting the group as relevant to the subject.[8]

Reference groups are only one kind of standard that receivers use in developing frames of reference. Our discussion in previous chapters suggested that *any* information a person acquires may be used in the development of reference frames. The experiences that people have may be enhanced, however, by associating with people who think them to be important. Thus, associating with a particular group, or learning that some group has spoken out on a particular topic, may make it more likely that one attitude will be developed rather than another, or that one belief will be adopted and another denied. For this reason, further examination of the characteristics of various groups that may serve as reference groups is warranted.

Membership groups

Every individual belongs to many groups. There are some kinds of group membership in which the individual has little or no control. These are *demographic groups*, or *involuntary groups*, and are indicated by such variables as age, sex, ethnic origin, and occupation. People cannot control how old they are, or whether they are born black or white. We might argue that the matter of being born at a particular time in history or being born of parents of a particular race ought not to make any difference in individual beliefs and attitudes. The evidence suggests, however, that these demographic groupings *do* make a difference, since individuals sharing demographic characteristics may also have increased interaction with one another.

The second type of membership group is that which people join voluntarily. These are *voluntary groups* and include such associations as religious groups, social groups, and political groups. We shall discuss both demographic and voluntary groups and their relationship to persuasive communication.

Demographic groups

In examining demographic characteristics, we should remember that they can serve only as general guides. Predicting the characteristics of a particular audience or individual from a knowledge of their demographic characteristics is helpful as long as the persuasive communicator realizes that the predictions may not apply to any one member of the audience.

Aging: the young and the old

Much research on persuasion is biased toward studying the effects messages have on children. Only recently has some attention focused on persuasion aimed at older segments of the population. America is aging, however, since over 11 percent of the total population is now 65 or older, and it is anticipated that by the year 2000 over 15 percent of the population (30 million people) will be in this age group.[9] As a general rule, however, there are relatively few differences between parents and their children in terms of values, expectations, degree of liberalness or conservativeness, and so on.[10] However, fundamental differences exist between age groups on the basis of habits, in terms of the development of frames of reference, and in terms of the receiver's ability to process information as it is transmitted to the receivers. In this part of the chapter we will talk about persuasion at the two extreme ends of the age continuum: the young and the old.

Probably no one is more susceptible to persuasion than the 3–7 year old. Members in this age group do not even know what a commercial is, when a commercial ends and begins, what function a commercial is supposed to serve, and members at this age are susceptible to "celebrity endorsements" by their real or cartoon idols.[11] On the other hand, by the time children reach the fifth grade 99 percent of them understand the purpose of a commercial, few are uncritically accepting of the message's content (for example, 66 percent of sixth graders claim that a product in real life is not as good as it is shown on television),[12] and few rely solely on television as a source of information about clothes, and so on, as they begin to read magazines and experience social or peer pressure.

Since children in the 3–7 age group are so susceptible to persuasion, several steps were taken in the 1970s to safeguard this particular group.[13] First, program personalities or program characters (live or animated) were prohibited from endorsing a product during a show or during any time slot adjacent to the show. Thus it does not appear to the three-year-old viewer that his or her favorite character on "Flintstones" walks into the bathroom and swallows pills. *Flintstones Vitamins* must be advertised on shows other than the "Flintstones." Second, a separator device should be inserted before a commercial that says, in both video and audio, "We [or name of program] will

return after these messages." This device must remain on the screen for at least five seconds but not more than ten seconds, and a device must be inserted on returning from the commercial to the program, using language such as "We now return to [name of program]." Why? We adults habitually look away from a significant portion of advertisements, but some children may be glued in some zombie-like fashion to the television screen, and these children should be informed that a break from the television show is occurring and informed that what follows is a commercial.

Third, because the younger viewer may uncritically believe what he or she hears, attempts have been made to establish guidelines for the ethical use of persuasion aimed at children. Meringoff and Lesser[14] present a discussion of some of these guidelines. Generally speaking, one would like to see advertisements aimed at children avoid language and production techniques that may distort the characteristics of a product and give the child a false impression of what the toy does, how it works, its volume, and how it looks when it is bought in a box and parents have to put it together. Also, advertisements aimed at children should avoid employing strident audio techniques, video devices such as cuts, special effects using strobe lights or flashing colors or lights, and they should avoid relying on irritating and obtrusive sounds. Some specific guidelines include:[15]

1. Provide audio disclosure when a product requires assembly.

2. Provide audio or video disclosure as to a product's method of operation and source of power.

3. Provide simultaneous audio and video disclosures when items, such as batteries needed to operate a product as demonstrated in the advertising, are not included.

4. Avoid competitive/comparative/superiority claims about (toys and other durable) products.

(This last guideline is designed to protect a child's self-concept because a child will usually possess only one bicycle and if advertisers claim that bicycle X is superior to other bicycles, many young people may feel hurt or inferior. Also, since children have not cognitively matured yet, we can not assume that they understand concepts such as "comparison advertising.")

Rules specific to toys include:[15]

1. To present the toy on its actual merits as a plaything. (It shall neither exaggerate nor distort play value.)

2. To limit any view of a toy or demonstration of its performance to that which a child is reasonably capable of reproducing.

3. To employ the complete and authentic sound(s) of the toy.

4. To confine their use of generic stock film footage, real-life counterparts of toys, fantasy and animation (in none of which either a child or a toy appears) to the first one-third of the commercial.

5. To disclose clearly the original purchase in the body of the commercial and (by video, with audio disclosure where necessary for clarification) in the closing five seconds.

According to Meringoff and Lesser,[16] music, sound effects, volume level, tempo, and other audio techniques should be used with restraint and discretion. It is also recommended that caution be taken in the use of particular video techniques involving camera angles, special lenses, special lighting, and dazzling visual effects. All of these techniques give the child ideas about the toy's operation that reflect distorted and exaggerated perception.

The guidelines we've discussed so far are not *rules* in that they are enforced in the media. Rather, these guidelines are used as a general set of ethical considerations that serve to protect the more naïve and impressionable 3–7 year olds. They are only suggested guidelines, and are not completely effective when used. Research, for example, indicates that when no separator devices are used about 50 percent of the 4 year olds recognize when a commercial is shown to them. When a separator device is used, the figure jumps to 75–77 percent—25 percent of the 4 year olds still do not recognize that what they are watching is a commercial.

Several volumes are required to address all of the issues relevant to children and persuasion that have been researched in the last 10 years. Briefly, we summarize research on how children are persuaded:[18]

1. Children are susceptible to celebrity or authority endorsements. There are several reasons for this—children at young ages are generally prone to adopt the views of authority figures, and they imitate authority figures. Young children desiring to achieve cognitive mastery over their immediate environment are excited when they correctly recognize a celebrity and learn about the products that go along with the celebrity, and children learn over the years that certain characters are good, likeable, and trustworthy (for example, Ronald McDonald, Burger King, Fred Flintstone). In one study, 36 percent of children desired a Frisbee when they saw it advertised. Yet, when Muhammad Ali endorsed the product 60 percent of the children desired the Frisbee. Another study found that celebrities do not even have to endorse the product verbally in order to promote the product—merely the presence of a black athlete is sufficient to increase preference for a product. Research indicates that if the children in the audience do in fact like the source and identify the source, celebrity or authority endorsements prompt 57 percent to over 70 percent of the children to want the product.

2. Other source effects operate on different age groups. Younger children may not be influenced by sex-role stereotyping as much as older ones, but are possibly influenced more by fantasy characters and are more strongly influenced than older children by the presence of parents in commercials. Older children display more sex-role stereotyping, with boys being influenced by physical strength and action, and girls being influenced by physical attractiveness. Also, older children may be more

strongly influenced by endorsements by athletes.

3. Younger children (3 to 5 years old) seem to be more susceptible to blatant claims (for example, drinking a milk shake will make you grow up to be strong) than older children. But older children (5th graders) seem more susceptible to social status appeals (for example, buying a product will gain the buyer more friends and will increase his or her status) than younger children (2nd grade).

4. Simplified wording and use of more than one modality for some messages can increase children's leaning from advertisements. Children do not understand what the term "assembly required" means, and so it is common today for advertisements to report verbally "Your parents have to put it together." Also, disclosures such as "Batteries required" should appear on the screen as well as be communicated verbally in the audio channel—use of both modalities should increase the chance children will notice and remember the disclosure.

5. There are fundamental differences in how toys and food are advertised. These differences probably reflect what advertisers have found in successfully selling to children, and possibly reflect how advertisers target products for particular audiences. Advertisements of toy products, for example, depict small groups of Caucasians playing with products, while advertisements of food products (candy, cereal, fast food restaurants) display larger groups of children of different ethnic origins having fun eating. The main appeals in selling food are humor and fun. Advertisements for toys appeal to affiliation, fun, power, or being grown up. Both toy and food advertisements, however, involve frequent repetition of the name of the product (often over 3 times in 30 seconds), and 50 percent of commercials in both categories use jingles and slogans.

Special attention has focused on selling food to children, since children may learn from these messages and advertising may have a significant impact on childrens' beliefs about nutrition,

food, and health. Some general findings include:

a. Most cereal ads are totally or partially animated, whereas ads for candy/sweets are usually live-action; fast food restaurants use live adult males as spokespersons.

b. In general, food products are not promoted to children on the basis of their nutritional value. Only cereal ads will occasionally make a reference to the number of vitamins contained in the cereal. Because of ethical guidelines (as discussed previously), breakfast-types of products should indicate that the product is to be consumed as part of a full breakfast. The majority of cereal ads makes this disclosure in the last five seconds or less of the ad; and children may not recall having seen this disclosure. Candy/sweets are depicted, however, as being eaten in a wide range of settings, and not shown as part of a meal.

Can some of these findings be used to make children informed consumers and to be knowledgeable about nutrition? Yes, there is evidence that children learn from food advertisements, and work now focuses on how children may respond to celebrities telling them to exercise, to eat correctly, to behave equitably with other children, and so on. These Public Service Announcements may not be as flashy or as sophisticated as the regular toy advertisement, but it is hoped that children will learn about nutrition and health.[19]

Aging Americans

Ronch suggests that there may be different stresses in the life of the elderly person that can make a difference in what the person will consider important or worth paying attention to.[20] Some of these areas include: (1) family problems, as family members age, become ill, or die; (2) peer-group problems, as friends become separated or are lost to the person; (3) occupation problems, as people are forced to retire at certain ages; (4) recreation problems, as health or age forces changes in old habits; and (5) sexual problems, as loss of a partner or changes in health force new patterns of behavior. Not all aging Americans will necessarily face all or even any of these problems. In fact, a scant 5 percent of people over 65 years of age require physical assistance to be mobile.[21] However, concerns over one's ability to control the environment and doubt about financial security can make individuals older than 65 susceptible to appeals concerning how such worries may be alleviated. The last ten years, for example, have witnessed an increase in advertising concerning health-care insurance plans that will help to cover hospital costs apparently not covered by Medicare. Thus, in some cases, increases in age may impact on self-esteem and anxiety, which influence the susceptibility to persuasion we discussed in Chapter 3.

Stress caused by changes in one's life status is not limited to aging Americans. Andreasen recently outlined work that indicated that any serious change in one's status may influence stress, which creates dissatisfaction with one's routine purchasing behaviors.[22] That is, negative changes in one's status, such as divorce, retirement, changes in jobs, losing a loved one, having a person move out of the household, and so on, prompt individuals to reassess the quality of, and loyalty to, brand products and to become less satisfied with products they may have been using for years. Some people may change consumer goods in order to effect some improvement in their social environment, and they can be susceptible to persuasion. Some general findings concerning persuasion and older receivers include:

1. The older American who was socialized into voting behaviors during the presidential terms of FDR and Truman are much more likely to identify themselves as strongly partisan and to use party membership as a reference group in deciding how to vote. They not only identify more with party labels, they are more likely to vote, and are more likely to vote Republican. Further, older individuals (especially if they identify themselves as similar to other older Americans) are more conservative on a number of beliefs about crime, drugs, sex roles, and so on. Some studies also suggest that older Americans are more likely to contribute to political campaigns, particularly when candidate-oriented direct mailing appeals are used. Older Americans are also more likely than younger ones to claim that political campaigns did not influence how they voted (which is compatible with the idea that older Americans vote along party lines). As a *general rule*, younger voters may be expected to vote according to issues and on the basis of quality of arguments and economic considerations.[23]

2. Children watch hours of television during certain blocks of time during the week, thus making it easy to reach this segment with persuasive messages. Further, there are shows clearly targeted for younger viewers, sports fanatics, businesspersons, and so on, so that a persuader has some idea about how to reach particular receivers. What about the aging Americans, what shows do they watch, why? Since television viewing is inexpensive and easily accessible, older viewers watch a good deal of television, and do so for reasons dealing with *information, entertainment, companionship,* and *relaxation*.[24] However, not all aging Americans rate these reasons as equally important. First, the companionship viewer is often a female or a person who lives alone and watches a number of game shows, daytime serials, and dramas. This type of viewer is more likely to tune in on television during early afternoon, prime time, and late night viewing. Viewers who rate information as important watch more news and talk shows, since they desire to learn about people and events in the world at large. Also, information about the weather seems particularly important, since it affects mobility, social activity, and feelings (hot or cold temperatures). Entertainment viewers watch high levels of television, including game shows, adventure programs, comedies, musical productions, and so on. This group is very selective in viewing, and easily defect to cable systems, and

so on, to watch what they believe is most entertaining. Relaxation viewers prefer general comedies and situation comedies. Studies that give us information like the kind we just summarized provide us first with an idea of how we might find the aging American audience for our messages. Second, we might use information such as this to prepare messages for particular audiences better—the informed viewer, for example, is more likely to be persuaded by facts, figures, data, and information, while the entertainment viewer might be more difficult to reach, generally speaking, and would be persuaded by different appeals.

3. Some types of appeals that help to persuade younger receivers do not apply to older receivers. First, several studies indicate that younger receivers are more susceptible to celebrity endorsements than older receivers and indicate that younger receivers have a more positive attitude toward advertisements and rate them as more trustworthy.[25] These studies used Paul Newman, Linda Evans, and Telly Savalas as endorsers, and it may be possible that only a set of particular endorsers is important to the aging American. Also, advertising executives indicate that they feel that humorous advertisements are inappropriate for older receivers.[26]

4. Aging Americans are less likely to take risks and therefore are less likely to be among the first to adopt new innovations or ideas. Younger receivers are among the first to use bank cards, automatic tellers, solar energy machines, and so on. In fact, the profile of an innovator or an "early adopter" of products include: higher income, higher education, younger, increased social mobility, more favorable attitude toward risk, greater social participation, and higher opinion leadership (see next chapter).[27] One of the few exceptions to this profile is the adaption of home computers; some of the earlier adopters were in the 30–40-year-old bracket—presumably because home computers were expensive when first introduced into the market and only established receivers could afford the product. But the profile of the early adopter of the home computer was similar in many ways to the general innovator: homeowner, more educated, more likely to claim to be an innovator, more positive attitude toward technical products, higher income, and more creative-minded. As a general rule, older receivers are rarely the ones who adopt innovations early.

5. Part of the stereotype of the elder American is loss of memory and/or a decrease in recall of message content. Few persuasion scholars, however, have documented this relationship. One study compared younger (less than 36 years old) and older (54+) receivers and found few important differences in recall.[28] Low comprehension or low recall of message content may not actually occur until receivers enter into their 70s, and even then poor recall is undoubtedly affected by a host of other factors related to health, stress, and so on. Generally speaking, however, the persuader may want to keep in mind that older receivers may not have attended college as commonly as younger receivers, and that messages should be tailored to increase comprehension and recall (for example, repetition, use of more than one modality, and so on).

Sex

A number of studies suggest differences between men and women in the ways they react to persuasive messages. Yet, for every study that indicates women might be more easily persuaded than men, another study indicates that there are no differences between the sexes. Perhaps the most accurate conclusion is that sex may become a significant variable if the *topic* of a message can be expected to elicit different attitudes from men and women. For example, imagine that the subject of a persuasive speech is compulsory arbitration of labor disputes and that the audience is composed of equal numbers of men and women drawn from a general population. When the speech is presented, striking attitude changes would not be expected from the men in the audience, since the information presented would have to fit into an already existing reference frame. For the women in our general audience, however, expectations are somewhat different. There will certainly be some in the audience who are members of labor unions, or who work with companies that are concerned with the arbitration of labor disputes. These women will already have formed reference frames about the topic, and their reactions to the message may be very much like those of the men in the audience. Many other women will not have developed reference frames about labor-management problems, and their reactions may be more pronounced than the reactions of those members of the audience who do have such structured reference frames. Given equal attention on the part of all members of the audience, a researcher might find that women made more changes in their attitudes than men, since they were moving from knowing little about the topic to knowing at least the content of the speech, without, however, being able to evaluate it from a specific frame of reference. The conclusion of the researcher in this situation would be that women are more persuasible than men.

The example we have used suggests that caution must be exercised in making judgments about the persuasibility of any demographic group. Persuasibility is probably related more to the topic or the situation than it is to any set of personal characteristics. If we had changed the topic of the speech from compulsory arbitration to abortion, we might have found the opposite results, and would thus have concluded that men were more persuasible.

In fact, Eagly's[29] extensive review of the sex-influencibility literature similarly suggests the importance of the topic. Eagly found that there was little evidence in support for the sex-influencibility hypotheses in persuasion studies and in conformity studies *not* involving *group* pressure and that the trend toward female influencibility ". . . in

these settings can be readily explained by researchers' tendency to choose experimental materials somewhat biased against the interests and expertise of women" (p. 103).

However, in group-pressure settings, females conformed more than did men. Eagly explored three explanations for why women might conform more than men: (a) that sex roles prescribe differences in yielding, with the female role implying submissiveness to influence; (b) that the superior verbal ability of females predisposes them to be influenced; and (c) that females' greater concern with interpersonal aspects of situations, in particular with maintaining social harmony, predisposes them to be influenced. She concluded that only the latter explanation, that females desire to have harmonious relationships (or to at least avoid conflict), received some support in the literature. Hence, there are two major concerns one should keep in mind when dealing with gender: Is this a topic biased in favor or against men or women? Is there likely to be pressure on audience members such that conformity is important in order to reduce conflict?

There is strong evidence that many traditional roles are changing. For example, in the Eagly review cited above it was noted that 32 percent of the studies published before 1970 indicated that females were more persuasible than males, while only 8 percent of the studies published after 1970 indicated such a trend. The growth of the National Organization for Women, the continuing support of millions of Americans of both sexes to advance equality of the sexes, and the opening of roles traditionally held by only one sex to both argues that *role position*, not sex, may provide the best predictor in the future.

All of the studies we have cited thus far make use of sex defined as a biological variable. There is another way of looking at sex. Bem[30] feels that perhaps the better variable is sexuality, not biological sex. She investigated the "androgynous personality," and found that those individuals who were able to assume both masculine and feminine roles do not conform in their attitudes or behavior to the ways in which men or women are *supposed* to behave. These studies suggest that the future might bring quite a different type of analysis for the variable of sex.

A number of studies have investigated the impact of sexuality on persuasibility. Two can be noted here. Montgomery and Burgoon[31] provided students with Bem's measure and classified individuals into four groups, traditionally sex-typed males and females, androgynous males, and androgynous females. The students later received a written message, attributed to an independent educational consulting firm, which argued that admission to the university should be restricted to juniors and seniors. (The topic was found to be equally salient to both males and females in a pretest.) The authors found that sex-typed females (females who were high on femininity and low on masculinity) were persuaded most, followed by androgynous females and androgynous males, while traditionally sex-typed males (high masculinity and low femininity) were least persuaded. In a later study, Montgomery and Burgoon[32] similarly found that the androgynous measure was a better predictor of persuasion than biological sex.

Advertisers would similarly argue that the general category of "women" is too broad and that one needs to take into consideration age (or life status) and career expectations.[33] Research indicates that women at home with preschool children experience little power and freedom and it is for them that the words "Calgon take me away" ring true. On the other hand, 28 percent of the women in America are stay-at-homes, 13 percent of the women plan to work (at some time), 37 percent simply want a job, and 22 percent are career-oriented workers. Simply studying the working women versus the housewife provides substantial differences in persuasibility. Not surprisingly, advertisements that appeal to the woman as a "Career Partner" are more appealing and persuasive to the working woman than the "Homemaker's Helper" type of ad. Differences in consumer behavior are also pervasive. Housewives are more likely to claim that serving nutritious meals and gaining praise for cooking is im-

portant, while working women rate shopping as a disliked chore and rate ease of preparation and ease of cleaning as important. Both housewives and career women rate novelty and variety as important in meal preparation, and both considered expense as an important consideration when purchasing food. It is not surprising, then, that frozen food companies offering products such as *Lean Cuisine* have profited so well in the 1980s by offering what 30 to 50 percent of women (not to mention men) are looking for: variety, ease of preparation, quality taste, and fewer calories.

Social class, education, occupation, and income

Although these four variables are frequently separated in research studies, they tend to be highly correlated. The level of education that people have tends to determine occupation, which is highly related to income level, and that in turn to social class. Knowing that these relationships *are* interrelated suggests that we can make use of one of the variables as a standard against which to make at least *some* estimate of the others. Social class is the variable about which we have the most evidence, and a number of different studies indicate that there are important differences in attitudes and beliefs between various social classes.

The term "social class" is a label for a series of categories into which people can be placed. Generally, social classes are labeled as lower, middle, and upper, with many researchers further subdividing each class into two or three additional subcategories. Thus, one can talk about the *Upper Americans* (upper-upper class representing 0.3 percent of Americans, lower-upper 1.2 percent, and upper-middle, 12.5 percent), the *Middle Americans* (middle class, 32 percent, and working class, 38 percent), and *Lower Americans* (working poor, 9 percent to 12 percent, and lower-lower, 7 percent).[34] Different Americans can be characterized according to values and according to interests. The working American is interested more in local events than the Upper American, who is likely to be interested in national and world events. The working American attends more closely to local news items and to local sports heroes than the Upper American. Further, working Americans appear to be particularly interested in family matters and place greater emphasis on family and on the extended family. Working class individuals rely on family for a number of purposes—help getting jobs, advice, help getting through crises. One study even found that only 12 percent of the Upper Americans lived within a mile of a close relative, while 45 to 55 percent of the working class lived close to relatives.[35]

Laborers in America also place greater emphasis on the needs of other laborers. Colemen,[36] for example, noted that American laborers were the last to buy foreign cars during the oil shortages of the 1970s. Even three years after the first oil price shock only 10 percent of the working Americans had purchased a fuel-economy foreign car, as compared to 40 percent of the Upper Americans. In terms of vacationing, laborers in America strongly prefer to stay in America. The typical working class American vacations at home or vacations within a few hours of home. If they travel far to vacation, it usually means that they will stay with relatives. Further, even when blue-collar workers were making significant advances in pay raises some years ago, they did not expect to change their status significantly. Rather, extra money was spent on improving the position of all family members—improved schools, better brand name products for school clothes, and so on.

The most obvious recommendation when dealing with social class involves adjusting the persuasive message to make it suitable to the values of the receivers. Working class Americans are more susceptible to claims concerning how one can achieve improvements for one's family, and are susceptible to appeals to patriotism. Further, they are likely to be suspicious of claims concerning how they can benefit greatly from a course of action—their expectations of achievement are likely to be limited to practical and short-term gains.[37] On the other hand, Upper Americans are likely to be persuaded by appeals concerning achievement, larger gains, more international or cosmopolitan interests, appeals to different reference groups (exclusive clubs to which they belong), and appeals of a more personal nature.

Religion and values

Over 50 percent of the American population is formally connected with a church, and an even larger percentage acknowledges having some set of formal religious beliefs. Like social class, the religious affiliations held by an individual tend to affect responses made to persuasive messages. Rossi and Rossi[38] asked a group of people in an industrial community in Massachusetts to designate the individuals and groups to whom they would go for advice or help in making decisions about local affairs. They also asked to whom the respondents had gone in the past. The results showed that Roman Catholics who had attended parochial schools named religious leaders 53 percent of the time. Catholics who attended public schools named religious leaders 43 percent of the time, while Protestants named such leaders only 22 percent of the time.

The Rossi and Rossi study shows that religion is an important determinant of the ways in which persuasive messages will be received. Religion is a variable whose importance depends to a great extent on the *intensity* of belief and commitment, and not merely on a simple acknowledgement of a religious affiliation. Individuals from strongly fundamentalist religions tend to bring their religious reference frames into play in many areas other than religion. Thus their religious beliefs may affect their attitudes about education, taxes, politics, and war. Religion plays a dominant role in the lives of these people, and their religion becomes their single most important reference frame.

For some Americans religious upbringing and religious participation reflect the individual's values, beliefs, and desires. Religious beliefs do not occur in isolation to other beliefs. While marketing experts have a number of ways of "segmenting" the American market, one recent analysis of interest to us identified different profiles of Americans based on values, health matters, religion (when applicable), beliefs, satisfactions, and probable consumer behaviors. Kahle[39] discussed eight basic types of individuals (the reader should keep in mind that what follows is a global profile that describes generalities about groups—it is possible that an individual does not "fit" into any of these groups):

1. Roughly 21.1 percent of the sample indicated that *self-respect* was the most important value. These Americans tended to have good jobs that involved a lot of data, a lot of work with other people, high prestige, and jobs involving complex work. They tended to be Jewish or Presbyterian and middle-aged. Kahl speculates that these Americans, as consumers, probably buy quality brand name products and look for quality durable goods. They are probably low in innovativeness.

2. Roughly 20.6 percent of the sample selected *security* as the most important value. This sample of Americans makes little money, includes many widows, retired Americans, and blacks and includes individuals who have jobs considered low in prestige. They are likely to have some type of health problem (most likely shortness of breath, trouble sleeping, dizziness) and to be extremely anxious. Obviously, consumers in this group are susceptible to messages that help to reduce anxiety, including medical remedies, deodorants, mouthwashes, insurance coverage, and used cars, and are likely to be susceptible to appeals of affection and social support.

3. Sixteen percent of Americans sampled indicated that *warm interpersonal relationships* was their most important value. Americans most likely to emphasize this value were Lutherans, Fundamentalists, and frequent churchgoers. Marriage and parenting are important to these Americans, along with social support networks and a desire to increase the number of one's friends. Kahle argues that these Americans probably spend a good deal of time entertaining at both the community and family level, and probably engage in a good deal of gift giving. They are also more likely, in our opinion, to be susceptible to the "warmth" factor in advertising discussed later in this book.

4. Roughly 11.4 percent of the sample considered a *sense of accomplishment* as their most important value. Well-educated, well-payed managers and professionals with complex and prestigious jobs and who are their own bosses fit into this category. They are likely to be young and male, to be Jewish or Methodist (or have no particular religion), and to be healthy, confident, and capable. However, they are also more likely to believe that relationships might distract from accomplishment. As consumers, these individuals are likely to buy quality products, to enjoy symbols of achievement, and to be persuaded much like the high need for achievement individuals described in Chapter 3.

5. Almost 10 percent of the sample indicated that *self-fulfillment* was the most important value. These receivers are optimistic, internally motivated, young, educated, well-to-do, successful, and healthy. The major source of unhappiness for the self-fulfillment American involved family roles. These individuals hate housework, question whether they could be better parents, and question whether they could be better spouses. Just like the high self-esteem receiver described in the last chapter, these Americans are likely to buy products that help them fulfill their view of themselves and that would help them retain an optimistic view of the world—products like hot tubs, exercise equipment, home computers, and so on.

6. Roughly 9 percent of Americans rated *well-respected* as the most important value. These individuals generally are over 50 years old and tend to be farmers, craftsmen, machine operators, or retired. They tend to be Baptist, Methodist, or Fundamentalist churchgoers, to be externally motivated, and to make less money than the average American. These individuals sought fulfillment in home life, al-

though they were often divorced. As consumers these individuals may purchase some items in order to enhance respect, but may not be able to afford status-related objects or symbols. They probably buy conventional clothing, furniture, and cars and may be prone to conformity—since gaining respect from others may sometimes entail complying with what the receiver thinks other individuals desire.

7. Individuals who value a *sense of belonging* are likely to attend church on a regular basis, and are likely to be Presbyterian, Lutheran, or Catholic. Only 7.9 percent of the sample rated this value as the most important—individuals who also tended to be middle income and middle-aged. They derived, however, significant satisfaction out of marriage and derived fulfillment out of marriage (although they often felt they could be better spouses). Women in this category devote their lives to family and spouses and when they shop, they have the family in mind. This group of consumers is fascinated by toys and fascinated with cleanliness—hence, they buy many toys for family members, and are concerned with buying products that keep clothes the cleanest and teeth the whitest and most decay free, the deodorant that works the best, and the coffee that is the tastiest (after all, the 1980s is known for introducing the "specialized coffee" to share with a close loved one).

8. The final group rated *fun, enjoyment, and excitement* as the most important value (4.5 percent of sample). Typically young males, this group seeks fulfillment from leisure. Its representatives are childless, heavy drinkers (of alcohol), and rarely go to any church. Obviously, members of this group spend money on themselves—exercise equipment, sporty cars, vacations, and products to enhance attractiveness to members of the opposite sex.

Along with the variables of age, income, status, and gender, religious participation affects the receivers' values and purchasing intentions. Only a few of these receiver-types are likely to watch Christian Broadcast Network, to donate money to African relief organizations, to behave in altruistic ways routinely, and so on, while other receiver-types may spend a good deal of time thinking about and worrying about their loved ones, and are willing to help loved ones and family members. Understanding profiles such as these is often critical in understanding how people are persuaded, and in understanding how messages should be prepared.

Racial and ethnic background

Every individual in the United States has a racial and ethnic background. We are white, brown, black, or yellow. We, or our fathers or grandfathers, came from such countries as England, Japan, India, Mexico, or Poland. We may be able to trace our ancestry back to a single foreign country, or to many countries, but we all belong to racial and ethnic groups.

For many Americans, the fact that ancestors of several generations back emigrated from England, France, or Sweden is of little importance in persuasion. Only on rare occasions will they bring that reference frame into play as important to a persuasive message. The persuasive communicator who knows the ethnic background of a particular audience may use that fact to gain the attention and goodwill of the audience, but it will probably have little to do with the eventual reaction to the speech.

Although racial and ethnic group identification does not play an important part for many Americans, others do have racial and ethnic memberships that dramatically affect the way in which they approach persuasive communication and are affected by it. Black Americans, Mexican Americans, Jewish Americans, Polish Americans, Japanese Americans, and other groups do have attitude and belief systems that are identifiable in part by their racial and ethnic background. This happens whenever people have been set apart in some manner from the rest of society, and thus base their attitudes and beliefs on associations with people of similar background.

Many of our large cities have ethnic pockets where individuals retain some of their old-world customs, beliefs, and attitudes. Detroit, Los Angeles, Miami, and other large cities possess racial and ethnic clustering. There are neighborhoods in which a large percentage of the inhabitants still speak Polish, listen to Polish language programs on the radio, go to churches in which Mass is conducted in Polish, and read Polish language newspapers. The same city also has neighborhoods that are largely populated by black Americans; the people read a black-owned-and-operated newspaper, and tend to listen to one of the radio stations with programming by black personnel. Similar examples can be found in almost every section of the United States. Japanese, Korean, and Chinese programs are common in Los Angeles, and Spanish-language programming is now common in most states. For a persuasive communicator to work successfully with a group of individuals who do maintain racial or ethnic identities, a knowledge of their racial or ethnic background may be important in understanding their beliefs and attitudes.

There are three important considerations the persuasive communicator needs to keep in mind when it comes to persuading members of ethnic groups, or when trying to rely on receivers' identification with an ethnic group as a positive reference group. First, the persuader must consider the extent to which members of a particular ethnic group are strongly or weakly associated with the reference group. In Boston many receivers are much more strongly associated with their Irish origins than in other parts of America, and while many Irish Americans have donated money to Irish causes, millions of third, fourth, or fifth generation Irish Americans have given little thought to the needs of Catholics in Northern Ireland. In the 1980s there has been considerable activity, debate, and pressure applied to create group cohesiveness among Polish Americans, Armenian Americans, Vietnamese Americans, and Chinese Americans (to mention a few groups), so

there is likely to be a stronger impact among these types of groups. If receivers do not identify with a group, little persuasion will be evidenced by appealing to the group.

Second, the persuasive communicator needs to attend daily or weekly to the relevant issues that emerge and are resolved in these various groups. Some groups rarely change; other groups subgroup with one faction changing as its members reject language and customs and gain aspirations of upward mobility while a second faction retains more of its ethnic orientation. Consider the case of the Hispanic American.[40] Over the years we have learned that Hispanic Americans are highly loyal to the brands of products they use, prefer to shop in familiar stores, and are price conscious. However, not all studies show these trends, since some studies indicate that while Hispanics do in fact prefer to shop in familiar stores and are price conscious, they may not be as loyal to brands as other Americans. However, recent evidence also indicates that Hispanic consumers ought to be segmented into a Spanish Language Radio group and an English Language Radio group, where the Spanish Language Radio receivers are older, more likely to be married, less educated, and are more likely to speak Spanish in their home than the English Language Radio group. Further, the Spanish Language Radio group attend to media (and are more easily reached) via midday news reports and spend more money on soft drinks and records than the English Language Radio group, who attend to morning and evening news reports. It is probable that the Spanish Language Radio group reflects the characterization noted earlier about brand loyalty, and so on, more than the younger Hispanics who rely on English.

Third, the potential persuader must keep in mind that some English slogans and appeals have difficulty translating into different cultures and different languages. In one mishap, Frank Perdue of Perdue Chickens had the sentence "It takes a tough man to make a tender chicken" translated too literally into Spanish, and the translation was understood to mean "It takes a sexually excited man to make a chick sensual." In another mishap, the word *Espiritu* was used in a "Catch the Pepsi Spirit" campaign, although the word *espiritu* normally is associated with spirits of the dead or of evil. Care must be taken in translating messages, in attending to whether a phrase means the same thing to ethnic groups in Texas, Miami, New York, and California, and attention must also focus on differences in cultural beliefs. In one campaign, a wife was portrayed saying to her husband, "Run downstairs and phone Maria. Tell her we'll be a little late." Traditionally, it is customary for Hispanics to be a little late, and it is not socially acceptable for a women to tell her husband what to do.[41] Such blunders fail to persuade receivers.

Voluntary groups

The membership groups we have discussed thus far are ones over which individuals seem to have little, if any, control. Most people, however, also belong to reference groups they have voluntarily joined. These groups may be either formal, organized groups, or relatively informal groups.

Formal groups

It has often been said that Americans are "joiners." Any look at the number of formal organizations available in even a small community bears out this observation. There are chess clubs, stamp clubs, service organizations, fraternities and sororities, bridge clubs, child-study clubs, and hundreds of other formal clubs or groups that people can join. These are all voluntary organizations. Each one has a roughly outlined set of goals and values it supports and defends. The chess club may provide better facilities for playing chess; the Kiwanis club may support a children's hospital; the bridge club may have been organized so that a group of people could enjoy themselves. We do not have to agree with all of the stated objectives and goals of the organizations of which we are

members, but the probability is high that we will be influenced by those goals and by other members in the groups.

There are a few empirical studies assessing the effects of social clubs on attitude change. Those of Newcomb[42] and Homans[43] tend to support the proposition that social groups serve to direct decision making about persuasive messages. The members of an organization tend to influence the attitudes of each other member of the organization. Furthermore, people tend to join groups that espouse the same values or have the same interests. Thus, the process of joining various groups produces constant reinforcement. Knowing the values and goals of a particular organization becomes of extreme importance when working with the members of that organization.

The kind of effect that membership in a social group will have depends upon the complexity and strength of the attitudinal structure associated with the group and the individual's particular association with it. Many boys join the Boy Scouts of America. The organization has a set of goals and stated values for each member of the organization to follow. These values include proper conservation practices. The probability is high that when an individual is actually with his Boy Scout troop on a camping trip, he will conform to the expectations of the organization and refuse to be persuaded by messages urging him to destructive practices. For some, identification with the Boy Scouts is so strong that it becomes a reference group even when they are not with the troop. For the majority of boys, however, absence from the troop is likely to mean that the Scouts will not be used as a reference group, and that persuasion that goes against Boy Scout values has a chance of being successful. In this case, the individual's identification with the group is weak, and it serves as a reference group only when the individual is with it.

What is true of the Boy Scouts is undoubtedly true of membership in other formal organizations. People are influenced by the organizations they belong to when they are in contact with it or are with other members, but the influence of the organization is lessened when the person leaves the group situation. Some organizations may exert only trivial influence on the attitudes of its members—a bridge club, for example. Others, like a fraternity, may have great influence on the formation of attitudes and beliefs. Knowing an individual's role in an organization can also help improve predictions about the influence of the group. For example, the attitudes of a club officer or a long-time member are more likely to reflect the objectives of the group, while a new member or someone who is on the fringes of the group may be influenced very little.

Informal groups

Not all persuasive communication situations occur in large, formal group situations. In fact, if we were to keep a log of the number of times a day we are exposed to persuasion, we would find that the majority of the time it is our friends and acquaintances who are attempting to persuade us to go to a movie, have a beer, vote in a campus election, take a trip, buy a car, or date a particular girl. Our reactions to these messages are, in part, conditioned by the kind of social groupings we have formed. Informal associations help to determine our norms of behavior. This is brought about by social pressures to which we are subjected. For example, a study of preteenage smoking behavior done in several cities in Michigan showed that for those children aged from nine to 13 who smoked regularly, it was almost always the case that their parents, older brothers and sisters, and friends did also.[44] Their associations determined this set of behavioral norms. One might imagine that any persuasive communicator attempting to convince these youths that smoking was harmful would have a difficult time if the youths' associates could not also be convinced.

For all of the membership groups to which we belong, the voluntary groups we join, the formal associations we make, and the demographic groups with which we are associated, there seems to be a set of relatively constant factors that gov-

erns behavior. Simple membership, however, in one group or another is usually not enough to ensure that a particular receiver will utilize that membership as a reference group. Mr. John Doakes may be a member of the Junior Chamber of Commerce in his community, but merely knowing that fact may be of little use in making a speech about the necessity of building a new civic center in the community. Mr. Doakes may or may not react to the speech in a fashion that reflects the reference frame built up as a result of membership in the Junior Chamber of Commerce. If, however, the persuasive communicator mentions the support of the new civic center by some prominent member, the probability is strongly increased that Mr. Doakes will respond by making use of this particular reference group. The communicator *must* design the message in such a manner so as to ensure that a desired frame of reference will be brought into play by the receiver.

Nonmembership groups

The discussion up to this point has concentrated on membership groups that are used as reference groups by people. Reference groups, however, need not be membership groups to be used in this fashion. Any nonmembership group used as a standard of comparison, either positive or negative, may be defined as a reference group for an individual.

Selection of nonmembership reference groups

A common belief is that everyone strives to be better than he or she is at present. Sometimes such a belief is expressed as "keeping up with the Joneses," "social climbing," or "status seeking." In terms of reference-group theory, this belief would indicate that people may be expected to use groups to which they aspire, but do not belong, as positive reference groups. Conversely, groups to which the individual does not aspire and may want to avoid are more likely to be selected as negative reference groups.

Siegel and Siegel[45] did a study using college women and compared their membership and non-membership reference groups. They found that both types of groups were effective in helping to determine attitudes. The nonmembership groups used were ones to which the girls aspired, and these groups proved to be even more effective in determining attitudes and behavior than did the simple association groups to which the girls were assigned for purposes of the study.

Maccoby and her associates[46] conclude that people who wish to move up in social class are more likely to vote Republican than Democratic, thus suggesting that such "climbers" are using groups to which they aspire as reference groups. In large corporations, rising executives behave as they believe immediate superiors would behave in similar situations. It is quite possible that receivers will use the class of Upper Americans as a reference group in deciding how to vote, in deciding to lease a Volvo or a BMW, and in deciding where to send their children to school. Other referents, however, may be used in deciding where to take a vacation, where to shop, and in deciding which spa one should join.

Utilizing reference groups in persuasive communication

People do not form all their judgments about persuasion on the basis of the reference groups they use. In succeeding chapters, we will examine other factors, and varying strategies regarding reference groups. Below, we offer advice on some of the ways the persuasive communicator may improve messages by taking account of the reference groups to which receivers belong.

1. When there is information about the probable reference groups of individuals, mes-sages can call a particular reference group to the attention of the receiver. What the communicator intends to do in this situation is focus attention on a reference group that is favorable to the message. Thus, the probability that the receiver will utilize the group named as a reference frame by which to judge the message is increased.

2. Different groups have different values as reference groups to the receiver. Some are used more frequently than others. For many individuals, their family, church, occupational association, neighbors, and close friends are more important than political affiliations, veterans' organizations, alumni groups, or other groups with which the individual does not have frequent contact. The persuasive communicator can use the probability that a particular group will be either an important or relatively unimportant group to the individual in planning the content of the message.

3. Many membership groups set certain standards of conduct for their members. These standards can be used to increase the probability that receivers will take desired actions. Frequently, an occupational group will also set standards of behavior for its members. These standards can be invoked to enhance the probability that an individual will respond appropriately.

4. The physical setting for communication may increase the probability that one reference group will be used in preference to another. A man watching the Detroit Lions perform on the field is not likely to attend to any message he receives regarding the church to which he belongs. Communicators may have to arrange for appropriate physical settings in order to be successful with the message.

5. Sometimes a favored reference group can be quoted directly in a message, again enhancing response on the part of the receiver. Thus the student who belongs to a particular organization may respond favorably if the communicator uses a quote by another individual within the organization.

Summary

Our frames of reference are built in many ways. The experiences we have as children, the books we have read, the friends we make, all contribute to the development of our frames of reference. These frames mediate the way in which we will view the world around us and the ways in which we will listen to and react to persuasive messages. We are gregarious animals, and we tend not to live in solitude. We all associate with others, sometimes formally, sometimes informally. Furthermore, these associations also help in the development of our reference frames. The people with whom we associate, and even those with whom we do not, form the reference groups we use as standards or comparisons in judging persuasive messages. Our study of the participants in persuasion cannot be complete without a discussion of the role played by reference groups.

Footnotes

1. H. H. Kelley, "Two Functions of Reference Groups," in H. Prohansky and B. Seidenberg, eds., *Basic Studies in Social Psychology* (New York: Holt, Rinehart and Winston, 1965), pp. 210–214.

2. T. M. Newcomb, "Attitude Development as a Function of Reference Groups," in H. Prohansky and B. Seidenberg, eds., *Basic Studies in Social Psychology* (New York: Holt, Rinehart and Winston, 1965), pp. 215–225.

3. L. Festinger, "A Theory of Social Comparison Processes," *Human Relations,* vol. 7 (1954), pp. 117–140.

4. G. Gothals and J. Darley, "Social Comparison Theory: An Attributional Approach," in J. M. Suls and R. L. Miller, eds., *Social Comparison Processes: Theoretical and Empirical Perspectives* (Washington, D.C.: Halsted-Wiley, 1977), pp. 259–278); C. T. Miller, "The Role of Performance-Related Similarity in Social Comparison of Abilities: A Test of the Related Attributes Hypothesis," *Journal of Experimental Social Psychology,* vol. 18 (1982), pp. 513–523; J. Suls, G. Gaes, and J. Gastorf, "Evaluating a Sex-Related Ability: Comparison with Same-, Opposite-, and Combined-Sex Norms," *Journal of Research in Personality,* vol. 13 (1979), pp. 294–304; J. M. Suls, J. Gastorf, and J. Lawhon, "Social Comparison Choices for Evaluating a Sex- and Age-Related Ability," *Personality and Social Psychology Bulletin,* vol. 4 (1978), pp. 102–105.

5. Suls, Gastorf, and Lawhon, "Social Comparison Choices."

6. L. Wheeler, R. Koestner, and R. E. Driver, "Related Attributes in the Choice of Comparison Others," *Journal of Experimental Social Psychology,* vol. 18 (1982), pp. 489–500.

7. Miller, "The Role of Performance-Related Similarity."

8. P. G. Zimbardo, E. E. Ebbesen, and C. Maslach, *Influencing Attitudes and Changing Behavior* (Reading, Mass.: Addison-Wesley, 1977).

9. H. Oyer and E. J. Oyer, *Aging and Communication* (Baltimore: University Park Press, 1976); J. Rodin and E. Larga, "Aging Labels: The Decline and the Fall of Self-Esteem," *Journal of Social Issues,* vol. 36 (1980), pp. 12–29; J. L. Ronch, "Who Are These Aging Persons?," in R. H. Hull, ed., *Rehabilitation Audiology* (New York: Grune and Stratton, 1982), p. 185.

10. R. D. Hess and J. Torney, *The Development of Political Attitudes in Children* (New York: Anchor Books, 1967); R. S. Lynd and H. M. Lynd, *Middletown: A Study in Contemporary American Culture* (New York: Harcourt Brace, 1929); R. S. Lynd and H. M. Lynd, *Middletown in Transition: A Study in Cultural Conflicts* (New York: Harcourt Brace, 1937); "Middletown Revisited," *Time,* vol. 112, no. 16 (Oct. 16, 1978); K. P. Langton, *Political Socialization* (New York: Oxford University Press, 1969).

11. L. K. Meringoff and G. S. Lesser, "Children's Ability to Distinguish Television Commercials from Program Material," in R. P. Adler, G. S. Lesser, L. K. Meringoff, T. S. Robertson, J. R. Rossiter, and S. Ward, eds., *The Effects of Televi-*

sion Advertising on Children (Lexington, Mass.: Lexington Books, 1980), pp. 29–42.

12. S. Ward, D. B. Wackman, and E. Wartella, *How Children Learn to Buy* (Beverly Hills: Sage, 1977).

13. Meringoff and Lesser, "Children's Ability to Distinguish Television Commercials."

14. L. K. Meringoff and G. S. Lesser, "The Influence of Format and Audiovisual Techniques on Children's Perceptions of Commercial Messages," in R. P. Adler, G. S. Lesser, L. K. Meringoff, T. S. Robertson, J. R. Rossiter, and S. Ward, eds., *The Effects of Television Advertising on Children* (Lexington, Mass.: Lexington Books, 1980), pp. 43–59.

15. Meringoff and Lesser, "The Influence of Format and Audiovisual Techniques," p. 44.

16. Meringoff and Lesser, "The Influence of Format and Audiovisual Techniques," p. 44.

17. Meringoff and Lesser, "The Influence of Format and Audiovisual Techniques," p. 45.

18. R. P. Adler, G. S. Lesser, L. K. Meringoff, T. S. Robertson, J. R. Rossiter, and S. Ward, *The Effects of Television Advertising on Children* (Lexington, Mass.: Lexington Books, 1980); C. Atkin and G. Heald, "The Content of Children's Toy and Food Commercials," *Journal of Communication*, vol. 27 (1977), pp. 107–144; J. Bryant and D. R. Anderson, eds., *Children's Understanding of Television* (New York: Academic, 1983); B. Reeves and B. S. Greenberg, "Children's Perceptions of Television Characters," *Human Communication Research,* vol. 3 (1977), pp. 113–127; S. Ward, D. B. Wackman, and E. Wartella, *How Children Learn to Buy* (Beverly Hills: Sage, 1977).

19. P. G. Christenson, "Children's Perceptions of TV Commercials and Products the Effects of PSAs," *Communication Research*, vol. 9 (1982), pp. 491–524.

20. J. L. Ronch, "Who Are These Aging Persons?," in R. H. Hull, ed., *Rehabilitative Audiology* (New York: Grune and Stratton, 1982), pp. 185–195.

21. Rodin and Larga, "Aging Labels."

22. A. R. Andreasen, "Life Status Changes and Changes in Consumer Preferences and Satisfac-

tion," *Journal of Consumer Research*, vol. 11 (1984), pp. 784–794.

23. See D. Granberg, N. L. Jefferson, E. E. Brent, and M. King, "Membership Group, Reference Group, and the Attribution of Attitudes to Groups," *Journal of Personality and Social Psychology*, vol. 40 (1981), pp. 833–842; N. H. Nie, S. Verba, and J. R. Petrocik, *The Changing American Voter* (Cambridge, Mass.: Harvard University Press, 1976); N. W. Polsby and A. Wildavsky, *Presidential Elections: Strategies of American Electoral Politics* (New York: Charles Scribner's Sons, 1980); N. Stephens and B. D. Merrill, "Targeting the Over Sixty-Five Vote in Political Campaigns," *Journal of Advertising*, vol. 13 (1984), pp. 17–20, 49.

24. A. M. Rubin and R. B. Rubin, "Older Persons' TV Viewing Patterns and Motivations," *Communication Research*, vol. 9 (1982), pp. 287–313.

25. C. Atkin and M. Block, "Effectiveness of Celebrity Endorsers," *Journal of Advertising Research*, vol. 23 (1983), pp. 57–62; J. B. Frieden, "Advertising Spokesperson Effects: An Examination of Endorser Type and Gender on Two Audiences," *Journal of Advertising Research*, vol. 24 (1984), pp. 33–41.

26. T. J. Madden and M. G. Weinberger, "Humor in Advertising: A Practitioner View," *Journal of Advertising Research*, vol. 24 (1984), pp. 23–29.

27. M. D. Dickerson and J. W. Gentry, "Characteristics of Adopters and Non-Adopters of Home Computers," *Journal of Consumer Research*, vol. 10 (1983), pp. 225–234; H. Gatignon and T. S. Robertson, "A Propositional Inventory for New Diffusion Research," *Journal of Consumer Research*, vol. 11 (1985), pp. 849–867.

28. N. Stephens and R. A. Warrens, "Advertising Frequency Requirements for Older Adults," *Journal of Advertising Research,* vol. 23 (1984), pp. 23–32.

29. Alice H. Eagly, "Sex Differences in Influenceability," *Psychological Bulletin,* vol. 85 (1978), pp. 86–116.

30. S. L. Bem, "Androgyny vs. Tight Little Lives

of Fluffy Women and Chesty Men," *Psychology Today*, vol. 9 (1975), pp. 58–62.

31. C. L. Montgomery and M. Burgoon, "An Experimental Study of the Interactive Effects of Sex and Androgyny on Attitude Change," *Communication Monographs*, vol. 44 (1980), pp. 130–135.

32. C. L. Montgomery and M. Burgoon, "The Effects of Androgyny and Message Expectations on Resistance to Persuasive Communication," *Communication Monographs*, vol. 47 (1983), pp. 56–67.

33. See B. Barak and B. Stern, "Women's Age in Advertising: An Examination of Two Consumer Age Profiles," *Journal of Advertising Research*, vol. 25 (1986), pp. 38–47; T. E. Barry, M. C. Gilly, and L. E. Doran, "Advertising to Women with Different Career Orientations," *Journal of Advertising Research*, vol. 25 (1985), pp. 26–35; R. Bartos, *The Moving Target* (New York: The Free Press, 1982); D. Bellante and A. C. Foster, "Working Wives and Expenditure on Services," *Journal of Consumer Research*, vol. 11 (1984), pp. 700–707; R. W. Jackson, S. W. McDaniel, and C. P. Rao, "Food Shopping and Preparation: Psychographic Differences of Working Wives and Housewives," *Journal of Consumer Research,* vol. 12 (1985), pp. 110–113; J. A. Lesser and M. A. Hughes, "The Generalizability of Psychographic Market Segments Across Geographic Locations," *Journal of Marketing*, vol. 50 (1986), pp. 18–27; V. A. Zeithaml, "The New Demographics and Market Fragmentation," *Journal of Marketing*, vol. 49 (1985), pp. 64–75.

34. R. P. Coleman, "The Continuing Significance of Social Class to Marketing," *Journal of Consumer Research*, vol. 10 (1983), pp. 265–280; K. Auletta, *The Underclass* (New York: Random House, 1982); R. P. Coleman and L. P. Rainwater, with K. A. McClelland, *Social Standing in America: New Dimensions of Class* (New York: Basic Books, 1978).

35. Coleman, "The Continuing Significance."

36. Coleman, "The Continuing Significance."

37. In fact, work from even 20 years ago suggests that receivers in the lower classes were susceptible to messages that told them how to achieve the next higher class, not to social classes two or more levels above the receiver's current level. See J. F. Short and F. Strodtbeck, *Group Process and Gang Delinquency* (Chicago: University of Chicago Press, 1965).

38. P. H. Rossi and A. S. Rossi, "Some Effects of Parochial School Education in America," *Daedalus* (Spring, 1961), pp. 300–328.

39. L. R. Kahle, ed., *Social Values and Adaption to Life in America* (New York: Praeger, 1984); L. R. Kahle, "The Values of Americans: Implications for Consumer Adaptation," in R. E. Pitts and A. G. Woodside, eds., *Personal Values and Consumer Psychology* (Lexington, Mass.: Lexington Books, 1984), pp. 77–84.

40. T. C. O'Guinn and T. P. Meyer, "Segmenting the Hispanic Market: The Use of Spanish-Language Radio," *Journal of Advertising Research,* vol. 23 (1983), pp. 9–16; J. Saegert, R. J. Hoover, and M. T. Hilger, "Characteristics of Mexican American Consumers," *Journal of Consumer Research,* vol. 12 (1985), pp. 104–109; H. Valencia, "Point of View: Avoiding Hispanic Market Blunders," *Journal of Advertising Research,* vol. 23 (1984), pp. 19–22.

41. Valencia, "Point of View."

42. T. Newcomb, "Attitude Development as a Function of Reference Groups: The Bennington Study," in E. E. Maccoby, T. H. Newcomb, and E. L. Hartley, eds., *Readings in Social Psychology* (New York: Holt, Rinehart and Winston, 1958), pp. 265–275.

43. G. C. Homans, *The Human Group* (New York: Harcourt, Brace, and World, 1950).

44. E. Bettinghaus, "Michigan Survey of Preteenage Smoking Behavior," mimeo Michigan Youth Council, State of Michigan, 1970.

45. A. E. Siegel and S. Siegel, "Reference Groups, Membership Groups, and Attitude Change," *Journal of Abnormal and Social Psychology,* vol. 55 (1957), pp. 360–364.

46. E. Maccoby, R. Mathews, and A. Morton, "Youth and Political Change," *Public Opinion Quarterly,* vol. 19 (1954), pp. 23–39.

CHAPTER FIVE

The Influence of the Communicator

Some speakers are better than others. Some writers are more effective than other writers. All of us have been in a situation where we listened to two people deliver speeches on exactly the same topic, and were more impressed by one speaker than the other. Most receivers are aware of differences in the communicators they attend to, although usually they do not try to specify why they are more impressed by one speaker than another. If we ask receivers, they might say, "I don't know why! But I know who I like when I hear him." If we were to push the receiver just a bit further, we might get some more specific statements such as: "She sounds really honest and sincere"; "He is a really smooth speaker." This chapter examines the communicator's role in persuasion, attempting to isolate that quality that some people have and others apparently do not.

That some communicators are better at persuasion than others is not a new idea. In ancient Greece, Aristotle believed the speaker was as important as the message. His observations are pertinent today: Persuasion is achieved by the speaker's personal character when the speech is so spoken as to make us think him (or her) credible. We believe good men (and women) more fully and more readily than others. This is true generally whatever the question is, and absolutely true where exact certainty is impossible and opinions are divided. . . . It is not true, as some writers assume, that the personal goodness revealed by the speaker contributes nothing to his (or her) power of persuasion; on the contrary, her (or his) character may almost be called the most effective means of persuasion he or she possesses.[1] Aristotle was not the only early writer who emphasized the importance of being a "good man." A few centuries after Aristotle, Quintilian, a Roman rhetorician, said that the ideal communicator was "A good man, speaking well."[2]

In examining research studies, it soon becomes obvious that there are a number of different types of research that examine personal influence in persuasion. These studies have looked at different types of communication situations. In some studies, the influence variable has been labeled "ethos"; in others, "source credibility," "differential status," "opinion leadership," and "charisma." We take the position that each of these labels refers to essentially the same variable. We shall, therefore, refer to the variable of communicator influence in persuasion as *source credibility*. This term has been more frequently used in recent research, and seems to be more applicable to the general persuasive situation than any of the other terms. We shall first look at cases subsumed under the general heading of source credibility, and then look at more specific situations in which other terms have been used.

Source credibility: the general case

How can we be sure that the source of a message is having an influence on the receiver? Imagine that a speech is prepared that calls for an amendment to the U.S. Constitution that would mandate a balanced budget. Then a speaker is selected, and the message is audio-taped. Researchers then select and assemble two audiences with members chosen randomly from a large city. After the two audiences are assembled in two different auditoriums, the researchers give the audience members a test to determine their attitudes toward taxes, a balanced budget amendment, and other topics relevant to the subject. The investigators conclude that there are no apparent differences between the two audiences. Then the researchers ask the audiences to listen to the speech that had been previ-

ously taped. Both groups hear exactly the same tape. For one group, however, the investigators announce that the person being heard on the tape is a nationally famous economist and expert on taxation. For the other group, the researchers announce that the person being heard on the tape is a student in engineering who attends the University of Michigan. After the tape is finished, the researchers again ask the members of both audiences questions about their attitudes and beliefs about taxes and the balanced budget amendment.

The group that thought it had listened to the economist and tax expert changed more in favor of the topic than had the audience that thought it was listening to a student speaker. Since both groups heard exactly the same tape, and since the groups were similar in their original attitudes, the only conclusion that can be drawn is that the differences between the two groups must be because of a difference in perceived *credibility* between the two imaginary sources. This hypothetical example represents the basic paradigm under which much credibility research has been conducted. The experimenter holds the message constant, uses equivalent audiences, and then systematically varies the characteristics of the communicator to find out what source factors are persuasive.

There are a number of early studies that clearly establish credibility as an important factor in persuasion. Haiman[3] used a design almost exactly like our hypothetical example, with the topic of the speech being socialized medicine, and the supposed speakers being Dr. Thomas Parran, then Surgeon General of the United States, Eugene Dennis, Secretary General of the Communist Party of the United States, and an anonymous university sophomore from Northwestern University. The results showed significantly more change for the group that thought it was listening to the Surgeon General. In another early study, Hovland and Weiss[4] used written messages, and tested the credibility of both individuals and institutions, for example, J. Robert Oppenheimer, the physicist, and *Pravda*, the Russian newspaper. The result of their study again suggested that sources possessing more credibility for a given audience were more effective in persuasion.

The way in which we have described these early studies might suggest to the reader that credibility is a single dimension characteristic, that is, a source either *is* or *is not* credible. The researchers we have discussed knew that credibility is not a single demographic characteristic of an individual, such as age or sex. It is not represented by variables like socioeconomic status or occupation. *Credibility is a set of perceptions about sources held by receivers.* If we want to find out whether a particular source is credible, we should ask potential receivers about the source. One way of going about this is to ask receivers to rate the source on a number of different characteristics. In this way the researcher could discover just what factors seemed to be important in establishing credibility and could also determine just how credible speakers having different characteristics were likely to be preceived by a given audience.

In describing some early studies, Hovland, Janis, and Kelley[5] suggest that there are two main variables that determine credibility: the *trustworthiness* that the receiver perceives in the source, and the *expertise or competence* that the receiver ascribes to the source. Although later researchers identify other factors also relevant to credibility, trustworthiness and expertness continue to emerge as major factors in studies associated with source credibility. Andersen[6] reports a *dynamism* factor, and an *evaluative* factor (good versus bad) that seems to parallel trustworthiness. McCroskey[7] reports somewhat similar findings, and labels his two factors as perceived *authoritativeness* and *character*. Markham[8] used different questions in his study of television newscasters, and reports three major credibility factors labeled as *logical*, *showmanship*, and *trustworthiness*.

One of the most careful examinations of source credibility has been made by Berlo, Lemert, and Mertz.[9] Like Andersen and Markham, they followed procedures developed by Osgood, Tannenbaum, and Suci[10] that consisted of developing sets of polar adjectives such as: good-bad, right-

wrong, and competent-incompetent, placing the adjectives at either end of a seven-point scale, and having groups of subjects rate a number of sources on each scale.

The results of these studies suggested that there were three independent dimensions or factors that people used in judging the credibility of the four kinds of sources. They termed the first factor identified a *safety* factor. It seems analogous to the trustworthiness factor hypothesized by Hovland, Janis, and Kelley and by Markham. A second factor was labeled a *qualification* factor, which seems much like the expertise factor of Hovland, Janis, and Kelley and like McCroskey's authoritativeness factor. The third factor was labeled as *dynamism*.

Almost every study on source credibility seems to agree on the existence of both a safety or trustworthiness factor and a competence or expertise factor. Not all researchers identified the dynamism factor that Berlo, Lemert, and Mertz found. McCroskey,[11] for example, suggests that only the factors of trustworthiness and expertness are stable factors. Whitehead,[12] on the other hand, repeated the Berlo, Lemert, and Mertz study and obtained essentially the same three factors. In a more extensive study, McCroskey, Jensen, and Valencia suggest the use of three additional factors of *composure*, *sociability*, and *extroversion*.[13] Their description of these factors suggests a similarity to the dynamism factor. We will discuss three features of credibility: safety, qualification, and general "personal characteristics."

Safety (or trustworthiness)

The safety dimension as reported by Berlo, Lemert, and Mertz is reflected in the use of scales having some relation to general personality traits. Thus, a communicator rating high on this factor might be described as kind, congenial, friendly, warm, agreeable, pleasant, gentle, unselfish, just, forgiving, fair, hospitable, sociable, ethical, calm, and patient. On the other hand, individuals perceived to have low credibility would tend to be rated at the other ends of these scales. Such an individual might be rated as untrustworthy, cruel, or unfair.

The safety or trustworthiness factor is a general factor. For topics that do not require a lot of expertise, or where the receiver does not have much specific knowledge, the safety factor tends to come into play. Many ministers have experienced a situation in which a member of the congregation comes to seek advice on personal finances, health problems, or even advice as to the best school for the member's children. The minister is seen as trustworthy, although he may have no special qualifications in any of these areas.

Qualification (or expertise)

The qualification or expertise dimension is reflected in the use of scales that indicate the source's competence or training as it relates to the topic. It is assumed to be an independent dimension from either dynamism or safety. Knowing how individuals mark scales on the safety dimension is of no help in predicting how they will mark scales on the qualification dimension. A person rated high on the qualification factor might be described as trained, experienced, skillful, informed, authoritative, able, and intelligent. Sources rated low on this dimension might be characterized as untrained, unskilled, or incompetent.

While the safety dimension seems to be a fairly general factor, the qualification or expertness factor is applied when people are faced with topics or situations where skill may be perceived as necessary. Thus, we might expect an individual to decide between two potential tennis teachers on the basis of their actual skill at the game.

Personal characteristics

Source credibility factors that fall into this third category tend not to be as important as either safety or qualification. When receivers do not have firmly fixed impressions about an individual's competence or trustworthiness, however, the receiver is likely to make a credibility judgment based on personal characteristics. Thus, an individual who stuttered or had a nervous mannerism might be rated low on composure. A person who came across as friendly would be seen as more sociable, while a person with a forceful vocal style might be perceived as dynamic or extroverted.

Personal characteristics are important in a variety of communication situations. Most of the people we communicate with are individuals we meet only a few times, and our first impression may be our only impression. In those kinds of persuasive situations, the personal characteristics we perceive will have to be the basis for some judgments.

There seems to be general agreement among researchers that source credibility is an important variable in persuasion. Some researchers suggest that it may take more than three dimensions to adequately characterize credibility, or that other measuring instruments are more appropriate.[14] An examination of some of the further factors will be useful to an understanding of source credibility.

Most importantly, the *situation* in which persuasive communication takes place may help determine the ways in which receivers perceive the source. As Cronkhite and Liska[15] noted: "People choose to participate in the process of persuasion with others who are most likely to satisfy needs and achieve goals which are most salient and important at the moment of choice." In their view, receivers' goals and needs differ from one situation to another (to avoid fear, gain esteem, to make good investments, and so on) and therefore, receivers will pay more attention to a particular source who possesses some characteristic relevant to satisfying their needs or goals. Thus, receivers who debate the relative merits of different birth control devices may *trust* the opinion of a person who is *similar* in age to the receivers and has had first-hand experience with such personal materials, while in another setting receivers may seek out the advice of an *expert*, and in others they might be influenced by a beautiful person, or by a celebrity. In a later section of this chapter we will discuss the relative effectiveness of each of these source characteristics.

BOX 5.1
THE SLEEPER EFFECT: A CAUTION TO SOURCES

A single message from a highly credible source elicits attitude change. However, once receivers change their attitude after hearing a speech or debate, their attitude is likely to revert to its original position unless the message is reinforced by other messages. The exception to this rule is the "sleeper effect" (that is, there is *more* attitude change days or weeks after the speech than *immediately* after the speech). Hovland and his associates at Yale coined the term when they were doing research on American soldiers' attitudes toward our British allies during World War II. One of the movies they showed to the Americans was called *Battle of Britain*, and the movie was effective in changing attitudes when the attitudes were assessed immediately after the film. Surprising, they found somewhat more attitude change *nine* weeks later.

Why does the sleeper effect exist? Research in the area occurred in two phases. First, Kelman and Hovland, in 1953, argued that there are different *cues* operating in persuasion. First, recall in the message-learning approach to persuasion that message arguments are associated with the amount of attitude change. However, also involved in the process is a special *cue* we call a *discounting cue*. It is anything that helps the receiver discount or discredit the conclusion.

A sleeper effect occurs when the message arguments and conclusion are remembered over time, while the discounting cue is forgotten. That is, the arguments (statistics, and so on) are so impressive and the conclusion is so persuasive that we could have been persuaded if we could have placed trust or confidence in the source. The immediate consequence of the message is for us to take a "wait and see" attitude. Later, we know the facts and figures, but we cannot remember where we heard them. Hence, the sleeper effect takes place. The Kelman and Hovland study also demonstrated that reinstating the source eliminates the sleeper effect.

Through the 1950s and 1960s the sleeper effect had a place in persuasion literature. However, in 1974 Gillig and Greenwald put the sleeper effect under close scrutiny and argued that it could not be reliably produced. Thus, a second phase of research on the sleeper effect was initiated. As a consequence, Cook and his colleagues are quite specific in identifying the conditions necessary for eliciting a sleeper effect:

1. A message must be persuasive on its own merits. If this is not true, then simply removing a discounting cue won't affect attitudes;

2. The discounting cue must severely suppress the amount of immediate attitude change. The receiver must feel that the source cannot be trusted, and therefore puts up some resistance to changing attitudes at the time of receiving the speech;

3. Over time, the discounting cue must be dissociated from the message;

4. The receivers must dissociate the discounting cue from the message *before* they also forget all of the message and message content. That is, after a year or so, there will be no sleeper effect because everything was forgotten.

BOX 5.1 (Continued)

To learn more about the sleeper effect, consult:

Thomas D. Cook and Brian Flay, "The Temporal Persistence of Experimentally Induced Attitude Change: An Evaluative Review," in Leonard Berkowitz, ed., *Advances in Experimental Social Psychology* (vol. 11) (New York: Academic, 1978), pp. 2–59.

Paulette M. Gillig and Anthony G. Greenwald, "Is It Time to Lay the Sleeper Effect to Rest?" *Journal of Personality and Social Psychology*, vol. 29 (1974), pp. 132–139.

Charles L. Gruder, Thomas D. Cook, Karen M. Hennigan, Brian Flay, Cynthia Alessis, and Jerome Halamaj, "Empirical Tests of the Absolute Sleeper Effect Predicted from the Discounting Cue Hypothesis," *Journal of Personality and Social Psychology*, vol. 36 (1978), pp. 1061–1074.

H. C. Kelman and Carl I. Hovland, "'Reinstatement' of the Communicator in Delayed Measurement of Opinion Change," *Journal of Abnormal and Social Psychology*, vol. 48 (1953), pp. 327–335.

Remember that *credibility is dependent on the perceptions of the receiver, and not necessarily on any actual characteristics of the source.* The local congressman will be perceived differently by strong Democrats and by strong Republicans. The president of a university may be perceived differently by faculty and by students. The head of the AFL-CIO will be perceived differently by union members and by management members.

Status differential research: perceived role difference

People play a number of different roles as they go about the business of life. The same person may be a student during the day and a husband at night. Another may be an office manager, a father, president of the Kiwanis Club, and an elder in the church. Some of the roles that people play occupy large amounts of time, such as the job role, or the family role. Others are secondary and are assumed only on rare occasions, such as the role of voter, which people assume once a year, or even less frequently. When people occupy particular role positions, some of their behavior is predictable by the behavior prescribed for that role. The behavior that people exhibit in any role is thus composed of behavior stemming from unique personal characteristics and behavior determined by the nature of the role position.

In persuasion, with either a one-way or a two-way relationship, what is important is not the actual role that any communicator or receiver is occupying, but the relationship between the roles of the source and the receiver. Each role can be described in terms of the *status* or prestige assumed to go with that role. The president of the United States has higher prestige because of his role than does the governor of a state. The foreman within an automobile plant has more status than does the worker on the production line. The college teacher has more status than does a high-school or elementary-school teacher. When any two role positions are compared, it is usually possible to determine which one would be accorded higher status by a general audience. In the following table (Figure 5.1), a number of pairs of role positions are compared. The importance of the differential status attached to role positions is that the higher a receiver views the prestige of a given position, the more likely is the individual occupying such a position to be influential in a persuasive situation.

A few years ago, the U.S. Public Health Service published a report dealing with the relationship between smoking and lung cancer. Many of the items in the report were not new and had been the subject of messages from a number of researchers. There was, however, little decrease in smoking as a result of these earlier messages. Then the Surgeon General held a news conference at which he released the Service's report summarizing the various studies. As a result, a large number of individuals stated that they had stopped smoking (at least temporarily). Many things may help explain the apparent persuasiveness of the Surgeon General in this situation. The timing of the message, the length, the language used, the amount of publicity, and the size of the viewing audience are all factors that may have contributed to the effect of the message, but doubtless the status associated with the Surgeon General's position was a strong contributor to the effect of the message. In fact, it may have been status alone in this case, and not the person actually occupying the position. Ask yourself whether you could name the Surgeon General who actually issued the 1964 Smoking and Cancer report. (Or ask yourself whether you can name either the current Surgeon General, or *any* past Surgeon General.) The newspapers who reported on the release of the report usually used headlines such as "Surgeon General Links Smoking to Lung Cancer." The actual name of the individual holding that position was usually "buried" deep within the story itself.

Perhaps the best situation in which to be a source is to occupy a position of high status *and* possess high personal credibility. In Michigan, for example, such an individual was one of the long-time governors, William G. Milliken, who could speak from a position of high status, but who also possessed very high personal credibility. Even his Democratic Party opponents, while arguing that he wasn't a very good leader, were forced to declare openly that he was a "very nice guy." Status and credibility are linked, but the linkage is neither direct nor complete. A source can have high status and low credibility, or high credibility and low status.

Dynamism, expertise, status, or similarity?

Obviously, we are more likely to buy stock in a company, vote for a candidate, adopt beliefs about low-tar cigarettes, and vote for or against

Higher Status	Lower Status
President of the United States	United States congressman
Mayor of New York City	Chief of Police, New York City
President, General Motors Corporation	Colonel, United States Army
President, Stanford University	Professor, University of Michigan
Policeman, city of Detroit	Fireman, city of Detroit
Master plumber	Carpenter
Boy Scout leader	Usher, Methodist Church
President, Parent-Teacher Association	Secretary, League of Women Voters
President, Chamber of Commerce	Chairman, Building Committee of Baptist Church
Senior, Michigan State University	Sophomore, Michigan State University
Prosecuting Attorney	Defense Attorney

Figure 5.1. Relative Role Position Rankings

various propositions, and so on, when a communicator is credible and has relatively high status. However, there are many instances where similarity with the communicator may be just as important as (if not more so than) credibility factors. In fact, the chances are that a number of behaviors you engaged in recently were due to what people similar to you have told you—who is a "nice" hairstylist, where are the "best" cheese enchiladas in town, or do you look more (or less) attractive in a particular bathing suit? When is it important for the communication scholar to emphasize the importance of similarity or to emphasize the importance of status or expertise in his/her program to influence others?

Weiss[16] conducted one of the first studies on similarity. He argued that a speaker may "flog a dead horse" by starting the speech with a message that points out similarities in attitudes between the speaker and the audience. Since people like others who share their attitudes, flogging the dead horse should result in less counterarguing: Audience members should be more open and receptive. Weiss constructed a persuasive message that argued against fluoridation of water. (The topic was selected because the college students had previously indicated on a pre-experimental questionnaire that they were profluoridation, but that they did not feel strongly about the topic.) In the experiment, some students heard a message where the speaker first argued in favor of academic freedom (a topic students not only agreed with but also felt strongly about). This "flogging" was followed by the antifluoridation message. A second group of students received a neutral "prepersuasion" message, followed by the anti-fluoridation communication (a control group). As expected, the students who believed that the speaker shared the same attitude concerning academic freedom elicited more attitude change toward the antifluoridation position. It should be noted that this tactic works if receivers believe that the expression of attitude similarity is sincere and that the expression of the agreement is not used solely for the ulterior motive of influencing the audience.

One of the classic studies on the effects of similarity is the *field experiment* conducted by Brock.[17] In this study, customers were selected at a paint store in an Eastern city after they had selected the paint they wanted to buy. On the way to the cash-register table, the salesperson introduced himself as a college student who worked part-time at the paint store and who had some advice to give the purchaser. The salesperson claimed that he had finished a job two weeks earlier using two types of paint and had used the same amount of paint as the purchaser was planning to buy (similar), or had used 20 times the amount of paint the purchaser was planning to buy (dissimilar). Not surprisingly, raters (external to the study) perceived the dissimilar speaker who used a lot of paint as more expert (more experienced in the area of painting). Since the speaker had compared paints, he recommended a paint that was either more expensive or less expensive than the one the purchaser was planning to buy. The results indicated that people followed the recommendation of the similar salesperson: 64 percent of the people complied with the request of the similar clerk versus 39 percent for the dissimilar clerk. Further, in the "similar condition," 73 percent of the subjects complied when the similar salesperson recommended less expensive paint; 55 percent of them did so when the similar salesperson recommended a higher-priced paint. For the interested reader, we have included the statistics from Brock's study in Table 5.1.

Building on the Brock study, Woodside and Davenport[18] demonstrated that *both* expertise and similarity are important in sales. In this study, a field experiment conducted in a stereo store, salespersons introduced customers to a head and capstan cleaning kit for tape decks as the customers purchased tapes. The salesperson manipulated similarity by stating that they owned the same tapes and enjoyed the same type of music as did the customer (similarity), or by stating that they preferred a different type of music (dissimilar). In some of the sales appeals the salespersons demonstrated either expertise, or lack of expertise, as follows:

EXPERT: Here is a device we have on special that will clean the dirt and tape oxide from the guides, the head, and especially the drive wheels of your tape player. You just put a few drops of this cleaner on these two pads, stick it in just like a tape, let it run for about ten seconds while you wiggle this [points to head of cleaning bar]. It will keep the music clear and keep the tapes from tearing up by winding up inside the player. It's only $1.98. Would you like one?

NONEXPERT: Here is a thing we have on special that they tell me will keep your tape player clean. I don't really know how it works, but

Table 5.1. Comparisons of Expert and Similarity Manipulations in Personal Sales Research Comparisons

| | Brock Study | | |
	Similar Salesperson	Dissimilar Salesperson	Total
Lower-priced paint	73%	45%	59%
Higher-priced paint	55%	32%	43%
Totals	64%	39%	

Woodside and Davenport Study		
	Purchase	No Purchase
Expert salesperson		
Similar	80.0%	20.0%
Dissimilar	53.3%	46.7%
Nonexpert salesperson		
Similar	30.0%	70.0%
Dissimilar	13.3%	86.7%
Control group	13.3%	86.7%

Woodside and Davenport Study, Comparing Expert and Nonexpert Salespersons		
	Purchase	No Purchase
Expert	66.7%	33.3%
Nonexpert	21.6%	77.4%

Woodside and Davenport Study, Comparing Similar and Dissimilar Salespersons		
	Purchase	No Purchase
Similar	55.0%	45.0%
Dissimilar	33.3%	66.7%

SOURCES: T. C. Brock, "Communicator-Recipient Similarity and Decision Change," *Journal of Personality and Social Psychology,* vol. 1 (1965), pp. 650–655; A. G. Woodside and J. W. Davenport, "The Effect of Salesman Similarity and Expertise on Consumer Purchasing Behavior," *Journal of Marketing Research,* vol. 11 (1974), pp. 198–202.

you can read the directions right here on the package as to how to use it and what it does. I never have used one, and really don't know anything about playing tapes except how to listen to them, but this thing is supposed to help the tape player a lot. It's only $1.98. Would you like one?

Clearly, if a salesperson seemed as inept as the above manipulation would make him or her appear, few people would buy the product; in fact 77.4 percent of the customers in the "nonexpert" condition *declined* to go along with the purchase of a two-dollar cleaner. Table 5.1 presents the full results of the Woodside and Davenport study, including the expert versus similarity breakdown, the expert versus nonexpert comparison, and the similar versus dissimilar comparison. Clearly, if a salesperson desired to sell the cleaner, it pays to be both expert and similar, since 80 percent of the customers bought the product when they were approached in this manner, as compared to 53 percent who were approached by expert but dissimilar salespersons. However, this study found that expertise had a stronger impact on compliance (66.7 percent versus 21.6 percent) than similarity (55 percent versus 33 percent).

In what kinds of situations should similarity be emphasized in order to increase attitude or belief change? There are two answers to this question. One of the reasons why similarity has an influence on our attitudes (and behaviors) stems from Festinger's social-comparison process (discussed in earlier chapters). Recall that people evaluate their competencies by comparing them with those of others who are similar. They make the same type of comparison when evaluating their attitudes. However, by agreeing with others (and adjusting attitudes to that of similar others), the individual runs the risk of being incorrect about the *facts* in the environment. For example, if a person joined many pro-Democratic groups, one of the outcomes of social comparison processes is that he or she probably would *prefer* Mondale in the 1984 election. However, since all the persons in the

groups tend to have the same or similar source(s) of information, there are biases in making decisions about *facts* in the world—such as how well Mondale may do in the election in the states of Montana or Wyoming. In the latter, information that came from someone *outside* his or her circle of similar peers may elicit more attitude change because a dissimilar source possibly has different sources of evidence. Thus, according to Goethals and Nelson,[19] when a *belief* is at issue, agreement from a dissimilar person should increase one's confidence in adopting the belief because a dissimilar person may be expected to have different sources of evidence. When an issue deals with *values*, agreement with a similar person would be more influential. In sum, if the persuasive message dealt with facts (Is there a high amount of salt in commercially processed baby food? What's a recommended level of pH for shampoo? What kind of car has the highest resale value in the Detroit market?) we ought to be influenced by credible speakers (especially ones who are expert and trustworthy) while similarity is relatively unimportant. If the issue at hand deals with *opinions* (Shampoo X did wonders for your hair. Blue really is your color. Villa Gordo really does have the best tasting cheese enchiladas. Soap Q makes your hands feel soft.), we often will be influenced by people we consider to be similar to ourselves.

To validate their hypothesis, Goethals and Nelson had groups of high-school students view a videotaped recording allegedly involving two applicants to a university. These observers were asked either to indicate the extent to which each student would be more academically successful at the university (belief condition) or to indicate the extent to which they liked the applicants (value condition). After the observers made their estimates, they were given an evaluation of the two applicants written by someone who had supposedly participated in the study previously. Half of the subjects were led to believe that the evaluation they would be receiving came from a person who was similar to themselves in judging others; the other half were led to believe that the evaluator judged others differently than they did. The evaluations that the subjects received also *agreed* with their own evaluations. After reading the other evaluator's comments, the subjects were again asked to indicate their estimates of success/liking and the level of confidence they had in making the estimates. The results indicate that when the subjects attempted to decide which of the two applicants had made a better record in college, *confidence* in their beliefs was enhanced more by *dissimilar agreers* than by *similar agreers*; *similar agreers* were more influential in raising confidence in estimates of likeability of the applicants than *dissimilar agreers*.

That similarity or "peer appeal" is successful for changing attitudes concerning personal preferences was demonstrated in an interesting study by Cantor, Alfonso, and Zillmann.[20] This study explored the impact of three source characteristics on attitudes toward birth-control devices: (1) *age similarity* (a 21-year-old peer versus a 39-year-old nonpeer); (2) level of *medical expertise* (the source was either a medical student or nurse versus a music student or music teacher); and (3) level of *personal experience* (the speaker was described as either having used an IUD for two years or as knowing a friend who used an IUD for two years). The results indicated that peer appeal had the strongest impact on attitudes of the three independent variables: Receivers who heard the same-age peer indicated that they were more likely to use an IUD than receivers who heard the same message from an "older" speaker. There was also a trend for receivers who heard the woman who personally used the IUD to rate the IUD higher in effectiveness (in preventing pregnancy) than women who only knew a friend who used the IUD. Level of expertise had little to do with preferences or perceptions of effectiveness of the IUD—and there are several reasons for this. First, since the topic involves a highly personal matter of preference, similarity between source and receiver was simply more relevant to persuasion than expertise. Second, as the researchers note, they may not have manipulated a very "high" degree of expertise (as in attributing one of the messages to "a leading gynecologist," and so on). Whatever the reason, the study provides clear evidence that for matters of preference, values, or personal tastes, peer appeal or similarity in the source-recipient relationship is an important determinant of persuasion.

In personal sales, a somewhat different approach is taken when addressing the issue of when one should emphasize similarity. Weitz[21] has developed a model of sales effectiveness and recommends that expertise should lead to success in sales when (1) the salesperson is recruiting new customers, (2) the salesperson does, indeed, possess a high level of knowledge, and (3) the customer is engaged in a complex buying task. In cases such as these, salespersons need to establish the image that they possess superior skills or knowledge relative to the decision maker. On the other hand, similarity leads to success in sales when (1) the salesperson and client may be expected to have future interactions over years, (2) the salesperson is actually similar to the client, and (3) the customer is engaged in simple, low-risk purchase decisions, or is involved in purchasing decisions involving social risks. It is little wonder, then, that life-insurance salespersons, Mary Kay representatives, Shaklee representatives, and so on, try to find commonalities between themselves and their customers.

Reviews on the impact of similarity conclude that similarity manipulations do not *always* work to increase sales. There are, in our opinion, two major shortcomings that a salesperson should avoid. First, while salespersons try to find some characteristic or attribute on which to claim similarity, it is clear that not all characteristics are equally important in establishing similarity. For example, suppose you were in the Air Force, and while you were stationed in Lubbock (Texas) you married a woman born in Lubbock. If a salesperson found this out and was quick to point out that his niece was born there you may not increase your intention to buy a $12,000 car—especially if you didn't like Lubbock. Thus, some consideration ought to be given to the basis of the similarity. Second, while it is true that we often prefer the opinion of a person who is similar to ourselves, it is also true that we do not like to feel manipulated.

Beauty and the celebrities

Many students who start studying persuasion have been exposed to thousands of messages by attractive communicators or celebrities, and they feel that these source characteristics must play a role in persuasion. Obviously, cereal can be advertised by a noted or qualified nutritionist or by a sports star—but it is usually the sports star who gets the contract. Why? Aronson[22] quotes the director of advertising of AT&T: "We have discovered through various surveys that the sports star enjoys a tremendous recognition factor—superior to that of Hollywood movie stars and nameless models picked on looks."[23] People recognize "Dr. Marcus Welby," O. J. Simpson, Michael Jackson, or Arnold Palmer, and this recognition draws attention to the advertisement and the product, and under ideal circumstances, the audience identifies so much with the public figure that the audience will both remember the celebrity-product, like and use the product (How many children in the United States in 1985 did *not* know Michael Jackson's favorite soft drink?). However, as Aronson goes on to note, the results of another survey indicate that the majority of heads of households do not believe that they are influenced by sports personalities. If we know an athlete has signed a million dollar contract for the purpose of influencing us, why should we trust the celebrity?

To us, it seems that a successful campaign is one in which the celebrities' ability to be recognized is paired with several of the credibility factors. While one can always point out exceptions to the rule, let's look at some classic celebrity-credibility combinations. What qualifies a professional golfer to sell motor oil? If you think back in time for a moment, you will recall that the motor oil was claimed to have kept an old tractor running smoothly for years back on a Pennsylvania golf course (and the advertisement showed a very old tractor). The celebrity testified to having first-hand *experience* with the positive consequences of the motor oil. In other commercials, a known attribute of the celebrity is used to highlight why the celebrity is relevant to the particular product. Robert Young (Dr. Welby) is not only readily recognized, but is perceived to be competent and trustworthy—ideal combinations for selling decaffeinated coffee. O. J. Simpson is known for being a fast runner and for being a successful businessman; hence, he seems a natural for car-rental advertisements. Our point is that the celebrity appeal gives the advertiser the advantage of instant recognition, but persuasive effects are usually enhanced by a mixture of credibility factors.

There is no disputing that *physically attractive* sources can be influential. There is considerable evidence that good-looking people are perceived to be more likeable, friendly, interesting, and poised, to be more likely to be successful, to make more money, and so on.[24] To date, the most impressive study that documented the effects of physical attractiveness was conducted by Chaiken.[25] This experimenter had students rehearse delivering a persuasive message, and later had them stop passersby on campus to ask if they would complete an opinion survey. If a passerby agreed, the student claimed that he or she belonged to a group who advocated that the university should stop serving meat at breakfast and lunch at all dining commons. The passersby were provided several reasons for this position and were given the questionnaire. The source later (after they completed the survey) asked the passerby to sign a petition banning meat at breakfast and lunch.

The results of the study indicated that attractive sources elicited greater attitude agreement (questionnaire response) as well as more petition signing. Further, attractive communicators (versus less attractive ones) were perceived as friendlier, judged as more fluent, and were slightly more likely to speak faster (all three of the latter are related to increased persuasiveness in their own right, regardless of the physical appearance of the speaker; see Chapter 7). Attractive communicators also had more positive views of themselves, compared to the less attractive.

Why does physical attractiveness influence us? While credibility causes attitude change primarily because of the apparent validity of the recommended position and the evidence presented, attitude change produced by an attractive source is caused, apparently, by our desire to identify with and be liked by good-looking persons. A study by Norman[26] demonstrated this nicely. In some experimental conditions, an expert (a 43-year-old professor who co-authored a book on sleep behavior) argued that sleeping less than 8 hours per night would prove beneficial to one's health; one-half of the subjects only heard the recommendation (no supporting evidence), while the other half heard six pieces of evidence that supported the claim. Other subjects heard either the "no evidence" or "evidence" message, but received the message from a physically-attractive undergraduate male. All subjects in the study were female. The results indicated that both expertise and attractiveness were effective in influencing attitudes. But, the expert was more influential if his message contained arguments as opposed to when he did not provide arguments, indicating that receivers listened to and responded to the message from expert sources. On the other hand, the attractive source was persuasive both with or without the supporting evidence: Attractive sources influence us because of their attractiveness, not because of message content. That is, since we identify with, and desire approval from, attractive sources, we respond to *them*, not the messages.

Studies in advertising also indicate that the main advantages in using beautiful models or celebrity endorsements are related to gaining attention and increasing liking for a product, not necessarily in increasing sales. Atkin and Block[27] compared celebrity endorsements and noncelebrity endorsements, and found that the two did not differ from one another in terms of the believability of the messages or in terms of receivers' purchasing intentions. However, advertisements employing celebrity endorsements received more overall favorable reactions, received higher ratings of trustworthiness and competence, and elicited a more favorable image of the product. Also, Atkin and Block found that teenage receivers (aged 13 to 17) were more strongly influenced by celebrity endorsements than were older receivers (aged 18 to 77). Another study found that younger receivers were more strongly influenced by spokesperson endorsers, and further found that celebrity endorsers elicited awareness of the product, but that technicians or experts were better equipped to create trust in selling televisions than celebrities.[28] Another study found that decorative female models gain the attention of male viewers.[29] One study found that a physically attractive celebrity endorser can have an impact on purchasing decisions—if the celebrity and product are matched appropriately.[30] That is, beautiful celebrities selling cosmetics, basketball stars selling basketball shoes, and so on, may provide more than simple recognition and may promote sales because some receivers may infer that the product helped cause the celebrities fame or success.

We conclude that attractive sources often influence us in face-to-face persuasion contexts and gain attention and interest when used in advertising. Celebrity endorsements are very effective at promoting prompt awareness and interest in the general population, yet celebrity endorsements by themselves do not guarantee sales. The celebrity's qualities should have some relevance to the product if purchasing intentions are to be influenced.

Opinion leadership research

Imagine a group of students collected in a dormitory lounge. They are listening to David Sharp, another student, argue over funds for doing animal research. David Sharp holds no official office. His status is no higher than that of any other students in the room. Yet after the speech, we find that most of the students agree with the speaker. Even those students who seemed to have earlier disagreed with Sharp appear to have swung over to agree with him. What has happened? Was the message so well prepared and delivered? Or does David Sharp have something else going for him?

One factor that might have resulted in the observed reactions is whether a source is regarded as an *opinion leader* by other members of a peer group. The pioneering study of opinion leadership was made by Katz and Lazarsfeld.[31] They examined the effects of the mass media on the attitudes and behavior of those who listened to radio and television or read the daily newspaper. Their initial conclusion, after presenting a message over one of the mass media and then measuring the effects of the message, was that there seemed to be little change in audience attitudes, but when they went back to the same group some weeks later, and again assessed attitudes, they found that there had been significant change. In looking for an explanation of the unexpected later shifts, they suggested that these individuals changed their attitudes only after they had talked to others in whom they had confidence. Katz and Lazarsfeld referred to the people conferred with as *opinion leaders*.

Opinion leadership has been studied (1) in looking at the diffusion and adoption of new farming practices and methods in the United States and in foreign countries, (2) in examining the adoption of new drugs by physicians, and (3) in trying to understand the adoption of educational innovations. While there are some conflicting findings among these studies, the opinion leadership studies offer important advice to the study of source credibility.

A brief description of the kind of situation in which opinion leadership seems to be most important will be helpful in understanding the characteristics of opinion leaders. A receiver obtains information or advice from some source, traditionally the mass media. For example, the receiver sees a news flash on television about a new drug available for headaches. Following the initial receipt of the mass-media message, the receiver talks to various friends about what has been received. One of those friends seems to know a good bit about the topic, and advises the receiver that the

new drug is ". . . much better than what has been available in the past." As a result of talking to the friend, the receiver gets a positive attitude about the new drug, and is likely to buy the drug at the first sign of the next headache. What has taken place in this situation is that the friend served as an "opinion leader" for the receiver. Essentially, the mass-media message and the friend's advice were the same, but the friend was directly influential in changing attitudes and beliefs, while the original mass-media message was not.

A number of characteristics of the opinion leader are of use to the persuasive communicator. The most general way of describing opinion leaders is that they tend to serve as *models* for the group members. They are asked for their opinions, and their advice is listened to. There seem to be few characteristics that all opinion leaders possess, but there are some factors that are useful in predicting opinion leadership.

Rogers has summarized the characteristics of opinion leaders across a wide variety of situations and cultures.[32] We have selected those factors most clearly related to persuasive communication, and we will discuss those characteristics in detail. *Opinion leaders tend to be better informed in those areas about which they are consulted.* They are better informed about the information transmitted by the mass media, particularly when it concerns the subjects on which they are influential. Berelson and his associates were concerned with an election study and the determination of opinion leaders in a political situation. They reported that leaders were more interested in the election, were better informed about it, held stronger opinions about it, and were more concerned about the election than nonleaders.[33]

One of the major factors that seems to emerge from the research is the amount of communication that is associated with being an opinion leader. *Opinion leaders talk to more people than nonleaders.* They know more people. They read more, listen more, and view more. They have more than one circle of acquaintances, although they may be opinion leaders in only one circle.

Opinion leaders tend to have more formal education than the people who consult them. They have a higher social status than the people to whom they give advice. They tend to have more empathy than the individuals to whom they offer opinions. Opinion leaders do not seem to possess any of these specific characteristics to an extraordinary degree. They cannot be compared on any characteristic with the population as a whole, but only with the group they serve as opinion leader.

Opinion leaders vary, depending on the topic under consideration. The opinion leader for the political arena is not likely to be the opinion leader for the latest in sports nor perhaps for the latest in stock-market activities. The student opinion leader in the dormitory who was influential in changing attitudes about funding animal research might not be successful in influencing attitudes about student government.

Opinion leadership is a relative variable. An opinion leader in one part of town can not be an opinion leader in another part of town. According to Rogers,[34] we select opinion leaders on the basis of perceived knowledge or superior expertise and on the basis of perceived similarity. We defer to the opinions of similar others who are more knowledgeable, better read, or possess greater technical skill. Opinion leaders may influence us on a number of topics, including fashion changes, political ideas, dental and medical products or procedures, solar water heaters, and so on.[35]

Charisma: a special case of credibility

Throughout history, individuals have appeared who seem to possess very high credibility. They have attracted large numbers of followers, followers who have attributed almost magical powers to these leaders. Napoleon in France, Gautama Buddha in the Far East, and Gandhi of India are well known examples. On a smaller scale, there are leaders of religious sects, like the Reverend Jim Jones or the Reverend Moon, who have been able to attract and hold the devotion of dedicated followers. Such individuals are said to possess *charisma*. The charismatic leader is one whose ability in persuasion and leadership seems to transcend any of the usual abilities of most individuals. Abraham Lincoln, Franklin Roosevelt, and Ho Chi Minh have all been called charismatic leaders. Originally, the term was applied to mean the "qualities of those who claim or are believed to possess powers of leadership derived from some unusual sanction—divine, magical, diabolic—or merely exceptional individuals.[36] Today the term is usually removed from the realm of magic, but it is still used to refer to unusual credibility or to the personal influence of an individual. People who are said to possess charisma seem to possess characteristics that cannot be easily defined or explained, but which permit the individual to have enormous personal influence regardless of the merit of the topic about which they are speaking.

Perhaps the best guess we have about the nature of charisma is that it is the possession of many dimensions of credibility by a single individual and possession of those factors to a greater degree than seen in other persuasive communicators. The student leader, the PTA president, the chamber of commerce leader, the state senator, the factory foreman, and the local physician can all improve their effectiveness in persuasion through an improvement in their perceived credibility, prestige, or status. Charismatic leaders, however, cannot be so easily produced. The charismatic leader is an individual whose effect on audiences and history is not easily explained by research literature.

Power

Our discussion of the influence of the source makes the assumption that receivers have a free choice to change their attitudes or not to change their attitudes as a result of attending to a persuasive message. The credibility model does not destroy the notions of free choice that underlie the model. It simply suggests that receivers may be influenced in their choice by perceptions held about the source. There is another view of the relationship between source and receiver. This view holds that behavior in many communication situations is dependent on the *power* that one individual can exert over another. In fact, we can define power as the *ability that individual A has to influence the behavior of individual B*. Generally speaking, individuals who are in a position of authority (police officers, firemen at the scene of a fire) often get us to comply with their requests to slow down our vehicle, to disperse, and so on. Other communicators might occupy roles where they have a legitimate right to make requests of us, and we are obliged to comply with their requests—librarians tell us to be quiet, teachers tell us not to pass notes in class, and so on. In later chapters of this book we will discuss the role power has in face-to-face persuasion (Chapters 10, 11, 12, and 13). In this chapter, we will discuss more generally the role of power in persuasion situations.

Jacobson,[37] in *Power and Interpersonal Relations*, provides an analysis of many ways in which power can influence our behavior. At the end of the volume, he provides a very useful set of 48 "power principles" derived from many different studies. Seven of these principles are directly related to persuasive communication situations:

1. The amount of communication is directly related to power. In any communication situation, the individual who can monopolize the communication is likely to have more power, and thus exert more influence.

2. The person in a persuasive communication situation with the most information about the topic will be the most powerful person. This suggests that the initial approach by a source may not be enough to influence change *if* the receiver has more information than the source.

3. The more a source can fulfill the receiver's wants or needs, the more influence is likely to be exerted in the situation. This principle emphasizes the need for an analysis of the audience before beginning persuasive communication.

4. In a group, people with less power communicate less frequently, but they tend to talk to people with more perceived power. This principle is related to the first principle we discussed, but turns the situation around to the receiver's viewpoint. This principle will help in making a prediction about the relative power held by members of the group.

5. To the extent that an individual has had a series of past successes that become known to the group, the individual will be perceived as having more power. This principle is directly related to the general credibility principles that we developed in the first part of this chapter. It suggests that power can be acquired sometimes if the group is informed about the source's past successes.

6. If there is a deviant member within the group, communication attempting to get that individual to conform will increase, until it becomes obvious that the person is not going to conform. At that point, communication will drop, and the individual will be isolated. This principle is closely related to some of the balance principles we discussed in an earlier chapter. The group can sometimes restore balance only by eliminating deviant members.

7. Groups with very sharp perceived power differences between members are likely to have poor social-emotional climates. Productivity in such groups may not suffer, but for long-term maintenance of the group, the power differences between the members of the group should be minimized. This suggests that it may be difficult to maintain large power differentials and still hope to keep a group happy.

Improving the influence of the persuasive communicator

What help can we give the college student who does not want to spend the next 20 years waiting to acquire status? Can we help the new teacher who wants to make an impact on the school system? Can a housewife become effective in spite of the fact that she is not a well-known personality? The literature does not provide a simple answer; rather, it indicates a series of suggestions and cautions:

1. In general, receivers do not ascribe negative characteristics to sources with which they are completely unfamiliar. Greenberg and Miller[38] found that when sources are not personally known to receivers, the sources are usually evaluated as positive rather than negative. They hypothesize that receivers may develop a cultural standard that in essence says, "I will remain open-minded, until I have seen or heard a source. Furthermore, I will err on the positive rather than the negative side." As an unknown source, then, we are at least not going into the persuasive communication situation with negative influence. If our influence becomes negative, it will be because of the way we handle the actual communication situation. The Greenberg and Miller findings suggest strongly that the beginning, unknown communicator is actually better off than the communicator who has already developed a negative image because of past actions.

2. As noted earlier, persuasive communication will be more effective if receivers view the source as being similar to themselves. This suggestion may help the beginning communicator locate audiences that will be receptive to the message. It may also help the communicator realize that perceived similarity helps in those situations where the source can do something to appear similar to the audiences that are being approached and where the persuasion involves values and preferences.

Several types of studies support this suggestion. Everett Rogers reviews a number of studies in this area.[39] He suggests that "homophily," the condition of being similar to a receiver, is almost always more effective than "heterophily," the opposite situation, where the source and receiver perceive themselves as quite different. This homophily-heterophily distinction seems to exist across a large number of factors, including socioeconomic status, education, attitudes, and beliefs. It may even extend to variables such as appearance or dress. Bettinghaus measured attitudes toward individuals with "normal" college clothing such as slacks and sweaters and sport coats, and toward "abnormal" dress, that is, dirty overalls and sweatshirts. The results showed that the abnormally dressed individuals were rated lower than were the more normally attired individuals.[40]

Rokeach[41] suggests that race may make a difference, but that race is not as important a variable as is the perception of similarity. Whites will prefer blacks if they see the black as being more like themselves than another white person. Again, similarity seems to be the preferred characteristic.

Through audience analysis, sources can isolate points of similarity between themselves and their audiences and can emphasize those items in the message. Through audience analysis, communicators can examine their own backgrounds and begin to make predictions as to the possible effects they might have on an audience. Perceived similarity can be a powerful variable in determining the effects of persuasion.

3. A persuasive communicator is seldom completely unknown to an audience prior to communicating. Before the listener starts to listen, before the reader starts to read, and before the viewer starts to view, they are making judgments about the source to which they are going to expose themselves. This suggests that it is not the first, momentary exposure to the source at the time of message transmission that is important, but the total set of impressions commencing from the time the receiver first becomes aware of the source.

We have already discussed the development of reference frames. We must remember that people are always viewed from within an already existing frame of reference. If the source seems to violate the receiver's expectations as to what sources should look like, talk like, and behave like, the probability is that the source will not be highly successful. The preconditions for persuasive communication are thus an important determiner of the eventual success of the message. In Chapter 7, we shall discuss the research literature on vocal characteristics, and nonverbal behavior as it relates to acceptability of the source.

4. Status level has been shown to relate to persuasion. Most sources cannot raise their social status for a specific occasion, yet a receiver may associate a source with one organization and be completely unaware of the level that the source has reached in another organization. For example, imagine that a group of social workers is listening to Danny Kaye talk about the problems of orphan children in Europe. The social worker may well wonder just why she, a professional, should be listening to an actor, no matter how good, talk about a subject that has no connection with acting. If, however, Kaye had been introduced to the group with a mention of the international commission dealing with children on which he has served as chairman, and a mention of the work he has been doing for the United Nations Educational, Scientific, and Cultural Organization (UNESCO), his status as perceived by the social worker might well have been improved and his influence increased.

There are few people who have absolutely no status at all. The fact that one is a college student may be important for the individual who has never been in college, or for the high-school student who aspires to college. Having been a leader in a church youth organization may well enhance credibility with some audiences. It is one of the tasks of persuasive communicators to examine themselves in the continuing attempt to determine how they might relate to a receiver or group of receivers.

5. It is not possible to become an instant opinion leader. It takes time to work with a group until they recognize you as an opinion leader, and you then have the opportunity to influence them. We can, however, suggest what sources might do to make themselves into opinion leaders for a particular group. Most important, perhaps, is a willingness to gather and dispense information. Opinion leaders must attend to the mass media, expose themselves to many different kinds of information, show a willingness to talk to others and to answer questions about interesting topics. Opinion leaders must digest information and then be willing to pass along that information to the members of the group.

Individuals serve as opinion leaders at the whim of the group, and they may move in and out of such an influential position as the group changes or the situation changes. Communicators can enhance their chances of being regarded as an opinion leader, thus enhancing their persuasive influence, by behaving as an opinion leader would.

6. Credibility has been studied largely as it affects a receiver's prior images of the speaker, but the communicator must remember that credibility, and thus influence, may well develop and change as a result of behavior during a speech. Brooks and Scheidel[42] had an audience rate the late Malcom X at various periods during a speech. The audience started with a somewhat low image of the speaker. There was a sharp rise shortly after the speech began, then a decline, another sharp rise, and then a final decline that lasted to the end of the speech. The final attitude toward Malcom X was lower than the image the audience brought with them as a result of the speaker's behavior during the speech.

What sources say is extremely important, but how they say it and how they behave while saying it does dramatically affect the receiver's perceptions of the source, thus influencing the extent of attitude change the receiver is likely to experience.

7. There is evidence that sources are more persuasive when receivers believe that the source is actually arguing against his or her own belief or position. This factor is based on one of our oldest beliefs. The Romans, for example, believed that "truth" could not be ob-

tained unless an individual were arguing against their own best interest. Today, we refer to a "reluctant witness," and most of us generally believe that such a witness is more believable than one who supports the side of an argument he or she would normally be expected to believe. Eagly, Chaiken, and Wood[43] discuss this position in detail and argue that what happens is that receivers tend to form a prior belief as to the position that the source is likely to take. If the subsequent message is seen as opposed to the prior position, the source may gain credibility and thus be more persuasive.

8. The credibility that people have can be affected by the people with whom they associate. If a potential audience sees a source as being associated with individuals who themselves possess high credibility, it is probable that some of that credibility will rub off on the source. Even the perceived credibility of the person introducing a persuasive speaker can affect the image of the speaker. In that way sources who are not well known can make use of a number of "sponsorship" techniques to increase their own influence.

McCroskey and Dunham[44] found that if a teacher remained in the room when an experiment was being conducted, the presence of the teacher influenced the ways in which the class responded to the experimenter. Harvey[45] also found that the credibility of the persuasive communicator is influenced by the audience's attitudes toward the person introducing the speaker. Thus, the relatively unknown source may enhance his influence by the individuals he invites to share the situation with him.

In a similar fashion, negative credibility may accrue if the source is introduced by, or associated with, an individual who possesses negative credibility. In 1971, the Gallup Polls showed President Richard Nixon had lost some of his support from the conservative members of his party when he sponsored the admission of the People's Republic of China to the United Nations. Even though his association with Communists was public and direct, the association

may have been enough to cause this loss in credibility.

9. Most of the research in credibility, and most of the suggestions offered to the communicator thus far, seem designed for traditional, one-way persuasive situations. Credibility, however, affects people who are trying to work together to achieve a goal. If you are working to reach agreement with a member of the City Council on rent control, you will be affected by his credibility as you perceive it and he will be affected by your credibility as he perceives it. Good, viable agreements may not result if the perceived credibility differences are too great between the two individuals. One party or the other would have to give up too much. Working together is essential to achieving many goals, but when people perceive too many differences between the parties, results are not likely to be easily achieved.

10. The results of a recent study by Chaiken and Eagly[46] indicate how a source might use media to their advantage. These researchers found that when receivers view a video-tape (or listen to an audio-taped version) of a speech the receivers spend more time thinking about the *communicator* (compared to thinking about the message itself), and that these positive reactions to the communicator significantly influence attitude change. Thus, if you have credibility or are "likeable" (friendly, good looking, and so on), using a medium that draws greater attention toward *you* will be beneficial. On the other hand, if a speaker is not liked by a set of receivers, then using a channel that draws attention toward the communicator will hurt the communicator in his or her efforts to persuade others. These researchers also found that communicator likeability had little impact on persuasion when the speech was given out in written form; in fact, the *only* variable that was significantly related to attitude change in this situation was the receiver's thoughts about the *message content*. By inference, such research indicates that speakers who feel that they possess credibility should capital-

ize on this advantage by making sure they select the appropriate medium, while those who may not possess credibility might use different channels in order to draw attention more to the content of the message (for example, charts, a video-tape segment of the shopping mall—or whatever—inserted sometime during the presentation, and so on) so that the receiver's thoughts will be directed more toward the message content.

Summary

We do not know all there is to know about the effects a source may have on the acceptance or rejection of a persuasive message. Some studies suggest that there may be few such effects with certain topics. For instance, the topic itself may be so important to the receiver that the nature of the source becomes less important, and the source thus becomes less influential. For most persuasive communication situations, however, sources who are perceived as having either high-positive or high-negative source credibility *can* make a difference in the attitude change of a receiver or group of receivers.

Each of the studies we have examined bears out the conclusion that source credibility is important. Regardless of whether it is called ethos, source credibility, status differential, opinion leadership, charisma, or power, the conclusion seems inescapable—who you are can influence how your messages are received.

Footnotes

1. W. R. Roberts, "Rhetorica," in W. D. Ross, ed., *The Works of Aristotle*, vol. 2 (New York: Oxford University Press), p. 7.

2. Quintilian, *Institutes of Oratory*, trans. by J. S. Watson (London, 1856), XII, ii, 1.

3. F. S. Haiman, "The Effects of Ethos in Public Speaking," *Speech Monographs,* vol. 16 (1949), p. 192.

4. C. I. Hovland and W. Weiss, "The Influence of Source Credibility on Communication Effectiveness," *Public Opinion Quarterly,* 16 (1961), pp. 635–650.

5. C. I. Hovland, I. L. Janis, and H. H. Kelley, *Communication and Persuasion* (New Haven, Conn.: Yale University Press, 1953), pp. 19–53.

6. K. E. Andersen, "An Experimental Study of the Interaction of Artistic and Non-Artistic Ethos in Persuasion" (Ph.D. dissertation, University of Wisconsin, 1961).

7. J. C. McCroskey, *An Introduction to Rhetorical Communication* (Englewood Cliffs, N.J.: Prentice-Hall, 1968), pp. 60–61.

8. D. Markham, "The Dimensions of Source Credibility of Television Newscasters," *Journal of Communication,* vol. 18 (1968), pp. 57–64.

9. D. K. Berlo, J. B. Lemert, and R. J. Mertz, "Dimensions for Evaluating the Acceptability of Message Sources" (Research Monograph, Department of Communication, Michigan State University, 1966).

10. C. Osgood, P. Tannenbaum, and G. Suci, *The Measurement of Meaning* (Urbana, Illinois: University of Illinois Press, 1957).

11. J. McCroskey, "Scales for the Measurement of Ethos," *Speech Monographs,* 1966, vol. 33, pp. 67–72.

12. J. Whitehead, "Effects of Authority-Based Assertion on Attitude and Credibility," *Speech Monographs,* 1971, vol. 38, pp. 311–315.

13. J. C. McCroskey, T. Jensen, and C. Valencia, "Measurement of the Credibility of Peers and Spouses," paper presented at the International Communication Association Convention, Montreal, 1973.

14. cf. R. F. Applbaum and K. W. Anatol, "The Factor Structure of Source Credibility as a Function of the Speaking Situation," *Speech Monographs,* vol. 39, no. 3 (August 1972), pp. 216–232, and G. Cronkhite and J. Liska, "A Critique of Factor Analytic Approaches to the Study of Credibility," *Communication Monographs,* vol. 43, no. 2 (June 1976), pp. 91–107.

15. G. Cronkhite and J. Liska, "The Judgment of Communicant Acceptability," in M. E. Rolloff and G. R. Miller, eds., *Persuasion: New Directions in Theory and Research* (Beverly Hills: Sage, 1980), p. 103.

16. W. Weiss, "Opinions Congruence With a Negative Source on One Issue as a Factor of Influencing Agreement on Another Issue," *Journal of Abnormal and Social Psychology,* vol. 54 (1957), pp. 180–187.

17. Timothy C. Brock, "Communicator-Recipient Similarity and Decision Change," *Journal of Personality and Social Psychology,* vol. 1 (1965), pp. 650–654.

18. A. G. Woodside and J. W. Davenport, "The Effect of Salesman Similarity and Expertise on Consumer Purchasing Behavior," *Journal of Marketing Research,* vol. 11 (1974), pp. 198–202.

19. George R. Goethals and R. Eric Nelson, "Similarity in the Influence Process: The Belief-Value Distinction," *Journal of Personality and Social Psychology,* vol. 25 (1973), pp. 117–122.

20. Joanne Cantor, Herminia Alfonso, and Dolf Zillmann, "The Persuasive Effectiveness of the Peer Appeal and a Communicator's First-Hand Experience," *Communication Research,* vol. 3 (1975), pp. 293–310.

21. B. Weitz, "Effectiveness in Sales Interactions: A Contingency Framework," *Journal of Marketing,* vol. 45 (1981), pp. 85–103.

22. Elliot Aronson, *The Social Animal,* 3rd edition (San Francisco: Freeman, 1980), p. 69.

23. *The New York Times,* February 17, 1974; see E. Aronson, *The Social Animal,* 3rd edition (San Francisco: Freeman, 1980), p. 69.

24. See Ellen Berscheid and Elaine Walster, "Physical Attractiveness," in L. Berkowitz, ed., *Advances in Experimental Social Psychology,* vol. 7 (New York: Academic, 1974), pp. 158–216.

25. Shelly Chaiken, "Communicator Physical Attractiveness and Persuasion," *Journal of Personality and Social Psychology,* vol. 37 (1979), pp. 1387–1397.

26. Ross Norman, "When What Is Said Is Important: A Comparison of Expert and Attractive Sources," *Journal of Experimental and Social Psychology,* vol. 12 (1976), pp. 294–300.

27. C. Atkin and M. Block, "Effectiveness of Celebrity Endorsers," *Journal of Advertising Research,* vol. 23 (1983), pp. 57–62.

28. J. B. Freiden, "Advertising Spokesperson Effects: An Examination of Endorser Type and Gender on Two Audiences," *Journal of Advertising Research,* vol. 24 (1984), pp. 33–41.

29. L. N. Reid and L. C. Soley, "Decorative Models and the Readership of Magazine Ads," *Journal of Advertising Research,* vol. 23 (1983), pp. 27–32.

30. L. R. Kahle and P. M. Homer, "Physical Attractiveness of the Celebrity Endorser: A Social Adaptation Perspective," *Journal of Consumer Research,* vol. 11 (1985), pp. 954–961.

31. E. Katz and P. F. Lazarsfeld, *Personal Influence* (New York: Free Press of Glencoe, 1955).

32. E. M. Rogers, *Modernization among Peasants: The Impact of Communication* (New York: Holt, Rinehart and Winston, 1969), p. 227.

33. B. Berelson, P. F. Lazarsfeld, and W. N. McPhee, *Voting: A Study of Opinion Formation during a Presidential Campaign* (Chicago: University of Chicago Press, 1954).

34. E. M. Rogers, *Diffusion of Innovations* (San Francisco: Free Press, 1983).

35. See H. Gatignon and T. S. Robertson, "A Propositional Inventory of New Diffusion Research," *Journal of Consumer Research,* vol. 11 (1985), pp. 849–867; D. Leonard-Barton, "The Diffusion of Energy Conservation Technologies," *Marketing of Solar Energy Innovations,* ed. Avraham Shama (New York: Praeger, 1981), pp. 145–183; D. Leonard-Barton, "Experts as Negative Opinion Leaders in the Diffusion of a Technological Innovation," *Journal of Consumer Research,* vol. 11 (1985), pp. 914–926.

36. J. Gould and W. L. Kolb, eds., *A Dictionary of the Social Sciences* (New York: Free Press of Glencoe, 1965), s.v. "charisma."

37. W. D. Jacobson, *Power and Interpersonal Relations* (Belmont, Ca.: Wadsworth Publishing Co., 1972).

38. B. S. Greenberg and G. R. Miller, "The Ef-

fects of Low Credible Sources on Message Acceptance," *Speech Monographs,* vol. 33 (1966), pp. 127–136.

39. E. M. Rogers and D. K. Bhowmik, "Homophily-Heterophily: Relational Concepts for Communication Research" (Paper presented at the Association for Education in Journalism, Berkeley, California, August 1969).

40. E. P. Bettinghaus, "The Operation of Congruity in an Oral Communication Situation" (Unpublished Ph.D. dissertation, University of Illinois, 1959).

41. M. Rokeach and L. Mezie, "Race and Shared Belief as Factors in Social Choice," *Science,* vol. 151 (January 1960), pp. 167–172.

42. R. D. Brooks and T. M. Scheidel, "Speech As Process: A Case Study," *Speech Monographs,* vol. 35 (1968), pp. 1–7.

43. Alice H. Eagly, Shelly Chaiken, and Wendy Wood, "An Attribution Analysis of Persuasion," in John H. Harvey, William Ickes, and Robert F. Kidd, eds., *New Directions in Attribution Research* (Hillsdale, N.J.: Erlbaum, 1981), pp. 37–62.

44. J. C. McCroskey and R. E. Dunham, "Ethos: A Confounding Element in Communication Research," *Speech Monographs,* vol. 32 (1966), pp. 456–463.

45. J. G. Harvey, "An Experimental Study of the Influence of the Ethos of the Introducer As It Affects the Ethos and the Persuasiveness of the Speaker" (Ph.D. dissertation, University of Michigan, 1968).

46. S. Chaiken and A. H. Eagly, "Communication Modality As a Determinant of Persuasion: The Role of Communicator Salience," *Journal of Personality and Social Psychology,* vol. 45 (1983), pp. 241–256.

CHAPTER SIX

The Persuasive Message: Using Code Systems Effectively

In this and in the several chapters that follow we will focus attention on how language, nonverbal communication, and message organization are used in order to persuade others. In this chapter, we will introduce the notion of a "code system," discuss how meanings of words are learned, discuss how one can use code systems effectively, and present guidelines for the effective use of language in persuasion. Persuasive communicators routinely make choices about the use of graphic terms, scientific terms, abstract terms, intense language, and so forth, when constructing persuasive messages. In this chapter we will discuss the topics that are important when making the correct decisions about the use of language in persuasion.

Code systems

What is a code system? *It is a group of symbols and a set of rules for combining those symbols into larger units*. It has a set of symbols and a set of rules for combining the symbols into larger meaningful units. The basic elements in English are words, transmitted either as sounds or as marks on paper. Each symbol has meaning to the individuals sharing the code system. The set of rules for combining words into larger structures is called grammar or syntax. This set of rules has to be understood by all users of the code system. Otherwise, a source could produce sentences such as "Away Calgon me take." We do not produce such combinations of symbols because sources and receivers must follow the rules of syntax.

Two kinds of code systems are utilized in persuasive communication. One system is the *verbal system*, illustrated by the words that speakers use. While speaking, however, speakers may speak quickly or slowly, they may be moving their hands up and down, they might smile, or frown, and so on. These behaviors are part of the *nonverbal code system*. The nonverbal code system is so important that we discuss it in its own chapter (Chapter 7). In this chapter we will concentrate on an examination of the *verbal code system*.

Developing meaning

For centuries, scholars have been interested in attempting to explain just how a baby, born without language, can within a very few years acquire the ability to use an elaborate code system with competence and fluency. Today, we know that code systems are *learned*, and learned according to many of the same principles of learning theory we discussed in Chapter 2.

Any discussion of the acquisition of language must begin with the birth of the child. When Karen Child is born, her eyesight is relatively poor and it usually does not develop fully until she is several weeks or months old. Karen's hearing, however, is fully developed at birth, and she is immediately able to assimilate the sounds that are made around her. Despite the lack of development in eyesight and in certain portions of the nervous system, and despite the lack of growth in the muscle systems of the newborn child, each human being has the biological capacity to develop language. Contrary to many popular beliefs, the process of developing language does not start when the baby is a year old and first says "Ma Ma." The process of developing language starts when the child first begins to hear sounds and first sees things in the surrounding environment.

Noam Chomsky has suggested that children have some built-in mechanisms that help control acquisition of language.[1] If each of us had to learn every aspect of language at the same slow rate that it takes us to learn to swim or to ride a bicycle, we could never develop the rich code system that the average individual possesses. Chomsky suggests that there is a "grammar" of baby talk that enables children to express certain fundamental language relationships, such as subject and predicate, noun and verb, or possession, even before they have been exposed to formal learning of grammatical rules. This capacity, present in all normal children, helps explain Karen's behavior as she responds to the world around her

As Karen matures in terms of her reactions to the sounds she makes, she also matures in her ability to respond to the objects she encounters. Her first cries are relatively simple, and it is difficult to make distinctions between the cries. Later, she can respond with a whole series of distinct sounds that are not language, but are clearly the forerunners of language. It is at this point that language learning can begin. Imagine that Karen is handed a bright, shiny ball for the first time. She will have a number of possible responses to the object—she may smile, kick her feet, smell, squeeze, or put her arms around the ball. The chances are that when the ball is handed to Karen, her mother will say, "ball." If Karen is handed the ball several times, and each time her mother says, "ball," the process of association of the sound and the object will take place. If Karen's mother then walks into the room and says, "Ball, Karen," the probability is that Karen will respond to that series of sounds in much the same fashion as she responds to the ball being handed to her. The sound "ball" becomes part of what the child is responding to, and through processes of contiguity and generalization, the time will come when Karen will respond to the sound alone *with many of the same responses that she made to the object*. Karen may smile, kick her feet, or even reach out with her hands as if to grasp the ball. At this point, an onlooker might be likely to remark, "The baby knows what the word means."

We have discussed the process of acquiring meaning in some detail, because the process, as described, indicates that at least two types of meaning are learned. The first is *denotative* meaning, or that meaning that serves as a link between word and referent. Denotative meaning is sometimes referred to as "dictionary meaning," since it indicates the references that a language community has for a particular word. Persuasive communicators usually assume that their receivers will use the same denotative meanings for words as they themselves do.

The second type of meaning acquired is *connotative* meaning. This meaning is reflected in the attitudes that people develop toward words. Karen's experiences with the bright, shiny ball have been pleasant. We expect her to have developed positive attitudes about that particular object. If, on the other hand, we had not handed her the ball, but had thrown it at her each time, we might expect her attitudes to be highly negative. In either case, Karen will develop connotative meanings associated with the words she learns.

Connotative meaning becomes important to persuasion because such meanings are more highly variable than are denotative meanings, and cannot be easily predicted. If we chose two children, placed one child in a very loving home, and the other in a home where the mother and father periodically indulged in child beating, just what kind of connotative meanings would those children develop? Both children might have the same denotative meanings for the words "mother" and "father," but we would certainly expect different connotative meanings to develop. Furthermore, we would expect the children to react differently to a persuasive message that suggested that the child do something "because your mother and father think it best."

We cannot help developing meanings toward the stimuli we encounter. Whether we are talking about verbal or nonverbal code systems, meaning becomes an important part of our consideration of persuasive messages. This discussion of meaning may be concluded by pointing out several implications for the persuasive communicator:

1. People *learn* the meanings they associate with words and gestures.
2. People will have similar meanings, either denotative or connotative, only to the extent that their learning experiences have been similar. When meanings are different, they can be made similar only through the application of learning principles.
3. Because meanings are learned, it is incorrect to say that meanings are in words or gestures. Words or gestures serve only as the stimuli to elicit meaning responses. The meanings are in the people, not in the words or gestures.
4. Because meanings mediate responses, they may serve as reinforcers of behavior. Thus, the meanings that receivers possess will help determine perceptions of the world, the messages attended to, and the responses that are made.

Using code systems effectively

Messages are composed of complex sets of stimuli. When a speaker addresses a large audience, a receiver can attend to a wide range of stimuli in his or her field of vision. The receiver can focus attention on the words being spoken, vocal inflections, gestures, the emotional expression on the face of the speaker, the reactions of the crowd. These elements interact with one another to impact on the receiver. It is, therefore, not completely realistic to take a persuasive message and examine its parts separately. But if we are going to help sources improve their speaking and writing, we must look at variables independently and attempt to make assessments of the role they play in effective persuasion.

Problems in denotation

We engage in persuasion to affect changes in the people around us. Whether we are acting as a source in attempting to change the behavior of some receiver, or engaging in an interaction to reach some consensus on a problem, we persuade with intent. One of the major problems in successful persuasion comes from a failure to elicit a response from another individual equivalent to the one intended. In other words, the receiver may not have the same meaning for the term used in a message as did the source. Several variables can be cited that may contribute to the failure to secure similar responses to the same word or phrase.

1. Abstractness. S. I. Hayakawa[2] and other semanticists point to abstract language as a problem in communication. The more abstract a term is, the less likely it is to elicit similar meanings from a group of receivers. Look at Figure 6.1. The terms on the left are relatively specific in meaning. There can be differences in meaning between receivers even with relatively concrete terms, but the probability is that the *range* of meanings will be narrower with concrete terms than with abstract terms. Most people will have approximately the same meaning for the term "book," although one individual may be thinking of a paperback while another thinks of a hardcover book. Nevertheless, the differences in meaning are not likely to be serious. If the communicator refers to a "teaching aid," however, the receiver may be thinking of a book, a film, a picture, or even a teacher. The more abstract the term, the more necessary careful definition becomes.

2. Technological Terms. As our country grows in technological complexity, there is a tendency for words to move from ordinary to more specialized meanings for the scientist or engineer.

Less Abstract	More Abstract
cat	feline
mother	relative
cow	cattle
bees	insects
teacher	educator
book	teaching aid
contraception	family planning
littering	polluting
war	border adjustment

Figure 6.1. Words and Pairs

Similarly, words that were part of a technological vocabulary sometimes become part of the common language, but with slightly different meanings.

The introduction of computers, particularly the microcomputers in home use, has brought to the daily newspaper terms like "bits," "bytes," "RAM," "processor," and "terminal." The newspaper seldom provides definitions, and there are surprisingly few people who could provide definitions of those terms that would correspond to the definitions that a computer manufacturer might use. Many people will nod their head as if they are understanding, but if a speaker were to ask only a few questions, it would become obvious that receivers do not have common denotative meanings for these terms. In many messages it may not make a difference that there is a lack of common meanings for technological terms. In other messages, such misunderstandings can lead to failures on the part of a communicator.

3. Euphemisms. One of the major problems in language use has arisen from the attempts by speakers and writers to make language pleasant to receivers. This results in the use of euphemisms that do not have precise meaning, and that may produce wide variation in response.

During the Vietnam War, the term "waste" was frequently substituted for the term "kill" by soldiers. To say, "We wasted them," rather than, "We killed them," is a clear example of a euphemism. The denotative meanings may be exactly the same, but the connotative meanings are different, and we expect different persuasive effects. The euphemism may have value in many persuasive situations. There are audiences that would react more favorably to the use of a euphemism than to a blunter term, but the persuasive communicator must be able to make an analysis of the audience before composing the speech, or denotative meanings are likely to be confusing for the audience.

4. Legalese. Closely related to the problem of using language drawn from technology is the problem of using language drawn from law. Lawyers have, over the centuries, developed precise meanings for words within the law. Those same words, however, may have quite different meanings to the layperson. As a general concern within society, this confusion has led to bills in state legislatures that require legal documents to be rewritten into "plain English." It has also led some insurance companies to issue their policies in a form that is far less legalistic.

Each of these problems relates to variations in meanings that are elicited for the same word. As time passes, there are always changes in meaning for the elements of any code system. Different areas of the country tend to develop new terms or acquire new meanings for old terms. The advent of any new technology brings new words into the language and existing words are given new meanings by the users of the new technology. Teenagers use words amongst themselves, give the words new meanings, and the new meanings spread to the rest of the population. These changes in the language we use are natural, but they pose a serious problem for the persuasive communicator. Once the communicator has selected a topic, and cast it into a preliminary message, there is the problem of deciding whether there are terms or propositions that will need clarification. If there is a high probability that the terms will be misunderstood, the communicator must use one or more of the following methods to increase the likelihood of a desired response.

1. Relearning. For those words or concepts that have a specific object, person, or event as a referent, the receiver can be led through a relearning process. The source can use scale models, visual aids, or other nonverbal clues to assist in demonstrating a complicated process or object.

2. Classification. In one of the most frequently used types of definition, a source places an unfamiliar term or phrase within a category of other similar objects and then specifies the term's position within this category. For example, the phrase "clearcutting" might be defined as "a

method of lumbering where all the trees in an area are cut down, rather than just selected trees." The source has placed the term "clearcutting" as one member of a class called "lumbering," and then specified just how clearcutting differs from other kinds of lumbering.

3. Negation. A variation of definition by classification has been termed *definition by negation*. The procedure is for the source to define a term by telling the receiver what is *not* being referred to. For example, a source may refer to "drug users" in talking to a college audience. That term could cover many different activities. The source may attempt to define the term by telling the audience, "I am not talking about the use of marijuana, alcohol, tobacco, or legitimate prescription drugs, but only about hard drugs such as heroin or cocaine." The source has defined the term by eliminating some possible interpretations.

4. Operational definition. Here, the communicator specifies a set of operations, which, if performed, will identify the term being defined. For example, the term "socialized medicine" might be defined operationally as "payment of all medical bills by an agency of the federal government."

The operational definition is one of the most useful tools for the persuasive speaker or writer. Many of the terms in political discussions, religious arguments, social situations, and similar persuasive situations refer to complex behaviors. The communicator can help clarify meanings for such terms by specifying the *steps*. As terms become more and more abstract, the difficulties of providing an operational definition increase. Let the reader try his hand at terms such as "technological insufficiency," "education," "socially deprived," or "racial discrimination."

Each of the types of definition cited is designed to provide assistance to a source in eliciting a desired response, but we cannot use the entire message to define terms. If we did, we would have no time for argument in favor of a particular position. A careful examination of a message may show where a simpler word can be used, or a more familiar one, and the necessity for a definition eliminated. Such an analysis may reduce the complexity of a message, provide more time for argument and appeal, and make the message far more effective in eliciting a desired response.

Problems in connotation

We have defined connotative meanings as the attitudinal meanings people develop as they acquire various code systems. Before we can look at some of the problems that arise in persuasion because of connotative components of a code system, a brief look at the measurement of connotative meaning will be useful.

Measuring connotative meaning

Charles Osgood and his associates have suggested useful ways of measuring connotative meanings.[3] The problem in making such measurements is that connotative meanings are internal, and do not lend themselves to the same type of analysis as do denotative meanings (for example, a dictionary definition). Osgood suggests the use of the *semantic differential* scaling technique to measure the intensity of reaction individuals have toward words and concepts.

When you ask people about the feelings they have toward words, the answers are frequently given in terms of *descriptive adjectives* of varying kinds. For example, ask a man what he thinks about "government," and he may answer with terms such as "strong," "weak," "necessary," and "bureaucratic." Osgood assembled a large number of pairs of polar adjectives, such as pleasant-unpleasant, smooth-rough, active-passive, low-high, good-bad, clean-dirty, and happy-sad. Each polar adjective is placed at the end of a seven-point scale, and individuals are asked to indicate how they feel about particular concepts.

If a large number of people make responses to a number of concepts and the results are then subjected to a factor analysis, three major factors or dimensions tend to emerge. These are called the *dimensions of connotative meaning*.

The first dimension is a general *evaluative* one, in which the scales express the degree of favorableness a person feels toward the word. Scales connected with the *evaluative dimension* include good-bad, valuable-worthless, fair-unfair, honest-dishonest, and so on. The second dimension is an *activity dimension*, which expresses the perceptions of a receiver toward the amount of movement or activity in an object or event. Activity scales include active-passive, fast-slow, vibrant-still, dynamic-static, and varied-repetitive. The third has been termed the *potency dimension*, which represents the feelings of strength and weakness that are perceived by an individual. Potency scales include serious-humorous, potent-impotent, strong-weak, heavy-light, and hard-soft.

These dimensions of connotative meaning seem to be stable for a number of concepts and even for a number of different languages (Kumata,[4] Suci,[5] Triandis and Osgood,[6] Osgood, Ware, and Morris[7]). This stability does not mean that people have the same connotative meanings for words, but simply that they tend to use the same dimensions with which to judge words. You may feel that "roast pork" is a concept that ought to be judged as highly favorable, and a Moslem friend may feel that the same concept ought to be judged as highly unfavorable. We are, however, using the same *dimension* of evaluation to make our judgment.

Many of the most important studies in persuasion have looked at the effects of the use of language that varies with respect to connotative meanings. In the sections below, we illustrate some of the ways in which the connotative aspects of meaning may affect persuasive communication.

Language intensity

What is the effect of using words that may elicit highly effective responses from an audience? There have been a number of studies that attempted to examine just how using intense language affects persuasion. For example, McEwen and Greenberg[8] did a study that suggested that credibility was affected by the use of intense language. Speakers using highly intense language were perceived as more credible than those who did not. The same study, however, was unable to conclude that speakers using highly intense language were also more effective in persuasion. Burgoon and Stewart[9] suggest that there may also be a sex difference. Male communicators were more effective than female communicators when using high-intensity language. Miller and Lobe[10] suggest that the nature of the receivers' involvement is related to the use of intense language. Audiences that are neutral to a topic are more influenced by highly opinionated language, while audiences where the members are already involved are less likely to be influenced. Burgoon and King[11] manipulated intensity of language in communication situations where active and passive participation were used. They found that intense language was useful in situations that had active participation built in.

Bradac, Bowers, and Courtright[12] reviewed all of the studies associated with language and communication in an attempt to isolate or identify those language variables that are most closely associated with communication. They suggest that the three most important variables are (1) intensity, (2) immediacy, and (3) diversity. Of these three, they claim that intensity is the one that most directly affects attitude change, and thus is most directly tied to persuasion.

Bradac, Bowers, and Courtright make a number of specific conclusions about the role of language intensity in persuasion. Five of their general conclusions are summarized as follows:

1. If a speaker experiences stress while speaking, he or she is not likely to use intense language. That is, when speakers are anxious, nervous, or worried, they tend to use "powerless" styles of speaking and avoid intense language.

2. The use of obscenity (at least by male speakers) **results in a reduction of persuasibility; also, the use of obscenity is related to the source's being rated lower in com-**

petence. No speaker can be rated high in competence (trained, experienced, and so on) if he or she uses foul language. Second, the research to date does *not* indicate that females are *more persuasive* than males when using obscenity—only that the effectiveness of male speakers is more likely to be adversely affected by the use of obscenity in a public speaking context.

3. Receivers are more likely to be persuaded by an intensely-worded message if they initially agree with the speaker's conclusion, but receivers are less likely to be persuaded by an intensely-worded message if they initially disagree with the speaker's conclusion.

4. Language intensity and initial source credibility interact in the production of attitude change, where intensity of language by high-credible sources increases persuasion but use of intense language by low-credible sources decreases persuasion.

5. Intensity of language (of a nonobscene type) **aids a male speaker in being persuasive; but reduces the effectiveness of female sources.**

The use of obscenity may also be seen as a special case of intense language. Does it help to use "gutter" language in a persuasive speech? A study by Bostrom, Baseheart, and Rossiter[13] suggests that the answer to the question is usually "no." They concluded that the use of obscenity tended to lower the receiver's appraisals of a speaker's credibility, and it also lowered the overall effect of a persuasive speech.

There may be times when the use of obscenity would have a positive effect. For example, in the Bostrom, Baseheart, and Rossiter study male receivers who heard obscene messages delivered by females tended to react positively toward the speaker. The authors suggest, however, that this might be a "titillation" effect. With that single possible exception, the use of obscenity in persuasive messages designed for general audiences is probably unwise.

In sum, there are certain contexts where the use of intense language aids in persuasion. On the other hand, obscenity rarely helps persuade others (but may serve some different functions, such as entertainment, and so on). We should further note in passing that the use of intense language may be of some benefit in several types of occupations. For example, if a prosecution lawyer routinely used the words "rape," "murder," "dead baby," "dead baby boy," and "smother" instead of "alleged assault," "accident," and "fetus," then the words should have a significant effect on the attitudes of the jurors. Also, more "vivid" descriptions are helpful in prompting receivers to have fuller and more detailed memory for an alleged offense than less vivid descriptions (see below).

Combining words for persuasive effect

Most of the language that a persuasive communicator uses in a message contains words that already have both connotative and denotative meanings for the members of an audience. Messages about education, medicine, abortion, juvenile delinquency, gambling, drug usage, or racial discrimination are messages for which the average receiver already has some meaning. Can the connotative meanings a receiver holds be changed substantially? How should a source proceed if changes in connotation are desired?

Howes and Osgood[14] and Bettinghaus[15] report that evaluative meanings are affected by the adjectives used to describe a noun. We might expect this to be the case, but their results suggest that the communicator can predict rather precisely the direction of the shift after the presentation of a message.

Basically, the methodology in both studies involved measuring evaluative meanings toward a series of nouns, such as "secretary," "student," "doctor," "spider," "wrestler," and "nurse." They also measured evaluative meanings toward a similar set of descriptive adjectives, such as "wonderful," "horrible," "shy," "gregarious," "sincere," and "miserable." Then the words were presented a second time to the subjects in word pairs such as "horrible doctor," "sincere spider," "miserable student," "wonderful doctor," "turbulent wrestler," and similar pairs. The results in both the Howes and Osgood study and in the Bettinghaus study showed that the adjectives did affect the way in which judgments were made. Significant predictions could be made by taking the original meaning for both words and applying a *consistency* theory prediction to obtain an estimate of the direction and amount of the connotative shift that the subject would make. For example, if the evaluative meaning for "spider" was negative, and for "wonderful" was highly positive, we can predict that when a subject is asked to rate "wonderful spider," he will show a rating lower than that of "wonderful," and higher than that of "spider." Similar results were obtained for the majority of combinations tested.

In a second phase, Bettinghaus tested the hypothesis that the results would be persistent, that is, the results of seeing the pair of words together would rub off on the subject. So three days after presenting the pairs of words, the subjects were asked to rate the noun alone. Again, the hypothesis was supported. Imagine that one group had originally judged the combination "wonderful doctor," and another group had judged the concept "horrible doctor." Three days later, both groups rated "doctor" alone. The group originally rating "wonderful doctor" rated the noun alone more favorably than did the group who had rated the combination "horrible doctor."

These studies indicate that adjectives do have an effect on the way in which terms are perceived. The motion picture described as "stupendous" or "mystifying" will acquire some of the characteristics of the adjective used to describe it. The studies also indicate that even when a word has a connotation already attached to it, the appropriate use of language may change the connotation.

Vividness: making the message memorable

Persuasion usually requires that a comprehensible message is created that is capable of gaining and keeping the audience's attention and is constructed in such a way as to be memorable (that is, information about the message or thoughts generated by the receiver are retained in memory). Two overall approaches to gaining attention and to making messages memorable are *saliency and vividness*.[16] A message is said to be salient if there is something unique or out of place in the message, something unexpected occurs, or something is out of context with the immediate surroundings. Many print advertisements rely on saliency or novelty: In one a man in a hotel room climbs out of his suitcase that is lying open on the bed, another has a woman wearing pink underwear as she appears to be refereeing a professional basketball game, another has a car parked on top of a cliff, another has a car parked on top of water, another drops a car from an airplane, and another has a woman wearing an expensive evening gown asleep on the beach, rolled into a ball with sand thrown over her. In each of these cases the advertiser wants you to stop flipping through the magazine and attend to his or her advertisement. Confronted with novelty and a mild controversy or question, the receiver is supposed to engage in some minimal amount of cognitive elaboration (see Chapter 3) to give some thought to resolving the controversy (for example, "Why is this apparently naked woman with a bottle of perfume wearing a snake around her neck?").

A second characteristic, vividness, is constructed in ways so as to gain and hold attention and to excite the receivers' imagination by making the message either emotionally interesting or concrete and image-provoking. A vivid message is one where a quality of an object is stunning in and of itself, where an object in the message is vividly beautiful, striking, or emotionally arousing or where descriptions of events are highly concrete and image-provoking. There is very good evidence to suggest that vivid messages are recalled more fully than nonvivid or "pallid" messages, and that sometimes vivid messages are related to persuasion. One area where the use of vividness is expected to be effective is in the courtroom.[17] In one recent study different versions of a drunk driving case were constructed. In some versions the prosecutor's case was described in a pallid

manner—the accused was described as knocking into a table and knocking a bowl to the ground before getting into his car and driving away. In the vivid portrayal, however, the accused was described as knocking over a bowl of guacamole dip that splattered all over a white shag carpet before the accused got into his bright orange Volkswagen and drove off. The vividly portrayed description was more fully recalled 24 hours later, and receivers who heard the vivid description were more likely to find the accused guilty.[18] Thus, in trials lasting days, weeks, or months, lawyers should rely on the most detailed, most highly descriptive and thought-provoking descriptions than on more pallidly described material.[19]

Psychologists have found that simply making any message vivid does not necessarily make the message persuasive.[20] There are at least three considerations a persuasive communicator should keep in mind when attempting to make a vivid message one that persuades. First, the reader should keep in mind that vividness is not a yes/no or high/low variable—there are degrees by which messages arouse emotions and degrees by which a message provokes images in the receivers' minds. Vividness probably helps in persuasion if at least some minimal level of emotional response is manipulated. Some research has called presentations vivid simply when the researchers used pie chart diagrams and figures, and such presentations may not have been as image-provoking as other presentations that are truly vivid.[21] Manipulations of vivid material in advertising, for example, are much more sophisticated and probably succeed in inducing emotional arousal in receivers.

Second, to be persuasive vivid messages must prompt receivers to engage in *cognitive elaboration*, by which we mean that when the receiver is exposed to the message, the receiver can easily process the material because he or she possesses a framework for evaluating the content.[22] For example, a former astronaut may vividly describe mobility in zero-gravity to a junior high school audience, yet the audience may not be able to elaborate on the material cognitively. Third, if vivid material is to be persuasive, then the emotional response receivers experience should be the one the persuasive communicator desires. For example, if receivers view a petite model dancing in front of a mirror trying on the latest fashions, the segment of the viewing audience who have failed repeatedly to lose weight may feel sad. Similarly, a commercial for special coffees that shows a loving couple sharing a cup of coffee may prompt the newly divorced or widowed to feel sad.[23] In both of these examples, probably the majority of viewers in the target market responded as the persuader desired them to—but perhaps there exists some small percentage who felt sad or depressed and who would not purchase the advertised products.

In sum, vivid material is useful in many contexts where the persuader wants the audience members to remember material. In marketing contexts, vivid material may help to persuade receivers if the material is in fact vivid, if the material in the message succeeds in prompting the receivers to respond by elaborating on the message, and if the material is viewed favorably by the receivers.

Vividness can be created either by the use of visual representations (pictures) or by the use of the type of language used in the message. Before concluding this section on vividness and persuasion, we should note that research has focused on the role of pictures and verbal content in print messages. Lutz and Lutz,[24] for example, found that a Yellow Pages advertisement that integrated the brand name and the product into a picture was later recalled better than an advertisement where the written form of the brand name appeared separate from the depiction of the product. Rossiter and Percy[25] found that receivers have more positive attitudes toward a brand name product when the picture was large and the print was small. Mitchell and Olson[26] found that advertisements for a soft facial tissue received highest ratings when a picture of a "fluffy kitten" was employed in the advertisement (as compared to rival pictures of pleasant scenes).

Research on print advertisements generally indicate that a verbal-only ad does not capture the receivers' attention as well as a picture + verbal message ad, and that the picture + verbal message ad is more easily and fully recalled than the verbal-only advertisement. Further, Edell and Staelin[27] reasoned that receivers probably respond to verbal print advertisements and pictorial print advertisements differently. A pictorial one is more attention-getting, pleasant, and easier to process than a verbal-only ad, but the verbal-only ad can convey more information. Also, Edell and Staelin reasoned that a large dominant pictorial advertisement with a reinforcing message (or "framed" picture) could be effective in gaining attention, creating a favorable attitude, and prompting greater recall of the brand name. By "framed" picture advertisement, we mean one where the verbal message is relevant to the picture of the brand name product, usually placed in one of the margins of the page. For example, the words "tough," "strong," or "absorbent" are used with the brand name (for example, "Brawny") along with a photograph of a giant lumberjack's shadow being cast over the school yard.

However, it is also possible that the picture advertisement has little to do with the verbal component. In some advertisements the verbal component is "unframed" in that it does not reinforce the message being sent in the visual channel. For example, a photograph taking up 75 percent of the space of a page shows young, healthy, college-aged individuals playing in the snow. At the bottom of the page are the words "Now, 10 percent less tar" or "One free pack in every carton." In advertisements such as these receivers will place much greater attention on the visual presentation, which could *distract* the receiver from generating thoughts about the advertisement (see Chapter 3 concerning "thought listing"). In their own experiment, Edell and Staelin found that receivers responded more favorably to the visual advertisement that was framed than to the unframed versions. Receivers listed relatively few favorable or unfavorable thoughts when exposed to the visual-unframed advertisements. Also, receivers recalled fewer of the brand names after having viewed the unframed versions. Thus, it appears that picture + relevant claim produce a desirable outcome compared to picture + irrelevant claim. Note, however, that it is still possible that the purpose of advertisements such as the one for selling cigarettes is not really to induce brand name recall, but simply to attempt to induce a favorable attitude toward the cigarette brand by repeatedly matching or pairing (see Chapter 2) the product with positive activities such as surfing, swimming, skiing, flirting, and so on—events that do not have anything to do with smoking tobacco. The unframed visual ad also draws attention *away* from the surgeon general's warning.

Guidelines for the use of language in persuasion

So far we have talked about how language is learned, how code systems can be used effectively, language intensity, combining words, and vividness. In this last section we will briefly summarize several other topics relevant to the use of persuasion. Many of the topics are important in legal settings and since we cannot deal with all issues of importance concerning language in legal settings, the reader is referred to Chapter 12, and to Kerr and Bray,[28] Loftus and Goodman,[29] Ficaro,[30] O'Barr,[31] and Matlon and Crawford.[32]

1. Speech style. Research has focused attention on powerless style of speaking and powerful style of speaking. Powerless users employ many more hedges ("kind of," "sort of," "it seemed to me"), more frequent hesitations ("er" or "umm"), and are more overtly polite ("sir," "please") than powerful style speakers. Powerless style speakers are rated as less competent, less intelligent, less credible, and less trustworthy. Further, witnesses who appear to be adopting a style of speech just for the courtroom situation by mimicking how they think lawyers talk, by mimicking legal terminology, or by acting in a "hypercorrect" manner are rated as less convincing, less competent, less qualified, and less intelligent than speakers using standard English.

2. Preparation and speech dialects. Americans do not by and large prefer their own regional dialect when it comes to persuasion. Defendants and witnesses are encouraged, in fact, to rely on "standard American dialect" (spoken in the Midwest) to other dialects (for example, the lack of a strong dialect like Walter Cronkite's).[33] Also, jurors and observers in the courtroom are not impressed with any speaker who relies on jargon. Further, some studies indicate that defendants who are polite and articulate (few grammatical errors) are more likely to be treated leniently than defendants who display frequent speech errors and who are less polite.[34] Given these results, one can ask the question of whether preparing a witness helps build confidence and competence, and improves performance. As a general rule, witness preparation does enhance performance in the courtroom situation and more lawyers (in major suits) are routinely having defendants prepared before testimony is given. One study found that only a 7-minute preparation concerning what was to happen in the cross-examination increased the witness's confidence and presentation to the court.[35]

3. Beginning and ending. Jurors have no knowledge of what might happen in any given trial, and they cannot be expected to draw conclusions on their own as the trial progresses. Thus, it is recommended that during the opening statements, the lawyer secure a favorable response from the jury, give an accurate (and comprehensible) impression of what will follow, and provide a framework for the jury so that the evidence and presentations that follow can more easily be understood. A study by Pyszczynski and Wrightsman[36] found that extensive opening previews helped to shape jurors' attitudes throughout much of the trial. Thus, a complete and easy-to-understand overview of the trial could help in the persuasion process. Further, the advice consistently given by attorneys, psychologists, and communication scholars is to start a case with a strong piece of evidence and to end the case with a strong piece of evidence. If weaker evidence has to be presented, it should be buried in the middle, where less attention is likely to focus on it. Some attorneys also feel it is important to provide summaries routinely during the cross-examination and to end each cross-examination on a high note. Some jurors cannot be expected to understand why every line of questioning is taking place, so summaries or comments about concluding points help them to follow the case and possibly increase their comprehension of the case.

4. Asking questions and managing the image of witnesses and defendants. Ficaro[37] has argued that by asking questions of many details where a witness correctly recalls what took place during an event increases the credibility of the witness with the jury. Thus, either a vivid portrayal by an eyewitness account or sheer quantity of material being recalled by a witness will prompt more of the jurors to believe that the witness is probably accurate when identifying the defendant. (There is no empirical evidence, however, to support this notion—that a witness who is accurate at recalling a wide range of details about an accident or a crime is more accurate about eyewitness identification of the alleged offender.) Other details of questioning affect witness credibility. In using a "narrative" questioning format a lawyer asks fewer questions, but allows the witness to tell her or his own story (for example, "Tell us about the evening of July 29?"). In a fragmented questioning format a lawyer will ask 100 to 200 short, closed-ended questions ("So you got gas Thursday evening, yes?"). Research indicates that jurors or observers who watch the fragmented questioning format take place believe that the lawyer has little faith, confidence, or trust in the witness that she or he is questioning. Further, jurors rated the witness who answers questions in the fragmented format low in competence, low in intelligence, and low in assertiveness. To reduce the credibility of the witness further, a lawyer might ask many questions where the witness has to answer "I don't know." Finally, it is advisable for a lawyer to avoid negative constructions in sentences (either in her/his

opening or closing statements or during the questioning of witnesses). Multiple negatives ("You never left the room, is that not correct?") take longer for receivers to process and are harder to understand.[38]

Summary

In this chapter, we have concentrated on the ways in which code systems can be used to build successful messages. The elements of any code system have meanings for each receiver who shares the code system. These meanings may be denotative or referential, connotative or evaluative, in nature, or arise from the ways in which the elements are structured. Any element will have both connotative and denotative meanings. All meanings are learned, and all meanings are in people, not in the referents themselves.

For successful persuasive communication, the source must be able to predict what meanings will be elicited from a receiver when a term is used in a message. We may have problems in predicting either the denotative or the connotative aspects of meaning, and we must consider the role that the verbal code systems will play in eliciting a successful response from a receiver.

Footnotes

1. Noam Chomsky, *Aspects of the Theory of Syntax* (Cambridge, Mass.: M.I.T. Press, 1965).

2. S. I. Hayakawa, *Language in Thought and Action* (New York: Harcourt, Brace & World, 1964).

3. C. Osgood, P. Tannenbaum, and G. Suci, *The Measurement of Meaning* (Urbana, Ill.: University of Illinois Press, 1957). See also J. Snider and C. Osgood, eds., *Semantic Differential Technique* (Chicago: Aldine, 1969).

4. H. Kumata, "A Factor Analytic Investigation of the Generality of Semantic Structures across

Two Selected Cultures" (Ph.D. dissertation, University of Illinois, 1957).

5. G. J. Suci, "A Comparison of Semantic Structures in American Southwest Culture Groups," *Journal of Abnormal and Social Psychology*, vol. 61 (1960), pp. 25–30.

6. H. C. Triandis and C. E. Osgood, "A Comparative Factorial Analysis of Semantic Structures in Monolingual Greek and American College Students," *Journal of Abnormal and Social Psychology*, vol. 57 (1958), pp. 187–196.

7. C. E. Osgood, R. E. Ware, and C. Morris, "Analysis of the Connotative Meanings of a Variety of Human Values as Expressed by American College Students," *Journal of Abnormal and Social Psychology*, vol. 62 (1961), pp. 62–73.

8. W. J. McEwen and B. S. Greenberg, "The Effects of Message Intensity on Receiver Evaluation of Source, Message and Topic," *Journal of Communication*, vol. 13 (1963), pp. 94–105.

9. M. Burgoon and D. Stewart, "Empirical Investigations of Language Intensity: I. The Effects of Sex of Source, Receiver, and Language Intensity on Attitude Change," *Human Communication Research*, 1 (1975), pp. 244–248.

10. G. R. Miller and J. Lobe, "Opinionated Language, Open- and Closed-Mindedness and Responses to Persuasive Communications," *Journal of Communication*, 17 (1967), pp. 333–341.

11. M. Burgoon and L. King, "The Mediation of Resistance to Persuasion Strategies by Language Variables and Active-Passive Participation," *Human Communication Research*, vol. 1 (1974), pp. 30–41.

12. J. Bradac, J. Bowers, and J. Courtright, "Three Language Variables in Communication Research: Intensity, Immediacy, and Diversity," *Human Communication Research*, vol. 7 (1979), pp. 257–269.

13. R. Bostrom, J. Baseheart, and C. Rossiter, "The Effects of Three Types of Profane Language in Persuasive Messages," *Journal of Communication*, vol. 23 (1973), pp. 461–475.

14. D. Howes and C. E. Osgood, "On the Combination of Associative Probabilities in Linguistic Context," *American Journal of Psychology*, vol. 67 (1954), pp. 241–258.

15. E. Bettinghaus, "Cognitive Balance and the Development of Meaning," *Journal of Communication*, vol. 13 (1963), pp. 94–105.

16. For more of a discussion of salience and vividness, see S. T. Fiske and S. E. Taylor, *Social Cognition* (New York: Random House, 1984).

17. S. M. Kassin and L. W. Wrightsman, eds., *The Psychology of Evidence and Trial Procedure* (Beverly Hills: Sage, 1985).

18. R. M. Reyes, W. C. Thompson, and G. H. Bower, "Judgmental Biases Resulting from Differing Availabilities of Arguments," *Journal of Personality and Social Psychology*, vol. 39 (1980), pp. 2–12.

19. See Kassin and Wrightsman, eds., *The Psychology of Evidence and Trial Procedure*.

20. J. Kisielius and B. Sternthal, "Detecting and Explaining the Vividness Effects in Attitudinal Judgments," *Journal of Marketing Research*, vol. 21 (1984), pp. 54–64; J. Kisielius and B. Sternthal, "Examining the Vividness Controversy: An Availability-Valence Interpretation," *Journal of Consumer Research*, vol. 12 (1986), pp. 418–431.

21. See Kisielius and Sternthal, "Examining the Vividness Controversy."

22. See Kisielius and Sternthal, "Examining the Vividness Controversy."

23. This example appears in P. A. Stout and J. D. Leckenby, "A Typology of Identifying Emotional Response to Advertising" (paper, Department of Advertising, University of Texas–Austin, 1985).

24. K. A. Lutz and R. J. Lutz, "Effects of Interactive Imagery on Learning: Applications to Advertising," *Journal of Applied Psychology*, vol. 62 (1977), pp. 493–498.

25. J. R. Rossiter and L. Percy, "A Visual and Verbal Loop Theory of the Classical Effect of Advertising on Product Attitude" (paper, Department of Advertising, University of Pennsylvania, 1978).

26. A. A. Mitchell and J. C. Olson, "Are Product Attribute Beliefs the Only Mediator of Advertising Effects on Brand Attitudes?" *Journal of Marketing Research*, vol. 18 (1981), pp. 318–332.

27. J. A. Edell and R. Staelin, "The Information Processing of Pictures in Print Advertisements," *Journal of Consumer Research,* vol. 10 (1983), pp. 45–61; see also T. L. Childers and M. J. Houston, "Conditions for a Picture Superiority Effect on Consumer Memory," *Journal of Consumer Research,* vol. 11 (1984), pp. 643–654.

28. N. L. Kerr and R. M. Bray, eds., *The Psychology of the Courtroom* (New York: Academic, 1982).

29. E. F. Loftus and J. Goodman, "Questioning Witnesses," in S. M. Kassin and L. S. Wrightsman, eds., *The Psychology of Evidence and Trial Procedure* (Beverly Hills: Sage, 1985), pp. 253–279; see also E. A. Lind and G. Y. Ke, "Opening and Closing Statements," in S. M. Kassin and L. S. Wrightsman, eds., *The Psychology of Evidence and Trial Procedure* (Beverly Hills: Sage, 1985), pp. 229–252.

30. M. Ficaro, "Prosecution of Violent Crimes" (paper presented to a seminar at the National College of District Attorneys, Colorado Springs, Colorado, 1982).

31. W. O'Barr, "The Language of the Law," in C. A. Ferguson and S. B. Heath, eds., *Language in the U.S.A.* (New York: Cambridge University Press, 1981), pp. 386–406.

32. R. J. Matlon and R. J. Crawford, eds., *Communication Strategies in the Practice of Lawyering* (Annandale, VA: Speech Communication Association, 1983).

33. H. Giles and P. F. Powesland, *Speech Style and Social Evaluation* (New York: Academic, 1975).

34. Loftus and Goodman, "Questioning Witnesses."

35. G. L. Wells, R. C. L. Lindsay, and T. J. Ferguson, "Accuracy, Confidence, and Juror Perceptions of Eyewitness Identification," *Journal of Applied Psychology,* vol. 64 (1979), pp. 440–448; see also R. E. Oliphant, ed., *Trial Techniques with Irving Younger* (Minneapolis, MN: National Practice Institute, 1978); Loftus and Goodman, "Questioning Witnesses."

36. T. Pyszczynski and L. S. Wrightsman, "Effects of Opening Statements on Mock Jurors," *Journal of Applied Social Psychology,* vol. 11 (1981), pp. 301–313.

37. Ficaro, "Prosecution of Violent Crimes."

38. Loftus and Goodman, "Questioning Witnesses."

CHAPTER SEVEN

The Persuasive Message: Using Nonverbal Code Systems Effectively

Communication is dependent upon the development and use of sets of symbols that have shared meanings for sources and receivers. Nonverbal code systems have the same general characteristics as verbal systems. They have elements and symbols with shared meanings. Thus, in our society, the handshake has a meaning of friendliness and is used as a greeting. Facial expressions—frowns, smiles, grimaces—come to have meanings for receivers, and form part of the general code system. Nonverbal code systems also have rules for the combination of elements. Frowning eyebrows are not combined with an upturned mouth when the individual wants to show displeasure.

We all use nonverbal code systems, but most of us receive little information about them through formal education. In part, this neglect stems from the fact that until relatively recently, there were few scholars studying nonverbal systems. The picture is changing, and changing rapidly. The past ten years have seen a virtual explosion in the number and variety of research studies concerned with nonverbal communication. Our concentration is in three areas. First, we will discuss what is included in the nonverbal code system and present an overview of the terms used to define its various features. Second, we will discuss what nonverbal behaviors are linked to credibility and persuasiveness. Third, we will discuss research on honesty and deception—can you tell when someone is lying to you? There are, of course, many topics in nonverbal communication that we cannot detail. However, the interested reader can find a more complete picture in Burgoon and Saine's *The Unspoken Dialogue: An Introduction to Nonverbal Communication*,[1] Knapp's excellent review of the research literature in *Nonverbal Communication in Human Interaction,*[2] or the recent books by Patterson (*Nonverbal Behavior: A Functional Perspective*)[3] and Wiemann and Harrison (*Nonverbal Interaction*).[4]

The nonverbal code system

Gestural codes

All of us use gestures to accompany our speech. We point, smile, shrug our shoulders, turn one way or the other, or shake our fist at someone. How should we classify such behavior? There are a number of options, ranging from Birdwhistell's system that includes a muscle-by-muscle examination of a person's gestures,[5] to some nineteenth-century elocutionists' attempts at tying certain gestures to particular words in the language. A most useful analysis is provided by Ekman and Friesen,[6] who suggest that our gestures can be divided into five categories:

1. Emblems. Emblems are gestures that can be translated directly into the verbal code system. Emblems may accompany a verbal message or be used alone. However, since it is not very effective for a referee to shout "touchdown," or for a hitchhiker to shout, "Give me a ride," many emblems are used without verbal accompaniment. If you are a fully socialized American, you should be able to recognize and use the following emblems:[7] hitchhiking; shrug of uncertainty; fighting; money; suicide; a woman's nice figure; something stinks; stating "OK, I don't know, he's crazy, shame on you!, stop, go away, come here, do you have a cigarette?, I'm hot, a close shave, tastes good, I'm smart, how could I be so dumb!"[11]; counting; and various insults.

Sometimes elaborate code systems are actually created for a purpose, as in the case of the sign language of the deaf. On the other hand, there are some emblems that change in frequency of occurrence because of popularity and the times. The emblems for peace and black power, for example, went out of fashion in the early 1970s. Today, advertisers commonly employ the "thumbs up" emblem, but this too may not last for long. Finally, it is important to understand that any system of emblems is influenced by culture, and what an emblem signifies in one culture may mean nothing in another (or worse, something different). Scholars have begun to document the common emblems of other cultures so that fewer instances of miscommunication may emerge, yet today's travelers must be aware of many subtle nuances. For example, Kendon,[8] and Morris et al.[9] note that some gestures become so offensive they are made illegal—only to evolve into more subtle variations. Hence, the "Italian salute" was altered on Malta to appear to be a gesture similar to what we refer to below as a self-adaptor—the left arm is held straight, with the hand clenched in a fist, while the right arm rubs the inside of the left elbow. Not only do emblems fascinate us, they also amuse—a point that Latka on *Taxi* exploits when he engages in ritualistic (and quite different) emblems for insulting others.

2. Illustrators. Illustrators are body movements or other nonverbal acts that accompany speech. They are called illustrators because they help illustrate the point the speaker is making. The gesture of holding one's hands apart when telling someone the size of a just-caught fish is an example of an illustrator. Movements emphasizing a word, pointing to an object when talking about the object, or indicating some action are all illustrators. Sometimes a refined subset of categories is employed. For example, some common forms of illustrators include, according to Ekman and Friesen, *deictic* movements (pointing to objects, places, or events), *rhythmic* movements (depicting the timing or rhythm of an event), and *pictographs* (showing the shape of what is referenced verbally). Sometimes it is useful to distinguish between illustrators and expansive illustrators—sweeping gestures outside the area of the shoulder and hip area (that is, movement away from the torso). People use more illustrators when they are excited or enthusiastic, and cultures differ in how much illustrating is typical or normal.

In this chapter we will emphasize the role illustrators and other hand gestures play in creating an image of the credible communicator. Yet, it should be noted that hand gestures are also related to recall of the message content. In a series of studies, Woodall and Folger[10] recorded conversations where an utterance (for example, "Really, I can't keep up with him, he just sits there and shovels it in") was accompanied either with (1) no hand gestures, (2) an *emphasizing* gesture (such as rhythmic motion like pounding or pointing), or (3) an *emblematic* gesture, where a gesture is related semantically with the utterance (in our example, with a sweeping motion of the speaker's hand toward the mouth). (We say the emblematic gesture is *semantically* related to the utterance because the nonverbal gesture transcribes to the words "shovels it in.") Observers viewed the different versions of the video-tapes and later were asked to recall parts of the conversations. Observers recalled utterances better if the utterances were communicated with emblematic gestures. Thus, hand gestures may be used strategically in order to highlight parts of a message the persuader wants receivers to emphasize—and hand gestures best able to secure receiver recall are ones that are closely linked to the words the speaker is communicating.

3. Affect displays. Affect displays are expressions or motions that indicate the state of our emotions. Frowns, smiles, grins, and hand motions all may be used to communicate our affective states. Affect displays may accompany the use of verbal codes, or they may be used apart from the verbal code system. There may be a high degree of variance among individuals in their use of affect displays, but all of us use such nonverbal clues to indicate to others how we feel.

4. Regulators. Regulators are gestures and facial movements that help control the flow of communication in an interaction situation. They are used by the source and receiver to indicate the way in which the conversation is to continue, or to change the nature of the conversation. Such gestures include head nods, certain hand movements, and eye movements. They may tell the speaker that receivers are interested, want further information or want the speaker to repeat a statement, and so on. Used by the source, they may indicate to the receiver that the source is nearly done, that the speaker wants to elaborate on a point, or that the source wants to continue speaking after finishing a point.

5. Adaptors. Adaptors are employed to satisfy physical or emotional needs and often include rubbing, biting, scratching, and so on, of the body. One of your friends may play with her hair when anxious, while another rubs a particular spot on his chin, and another friend rubs her chin when involved in deep concentration. Obviously, an adaptor does not carry meaning in the same way that an emblem does, and you may need to get to know a person in order to know whether a particular adapting behavior reflects anxiety, arousal, deep concentration, or some other state. In general, however, frequent adapting seems to reflect anxiety and tends to reduce a speaker's effectiveness (see below). Further, sources are often quite unaware of their own adapting behaviors (unless they receive feedback from others), but learn to read the adaptors of others without difficulty. Adaptors are commonly divided into two types: *self* (including facial or head, and body) and *object* (playing with objects such as rubber bands, paper clips, and so on).

Paralinguistic codes

Most of our study of verbal code systems focuses on words and syntax. Thus, we learn that words convey denotative meanings, and that words can be constructed into sentences and paragraphs. All of us realize, however, that the same word, referring to the same object or event, can be said in many different ways. If we are talking about "Women's Lib," we can use these two words sneeringly, encouragingly, depreciatingly, humorously, defiantly, or sadly, all depending on the tone of voice used. The study of those nonverbal cues that surround the verbal code system is called *paralinguistics*. Unlike linguistics, which has been an object of scholarly study for many centuries, paralinguistics has been on the scene for only a few decades. Trager[11] suggested that the study of paralinguistics involves at least two major elements.

1. Voice qualities. Voice qualities include such things as speech rate, rhythm pattern, pitch, precision of articulation, and control of utterances by the lips, tongue, and other articulators. Such voice qualities do seem to convey meaning as they accompany words and statements. The high-pressure salesman who spits out his message at a very rapid rate conveys a sense of importance and urgency because of that rate. Thus, rate becomes a paralinguistic characteristic of the message.

2. Vocalizations. Vocalizations include a number of sounds that do not have specific meanings, but which can indicate emotions when they accompany verbal messages. Vocal characteristics such as swallowing, coughing, heavy breathing, sneezing, yawning, and signing may indicate importance, nervousness of the speaker, or other emotional states of the speaker or listener. *Vocal segregates* are interjections such as "uh," "uh-uh," or "ah," placed in the message. They may signal the source to continue, or to stop for a question, or they may tell the listener that the source has more to say, or is almost finished. By using *vocal qualifiers* we indicate intensity in a message by speaking loudly or softly, indicate emotion by using extremely high pitch, or convey importance by speaking slowly and very precisely.

In addition to the paralinguistic elements suggested by Trager, other writers, such as Malh[12] and Siegman,[13] have suggested that other message elements be studied. Since the 1950s considerable attention has focused on *speech disturbances*. As we

shall see later, many of these speech disturbances result in a loss of persuasiveness, and are related to deception. We need to point out *why* these nonfluencies emerge. As reviewed in Harper, Wiens, and Matarazzo,[14] it is important to distinguish between "ah" and "non-ah" speech disturbances because the two types of disturbances serve different functions. "Ah" disfluencies include any "ah," "er," "ummm" a speaker makes while presenting the speech. "Non-ah" disturbances include the following:

omissions—which occur during speech production when words or parts of words are omitted. For example: "It was East() Sunday. They were really hap() about the picnic."

stutter—which occurs when the speaker repeats a sound. For example: "Sh-she was mean to me. Bu-but I still love her."

word/phrase repetitions—which occur when a word or even a whole phrase is repeated. For example: "Then we-then we-then we went for a drive."

tongue slip—which occurs when a speaker makes an incorrect substitution of syllables. For example: A speaker says "darn bore" or "rage wait" for "barn door" and "wage rate."

sentence correction—occurs when a correction in a word choice is made by a speaker while she or he speaks. (This disfluency is different from grammatical error because in the grammatical error disfluency the speaker continues to speak as if he or she were unaware of the disfluency.) Example: ". . . Third World War (ah), I meant Third World *Nations*. . . ."

grammatical error—occurs whenever a grammatical error is made during the speech. For example, the speaker mixes present and past tense or mixes plural and singular.

A person who displays frequent non-ah disturbances when speaking, stutters, omits syllables or words, repeats words or phrases, engages in "Freudian slips" (or is "tongue tied"), and displays sentence corrections (also called "false starts") and speech errors. There is considerable evidence that "non-ah" disturbances are related to anxiety, while the use of "ah" may indicate several different variables: The speaker may be answering an ambiguous question, the speaker wants to "hold" the conversational floor so that another conversationist does not take the floor, or the speaker may have difficulty (cognitively speaking) in answering a question. "Ah" and "non-ah" speech errors play different roles in persuasion (see below). Finally, longer *response latencies* (the periods of silence that occur before the speaker starts to speak) and *silent pauses* (periods of silence that occur while the speaker holds the floor) reflect increased mental concentration, as well as anxiety.[15]

As noted earlier, research on nonverbal communication has accelerated in the last decade. What we have reviewed so far provides the reader with the major features of the nonverbal code system, and sufficient terminology to describe most of the specific behaviors that are employed in research. In the remainder of the chapter we will:

1. discuss how specific behaviors reflect extroversion, affiliation, and relaxation;

2. relate body movement, eye-contact rates, distance and touching, speech fluencies and delivery styles, speech rates, and vocal qualities to persuasiveness and/or speaker effectiveness; and

3. discuss what nonverbal cues you should attend to in order to increase your chance of detecting deception.

Behaviors associated with persuasiveness

A number of studies have attempted to group nonverbal behaviors together on the basis of what the behaviors communicate. While a number of typologies exist, and different researchers have used different labels, we shall discuss three general categories of behaviors that are relevant to persua-

sion.[16] First, there are cues associated with *extroversion* that reflect the speaker's level of animation and/or enthusiasm for the topic. These behaviors include forceful, rhythmic gestures of illustrators, high eye-contact rates, higher vocal volume, faster speaking rates, more affirmative head nodding, more facial activity, and greater variety of intonation. Second, there are a number of behaviors that reflect *affiliation* (liking and attraction) that communicate the speaker's attitude toward the audience. Behaviors included in this category are increased gesturing, forward leaning, increased head nodding, closer proximity, and increased smiling, touching, and eye contact. Third, behaviors can reflect the speaker's level of *relaxation* (or, conversely, anxiety). These include relaxed posture (asymmetry of arm/leg positions, sideways lean, backward reclining of the body, and relaxed hand and neck positions), anxiety cues (adaptors, vocal nervousness), and fluency of speech.

As a general rule, persuasiveness increases as the speaker engages in behaviors indicative of extroversion and affiliation while exhibiting few anxiety-related behaviors. More specific conclusions can be made after we examine more closely the impact on persuasiveness and speaker evaluations of each of the following: body movements, eye contact, distance and touching, speech fluency, speech rate, and vocal qualities.

Body movements

Mehrabian and Williams conducted a series of studies to see what behaviors persons exhibit when intending to be persuasive.[17] In one of the studies, for example, students were told either to be very persuasive, to be moderately persuasive, or simply to be neutral. The subjects were then allowed time to prepare speeches and delivered the speeches to an audience while being videotaped through a one-way mirror. Mehrabian and Williams found that as intention to persuade increased, speakers were more likely to increase eye contact, to increase affirmative head nodding, to illustrate or gesture more frequently, to increase facial activity, to speak more loudly, and to speak more quickly. Mehrabian and Williams also had observers view videotaped presentations and rate them on level of persuasiveness. The speaker was perceived as more persuasive when he/she maintained eye contact, engaged in more illustrating, engaged in fewer adaptors, spoke more quickly with greater volume and fluency, and engaged in more facial activity. LaCrosse similarly found that in counseling interactions, individuals were perceived as more persuasive when they maintained more eye contact, smiled more, exhibited more affirmative head nods, gestured frequently, and exhibited a body orientation where they directly faced the listener.[18] Maslow, Yoselson, and London paid an actor to deliver a speech in a confident, doubtful, or neutral manner.[19] Not only did confidence increase persuasiveness, but the "confident" speaker used more forceful and rhythmic gestures, maintained more eye contact, and exhibited a more relaxed posture. During the "doubtful" speech, the speaker engaged in more object and body adaptors, maintained less eye contact, and sat in a tense, upright position.

The above studies indicate that gestures dealing with both affiliation and extroversion are related to perceived persuasiveness. There are also studies that indicate that a number of the same cues elicit favorable evaluations in interviews.[20] Generally, these studies indicate the following:

high levels of eye contact, high energy levels, desirable paralinguistic cues (a low number of speech disturbances, fluent speech, and high modality), and frequent head and hand movements produce higher ratings of effectiveness in job interviews;

individuals who exhibit energy and involvement in the interview are liked better, and are judged as more competent, more qualified, more likely to be successful, and to be more motivated;

high nonverbal responsiveness (using vocal cues, facial expressiveness, increased nodding, gaze, and gesturing) led to enhanced ratings of

a counselor's expertise, trustworthiness, and attractiveness;

interviewers who are enthusiastic (versus unenthusiastic) emit high amounts of eye contact, smiling, and gesturing, and are perceived to be more job satisfied, more approachable, more interested, more enthusiastic, more considerate, and more intelligent.

Although many of these behaviors are related to affiliation, there is little doubt that cues associated with extroversion, such as high energy level, expansive gestures, and level of enthusiasm, are related to enhanced evaluations—both in public speaking and interview contexts.

In regards to social relaxation there is ample evidence that listeners have distinct preferences concerning levels of relaxation and, in general, do not care to be distracted by anxiety cues. It is clear, for example, that a large number of adaptors result in lower ratings of liking and speaker effectiveness. Persuasiveness is also influenced by body tension—females were considered more persuasive when they were slightly tense or slightly relaxed, while males were more persuasive when they were slightly relaxed.[21] The "very relaxed" position produced ratings very low in perceived persuasiveness. Further, it would appear to be the case that listeners prefer a speaker to sit directly in front of them, at least in a dyadic setting.[22] Finally, while it is clear that forward leaning (versus backward leaning) is associated with attraction and trust (that is, affiliation), the relationship between proximity and persuasion is complex (see below).

The preceding literature provides us with two conclusions concerning bodily movements and speaker effectiveness. First, there are a number of nonverbal behaviors that are *consistently* related to enhanced performance ratings in both public speaking and interview contexts: It is to the speaker's advantage to maintain eye contact, to nod, to smile, to illustrate, to avoid being too relaxed, and to refrain from using distracting adaptors. Second, there are additional behaviors indicative of extroversion (high energy level, level of enthusiasm, sweeping or expansive illustrating, and so on) and of affiliation (forward lean, direct body orientation, open hand movements, and so on) that are not *consistently* related to enhanced performance, but that are related to improved evaluations in certain contexts. In a face-to-face or dyadic context, affiliative cues can and often do help in persuasion (as in getting more tips, selling more encyclopedias, getting people to sign a petition, and so on), while in formal contexts persuasiveness can be enhanced by greater extroversion and animation and by less affiliation. There are, for example, studies that have found that forward lean and relaxed hand gestures often are unrelated to effectiveness in formal employment interviews, while verbal output, speech fluency, body composure, eye-contact rate, posture, and appearance are more important, and that too much emphasis on affiliative gestures in such a formal context may result in the speaker being perceived as failing to exhibit sufficient seriousness.[23]

Thus, we recommend that readers maintain eye contact, nod, smile, illustrate, and display few anxiety cues, and to adapt other behaviors for the particular context. The reader should be able to notice this recommendation in practice in television commercials. In some commercials, the president of airline X wants you to *trust* his or her airline; hence there are more facial close-ups, more eye contact, considerable smiling, open hands or open arms, and as the president walks by

happy workers they nod and smile—the message is laden with affiliative cues. Another company president, trying to convince the public that he can turn Company Dismal around, is filmed from the waist or knees up, gestures expansively, stands more erect (with less relaxation), pounds a fist into his hand once or twice, and so on, while attempting to appear dynamic and extroverted.

In passing, we should note that it is often easier to recommend that speakers increase illustrating than it is to implement the recommendation. Obviously, any illustrating should appear natural and spontaneous, and should be timed correctly with respect to the verbal message. However, what if some politicians and company presidents simply do not look natural when illustrating? In some cases, you will see the communicator walking through selected crowds of workers or supporters when the only movement required of him or her is to walk and point. However, if the communicator cannot at least walk with authority (like the president of Chrysler), then the communicator is given a prop to hold—babies or objects from the space program are ideal. An even more extreme example is the "slide show" political advertisement that became popular in the early 1970s. In this innovation, the candidate was seen in actual motion for a brief period of time (if at all) and the bulk of the advertisement dealt with voice-overs using a commanding voice, excerpts from the candidate's previous speeches, or from endorsements. Slides were shown of the candidate

---

To build the perception of *trustworthiness*, the speaker should maintain a high eye-contact rate, nod frequently, smile, display open arms and hands, and employ other behaviors associated with affiliation. The speaker should also avoid exhibiting anxiety related behaviors, and use a conversational style of delivery.

To build the perception of *dynamism*, the speaker should illustrate expansively, move energetically, speak relatively loudly, speak relatively quickly, display greater facial activity and greater intonation. The speaker should also use few nonfluencies, and use a "dynamic" style of delivery, including a greater range of inflections, and varying rate and pitch of speech.

interacting with various target groups. Emphasis was placed on persuasion via the auditory channel.

Eye-contact rate

We concluded that a high amount of eye contact consistently leads to improved performance. Why is this so? What do we mean by "high" amount of eye contact? A number of studies that focused attention solely on the effects of eye-contact rate demonstrate clearly that eye-contact rate is linked to perceived sincerity, trustworthiness, friendliness, and qualification, although not necessarily to dynamism, potency, or dominance.[24] For example, one study found that speakers who averaged 63 percent eye-contact rates were judged as more sincere than speakers who averaged 20 percent. Another had a speaker deliver a speech three times, each time manipulating eye-contact rates: 0 percent, 50 percent, and 90 percent. The results indicated that higher eye-contact rates led to improved ratings on Berlo, Lemert, and Mertz's honesty and qualification factors of credibility, but that the perception of dynamism was unaffected by eye-contact rate. In interview contexts, eye-contact rates were found to be related to perceptions of friendliness—but not to perceptions of dominance, potency, or confidence. Other aspects of the nonverbal code system determine perceptions of confidence, and so on. Clearly, then, when a person maintains a high rate of eye contact, we feel trusting and safe, and we believe he/she is friendly and sincere.

Burgoon and Saine noted that in any interaction, normal rates of eye contact range from 29 percent to 70 percent.[25] Studies indicate that rates of 20 percent to 40 percent are detrimental to persuasiveness, while much more persuasion occurs when eye-contact rates range from 60 percent to 90 percent.

Distance and touching

Increased proximity is associated with intimacy, liking, arousal, and attraction.[26] Similarly, touch is often discussed as one of the most powerful relational messages. Often touch elicits liking from recipients, and is linked to warmth, friendliness, and to love.[27] Thus, one might expect that proximity and touch may influence perceptions of social attractiveness and, thus, enhance persuasiveness. However, there is no simple relationship between proximity and persuasiveness.

First, Mehrabian and Williams found that decreased distance was associated with increased persuasiveness. However, Albert and Dabbs found that attitude change was obtained as distance *increased*.[28] That is, speakers obtained more attitude change when speaking 14 feet away from an audience than at four feet or one to two feet. The more reasonable explanation for these results is that closer approaches (especially one foot) make people defensive and resistant. More recently, however, Ellsworth and Langer, Kleinke, and others have argued that a brief touch during a compliance request elicits arousal and a sense of interpersonal involvement.[29] Staring also elicits arousal. However, the arousal that occurs when a stranger touches or stares at you may indicate either stress or attraction. Thus, there are only certain circumstances in which increased proximity or touching will enhance persuasiveness.

For example, when a request is not ambiguous (compared to an ambiguous or even illegitimate one) a high eye-contact rate or a slight touch on the arm can increase compliance. We may also add that this is true when the request is politely phrased and when the request does not involve a lot of effort or cost for the receiver.

We cannot make precise recommendations about distance or proximity in persuasion, although we can report that two models have been advanced that are worthy of consideration. Patterson proposed a model that focuses on the amount of effort or expense involved in complying.[30] According to Patterson, when a stranger approaches close to you or even touches you, you experience arousal, which can be linked to stress or can reflect arousal associated with involvement and attraction. In this situation, if you were asked to comply with a request that involved little effort or expense (loaning a dime, returning a dime left in the phone booth, briefly letting someone else use the copy machine, or signing a prosocial petition) you would probably comply with a request because of the high involvement (or stress reduction). On the other hand, if the request involved some cost or effort on your part, then having a person stand too close to you will make it harder for you to concentrate. Thus, if persuasion involves effort on the part of the audience, being too close to the receiver may make the receiver defensive.

Burgoon's model focuses attention on normative expectations and the general attractiveness of the speaker.[31] First, all receivers have expectations about how close and far away people will stand from them. You may expect, for example, that your neighbor will stand three and a half feet from you. Now, if you liked your physically attractive neighbor and she moved *closer* than you expected, you would experience heightened arousal (associated with interaction involvement and attraction), and she would become more persuasive. If you disliked the neighbor and she moved closer than you expected, you would experience stress and neither comprehension nor persuasion would increase.

Both of these models have their merits and should be kept in mind when you try to be persuasive or when you watch others trying to be persuasive. For example, it is occasionally amusing to watch eager used-car salespersons move closer toward and then further away from prospective buyers. People in such an occupation must be careful—they want to get closer to be friendly and persuasive, but they cannot stay too close without making the buyer defensive.

Speech fluencies and delivery style

Despite the fact that frequent speech disturbances grate on our nerves, there is no evidence that frequent disturbances reduce the receiver's *comprehension* of material. For instance, Burgoon and Saine cite one dissertation that varied the number of nonfluencies (repetitions, mispronunciations, hesitations) from four to 64 in a two-minute speech and found no decrease in comprehension.[32] In another dissertation, stuttering was found not to affect comprehension. However, frequent nonfluencies can reduce the speaker's credibility. Miller and Hewgill,[33] for example, constructed a number of versions of a speech by varying the frequency of repetitions and vocalized (filled) pauses. A repetition was defined as a repetition of an utterance (example: "For New-uh/Newman, it was. . . ."). (An example of a filler pause: "For uh Newman it was. . . .") Speeches were constructed that contained from 25 to 100 repetitions or pauses. The results were not surprising. Frequent repetitions resulted in a dramatic decrease in competency ratings, resulted in a reduction in perceived dynamism, and resulted in a small reduction in trustworthiness. Frequency of filled pauses had fewer overall effects on credibility ratings; frequent filled pauses led to a reduction in competency ratings and to a small reduction in ratings of trustworthiness. Frequency of filled pauses was weakly associated with ratings of dynamism.

These results are simple to explain. As listeners, we believe that if a person is competent and is speaking in the area of his or her expertise, then the speaker should neither be anxious nor have a difficult time thinking about what to say. Thus, too many nonfluencies lower ratings of competence. Also, a person who is dynamic is extroverted, active, potent, and charismatic—and displaying frequent anxiety-related disturbances is simply incompatible with the expectation of an extroverted speaker. Finally, trustworthiness ratings are only slightly affected by speech nonfluencies because we can still feel safe with a speaker even if he or she stutters or has frequent "ah" speech errors—how many of us question the sincerity of a stutterer or think that a person with frequent "ah" nonfluencies has a hidden or ulterior motive? One variable that is related to trustworthiness is the speaker's style of delivery.

Pearce and others indicate that the speaker's style of delivery influences a wide range of perceptions of the speaker. Pearce and Conklin,[34] for example, hired an actor to record a message either using a dynamic style of delivery or a conversational style of delivery. Conversational delivery involved a relatively smaller range of inflections, a greater consistency of rate and pitch, less volume, and generally lower pitch levels than dynamic delivery. A panel of trained observers judged the conversational speaker as more reasonable, sophisticated, knowledgeable, calm, and sincere, and the dynamic speaker as more emotional, excited, dynamic, and overbearing. When the speeches were played back to students, the researchers found that the conversational-style speaker was perceived as more trustworthy and more friendly and pleasant, while the dynamic speaker was rated as more dynamic. Generally, the students felt that the conversational-style speaker was more of an ideal speaker—he was judged as more attractive, better educated, more professional, more honest, person-oriented, self-assured, and assertive. Pearce and Brommel[35] found that these two delivery styles were significantly related to perceptions of the credibility factors of evaluation, dynamism, and trustworthiness (but not to competence). The results indicate that people found the conversational style of delivery considerably more pleasant and less dynamic than the dynamic style of delivery.

What the Pearce studies indicate is that people have a distinct stereotype of the calm conversational-style speaker and the more active, dynamic speaker, and that people prefer the conversational-style speaker. Neither of these results is surprising. In fact, late-night television reinforces the stereotypes as well as the preference. Johnny Carson (note that we even call him Johnny) is a conversational-style speaker who is popular. At the same time, however, we are bombarded by 30-second advertisements of hyperactive salespersons selling everything from used Vegas to new Veg-o-matics. The preference for the conversational-style is obvious—and not only are conversational-style speakers more pleasing to hear, they are also more likely to be trusted.

However, it is important to note that "conversational" and "dynamic" anchor two extremes, that there are degrees by which one is dynamic,

and that many contexts call for a more conversational style of delivery while others require an increase in dynamism. For example, if you want to convince people that you are dynamic, potent, toughminded, and sufficiently self-assured to turn around the fortunes of Company Dismal, then you would use more of the components of the dynamic style (cues associated with extroversion). But such a style is clearly less appropriate for the PTA or Rotary meetings. It is interesting to note, in passing, that our system of nominating presidential candidates requires that the candidate be effective at both styles—the conversational style in small-town caucuses and the dynamic style at the Jefferson-Jackson banquet or at the convention. Such a system clearly tests the candidates' flexibility in communication skills.

The Pearce studies found that style of delivery was not related to perceived competence. One may ask, aren't there vocal qualities that are related to competence? According to Scherer, London, and Wolf's "voice of confidence" study, the answer to this question is "yes."[36] Scherer et al. hired an actor to record a message using either a confident voice or a doubtful voice—where the confident voice was louder, faster, and contained fewer and shorter pauses than the doubtful voice. Results indicated that the confident voice was perceived as more fluent and more expressive than the doubtful voice. The confident speaker was also perceived as more enthusiastic, forceful, active, dominant, self-assured, and competent. Thus, it would appear that varying pitch and rate (as in the Pearce studies) has less to do with competency ratings than increased rate, loudness, and lack of pauses. Packwood has also found that loudness is related to the persuasiveness of statements made in counseling.[37] However, these studies only indicate that confident and persuasive communicators speak more loudly than doubtful speakers—one should not conclude that loudness leads directly to persuasion. There's obviously going to be some limit at which loudness becomes annoying, distracting, and even provokes hostility.

Speech rate

Most researchers who study the impact of speech rates argue that there exists a range of rates that listeners find acceptable. Once a speaker speaks slower or faster than the lower and upper thresholds, respectively, some less than desirable consequence may occur. Normal speech rates vary from 120 to 195 words per minute (wpm); research has employed rates of 102–111 wpm as slow, 140 wpm as moderate, and 191 wpm as fast. The results of research on rate of speech provide us with three general conclusions.

First, only at extremely fast speech rates does comprehension of material decline. Foulke and Sticht reviewed literature on speed of speaking and comprehension and found that the majority of studies found no significant relationship between the two.[38] When studies did find a significant relationship, faster rates resulted in lowered comprehension. The reason for these results is that speech must be accelerated considerably for there to be a decline in comprehension. The study by Fairbanks, Guttman, and Miron demonstrated this nicely.[39] In this study, the researchers used *compressed speech* methods to alter speech rate. The method of compressed speech increases speech rate by keeping the words on the tape-recording just as intelligible as when originally recorded, but removes brief segments of silence from the recording. This study varied speed of speech to see at what point comprehension declined. They found that even at 282 wpm (twice the normal rate) listeners could still comprehend 90 percent of the message. At 353 wpm the listeners could comprehend only about 50 percent of what was said. Orr similarly found that retention of material did not decline until speed of delivery reached 275–300 wpm.[40] Since normal speech rates vary from 120–195 wpm and radio announcers (who are fairly fast) range from 140–191 wpm, it is obvious that increased speed of delivery has a negative effect on comprehension only at *extremely* fast rates. Also, according to Street and others, speakers who exhibit extremely fast rates may be perceived as equally competent as speakers who use moderate to moderately fast rates, but ratings of how socially desirable the speaker is tends to decrease at extremely fast rates.[41]

The second conclusion is that speakers are considered more competent and socially attractive when speech rates are at moderate to relatively fast levels than at slow levels. In Street's studies, subjects listened to a person describe his summer activities. Listeners heard the speaker describe the activities at a slow rate, a moderate rate, or a fast rate. There was consistent evidence that listeners found the moderate-paced and fast-paced speakers to be more competent and more socially attractive than the slow speaker. These effects, not surprisingly, translate directly into increased persuasiveness. In a study by Miller, Maruyama, Beaber, and Valone, various speeches were made at slow, moderate, or fast speeds.[42] Results indicated that as speed of delivery increased, listeners were persuaded more and rated the speakers as more intelligent, more knowledgeable, and as possessing greater objectivity. Employing different topics and different speech rates, Apple, Streeter, and Krauss found that slower speakers were judged as less truthful, less fluent, and less persuasive than moderate to fast speakers.[43] Clearly, speakers who want to be persuasive must avoid the lower end of the speech-rate continuum.

Third, a person's preference for speech rates is partially influenced by their own speech rate. The Orr study above indicated that people prefer a speed of delivery one and one-half times the normal rate of delivery. It would appear that people can process and prefer to process information at a rate slightly faster than they can produce the information. The research by Street, also noted above, supports this trend. In several studies the listener's own speech rate was obtained by recording the listener as he or she read a statement as "naturally" as possible. Listeners generally rated speakers highest in competence and social attractiveness when the speaker's rates were similar to and up to 50-words-per-minute faster than the listener's. Ratings decreased as the speaker's rate exceeded 75-words-per-minute faster than the listener's own rate. Thus, if a campaign encompasses some areas where people typically speak slowly, or includes a subset of speakers who speak slowly (people speak more slowly, for example, as they age), then some adjustments in recorded messages may be beneficial.

Voice qualities

Although it is right "under your nose," one variable that is often related to success in many contexts, but receives little attention, is your voice quality. There is considerable evidence that we possess vocal stereotypes and use characteristics of the voice to make decisions about others. Addington, for example, has explored seven voice characteristics: thin, breathy, flat, tense, throaty, nasal, and orotund (orotund means that the voice possesses a deep resonating quality).[44] In one study, Addington explored the personality traits associated with the vocal characteristics. The results can be summarized as follows:

Nasality—Increased simulation of nasality by both sexes resulted in a wide array of socially-undesirable characteristics, including reduced intelligence, immaturity, being boorish and boring, and so on.

Breathiness—Increased breathiness on the part of males resulted in the speakers being perceived as younger and more artistic. Increased breathiness on the part of females resulted in the speakers being perceived as more feminine, prettier, more petite, more effervescent, more high strung, and more shallow.

Thinness—Increased thinness on the part of males was not associated with any of the 40 characteristics assessed. Increased thinness on the part of females was associated with immaturity, sensitivity, and a sense of humor.

Flatness—Increased flatness by both males and females resulted in perceptions of being more masculine, more sluggish, colder, and more withdrawn.

Tenseness—Increased tenseness by males led to their being perceived as older and more unyielding. Increased tenseness by females led to the perception of their being more emotional, more feminine, more high strung, and less intelligent.

Throatiness—Increased throatiness by males led to the perception of their being older, more realistic, sophisticated, mature, and well adjusted. Increased throatiness by females led to the perception of reduced intelligence, and their being more masculine, lazier, more boorish, unemotional, ugly, sickly, careless, inartistic, naïve, humble, neurotic, quiet, uninteresting, and apathetic. Female throatiness was related to the appearance of being more cloddish or oafish.

Orotund—Increased orotundity by males led listeners to believe that the speakers were more energetic, healthy, artistic, sophisticated, proud, interesting, and enthusiastic. Increased orotundity by females affected perceptions of increased liveliness, gregariousness, and aesthetic sensitivity, being proud, and also being humorless.

In another study, Addington found that, of these seven characteristics, orotundity is strongly related to perceptions of competence and dynamism (but not to trustworthiness), while throatiness, tenseness, and nasality led to low ratings on all three of the credibility factors. (Also, thinness, flatness, and breathiness were related to moderate ratings—although thinness was related to higher ratings of trustworthiness and increased breathiness was related to low ratings of dynamism.) More recently, Apple, Streeter, and Krauss found that speakers with higher pitch were perceived as less truthful, less emphatic, more nervous, and less "potent" than speakers who had lower pitch.[45] Also, Diehl and McDonald found that both nasal and breathy voices can reduce comprehension, while harsher-sounding voices appear to be unrelated to comprehension.[46] These studies indicate that people form distinct impressions of others from vocal characteristics and, generally, do not like the throaty, tense, or nasal voice.

Some readers may think that vocal characteristics are only a small part of the big picture—that persuasion requires the right combination of bodily movements, paralinguistic features, and so on. While this is true, we must point out that there are many contexts where one's voice is the *only* contact to the audience. In our classes, for example, we occasionally do an exercise where a tape of a telephone request is played to students, politely asking them if they would answer ten questions about student opinions. Different variations of voices have been used over the years, and certain consistencies have emerged: People are quick to agree to the survey if the voice is orotund or if a female uses a breathy voice. Also, consider what the media do with voice qualities—how many "breathy" females are there on situation comedies, how many negative characters have nasal voices, and how many "liars" have higher pitch?

We can summarize the work detailed above by providing four general statements:

1. To appear confident and persuasive, and to be persuasive, a speaker should engage in more eye contact, more smiling, more affirmative head nodding, more gestures (and more forceful gestures), few adaptors, and should not be too relaxed while standing directly in front of his or her audience. Vocally, one should speak quickly and loudly with few pauses (and brief pauses) and speak with few nonfluencies.

2. Many cues associated with affiliation facilitate communication, and a therapeutic climate, when employed by the interviewer. Many cues of affiliation can enhance persuasion in dyadic contexts. However, in more formal or task-oriented contexts, cues associated with extroversion (such as verbal output, fluency, body composure, and confident voice) are more important than cues of affiliation.

3. The perception of trustworthiness can be

enhanced by increasing eye contact, adopting a more conversational style of delivery, and by avoiding the higher pitched voice. Generally, the perception of competence and dynamism can be enhanced by employing a confident voice, speaking more quickly, adopting an orotund voice while avoiding a nasal, throaty, or tense voice, by avoiding cues to anxiety, and by displaying cues associated with extroversion (high energy level, expansive illustrating, and so on). The perception of dynamism can also be enhanced by adopting a dynamic style of delivery.

4. Increased proximity may enhance persuasion if the request requires little thought or effort on the part of the receiver, if the request is legitimate and politely stated, and if the person making the request is attractive.

Cues to deception: identifying the dishonest communicator

Since Watergate, researchers have focused considerable attention on a very specific question concerning nonverbal communication and persuasion—can a person tell when a politician, defendant, witness, bargaining opponent, job applicant, and so on, is engaging in deceit (that is, "intentionally fostering in another a false belief or opinion")? Obviously, if we think a person is lying to us, it is unlikely that he or she will persuade us—and their ratings of credibility will be harmed. Of course, there are a number of physiological means by which one can detect deception, but these require electronic surveillance.[47] The devices are not admissible as evidence in a courtroom, and some are so unobtrusive that they can be used with any simple audio cassette or used over the phone—and have consequently been banned from commercial use in some states. Our interest, of course, rests in the question of whether people can detect deception without the aid of sophisticated machinery.

We all have a stereotype of the "liar," but does this stereotype help in detecting deception? Specifically, the stereotype of the liar is that he or she avoids eye contact, smiles less, engages in more postural shifts, longer response latencies, slower speech rates, increased speech errors, higher pitch, and more speech hesitations (pauses).[48] In sum, liars are considered to be less affiliative, less extroverted, and more anxious than truth tellers. However, possessing a stereotype of the liar does not enable people to detect deception accurately. Generally, people who are untrained in nonverbal communication are moderately accurate at detecting deception on the part of friends and lovers, because we know their idiosyncratic behaviors.[49] However, we want to know which cues produce greater accuracy when we view communicators generally, and we want to know *why* some cues are helpful and others are not.

The single most important contribution to research on deception is the idea that speakers try to control some of their nonverbal behaviors when lying.[50] Ekman and Friesen argue that there are areas of the body that we monitor more closely and use more extensively when communicating. As a consequence, the area of the face is both the most expressive part of our body and the easiest to control. It is high in "sending capacity." On the other hand, adaptors, leg/foot movements, random hand-to-face movements, and so on, go unmonitored, are rarely (if ever) used for intentional communication, and are low in sending capacity. The Ekman and Friesen sending capacity hypothesis simply states that the channels high in sending capacity are less likely to reveal deception. The body should leak more deception cues than the face. (We use the term "leakage" to denote behaviors that reveal our true feeling without our control.) In fact, one study found that when liars had rehearsed their lies, the liars intentionally attempted to maintain eye contact.[51] In another study, liars *increased* eye contact and glanced more frequently at an interviewer who was an "expert."[52] Hence, people can rise to the occasion and control features of the face.[53] While it is true

that some studies may find liars to exhibit reduced eye contact, the typical study indicates that eye behavior is not a reliable or consistent source of leakage (see also Table 7.1 on page 133).

The sending capacity hypothesis has recently been extended to include the audio channel (speech)—under the notion that while we may monitor the words we select to speak, we do not monitor paralinguistic behaviors and we *cannot* control voice stress, and so on. As DePaulo, Stone, and Lassiter indicate, there are two sources of evidence that support the conclusion that the vocal channel is leakier than the body channel, which in turn is leakier than the face.[54] First, DePaulo et al. compared all studies that examined the different channels and found that speech as a single channel consistently led observers to be more accurate than observers who only had access to the body, and that the observers who only had access to the face were the least accurate in detecting deception. Second, DePaulo et al. identified, via statistical analyses, which cues were reliably associated with deception across all of the studies. The results are summarized in Table 7.1. As indicated in Table 7.1, the results indicate that the speech-body-face hierarchy is valid—eight out of eleven vocal cues were significantly related to deception, two out of five body cues were related to deception, and two out of five facial cues were associated with deception. Thus, the area of the face is a very poor place to look if you want to find out if a communicator is being dishonest. As a general rule, the DePaulo et al. results indicate that liars (compared to truth tellers) blink their eyes more, have dilated pupils, shrug more, have shorter messages, have less "immediacy" in how sentences are phrased, have move leveling terms (that is, liars are more likely to overgeneralize—"the usual stuff," "that sort of thing, you know?"), have more speech errors, have higher pitched voices, more speech hesitations, and more irrelevant and negative statements.

What specific cues, then, should an observer emphasize in order to detect liars, and why are specific behaviors "leaked"? To summarize:[55]

1. Liars experience increased *arousal* because of the fear of punishment, because liars know that lying is morally wrong, and so on. Because of the heightened arousal, liars can be detected via electronic surveillance devices. If unaided by such machines, the arousal is indicated by increased *pupil dilation*, more *speech errors,* and higher *pitch*. Note that these behaviors are rarely (if ever) controlled by the speaker.

2. Liars leak cues associated with *uncertainty*. Increased *hesitations* (pauses, especially silent pauses) indicate that the person is thinking about his or her message, while a *shrug*

(hand-arm emblem) likewise denotes uncertainty and difficulty in constructing and delivering the message. Further, liars may provide more *irrelevant statements* or be vague about details because they cannot provide specific or concrete details for events that never took place. Again, it is unlikely that speakers monitor and can control hesitations and shrugs (they simply slip out at certain times), and liars cannot communicate specific details of events that never occurred.

3. Due either to *anxiety* or to *negative affect* (liars have a negative attitude toward the role of "liar"), liars engage in more *adapting*, more

Table 7.1. Behaviors Associated with Deception[a]

Behaviors	*Number of Studies*	*Relationship with Deception[b]*
Facial channel		
Pupil dilation	5	+
Gaze	18	0
Blinking	8	+
Smiling	16	0
Head movements	10	0
Body channel		
Gestures	12	0
Shrugs	4	+
Adaptors	14	+
Foot/leg movements	9	0
Postural shifts	11	0
Speech channel		
Response latency	15	0
Response length	17	+
Speech rate	12	0
Immediacy	2	+
Leveling	4	+
Speech errors	12	+
Speech hesitations	11	+
Pitch	4	+
Negative statements	5	+
Irrelevant statements	6	+
Self-references	4	0

[a] Adapted from DePaulo, Stone, and Lassiter.
[b] A (+) denotes that the behavior is consistently related to deception. A (0) means that the behavior is not consistently related to deception.

negative statements, and more *speech errors* (speech errors are linked both to arousal and to anxiety). As noted above, we do not routinely monitor our adapting.

The general rule, then, for increasing accuracy in detecting deception is to (a) emphasize the leakage that occurs in the voice and in the body while de-emphasizing the face as a source of leakage, and (b) emphasize cues to arousal, anxiety, and uncertainty that are *less* likely to be controlled by the speaker.

Types of lies and types of liars

One of the most common questions asked by students is: Aren't some people better than others at lying? The answer to this question is "yes," although there is no simple relationship between traits of persons and quality of performance in deceit. Some personalities are related to quality of performance in deceit only for certain types of lies. Hence, a brief overview of different types of lies is called for:

1. Amount of preparation.[56] Some studies allow liars time to prepare and rehearse the lie while other studies entrap liars into telling lies when the liar did not know that the particular line of questioning was going to surface (that is, spontaneous lies). There is considerable evidence that when liars are prepared to lie they exhibit short response latencies, engage in less postural shifting and fewer gestures, and provide brief messages that lack spontaneity (the messages *seem* prepared, or rehearsed). Spontaneous lies, however, require the liar to create a message and transmit it off the top of his head—thus, spontaneous lies contain more pauses and nonfluencies, and lack specific detail. In terms of the general rules noted above, being prepared to lie decreases the liar's level of uncertainty while spontaneous lies increase the level of uncertainty.

2. Length of lie/narrative responses.[57] Some lies may be relatively easy to tell because they are relatively short—a "yes" or "no" lie un-

doubtedly reduces the extent to which liars leak clues to deception via speech errors and pauses. However, if a liar had to lie for a full minute or to list activities that occurred during a fictitious event, the liars cannot create as many specific details, and liars speak for a briefer period of time than truth tellers. Liars also leak the fact that they are uncertain by employing more "leveling" or "generalizing" terms, such as "the usual stuff," "stuff like that," "you know," and so on. Further, there is some recent evidence that as liars feel required to give more narrative responses, they sit in very rigid positions. This last outcome may be expected on the grounds that the more you concentrate, the more you freeze your body movement. In terms of the general rules noted above, longer or narrative lies increase the speaker's level of uncertainty.

3. Motivation to lie convincingly.[58] Some studies induce liars to lie convincingly by promising them payment or some type of reward for a quality performance. In the Exline, Thibaut, Hickey, and Gumpert study, liars were implicated in cheating, and successful lying (denying wrongdoing) meant that they would not be reported to the Dean's Office. In other studies, the only incentive to lie convincingly is some extra credit given for class participation. Highly motivated liars (versus less motivated ones) blink less, engage in less head nodding, fewer adaptors, fewer postural shifts, and higher pitch. In terms of the general rules noted above, high motivation increases arousal and the desire not to be detected (thus, liars control more behaviors).

Two personality types have been found to be successful in deceiving others.

One personality type that has received some attention in nonverbal research is the Machiavellian.[59] A high Machiavellian is an individual who manipulates others; low Machiavellians believe that people are good and can be trusted and believe that lying is inexcusable. Evidence to date indicates that high Machiavellians are no better at lying to others than their low Machiavellian counterparts when telling a prepared or rehearsed lie, when there is no motivation to lie convincingly.

However, if sufficiently motivated, high Machiavellians can lie quite effectively. In the Exline, Thibaut, Hickey, and Gumpert study, an elaborate experimental treatment was employed to implicate either the low Machiavellian or high Machiavellian subject in cheating. Later, the experimenter confronted the implicated person. The results indicated that when the experimenter asked if cheating had taken place, high Machiavellians managed to maintain more eye contact than low Machiavellians, and held out longer before confession. More recently, Geis and Moon entrapped either a low or high Machiavellian in a situation that required them to deny knowledge of a theft. Observers rated the high Machiavellian liars as more believable than low Machiavellian liars.

A second personality measure that is related to quality of performance during deception is *self-monitoring*.[60] People who score high on self-monitoring are more knowledgeable about how to manage their behaviors across a wide range of situations and search the environment for cues to know how to behave. Low self-monitors, however, prefer to behave in ways that are compatible with their own beliefs and dispositions, and select persons and situations compatible with their attitudes, and so on. As noted in Miller, deTurck, and Kalbfleisch,[61] the person who possesses greater "knowledge of others" (the high self-monitor) is more accurate in detecting deception, and prepares better than the low self-monitoring individual by finding out as much as possible about the target of the deceptive message. Miller et al. demonstrated that high self-monitors were less likely to be detected than low self-monitors, especially when allowed to rehearse a lie.

Thus, high Machiavellians are more skillful at lying than low Machiavellians when motivated to do so, and appear to be better liars when emotions are involved and when the situation is stressful. High self-monitors are sensitive to situational cues and at adapting to the environment, and benefit more than low self-monitors when preparing to deceive.

We have spent some time discussing the concept of deception detection because it is important in a number of situations—politics, eyewitness or defendant testimony, selling, bargaining, and so on. Lawyers may want to "read" nonverbal communication effectively in order to estimate the possible weaknesses in depositions or in courtroom testimony, journalists may want to identify fabrications on the part of politicians, and so on. As these studies indicate, individuals trying to detect deception are well advised to *listen* closely to what is being said and to watch what the speaker does with his or her body. However, the reader should also realize that if a liar is well prepared and has rehearsed a lie, then it might be difficult to detect the lie in some liars. One needs to keep in mind the kind of lie a liar is telling, as well as the personality of the liar, in order to become an effective lie detector.

Summary

In this chapter we have concentrated on the ways in which aspects of the nonverbal code system either aid the speaker or distract from the speaker's effectiveness. We have discussed the terms used to describe gestures and movements, and have surveyed the types of paralinguistic cues. We reviewed studies that linked specific aspects of the nonverbal code system to speaker effectiveness and persuasiveness and offered four general conclusions that linked nonverbal behaviors to positive evaluation. Generally, there are a number of nonverbal behaviors that lead to enhanced evaluations consistently across public speaking contexts and interviews, and there are cues associated with extroversion and with affiliation that can be used to advance the image appropriate to the context and to the speaker's intentions. However, behaviors associated with anxiety generally lead to a reduction in the speaker's effectiveness. Also, there are a number of variables one must take into consideration if one plans to use physical proximity as an aid to persuasion. Finally, we have noted that accuracy in detecting deception may be enhanced if observers pay closer attention to the auditory channel and to the body channel and de-emphasize the importance of the face as a source of information. We have noted the specific behaviors observers should emphasize if they are to be accurate decoders, that the type of lie people tell influences which of the behaviors one is likely to observe, and that some people are better liars in some contexts.

Footnotes

1. J. Burgoon and T. Saine, *The Unspoken Dialogue: An Introduction to Nonverbal Communication* (Boston: Houghton Mifflin, 1978).

2. M. L. Knapp, *Nonverbal Communication in Human Interaction,* 2nd edition (New York: Holt, Rinehart and Winston, 1978).

3. M. L. Patterson, *Nonverbal Behavior: A Functional Perspective* (New York: Springer-Verlag, 1983). Also consult: R. Heslin and M. L. Patterson, *Nonverbal Behavior and Social Psychology* (New York: Plenum, 1982); and C. Mayo and N. M. Henley, *Gender and Nonverbal Behavior* (New York: Springer-Verlag, 1981).

4. J. M. Wiemann and R. P. Harrison, eds., *Nonverbal Interaction* (Beverly Hills: Sage, 1983).

5. R. L. Birdwhistell, *Kinesics and Context* (Philadelphia: University of Pennsylvania Press, 1970).

6. P. Ekman and W. Friesen, "The Repertoire of Nonverbal Behavior: Categories, Origins, Usage, and Coding," *Semiotica,* vol. 1 (1969), pp. 49–98.

7. H. G. Johnson, P. Ekman, and W. V. Friesen, "Communicative Body Movements: American Emblems," *Semiotica,* vol. 15 (1975), pp. 335–353.

8. A. Kendon, "Gestures and Speech: How They Interact," in J. M. Wiemann and R. P. Harrison, eds., *Nonverbal Interaction* (Beverly Hills: Sage, 1983), pp. 13–46.

9. D. Morris, P. Collett, P. Marsh, and M. O'Shaughnessy, *Gestures: Their Origins and Distribution* (New York: Stein and Day, 1979). Also consult: M. R. Key, *Nonverbal Communication: A Research Guide and Bibliography* (Metuchen, N.J.: Scarecrow Press, 1977); M. R. Key, *Paralanguage and Kinesics* (Metuchen, N.J.: Scarecrow Press, 1975).

10. W. G. Woodall and J. P. Folger, "Encoding Specificity and Nonverbal Cue Context: An Expansion of Episodic Memory Research," *Communication Monographs,* vol. 49 (1981), pp. 39–53; W. G. Woodall and J. P. Folger, "Nonverbal Cue Context and Episodic Memory: On the Availability and Endurance of Nonverbal Behaviors as Retrieval Cues," *Communication Monographs,* vol. 52 (1985), pp. 319–333.

11. G. L. Trager, "Paralanguage: A First Approximation," *Studies in Linguistics,* vol. 13 (1958), pp. 1–12.

12. G. F. Malh, "Disturbances and Silences in the Patient's Speech in Psychotherapy," *Journal of Abnormal and Social Psychology,* vol. 53 (1956), pp. 1–15; G. F. Malh, "Measuring the Patient's Anxiety During Interviews From 'Expressive' Aspects of Speech," *Transactions of the New York Academy of Sciences,* vol. 21 (1959), pp. 249–257; S. V. Kasl and G. F. Mahl, "The Relationship of Disturbances and Hesitations in Spontaneous Speech to Anxiety," *Journal of Personality and Social Psychology,* vol. 1 (1965), pp. 425–433.

13. A. W. Siegman and B. Pope, "Effects of Question Specificity and Anxiety-Producing Messages on Verbal Fluency in the Initial Interview," *Journal of Personality and Social Psychology,* vol. 2 (1965), pp. 522–530; A. W. Siegman, "The Telltale Voice: Nonverbal Messages of Verbal Communication," in A. W. Siegman and S. Feldstein, eds., *Nonverbal Communication* (Hillsdale, N.J.: Lawrence Erlbaum, 1978), pp. 183–243.

14. R. G. Harper, A. N. Wiens, and J. D. Matarazzo, *Nonverbal Communications: The State of the Art* (New York: Wiley, 1978).

15. F. Goldman-Eisler, *Psycholinguistics: Experiments in Spontaneous Speech* (New York: Academic, 1968); Siegman, "The Telltale Voice."

16. For example, Miller and Burgoon refer to *extroversion* and *involvement,* to *relaxation* and *positivity,* and Cappella employs the terms *animated, aroused,* and *involved.* See G. R. Miller and J. K.

Burgoon, "Factors Affecting Assessments of Eyewitness Credibility," in N. L. Kerr and R. M. Bray, eds., *The Psychology of the Courtroom* (New York: Academic, 1982), pp. 169–194; J. N. Capella, "Conversational Involvement: Approaching and Avoiding Others," in J. M. Wiemann and R. P. Harrison, eds., *Nonverbal Interaction* (Beverly Hills: Sage, 1983), pp. 113–148.

17. A. Mehrabian and M. Williams, "Nonverbal Concomitants of Perceived and Intended Persuasiveness," *Journal of Personality and Social Psychology,* vol. 13 (1969), pp. 37–58.

18. M. B. LaCrosse, "Nonverbal Behavior and Perceived Counselor Attractiveness and Persuasiveness," *Journal of Counseling Psychology,* vol. 22 (1975), pp. 563–566.

19. C. Maslow, K. Yoselson, and H. London, "Persuasiveness of Confidence Expressed via Language and Body Language," *British Journal of Social and Clinical Psychology,* vol. 10 (1971), pp. 234–240.

20. T. V. McGovern, "The Making of a Job Interviewee: The Effect of Nonverbal Behavior on an Interviewer's Evaluations During a Selection Interview," *Dissertation Abstracts International,* vol. 37 (1977), pp. 4740B–4741B; D. M. Young and E. G. Beier, "The Role of Applicant Nonverbal Communication in the Employment Interview," *Journal of Employment Counseling,* vol. 14 (1977), pp. 154–165; R. J. Forbes and R. P. Jackson, "Nonverbal Behavior and the Outcome of Selection Interviews," *Journal of Occupational Psychology,* vol. 53 (1980), pp. 65–72; see also Patterson, *Nonverbal Behavior;* A. S. Imada and M. D. Hakel, "Influence of Nonverbal Communication and Rater Proximity on Impressions and Decisions in Simulated Employment Interviews," *Journal of Applied Psychology,* vol. 62 (1979), pp. 295–300; C. D. Claiborn, "Counselor Verbal Intervention, Nonverbal Behavior and Social Power," *Journal of Counseling Psychology,* vol. 26 (1979), pp. 378–383; P. V. Washburn and M. P. Hakel, "Visual Cues and Verbal Content as Influences in Impressions Formed After Simulated Employment Interviews," *Journal of Applied Psychology,* vol. 58 (1973), pp. 137–141.

21. Mehrabian and Williams, "Nonverbal Concomitants."

22. Mehrabian and Williams, "Nonverbal Concomitants." See also studies concerning effective interviewing.

23. J. G. Holandsworth, Jr., R. Kazelskis, J. Stevens, and M. E. Dressel, "Relative Contributions of Verbal, Articulative, and Nonverbal Communication to Employment Decisions in the Job Interview Setting," *Personnel Psychology,* vol. 32 (1979), pp. 359–367; S. R. Strong, R. G. Taylor, J. C. Bratton, and R. G. Loper, "Nonverbal Behavior and Perceived Counselor Characteristics," *Journal of Counseling Psychology,* vol. 18 (1971), pp. 554–561; see also M. L. Patterson, *Nonverbal Behavior.*

24. J. Wills, "An Empirical Study of the Behavior Characteristics of Sincere and Insincere Speakers" (dissertation, University of Southern California, Los Angeles, 1961); S. A. Beebe, "Eye-Contact: A Nonverbal Determinant of Speaker Credibility," *Speech Teacher,* vol. 23 (1974), pp. 21–25; J. M. Wiemann, "An Experimental Study of Visual Attention in Dyads: The Effects of Four Gaze Conditions on Evaluations by Applicants in Employment Interviewing" (paper presented to the Speech Communication Association Convention, Chicago, 1974).

25. Burgoon and Saine, *The Unspoken Dialogue.*

26. For an excellent review, consult J. K. Burgoon, D. B. Buller, J. L. Hale, and A. deTurck, "Relational Messages Associated with Nonverbal Behaviors," *Human Communication Research,* vol. 10 (1984), pp. 351–378.

27. The effects of being touched by strangers is a complicated matter; see R. Heslin and T. Alper, "Touching: A Bonding Gesture," in J. M. Wiemann and R. P. Harrison, eds., *Nonverbal Interaction* (Beverly Hills: Sage, 1983), pp. 47–75.

28. S. Albert and J. M. Dabbs, "Physical Distance and Persuasion," *Journal of Personality and Social Psychology,* vol. 15 (1970), pp. 265–270.

29. P. C. Ellsworth and E. J. Langer, "Staring and Approach: An Interpretation of the Stare As a Nonspecific Activator," *Journal of Personality and Social Psychology,* vol. 33 (1976), pp. 117–122;

C. L. Kleinke, "Compliance to Requests Made by Gazing and Touching Experimenters in Field Studies," *Journal of Experimental Social Psychology,* vol. 13 (1977), pp. 218–223.

30. Patterson, *Nonverbal Behavior.*

31. J. K. Burgoon, "Nonverbal Violations of Expectations," in J. M. Wiemann and R. P. Harrison, eds., *Nonverbal Interaction* (Beverly Hills: Sage, 1983), pp. 72–112.

32. Burgoon and Saine, *The Unspoken Dialogue;* H. M. Klinger, "The Effects of Verbal Fluency upon the Listener" (dissertation, University of Southern California, 1952).

33. G. R. Miller and M. A. Hewgill, "The Effect of Variations in Nonfluencies on Audience Ratings of Source Credibility," *Quarterly Journal of Speech,* vol. 50 (1964), pp. 36–44.

34. W. B. Pearce and F. Conklin, "Nonverbal Vocalic Communication and Perceptions of a Speaker," *Speech Monographs,* vol. 38 (1971), pp. 235–241.

35. W. B. Pearce and B. J. Brommel, "The Effects of Vocal Variations on Ratings of Source Credibility," *Quarterly Journal of Speech,* vol. 58 (1972), pp. 298–306.

36. K. R. Scherer, H. London, and J. J. Wolf, "The Voice of Confidence: Paralinguistic Cues and Audience Evaluation," *Journal of Research in Personality,* vol. 7 (1973), pp. 31–44.

37. W. T. Packwood, "Loudness As a Variable in Persuasion," *Journal of Counseling Psychology,* vol. 21 (1974), pp. 1–2; and K. Valone, "Speed of Speech and Persuasion," *Journal of Personality and Social Psychology,* vol. 34 (1976), pp. 615–624.

38. E. Foulke and T. G. Sticht, "A Review of Research on the Intelligibility and Comprehension of Accelerated Speech," *Psychological Bulletin,* vol. 72 (1969), pp. 10–19.

39. G. Fairbanks, N. Guttman, and M. Miron, "Effects of Time Compression Upon the Comprehension of Connected Speech," *Journal of Speech and Hearing Disorders,* vol. 22 (1957), pp. 10–19.

40. D. B. Orr, "Time Compressed Speech—A Perspective," *Journal of Communication,* vol. 18 (1968), pp. 288–292.

41. R. L. Street, Jr., and R. M. Brady, "Speech Rate Acceptance Ranges as a Function of Evaluative Domain, Listener Speech Rate and Communication Context," *Communication Monographs,* vol. 49 (1982), pp. 290–308; R. L. Street, Jr., R. M. Brady, and W. P. Putnam, "The Influence of Speech Rate Stereotypes and Rate Similarity on Listeners' Evaluations of Speakers," *Journal of Language and Social Psychology,* vol. 2 (1983), pp. 37–56; B. L. Brown, W. J. Strong, and A. C. Rencher, "Perceptions of Personality from Speech: Effects of Manipulations of Acoustical Parameters," *Journal of the Acoustical Society of America,* vol. 54 (1973), pp. 29–35.

42. N. Miller, G. Maruyama, R. J. Beaber, and K. Valone, "Speed of Speech and Persuasion," *Journal of Personality and Social Psychology,* vol. 34 (1976), pp. 615–624.

43. W. Apple, L. A. Streeter, and R. M. Krauss, "Effects of Pitch and Speech Rate on Personal Attributions," *Journal of Personality and Social Psychology,* vol. 37 (1979), pp. 715–727.

44. D. W. Addington, "The Relationship of Selected Vocal Characteristics to Personality Perception," *Speech Monographs,* vol. 39 (1971), pp. 242–247.

45. Apple, Streeter, and Krauss, "Effects of Pitch and Speech Rate."

46. C. F. Diehl and E. T. McDonald, "Effect of Voice Quality on Communication," *Journal of Speech and Hearing Disorders,* vol. 21 (1956), pp. 233–237.

47. For a recent review of polygraph techniques, consult W. M. Waid and M. T. Orne, "Cognitive, Social, and Personality Processes in the Physiological Detection of Deception," in L. Berkowitz, ed., *Advances in Experimental Social Psychology,* vol. 14 (New York: Academic, 1981), pp. 61–107.

48. J. E. Hocking and D. G. Leathers, "Nonverbal Indicators of Deception: A New Theoretical Perspective," *Communication Monographs,* vol. 47 (1980), pp. 119–131; B. M. DePaulo, J. I. Stone, and G. D. Lassiter, "Deceiving and Detecting Deceit," in B. R. Schlenker, ed., *The Self and Social Life* (New York: McGraw-Hill, 1985), pp. 323–370; M. Zuckerman, B. M. DePaulo, and R. Rosenthal, "Verbal and Nonverbal Communication

of Deception," in L. Berkowitz, ed., *Advances in Experimental Social Psychology,* vol. 14 (New York: Academic, 1981), pp. 2–60.

49. M. E. Comadena, "Accuracy in Detecting Deception: Intimate and Friendship Relationships," in M. Burgoon, ed., *Communication Yearbook 6* (Beverly Hills: Sage, 1982), pp. 446–472.

50. P. Ekman and W. V. Friesen, "Nonverbal Leakage and Clues to Deception," *Psychiatry,* vol. 32 (1969), pp. 88–106; P. Ekman and W. V. Friesen, "Hand Movements," *Journal of Communication,* vol. 22 (1972), pp. 353–374; P. Ekman and W. V. Friesen, "Detecting Deception from the Body or Face," *Journal of Personality and Social Psychology,* vol. 29 (1974), pp. 288–298; Hocking and Leathers, "Nonverbal Indicators of Deception."

51. J. K. Matarazzo, A. N. Wiens, R. H. Jackson, and T. S. Manaugh, "Interviewee Speech Behavior Under Conditions of Endogenously-Present and Exogenously-Induced Motivational States," *Journal of Clinical Psychology,* vol. 26 (1970), pp. 141–148.

52. S. S. Fugita, M. C. Hogrebe, and K. N. Wexley, "Perceptions of Deception: Perceived Expertise in Detecting Deception, Successfulness of Deception and Nonverbal Cues," *Personality and Social Psychology Bulletin,* vol. 6 (1980), pp. 637–643.

53. When liars lie about emotions, however, they may not be able to put on a full face of joy, sadness, or whatever. Some research indicates that liars may have "miserable" smiles and display "asymmetrical" faces of emotion—that is, a smile may be held more fully (and for a longer duration) on one half of the face—the strong side—than the other half of the face. Interested readers should consult: P. Ekman and W. V. Friesen, "Felt, False, and Miserable Smiles," *Journal of Nonverbal Behavior, 6* (1982), pp. 238–252; J. C. Hager and P. Ekman, "The Inner and Outer Meanings of Facial Expressions," in J. T. Cacioppo and R. E. Petty, eds., *Social Psychophysiology* (New York: Guilford Press, 1983), pp. 287–306; H. A. Sackeim and R. C. Gur, "Facial Asymmetry and the Communication of Emotion," in J. T.

Cacioppo and R. E. Petty, eds., *Social Psychophysiology* (New York: Guilford Press, 1983), pp. 307–352.

54. DePaulo, Stone, and Lassiter, "Deceiving and Detecting Deceit."

55. Some authors have proposed six categories of behaviors that may distinguish the liar from the truth teller. We have decided to list here only a few that seem to be consistently related to deception across studies. The interested reader should read M. L. Knapp, R. P. Hart, and H. S. Dennis, "An Exploration of Deception as a Communication Construct," *Human Communication Research,* vol. 1 (1974), pp. 15–29; also Miller and Burgoon, "Factors Affecting Assessments of Eyewitness Credibility." Besides the three types of lies listed here, one study has compared truthful responses with lies of emotions and lies of factual statements. Unfortunately, not a sufficient amount of research has been done concerning the difference between lying about feelings and facts. Consult J. E. Hocking, J. Bauchner, E. Kaminski, and G. R. Miller, "Detecting Deception Communication from Verbal, Visual, and Paralinguistic Cues, *Human Communication Research,* vol. 6 (1979), pp. 33–46.

56. Concerning prepared lies, consult M. J. Cody, P. J. Marston, and M. Foster, "Paralinguistic and Verbal Leakage of Deception as a Function of Attempted Control and Timing of Questions," in R. M. Bostrom, ed., *Communication Yearbook 7* (Beverly Hills: Sage: 1984), pp. 464–490; J. O. Greene, H. D. O'Hair, M. J. Cody, and C. Yen, "Planning and Control of Behavior During Deception," *Human Communication Research,* vol. 11 (1985), pp. 335–364; G. R. Miller, M. A. deTurck, and P. J. Kalbfleisch, "Self-Monitoring, Rehearsal, and Deceptive Communication," *Human Communication Research,* vol. 10 (1983), pp. 97–118; H. D. O'Hair, M. J. Cody, and M. L. McLaughlin, "Prepared Lies, Spontaneous Lies, Machiavellianism, and Nonverbal Communication," *Human Communication Research,* vol. 7 (1981), pp. 325–339.

57. Concerning longer or narrative lies, consult R. E. Kraut, "Verbal and Nonverbal Cues in the

Perception of Lying," *Journal of Personality and Social Psychology,* vol. 36 (1978), pp. 380–391; Cody, Marston, and Foster, "Paralinguistic and Verbal Leakage"; Zuckerman, DePaulo, and Rosenthal, "Verbal and Nonverbal Communication of Deception."

58. R. V. Exline, H. Thibaut, C. B. Hickey, and P. Gumpert, "Visual Interaction in Relation to Machiavellianism and an Unethical Act," in R. Christie and F. L. Geis, eds., *Studies in Machiavellianism* (New York: Academic, 1970), pp. 53–73; Zuckerman, DePaulo, and Rosenthal, "Verbal and Nonverbal Communication of Deception."

59. R. Christie and F. L. Geis, eds., *Studies in Machiavellianism* (New York: Academic, 1970); O'Hair, Cody, and McLaughlin, "Prepared Lies, Spontaneous Lies"; Knapp, Hart, and Dennis, "An Exploration of Deception"; F. L. Geis and T. H. Moon, "Machiavellianism and Deception," *Journal of Personality and Social Psychology,* vol. 41 (1981), pp. 766–775.

60. M. Snyder, "Self-Monitoring of Expressive Behavior," *Journal of Personality and Social Psychology,* vol. 30 (1974), pp. 526–537.

61. Miller, deTurck, and Kalbfleisch, "Self-Monitoring."

CHAPTER EIGHT

Structuring Messages and Appeals

In the two previous chapters, we noted that ideas can be expressed with different words from the same language code, and that nonverbal code elements can enhance or detract from the reception of an intended message. Messages, however, do not exist as single words or gestures. Messages are created through placement of single words into larger units (sentences, paragraphs, sections, and chapters). Each message could have many different structures, depending on where a particular sentence is placed, or how a chapter is organized. Are there more effective and less effective ways of organizing messages? Do some types of message structures have greater impact on receivers than others? Our first concern in this chapter will be to examine various ways of organizing messages. Our second concern deals with the problem of maximizing the effectiveness of the *appeals* that are

used in the message so that receivers will agree with the message. Should the source appeal to rationality? Or should the source try to scare receivers into agreeing with the message? Are there other appeals that would be effective with an audience?

Message organization

There is ample evidence to support the statement that *some* kind of organization is essential in a speech or an article. There are a number of studies that compare organized messages with disorganized messages in terms of their relative effectiveness. Petrie[1] examined a series of speech studies. He concluded that the evidence was inconclusive;

some studies showed that organized messages produced more retention of the speech materials, while others concluded that organization made no significant difference in retention. In two early studies, Kenneth Beighley came to somewhat conflicting conclusions.[2] In a review of the literature on *written messages,* however, Beighley found clear evidence that comprehension is greater for organized than for disorganized structures in messages.[3] More recently Eagly[4] took a speech and made three versions, *high comprehensibility, medium comprehensibility* (sentences were halved and reordered in a random fashion), and *low comprehensibility* (the words were randomized). Receivers who heard the comprehensible version were persuaded more and recalled more arguments about the topic.

The effect of organization on both retention and attitude change has been examined. Thompson[5] found that individuals listening to an organized message retained more of the material but that organization of a message did not seem to affect the amount of attitude change that occurred. Darnell,[6] on the other hand, using a written message, found that it took a great deal of disorganization of a message before retention was affected, but that even minimal amounts of disorganization affected attitude change. Darnell's results were confirmed by Kissler and Lloyd in a more recent study.[7] Sencer[8] manipulated the number of grammatical errors in a series of messages, and found that adding grammatical errors did not seem to affect learning, but did adversely affect attitude change.

To this point, we have simply asked how receivers responded to the materials or to the topic of speeches presented in organized versus disorganized fashion. McCroskey and Mehrley asked an equally important question. They asked whether the nature of the *source* would have any impact on receivers' responses to message organization. Their findings showed that a speaker who presented an organized message was seen as more credible than a speaker who presented a disorganized version. This is an important finding. Since we know that credibility is related to persuasibil-

ity, we should expect more credible sources to elicit greater attitude change than the less credible sources.

If some organization is preferable to no organization, the next question is whether there are any patterns or arrangements of material that are more effective than others. The most general principle we can mention deals with expectations: *Do not violate the expectations of your audience.* This principle, as stated by Burgoon and Miller,[10] rests on the assumption that receivers come to expect certain basic types of structure for messages they are exposed to. If we present our persuasive messages using familiar patterns, we may have some confidence that rejection of the message will not be due to its organizational structure. There are a number of familiar organizational patterns that have been used with success in communication:

1. Space pattern. In this pattern, the source organizes material in terms of geography or space. For example, in talking about the necessity for further increases in the efforts of the federal government in helping solve our population problems, the communicator might make an outline dividing the topic into sections that would cover the major areas in the United States. Such a basic outline might have five major sections:

  I. Problems in the eastern states
 II. Problems in the midwestern states
III. Problems in the southern states
 IV. Problems in the Far West
  V. Problems in Alaska and Hawaii

In each section of the message, the source would then proceed to discuss some of the specific problems associated with each area, and how federal effort might help alleviate the problem. Our example is simple, but the same plan can be used for more complicated material. Audiences find this type of organization to be familiar, and the communicator will seldom violate expectations with a space outline.

2. Time order. In this familiar pattern, the persuasive communicator outlines a sequence of events leading up to the problem as a historical background against which the proposed solution is judged. An editorial writer, arguing for the development of a mass transportation system as a way of alleviating the energy crisis, might organize materials as:

    I. The use of multipassenger vehicles—trolleys and buses—in the nineteenth and twentieth century.
   II. The development of the automobile in the twentieth century.
 III. The decline of mass transportation between 1945 and 1980.
 IV. The necessity for redevelopment of mass transportation in the 1980s.

A time order is useful when some problem has a clear history. A caution should be issued to the source who plans to use this particular organizational pattern. There is some danger that the source will get so wrapped up in the history that the persuasive message will fail to be received by the audience. The time order and the use of a historical approach is a convenience, and should not be the major thrust of the speech. All a time order does is to suggest that when a problem has a history, attention to that history may provide a useful organizational pattern.

3. Deductive order. In this organization, the communicator proceeds from a set of general statements to more specific materials or suggestions. In practice, the writer of an editorial might outline a number of areas on which general agreement is expected. Then the message is concluded by calling for some action that seems to follow logically from the earlier agreements.

    Note that in a deductive arrangement, the communicator engages in persuasion at each step of the way. The source has to get audience agreement on each of the major statements before asking for agreement on the final statement. The use of a deductive arrangement is based on the assumption that by agreeing to a series of more general statements, the receiver will find it easy to agree to a more specific proposition as the con-

cluding statement. In order for this chain of reasoning to be effective, the source must be careful to show the relationship between the general cases or statements that appear in this message and the specific final proposition.

4. Inductive order. An inductive arrangement attempts to let the reader or listener "reason with" the communicator. The communicator presents a number of specific examples and waits until the end of the message before drawing a conclusion. The following sentence outline illustrates an inductive arrangement.

    I. Pittfield has a public swimming pool and a low juvenile-delinquency rate.
   II. Omio has a new pool, and their juvenile delinquency has dropped drastically.
 III. Sunfield had two people killed in drag-racing accidents, built a new pool, and has had few problems since.
 IV. Therefore, if New Berlin were to build a pool, it could also reduce its delinquency problems.

This example represents an inductive pattern of organization, with an *explicit* drawing of the conclusion. At times, the communicator will give the audience a number of examples, but will allow the audience to draw the conclusion for themselves. This can be referred to as an *implicit* conclusion. For example, a political speaker may refer to the poor record the incumbent has generated, but never say the incumbent should be turned out of office. Obviously, there is a danger in using an implicit conclusion. The audience will probably draw a conclusion, but may *not* draw the conclusion intended by the speaker. In the case of the political speaker, the audience may decide not to vote for the incumbent, but may also decide not to vote for the person making the speech but for a third party. A conclusion was drawn, but not the one intended. The best advice to the communicator is to use the implicit method of organization only in those situations where the conclusion to be drawn is completely obvious to the audience. In most cases, the inductive or indirect organizational pattern should involve an explicit drawing of the conclusion.

5. Psychological organization.

Monroe and Ehninger suggest that organization be based on what they term the "motivated sequence," as a succession of steps that would lead a receiver through the same steps that the receiver might employ in making a decision.[11] They suggested that such a process would have five steps:

    I. Attention
    II. Need
    III. Satisfaction
    IV. Visualization
    V. Action

The "Motivated Sequence" is one of the most famous and successful ways of approaching the task of preparing a speech. First suggested by Alan Monroe in the mid 1930s, it has never actually received systematic testing in a research situation. It has, however, served literally millions of students from all walks of life as an organizing principle in the preparation of messages. Thus it seems a particularly appropriate one for the persuasive communicator to use in many communication situations. For example, imagine that the speaker wishes to convince an audience of the necessity for a new program of family planning. In the attention step, the source might point to the tremendous increase in population that the world is experiencing. In the need step, the speaker points out that current family-planning efforts are failing to have any effect on reducing population. In the satisfaction step, the speaker might point out that the new system of family planning would have a positive effect on a reduction of population as it has had in Japan. In the visualization step, the communicator outlines exactly how the plan would work. And, finally, the speaker will outline exactly what actions the audience might take to bring the new system into effect as a national policy.

The example we have used allows us to look more closely at each of the steps in this pattern, and to specify exactly what the source does for each step. The *attention* step is designed to prepare the audience for the message. Here, the communicator presents any materials that would serve to make the receiver aware of the problem and become interested in the problem. After all, just why should I be interested in listening to a speech on overpopulation? Unless the speaker does something that makes me interested, it is likely that I will simply turn off whatever the speaker is saying.

In the *need* step, the source presents any material that demonstrates exactly why there is a problem, and why we need to do something about the problem. There are many topics about which people can speak. Persuasion occurs every day, and most of us are bombarded with persuasive messages. Unless a source can tell us why this is an important problem, and just why we should do something about the problem, there is little reason for a receiver to be concerned.

The *satisfaction* step is the point in the message where the communicator tells the receiver that a proposed solution will work. In the example we have used, the speaker points to the results that were obtained when the solution was used in another country. The speaker could also have used statistics from research studies or from small trials here in the United States. The argument behind this type of reasoning is that audiences are not inclined to be persuaded about a potential solution unless they can see that the plan might work. Obviously, one of the best ways of making that demonstration is by showing that a similar plan has worked elsewhere.

The *visualization* step is the point in the message where the source tells the audience exactly how the plan would work. This might be done by simply suggesting that a law be passed, or it might require the presentation of a elaborate plan of work. If the source does not go through this step, the audience is being asked to accept a proposal with no indication of exactly how the proposal would work.

Finally, the *action* step tells the audience exactly what the speaker wants them to do. It may be to vote for a piece of legislation. It may be to write their congressman. But the action step gives the audience member something to do. Perhaps this step is the most important addition to persuasion that Monroe contributed. Speakers and writers for centuries have made suggestions to their audiences. Monroe was one of the first to recognize that the action step must be an integral part of almost every successful persuasive speech. What seems to be at work is involvement on the part of the receivers. People react more favorably to persuasion if they can be made to feel involved in the topic. One way to obtain involvement is to be able to propose some kind of activity that a receiver can do after being convinced of the merits of the proposal.

There are other organizational patterns based on the ways in which receivers are supposed to attack problems. Such patterns, like Monroe's "motivated sequence," can prove extremely useful to the persuasive communicator.

6. Problem-solution structure.

This is another popular and familiar type of organization. The communicator first details the nature of the problem, and then proceeds to discuss the steps that ought to be taken to solve the problem. An outline for a message organized in this fashion might be as follows:

I. We have had a number of riots in our community.
II. These riots are apparently located in areas where most individuals have low incomes and few opportunities for normal recreational activities.
III. When teenagers and young adults cannot participate in ordinary recreational activities, they are likely to make trouble.
IV. Perhaps we can solve some of our problems by passing a bond issue for a new park and a new swimming pool within the low-income area of the city, with free access for all residents.

Again, the problem-solution pattern of organization is one used frequently in persuasive communication, since many persuasive speeches suggest changes in attitude or action based on the existence of a specific problem.

7. The Toulmin pattern.

A pattern of message organization that is increasingly popular is based on an analysis of the way in which people actually make decisions. Stephen Toulmin, a British philosopher, suggested in his book *The Uses of Argument*[12] that people make decisions in everyday life based on a fairly limited number of argumentative patterns. Since his initial formulation, several people have extended his work into more elaborate schemes of argumentative analysis and message organization (cf. Ehninger and Brockriede,[13] Windes and Hastings,[14] and Bettinghaus[15]). In this section, we present only a simple organizational pattern appropriate to persuasion in order to illustrate this useful approach.

Figure 8.1 presents the Toulmin pattern in a basic form, and utilizes only three of the six elements that Toulmin describes. By *evidence,* we mean any data, observations, personal opinions, case histories, or other materials that are relevant to the issue under consideration. The *claim* is the statement that the communicator wishes people to believe, or the action that is desired. And the *warrant* is the linking statement between the evidence and claim. It is a statement showing why people ought to accept the source's conclusions. In the very simple argument below, each of these elements is present.

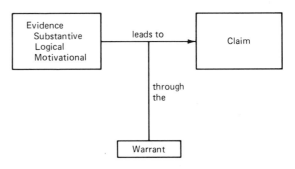

Figure 8.1. Basic Toulmin Model

The Federal deficit in the United States has risen almost to the 200-billion-dollars-a-year level. (*evidence*) During the next fiscal year, we absolutely must cut federal spending by at least 75 billion dollars (*claim*) because the high deficits will lead us into a renewal of inflation and another recession. (*warrant*)

Obviously, one could take these three simple statements and expand them into a lengthy speech by adding more evidence, expanding the claim into a specific plan, and adding support for the warrant so that the connection between the claim and evidence will become clear.

Toulmin would argue that his pattern of argument is valuable because it represents the way in which people actually think. We change our beliefs because someone asks us to, and in the asking gives both evidence and a reason for the change.

One of the advantages of the Toulmin method of message organization is that it allows even complex arguments to be analyzed and placed into an effective message form.

Figure 8.2 illustrates a more complex message, and one that makes use of all six of the elements that Toulmin identified. The more complex model presented in Figure 8.2 introduces three additional elements that need definition. By a *qualifier,* we normally mean the use of some adjective that softens or modifies the claim. In the sample we used, we could add a qualifier to the claim by saying, "We must cut government spending by *approximately* 75 billion dollars a year." Adding a qualifier may make it easier for a receiver to accept the claim. A *reservation to the claim* simply sets out any limitations that the source wishes to place on the claim. It sets the conditions under which the claim should or should not be accepted. Using the same example, we could add a reservation to the claim by rewriting it, "We must cut government spending by approximately 75 billion dollars a year, unless we find that Russia has drastically increased the size of their defense budget." By adding the last clause, the source suggests that there may be conditions that would make it impossible to accept the claim. Finally, the element *support for the warrant* adds material that adds further justification for the use of the warrant in linking evidence and claim. Again, using our example of inflation, the phrase ". . . since federal deficits allow too much money to be put into circulation" would be support for the warrant. Warrants can be supported by historical data, or statistical materials, or analogies from other situations. Support for the warrant helps to strengthen the warrant and make it more believable.

We began our discussion of the Toulmin approach to organization with a simple example, using only the three elements that Toulmin says are essential to any argument. Now let us use that same argument, but expand the argument to use all of the Toulmin elements:

The Federal deficit in the United States has risen almost to the 200-billion-dollars-a-year level. (*evidence*) The balance of payments deficit between the United States and our trading partners will account for at least 50 billion dollars of that amount. (*evidence*) Because of these facts, we must cut spending by the Federal government by at least 75 billion dollars a year, (*claim*) unless we find that the Soviet Union has drastically increased the size of their defense and that we might fall behind the Soviets in defense preparations. (*reservation to the claim*) Such a cut in spending is necessary because huge Federal deficits lead to higher interest rates (*sup-*

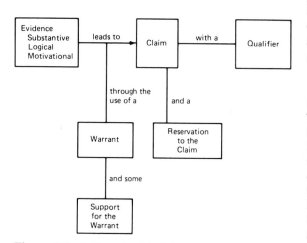

Figure 8.2. A Complex Model

port for warrant) and thus to a renewal of inflation and another recession. (*warrant*)

This message looks more complicated, but it consists of just the six elements that Toulmin identifies. You can take this message and diagram it in exactly the same form illustrated in Figure 8.2. Furthermore, the source could expand this short message into a much longer speech either by using a series of similar arguments, or by adding even more evidence in support of the claim.

Although there is little conclusive evidence of a scientific nature regarding the relative effectiveness of any of the patterns of organization discussed above, there is no justification in concluding that there is no research relating to message organization. There is, but the research available has not directly tested the patterns discussed. Instead, a number of questions that relate to several kinds of arrangements have been studied. These include: Where should the longest or the best arguments be placed within the persuasive message? Are people affected by the use of logical structures or patterns? Should persuasive messages present both sides of an issue or only the side that the source advocates? In discussing these questions below, the point must be emphasized that the answers to these questions may affect all the patterns we have already mentioned.

Order effects

Most messages will have more than one piece of evidence to support a given conclusion and more than one section in the entire speech. The communicator faces a decision regarding the placement of these materials. Some elements will be regarded as more persuasive than others, some sections will be longer than others. Is it more persuasive to place the most important materials at the beginning of the message, in the middle, or should the most important materials come at the end of the message?

One line of research deals with the order of the most important elements. The research model that is frequently employed presents messages having the same topic, but differing arrangements, to comparable audiences, and then sees which audience has the most response. The assumption is that if the messages all use the same topic, and if the audiences are actually comparable, any differences in response among the audiences must be due to the different types of order that the messages utilize. A *climax order* places the most important materials last; an *anticlimax order* arranges the most important materials first; and a *pyramidal order* places the most important materials in the middle of the message, with less important materials both first and last. The research has demonstrated a *primacy* effect if the material placed first in the message has the greatest effect. It is a *recency* effect if the element positioned last in the message has the most effect.

The study with the most complete design and analysis is by Gulley and Berlo,[16] who used organizational patterns of climax, anticlimax, and pyramidal structures in a series of persuasive speeches. Their results suggested that either climax or anticlimax orders are preferable to pyramidal orders. The data from their study show that the climax order was consistently slightly more effective than anticlimax order, but since the differences between the two forms were not statistically significant, we are really not justified in using the difference to support a recency hypothesis.

Years of research on order effects indicates, first, that the pyramidal order should be avoided, and, second, that primacy effects are often observed. However, the more important issue is whether we can predict *when* there will be a recency effect or a primacy effect. According to Rosnow and Robinson[17] one is more likely to observe a primacy effect when the topic is of interest to the receivers, materials are familiar to them, issues are seen as relatively unimportant, and the speech deals with controversial topics. In settings such as these, the receiver's interest in listening to the speech and level of attention is first high and then tends to decrease over a length of time; thus, the receiver attends more, comprehends more, and retains more from the beginning of the presentation than at the middle or end. More recently, a legal expert named Lind[18] reviewed communication principles as they apply to courtroom contexts and concluded that primacy effects may be observed when the receiver's primary goal is to make a decision about a particular person's character. This conclusion is compatible with work on interpersonal communication—work that suggests we make first impressions of others in the first few minutes of contact with them. The explanation for primacy effects according to this second conclusion is that we *normally* make quick decisions about others. These conclusions are rich in implications concerning persuasion. For example, in court cases dealing with a person's character (after being charged with embezzlement, and so on) one should emphasize early what will transpire in the court (the opening statements discussed briefly in Chapter 6) and move quickly to convince jurors that the defendant is a moral and trustworthy individual.

When will a recency effect be observed? According to Rosnow and Robinson[19] a recency effect is more likely to be observed when uninteresting topics are used, when receivers are unfamiliar with the issues, and when issues are seen as important. Under these conditions the receiver may be expected to attend to all of the message, since (1) the receiver feels the need to attend to all of the message in order to make an informed choice, and (2) the receiver probably expects to hear a summary statement that may help him or her to formulate a decision on matters of an unfamiliar nature. Lind[20] also notes that recency effects are more likely to be observed when the receiver is focusing on general issues, rather than on the specific issue of a speaker's character. Thus, one would expect courtroom cases where lawyers debate finer points of law and evidence to produce more recency effects.

Not all of the studies conducted have obtained a significant difference in persuasion that could be attributed to order effects. In fact, the majority of studies probably indicate no effect owing simply to the order of presentation. Why? Order of presentation is only one variable that operates on the receiver's attention, interest, memory, and yielding to messages. Certainly advertisers cannot worry about whether their advertisement is first or last in a series of advertisements. Instead, if a persuasive communicator does not know the order in which she or he will speak, then other tactics can and should be implemented in order to be persuasive. For example, one can make a message distinctive by making it novel or vivid, or one can make a message memorable by relying on vividness or by including jingles or slogans. Rhetorical questions could be used throughout a presentation to keep interest high; and different delivery styles may be used. Multiple sources communicating multiple messages may be especially helpful, since it appears that receivers listen to each new speaker with a fresh and open mind (see Chapter 3). Finally, research evidence indicates that strong evidence is more important than all of these other variables in legal settings and strength of evidence can completely wipe out any order effect.

In sum, primacy effects might be expected for some topics and events/recency effects might be expected in evaluating general issues or more unfamiliar and unusual issues. Given these trends, the persuasive communicator can adjust his or her approach to persuasion accordingly. On the other hand, a persuasive communicator should realize that a host of variables can be used to wipe out any effect owing only to order of presentation.

One-sided versus two-sided messages

For almost all persuasive communication situations, there will be those in favor of a course of action and those who are against any type of change. Also, there are arguments that can be used to support either side of a proposition. Should you vote in favor of a constitutional amendment reinstating the death penalty? Should you vote for or against a particular proposition? There are reasons for and against each decision. Most voters will reach a decision based on messages they hear from both sides of the position. If you were a speaker advocating a position, would you use the approach where you presented materials from only one side of the issue, or would you present both sides of an issue and advocate that one stand is better than the other?

Hovland, Lumsdaine, and Sheffield[21] conducted the first study on message sidedness when investigating propaganda during World War II. They constructed one message that was a straight presentation of materials arguing for the proposition supporting war with Japan, with no mention of the possibility of materials existing in support of the other side. A second message was constructed that presented arguments in favor of war with Japan, but also made specific mention of arguments from the other side. The two-sided presentation stressed only the side on which most of the material had been presented.

The study concluded that the one-sided presentation was more persuasive for men with lower educational attainment. For men with at least some high-school education the two-sided presentation was more effective. The one-sided presentation was also slightly more effective for men who had originally been in favor of the view expressed in the message, apparently serving as a reinforcing stimulus in this case.

A second study conducted by Lumsdaine and Janis[22] added another major finding to the literature in this area. They found that receivers who were in initial agreement with the position that was advocated in the message were more persuaded by the one-sided message, while those people who were initially opposed to the intent of the original message were more persuaded by the two-sided message. Thus, one might argue that if the persuasive communicator knows that the audience is in favor of the message, time and money do not have to be spent on mention of opposition arguments.

One factor that is extremely important in attempting to make a decision about whether to include opposing materials in a message is the extent to which the opposing side has received coverage in the mass media. Hovland, Lumsdaine, and Sheffield conducted their study during the middle of World War II. No television existed and any information that did reach the population as a whole was rather carefully controlled. Furthermore, the educational level of the population was significantly lower than it is today. If there is a strong chance that the audience members will either have information about the opposing sides, or if there is a strong chance that they will become aware of opposing arguments, then a two-sided message should be presented.[23] To do otherwise is to run the risk that audience members will later find out about the opposing side, and reject the communicator because no mention of it was made.

The studies considering the effect of message sidedness all suggest that this variable tends to interact with a set of other variables. Commitment, level of education, and prior information all interact with message sidedness. The research to date can be summarized by saying:

1. Two-sided messages seem to be preferable for audiences with higher educational levels, although the obtained differences are not supported in all studies.

2. Two-sided messages seem to be preferable when the audience initially disagrees with the communicator's position.

3. Two-sided messages seem to be preferable when there is a possibility that the audience will be exposed to messages opposing the source's position.

4. One-sided messages are more effective when the receiver is already in agreement with the source, *provided* that the receiver is not likely to be exposed to later opposing messages.

5. Prior attitude and commitment may interact with sidedness, tending to cover up the potential effects of message sidedness.

Considering all the problems that a source might have in attempting to deliver a one-sided message, perhaps the best advice is to be willing to acknowledge to your audience that there *are* opposing arguments. A church evangelical meeting, a meeting of a political party, or the advertisement of a product that is known to be extremely well liked are among the situations where a one-sided message might be effective.

The reader will also note that comparison advertising (one brand name product compares itself favorably with a competitor) has grown tremendously in the last several years, and now represents close to one-third of the print advertisements in leading magazines (up from 10 percent of all advertisements in the mid-1970s).[24] Also, virtually one-third of the comparison print ads relied on scientific evidence or research in making and advocating their favorable comparisons—apparently reflecting the belief that readers are smart consumers who pay attention to economics and to strong evidence. The comparison print advertisements contain more overall information than noncomparison print advertisements, and, because they aid the consumer and because they are likely to be persuasive, we will probably see even more comparison ads. However, we are not likely to see "category leaders" (that is, the companies with larger sales in the product area, such as IBM, and so on) use such comparison ads. Research indicates that comparative advertising by a challenger results in increased brand similarity between the challenger and leader;[25] and, by implication, whenever a brand leader mentions a challenger, the brand leader not only makes the challenger look more similar to the leader, but also gives the challenger free publicity. For example, no IBM personal computer advertisement mentions other brands by name, but all challengers make it a point to say they are just as good as an IBM, or that they are IBM compatible.

Logical arrangement in messages

Inductive and deductive patterns of organization have already been discussed. Presumably, receivers ought to respond to logical patterns, recognize their validity, and be more influenced by messages that are organized in either inductive or deductive arrangements. The research evidence, however, indicates that logical arrangement, or the use of formal logical structures within messages as proof units, is not necessarily persuasive.

In an early study, Knower's[26] results suggest that original commitment to the topic is a far more important variable than is the organizational pattern into which messages are cast.

Classic syllogisms such as the following have been used in a number of studies to test the effectiveness of logic upon judgments.

> All men are mortal.
> Socrates is a man.
> Therefore, Socrates is mortal.

Lefford[27] showed that when people are asked to judge the validity of syllogisms, the mistakes they make are likely to be in the direction of the bias they hold toward the concluding statement of the syllogism.

The Lefford results seem to hold up even when the subjects are given training in how to judge syllogisms. Bettinghaus and Swinney[28] asked a group of students to indicate their attitudes about a set of 30 statements relating to current events and student affairs. They then received training in how to judge the validity of syllogistic structures. One week later, they were again asked to judge the validity of a set of syllogisms that used the 30 statements as concluding statements. Training helped, but when the students made mistakes, they were almost always in the direction of the students' biases.

Feather[29] shows that the tendency to accept or reject the conclusions of formal syllogisms is related positively to the strength of attitude a receiver has toward a conclusion. Bettinghaus, Miller, and Steinfatt[30] show that there is more attitude change when the syllogism is attributed to a positive source than when it is attributed to a negative source. In a subsequent study, Steinfatt, Miller, and Bettinghaus[31] suggested that the more complex the syllogistic arrangement was, the more errors people were likely to make in judging validity. The error rate seems more dependent on complexity than on prior belief, but having logical arguments did not prove to have a positive effect.

Most studies of the effect of logical arrangement or the use of logical forms in persuasion show that receivers are frequently not able to make accurate judgments between logical and nonlogical arguments. In a review of the studies in this area, Miller[32] concluded that receivers have a tendency to accept arguments that the rules of formal logic would judge as invalid.

Why, then, do we tell communicators that having logical arrangement of messages is beneficial? It is a simplistic answer to say that logic does not make a difference. There is some merit in having the *appearance of logic* in a persuasive message, even if there is little merit in actually making sure that the materials are arranged in such a way as to ascertain their validity. In an unpublished study, Bettinghaus attempted to test this hypothesis. Two audiences listened to a persuasive speech. For one audience, each argument was introduced by, "Isn't it only logical that . . . ," while the other audience heard exactly the same speech except that it contained no cues to indicate that the speaker thought the speech was logical. The results showed a small but significant difference in favor of the speech having its arguments labeled as logical. What seemed to be operating was a feeling by audience members that "logic" ought to be a desirable thing. Stewart[33] argues that people have at least a general idea as to what constitutes a logical argument, while Cronen and Mihevic[34] suggest that our belief in the importance of logic is strong enough that we will mentally find a logical structure for illogical arguments if we are in agreement with the illogical argument's conclusion.

It is very doubtful that many communicators have the training or the inclination to produce speeches or messages that include arguments arranged according to a strict logical pattern that would be valid in a formal sense. There is evidence, however, which indicates that communicators would exercise good judgment if their messages and the arguments within the messages are made to *appear* logical, even if they cannot be easily tested.

Number of arguments in messages

One question that frequently arises from students of persuasive communication is whether it is better to concentrate on presenting a small number of arguments in favor of a position, or whether it might be more effective to present all possible arguments to the receiver. This question has been addressed in two types of research areas: quality versus quantity of arguments, and repetition of message components. The first issue was discussed in Chapter 3, when we discussed the fact that strong arguments are needed in order to persuade the receiver who is highly issued-involved in the topic. If receivers are less involved (and therefore are less motivated to think about each piece of evidence or argument), then messages are more likely to be persuasive if the messages *appear* to contain a lot of arguments. Note, of course, that for some advertised products advertisers are not "persuading" us per se to drink beverages, since we are going to drink some type of beverage *habitually* already. Instead, advertisements either simply attempt to get us to recall a brand name or attempt to elicit from us a particular emotional response (see later section in this chapter). Thus, the three-word sentence "Coke is it!" can hardly be construed as "persuasive" since it is ambiguous at best. However, when vividly photographed beautiful people sing the words and dance to upbeat music, the receivers are supposed to *like* the product more. The soft-beverage industry does not need to persuade us to buy colas, only to like and eventually buy one particular brand.

Another consideration the persuasive communicator needs to keep in mind is the receiver's expectations. If we think we are going to hear a speech by an "expert," then we expect to hear evidence and we are not going to be persuaded if an expert does not provide evidence. On the other hand, if we listen to a good-looking person we might be persuaded moderately—whether the speaker uses evidence or not. These trends were demonstrated in a study by Norman.[35] Norman had half of his subjects read a message that simply advocated that people sleep less. The other half also read three-and-a-half pages of additional arguments. Half of the subjects were led to believe that the communicator was an attractive speaker; half were told the speech was from a leading expert on sleep research who had published books on the area of sleep and its functions. Norman's results showed that when the source was perceived to be an "expert," adding arguments significantly improved the amount of attitude change obtained from the receivers. But when the source was physically attractive, it didn't make any difference whether there were added arguments or not. The results of this study clearly show the importance of the receiver's expectations—if an expert gives a speech, the more arguments presented the better. If, on the other hand, the persuasive communicator plans to change attitudes by relying on attractive sources, then the issue of the number of arguments is less relevant—Norman found that attractive sources without arguments elicited a moderate attitude change and that only a small and nonsignificant additional amount of attitude change was observed when the attractive source used many arguments.

How frequently should you repeat part of your message? In advertising Krugman[36] has recommended that the number three is magical. In fact, the typical commercial aimed at children repeats some slogan or brand name 3 to 4 times every 30 seconds. Research by Miller,[37] Grass and Wallace,[38] Ray, Sawyer, and Strong,[39] Ray and Sawyer,[40] Greenberg and Suttoni,[41] Gorn and Goldberg,[42] and others has provided us with a wealth of information about repetition in advertising. Repetition aids in consumer learning, but repeatedly showing the same advertisement results in saturation or satiation where the advertisement reaches "wear-out." In a typical case, a viewer who sees the same ad three times in an evening will get

bored with the advertisement in due time, but the advertisement may still be effective in influencing receivers' attitudes if the particular advertisement does not cross over a "wear-out threshold" or "satiation point." Continued exposure to the advertisement will result in receivers hating the ad. Research shows that in any single viewing (one hour or one evening), one showing of an advertisement is less effective than three airings of the advertisement—but that five advertisements provide no benefit beyond that which was achieved by three airings. Another study[43] indicated that when viewers were exposed to the same commercials from 4 to 24 times over an eight-week period interest gradually increased and peaked at 15 exposures and then declined after 15 exposures (which is, of course, seeing the advertisement twice an evening).

Here are some general conclusions about repetition and persuasion, the first two dealing with effects of repetition, the rest with ways to extend the wear-out threshold:[44]

1. Repetition aids consumer learning.
2. Repetition helps to establish new products or brands.
3. A group or pool of commercials should not wear out as fast as a single commercial given the same overall frequency of exposure.
4. Only *good* commercials wear out. A commercial that was ineffective to start with cannot lose what it never had.
5. Commercials wear out faster among those who are heavy TV viewers.
6. If the number of commercials to be produced is limited, one might consider using a subtle approach in the few commercials that can be made in order to lengthen the learning process.
7. Several commercials are frequently produced on a single creative theme, and the rate that the commercials will wear out does not depend as much on the actual numbers produced and aired as on the viewer perception of how similar or dissimilar they are. In other

words, one ad may be made that repeats a basic slogan or set of concepts ("Don't want to spend a lot of money," "Don't want fast food," and "Don't have a lot of time"), and a second ad may be made that also repeats the verbal component, but is sufficiently different from the first advertisement so that exposure to the first advertisement doesn't also make receivers tired of the second advertisement.

8. Commercials whose single point of humor is a gag or punch line tend to wear out more quickly than commercials relying on a narrative approach.

9. Commercials for infrequently purchased products have a longer life because there is a natural turnover in the market in terms of receivers who attend to the messages.

10. The greater the time span between commercial airings, the longer the single commercial can run.

11. Commercials can be removed and later reintroduced, but their second airing will wear out faster than the first. An added bonus occurs, of course, when particular advertisers re-run Christmas advertisements during the holidays. Since the average person has had happy and joyful Christmases in the past, such airings can also capitalize on generating positive feelings among receivers.

12. Commercials that involve the viewer have a longer effective life than commercials that simply present a straightforward product story. Thus, commercials with children clapping hands, dancing, challenging them to repeat what is on the hamburger, work to extend the wear-out threshold. Also, advertisements with varied and active backgrounds help to extend wear-out—as in the advertising campaign for a famous type of low-calorie beer.

Persuasive communicators should keep in mind that receivers benefit from hearing a message more than once but tire of hearing a message more than three times in any given block of time. To extend wear-out, the persuasive communica-tor can rely on subtler forms of humor, vary the background, increase receivers' participation, or rely on different versions of the same basic message.

Message appeals

As a general rule, the mere presentation of data and statistics is not sufficient to change a receiver's attitude or behavior. Some incentive or appeal must be used to get the receiver to stop smoking, to get a dental check-up, to switch brands of tooth-paste, and so on. We have already discussed the role of appeals in earlier chapters when we mentioned how to persuade certain types of indi-viduals or groups (Chapters 3 and 4). Most of the appeals we have discussed so far are what we call *reward appeals*. These types of appeals suggest some benefit the receiver will derive if she or he complies with the speaker's request. Rogers,[45] for example, found that monetary rewards increased the rate of voluntary vasectomies (useful in popu-lation control) in several Asian countries. The use of money, coupons, discounts, and the like are economically based rewards that tell receivers how they can benefit financially. Also, rewards include praise, social approval, a plaque for "worker of the month," and other personally important benefits. These types of appeals are useful in persuasion if used on the appropriate audience members and if audience members do in fact value the offered rewards.

A second type of appeal is called the *motiva-tional appeal*. Motivational appeals are a class of *learned motives*. Many textbooks on public speak-ing or persuasion will suggest that the speaker appeal to the receiver's sense of fair play, or to patriotism, humanity, religion, values, or any one of the many motives for action that seem to affect people. The few studies that have attempted to look at the value of appealing to learned motives, however, have reported very inconclusive results. It seems that these motives are highly dependent on the specific individual. For one person in an audience, patriotism might be an extremely important motive and she or he will react favorably to an appeal based on patriotism. Another person in the same audience may not be moved favorably by appeals to patriotism.

For motivational appeals to work, the persuasive communicator needs to know his or her audience. A message by President Reagan about religion and prayer in school would get a mixed reaction if played on network television—but on Christian Broadcast Network the political advertisement would be extremely effective and would help motivate the Christian viewers to show up at the poll sites the following Tuesday for the election. You may not be able to motivate a group in the eastern part of town to help with a fund drive—but knowing they are Catholic, getting the endorsement of the Knights of Columbus, and then appealing to family togetherness and to a sense of belonging may improve results (see Chapter 4).

A third type of appeal is called the *emotional appeal,* and we have not talked much about this type of appeal until now. Emotional appeals attempt to persuade receivers to take a course of action by playing on their feelings of fear, guilt, happiness, pride, warmth, nostalgia, or other feeling states. A common practice is to compare emotional appeals with logical appeals, and over the years the term "emotional appeals" has taken on a negative meaning. Some readers, when hearing the term "emotional appeals," think back to the days of the "Red Scare" in America when Americans feared Russian spies had infiltrated our country; they think about photographs of aborted fetuses used in antiabortion campaigns; they think about mudslinging political campaigns; or they think about a dynamic speaker condemning the behavior of some disliked group. True, some emotional appeals are irrational and are despicable from an ethical point of view. However, researchers and advertisers have found that a number of emotionally oriented messages can be constructed that are well-liked by receivers and effective at achieving certain goals helpful to the persuader.

Because of these positive outcomes, we have witnessed a tremendous growth in advertisements that are humorous, that appeal to our feelings of warmth (pride, love, affection, and so on), and that are exciting. Thus, we need to talk about how and why emotionally oriented advertisements work. Second, we will look at the research on humor, warmth, and fear.

Emotional appeals

We typically pay little attention to advertisements. Only when we are involved in a topic do we attend to one message out of a stream of messages from our radio or television, and only when we are involved in a topic do we bother to put out the energy to comprehend sentences in the message, to respond or elaborate cognitively on what is said, and to retain the information in long-term memory. For example, if I wanted to buy a computer printer for my home and was involved in checking advertisements and comparing prices, I would be very attentive to the one radio advertisement on computer printers I hear while driving to work—but I would totally ignore the advertisement for the BMW that preceded the commercial and totally ignore the advertisement for deodorant that followed. Yet, aren't these two *extremes*? Isn't there a middle ground between total concentration and totally ignoring stimuli? There are different stages by which we attend to varying stimuli, and we need to know what these stages are in order to understand fully why the humorous and "warmth" advertisements work the way they do.

In Chapter 3 we introduced the idea of the issue-involved receiver, and at that time we talked about whether receivers were involved or not involved with a particular issue. Now it is time to make finer distinctions than just high versus low involvement. According to Greenwald and Leavitt[46] four levels of involvement exist:

preattention—at this stage receivers perform some habitual behavior but are not aware of what they are doing. Example: Persons may hum a jingle or a slogan, but not be aware that they are doing so.

focal attention—at this stage the receiver gives minimal amount of attention to a given message out of all the incoming stimuli. Receivers pay attention to and process *sensory* material and focus on colors, music, novelty, laughter, and so on. They do not, however, process the words that are being said. Example: A person looks up to see beautiful people on a "Coke is it!" advertisement.

comprehension—at this stage the receiver attends to the message and attends to the verbal content. The receiver is interested in who says the message and whether the content of the message is agreeable to him or her. Example: A receiver listens to a message about three women trying to decide where to eat lunch, and they "Don't want fast food" and "Don't want to spend a lot of money." The receiver comprehends these sentences.

elaboration—at this stage the receivers generate their own thoughts about what they are hearing, they think about themselves in view of what the message is saying, they list favorable and unfavorable thoughts about what is being said, and they think about the message more critically. Example: When you are in the market for a computer printer, you attend to the message and inquire whether the asking price is a good one, what accessories you need, where the maintenance work is done, and so on.

For any given topic, persuasive communicators cannot assume that any large percentage of receivers will be involved sufficiently to engage in *elaboration*. At the other extreme, if you made messages and transmitted them to receivers and they never responded beyond the *preattention* level, then you will fail miserably because your message will have no lasting effect. What the typical persuasive communicator needs to do, then, is to make a message that at least achieves focal attention levels. The communicator must at least make messages that gain the receiver's attention to

sensory data. Next, the persuasive communicator must make a message that is simple to comprehend and where repetition is frequent. Why? Receivers do not focus much attention on verbal content when the advertisement is audiovisual, and receivers do not elaborate on verbal content when *any* emotional message is used—whether the emotion is humor, warmth, or fear. Thus, simple easy-to-comprehend messages are used to increase the chance that simple slogans will be stored in long-term memory ("Coke is it!"). These steps, along with making receivers feel positive and happy, will create advertisements that gain attention, make an impression, and create positive attitudes toward both the product and the commercial itself.

There are a number of desirable consequences that stem from emotional advertisements that induce either focal attention or comprehension levels of involvement.[47] Four will be mentioned here. First, and most obviously, emotional advertisements grab our attention. Emotional displays (laughter, voices, background music, and noises) grab our attention when we drive to work because we will tune in to hear something funny or dramatic. Also, considerable work[48] indicates that people selectively filter out information that is discrepant from the mood they are currently experiencing—suggesting that when millions of viewers tune into evening comedy shows they are likely to tune out boring advertisements, confusing advertisements, and irritating advertisements. They are likely to attend selectively to commercials with feelings. Commercials using humor, that portray human pride and warmth, that show excitement, are likely to be the ones attended.

Second, when we experience emotional responses to an advertisement, it is possible that we do not counterargue the verbal message. That is, if we were issue-involved to the point of reaching the elaboration stage, then we might list unfavorable thoughts about message content (along with favorable thoughts). However, if we watch, listen, and experience happiness by one advertisement, the excitement of another, and the feeling of pride by a third, we are likely to be experiencing the *feelings,* not thinking about the truthfulness of statements A through M, or looking for weak or poor arguments. Remember, the focal attention stage is where we attend to *sensory* material—we think about *verbal content* only at the comprehension and elaboration levels. Just what is meant by "Catch the wave!," "Coke is it!"? Consider the warmth/sympathy advertisement where the wife cannot sleep because she loves her husband so much and her life is so perfect. What does the husband do? He makes a pot of coffee! The idea is that if you sympathized with the woman portrayed, then you won't bother to be critical of content or story line.

Third, emotional advertisements are more likely to be vividly portrayed than "logical" ones, and are more likely to use all available channels in order to create successful emotional responses. Music, giggles, laughter, clinking glasses, facial displays, colors of soft tans, browns, and soft reds all help to communicate intimacy in a bar setting, with people flirting and having an exciting time. If you identified with the story line and put yourself into the picture, then you should have a positive attitude toward the beer or the wine cooler that is being advertised.

Fourth, creating a positive attitude toward the commercial and a product may be an important goal in and of itself, since doing so may make it difficult for competitors to attack the advertiser's claim. McDonald's has spent millions of dollars over the years to create and maintain the image that it is fun to eat at McDonald's. There are parties, singing, and dancing, young persons on dates, everyone at McDonald's is happy—even the meals for children are called "Happy Meals." Competitors may challenge the claim that the French fries are special or that the food is prepared freshly. Competitors may offer lower prices on some products for limited times. However, it would be very hard to change people's impressions, especially younger people, that it is fun to eat at McDonald's.

Given benefits such as these it is not surprising that the manipulation of emotions is one of the most popular means by which to persuade consumers in the last several years. Here, we will

briefly discuss the effects of two positive emotional appeals, humor and warmth, and then we will discuss fear appeals.

Humor

Humor may not be able to change people's attitudes or overcome resistance on the part of issue-involved receivers, but humor does have a place in persuasion. According to one survey of advertising experts,[49] advertisers have distinct ideas about when humor might be used appropriately: Humor can be used to draw attention to a product, it may help aid name recall and aid in the recall of simple copy (but not complex copy), it may aid in the retention of material, in persuading consumers to switch brands, and in creating a positive mood that may enhance persuasion. Humor is not very effective in bringing about action/sales—that is, it may not be able to prompt receivers to get out of their chairs and drive someplace to buy a product. However, humor can be used, perhaps, to get receivers to try a new brand of chip or soft drink (switch brands) once the receiver is in the store. Consumer nondurables and business services are best promoted by humor, while corporate advertisements and industrial products are least served by the use of humor. Humor should be related to the product, should not be used with sensitive goods or services, and is more appropriately used with younger, better educated, upscale, male, and professional receivers than with older, less educated receivers. Finally, radio and television are better suited to humorous advertisements than print media and direct mailing advertisements.

Research conducted in the last several years supports some of these claims. Lammers, Leibowitz, Seymour, and Hennessey[50] conducted a study where they used either a humorous message or a serious one and assessed attitudes either immediately after the receivers were exposed to the messages or after a time delay. They found that in the *delayed* measure humor produced more positive responses than did the serious message. The idea here is that a serious message usually produces an impact immediately upon reception, and then the effects start to decay as receivers forget; serious advertisements quickly reach the elaboration stage of involvement. On the other hand, since we enjoy the experience of being in a good mood, we spend more time reflecting on the humorous material and some of the effect of humor occurs over time. That is, first we *experience* humor and then later we think about the advertisement (that is, reach an elaboration stage). Also, Lammers et al. found that men generated more favorable thoughts about the product, but that women thought of more counterarguments. This finding, that men are more susceptible to humor, supports the advertisers' beliefs in the survey noted above, and is compatible with research that shows men are more likely to tell jokes and appreciate humor than are women.[51] In a more recent study, Aaker, Stayman, and Hagerty[52] found that humorous advertisements were better recalled than "warmth" advertisements or irritating advertisements.

Not every study on the effects of humor have found that humor is a successful means of persuading others. In fact, ten years ago we would have concluded that humor does not aid in persuasion, or, more precisely, that humor is not useful in persuading receivers about serious topics. The research indicates that a combination of topics (food, beverages, other types of consumable goods), mediums (television or radio), and receivers (young professional males) probably provide the ideal situation for successful persuasion using humor. As a general rule, however, it seems to be the case that humor can gain our attention, we often recall humorous better than nonhumorous material, we tend to be less resistant to persuasion when humor is used, we may think less critically about humorous advertisements, and we may think longer about a message if we experience a pleasant mood.

Warmth

Although "warmth" advertisements have been used for years, only recently have researchers focused attention on the operation of this construct in persuasion. Aaker and Bruzzone[53] associated warmth with sentimental feelings, the "feel-good-about-yourself" type of advertisement, and with advertisements dealing with friendships and feelings. An empathy appeal, according to Schlinger,[54] involves affectionate couples, warm relations, mother-child interactions, attractive products, vacation settings, and appealing characters. Some persuasive communicators would also consider appeals to one's sense of pride also to reflect a "warm" advertisement. These advertisements have increased in frequency over the years because they can be effective. They are effective because receivers identify with the portrayals (even though what is seen seems idealized) either because they like to "relive" a situation or because what is shown to them is an event they'd like to happen to them. The advertised products are wine, photography companies, coffee companies, telephone companies, and some restaurants.

A growing body of literature on warmth in advertising provides us with five overall conclusions, although the systematic research has only just begun in this area:

1. Warmth conveyed via characterizations of family reunions, loving relationships, sympathy, and the like are strongly related to galvanic skin responses—meaning that receivers do in fact experience a sense of arousal when viewing these commercials.

2. The experience of warmth during these advertisements changes quickly and substantially during viewing. That is, some advertisements are better equipped at creating and maintaining higher levels of warmth for an entire 60 seconds, while others show a dramatic tapering off of warmth.

3. Warmth in advertising is strongly associated with liking for the advertisement. Receivers seem to like watching advertisements that capitalize on feelings of love, pride, affection, and the like. As a general rule, warmth in advertising also results in more positive attitudes toward the products, and with intentions to buy the products.

4. Some studies (but not all studies) suggest that warmth in advertising is related to increased recall of message content (compared to logical advertisements or irritating advertisements). This issue of recall, however, is rather complex. First, for warm advertisements material should not be complex. In fact, the general rule of thumb for all messages relying on emotions, whether they be fear, humor, or warmth, is not to use complex material. Second, what is recalled from an advertisement depends partially on the sequence of presentations.

5. Ratings of liking for an advertisement, likelihood of purchasing the product, and recall of the content of the message depend on the type of appeal used and the sequence in which advertisements are shown. The Aaker et al. study cited above examined the impact of irritating advertisements, warm advertisements, and humorous advertisements. Generally speaking, humorous advertisements received higher recall of content (followed by warm advertisements), and both warm advertisements and humorous advertisements received high ratings of purchasing intention and liking for the advertisement. However, there were substantial differences in how an advertisement was judged depending upon when the ad was shown. That is, there were contrast effects—indicating that an irritating ad was judged as less irritating when the ad followed immediately behind an earlier irritating ad, a humorous ad wasn't quite as favorably received if it followed immediately after another humorous advertisement, and a warm ad wasn't quite as favorably received if it followed immediately after a warm advertisement. Persuasion was aided when advertisements were mixed—one a humorous advertisement, the second a warm advertisement.

Despite these rather complex contrast effects, there can be little doubt that the warmth concept can be very successful in persuasion—at least for some topics and when used on some people. Un-like humor, where a survey of experts gives us some rules of thumb about expectations concerning how to use the approach appropriately, no clear-cut guidelines are available yet for saying precisely when the persuasive communicator might best use a "warmth" appeal. At the moment it seems that any product dealing with interpersonal relationships might be sold using a warmth appeal—things people share (wine, coffee, family reunions, and so on) and things that are used in communicating between friends. Since this appeal works when the receiver identifies with what is portrayed, we can also infer some effects due to receivers. That is, advertisements that deal with family reunions, old friends who stay in touch, younger women calling "daddy" from college, and so on, seem to appeal to those receivers who desire a sense of belonging, while the advertisement of the professional woman proudly taking her husband out to dinner to break in her American Express card appeals more to the professional career woman than to any other type of woman (see Chapter 4).

Fear appeals

More research has been done on the effectiveness of fear appeals than on any other type of appeal. Examples of fear appeals might include: "Stop smoking, because smokers get lung cancer," or "Prepare a fallout shelter in your home to protect you in case of nuclear war." Essentially, the message built around a series of fear appeals tries to frighten the individual into thinking a certain way or into acting a certain way.

One of the earliest studies in fear appeals is that by Janis and Feshback.[56] They used groups of high-school students and the topic of tooth decay. Some groups received high-fear messages, while others received low-fear messages. Their results indicated that the *lower* levels of fear were more effective in changing attitudes toward tooth brushing. They suggested in the conclusion to the study that high levels of fear appeal seemed to produce an avoidance reaction, which negated the effects of the persuasive materials. The implication is that high-fear appeals produce high anxiety, and as a consequence, receivers paid little attention to the content of the messages, and much attention to their own state of anxiety.

For many years, the advice given persuasive communicators followed the Janis and Feshback findings, and sources were advised to use low levels of fear appeal to help ensure attitude change. Other studies have made us modify that advice. Hewgill and Miller[57] worked with materials relating to civil defense, specifically the building of home fallout shelters. They found that the level of fear appeals used varied with the credibility of the communicator. When highly credible sources were used, high levels of fear appeals could also be successfully used. When the source was not highly credible, however, low-fear appeals were more successful.

Hewgill and Miller also found that the success of fear appeals depended on the perceived relevance of the topic to a receiver. For example, they found that using fear appeals to try to get people to build a fallout shelter worked better with younger people who had children. Obviously, people without children had less concern for their own safety than did those who had the responsibility of providing for others. Other organizations have used this approach with some success. They will tell you to go to the doctor for a checkup because you owe it to your family. Colburn[58] found that the level of fear appeal used depends at least in part on the importance of the topic. When the receiver was faced with a topic that he considered to be extremely important to him, high-fear appeals were effective. As the importance of the topic to the receiver declined, the success of high-fear appeals also declined. One might suggest that what happened in the Colburn study was that when the topic was less important, the receiver was able to "step back" and reject the persuasive materials that were supported by a set of high-fear appeals. When the topic became extremely important to the receivers, they were not able to detach themselves, and consequently reacted to the appeals. Goldstein[59] looked at the relationship between the level of fear used in persuasive messages

and the personality types of the receivers. He suggested that receivers could be divided into "copers" and "avoiders." Copers could recognize their personal involvement in aggressive statements, while avoiders would read the same statements and find no personal implications in them. Goldstein reports that copers were responsive to much higher levels of fear than were avoiders.

From these and from many other studies it is clear that fear appeals can be emotionally arousing, they can result in the experience of fear, they can make people worry, and they can influence the receiver's *intentions* to change a behavior. However, as quality reviews by Boster and Mongeau,[60] Petty and Cacioppo,[61] Rogers,[62] and Sternthal and Craig[63] indicate, there is no simple relationship between fear and changes in behaviors. In order to make some recommendations helpful to the reader, we need to discuss two issues. First, there are specific guidelines that one can follow that may help to make fear appeals effective in changing attitudes and behaviors. Second, we need to discuss the issue of whether fear by itself is sufficiently motivating to change a person's behavior—especially if that behavior is a habit (smoking, drinking alcohol, and so on).

The history of research on fear appeals leads us to make a number of recommendations that the persuasive communicator should keep in mind:

1. A fear appeal message must provide strong arguments that the threat is real—that the receiver will experience some extremely negative consequence. Few Americans actually went to get a "Swine Flu" vaccination because they did not believe the threat was real. Few Americans went to Europe during the summer of 1986 because they felt the threat of terrorism was real.

2. The message must emphasize the likelihood that the receiver will experience undesirable consequences if the appeal is not accepted. Most states in America adopt the view that high school students may not take the responsibility of driving safely seriously. You are shown driver education films in high school

that involve fear because the state wants you to realize that accidents are deadly and horrifying—and they can happen to *you*.

3. The message provides strong assurances that adopting the recommendations can eliminate the negative consequences effectively. Telling receivers, for example, that a vaccination will reduce their chance of getting an infection by 50 percent is hardly comforting and motivating. To be effective, messages must reassure the receivers that adopting a "coping response" will protect them from the negative consequences.

4. It is helpful to convince receivers that the negative consequences of engaging in the behavior are greater than the costs or risks involved with the "coping response." An alcoholic who needs to begin treatment is likely to put off the treatment if he or she sees substantial costs—the loss of time from work, what others will say or think of him or her, the medical costs, a change in life-style, and so on. The message must tell the alcoholic that going for treatment (the coping response) is less costly in the long run than suffering the financial ruin of the life of the alcoholic, and dying an early death (among other things).

5. It is also helpful to convince receivers that they have the ability to engage in the coping response. That is, the message must help convince them that they are competent and effective individuals and they can change and/or adopt a coping response. If a particular high-fear appeal message makes smokers fearful, but also makes them depressed and feel helpless, then the persuasive communicator failed. The message (or someone) must help obese receivers, or smokers, or alcoholics to believe that they can start a treatment program and that they can maintain it.

Following these guidelines only helps to ensure that fear appeals may prove useful—they do not guarantee success.

As these guidelines indicate, we may sometimes expect that fear appeal messages can be effective when used in conjunction with factual information and positive appeals (appeals dealing with social support, encouraging the receiver to make an effort, and so on). This observation should not be surprising if we consider that many of the health behaviors that experts in fear appeals research study deal with the receiver's *habits* (smoking, drugs, dental care, diet, exercise, and so on). If we think back to what we said in earlier chapters about learning and habits, it is sensible to take a two-fold attack on changing people's habits—we use fear, punishments, and discouragement to keep them from engaging in poor habits, and we use praise, rewards, and encouragements to promote desirable behaviors. The advantage of using fear in this perspective is to prompt receivers to realize seriously that they should change their behaviors. But changing behaviors may best be achieved when we also add rewards for correct behaviors. Years ago, for example, Evan[64] and his colleagues found that high fear appeals concerning dental care were very successful at getting students to *intend* to change their behaviors. However, the students who actually improved dental care were the ones that either received elaborate instructions or received positive affects (for example, the researchers emphasized that students with good-looking teeth were more popular, and so on). McAlister,[65] in summarizing years of research on anti-smoking campaigns, concluded that information campaigns were not sufficient for reducing smoking behavior. McAlister recommended that media campaigns be reinforced by social support groups that help the ex-smoker learn to cope, and that encourage the ex-smoker to maintain the coping response. We can also note that the new wave of advertisements for alcohol abuse clinics seem to rely on five messages: (1) fear is vividly portrayed concerning the negative consequences of continued abuse; (2) messages emphasize that the treatment is effective and has a "high success rate"; (3) messages emphasize the low cost involved in seeking treatment—most insurance plans cover the cost, and the treatment only involves 10 days and a "couple of 2 day follow-ups"; (4) messages emphasize how the abuser's loved ones encourage him or her to go seek treatment—these loved ones are shown expressing concern and love, and praise the abuser for taking action; (5) messages emphasize that one should not be embarrassed by admitting that he or she has a drinking problem—the characters on the television screen are shown talking, nonchalantly, about drunk driving antics of running over the neighbor's mail boxes, and so on. As a total package, these messages try to shape the receiver's desired response—to admit fearfully that what he or she is doing is bad, that there is an effective coping mechanism to adopt, that the coping mechanism is effective and is not costly, that there are no other negative emotions (for example, embarrassment) that keeps the receiver from taking action, and that the receiver can regain the love of family members by going for treatment.

In sum, fear can be a very powerful motivator. It can make people afraid, and it can prompt receivers to decide to change their behaviors and to intend to change their behaviors. To use fear appeals effectively, however, the persuasive communicator needs to follow several guidelines and attend to the receivers' perceptions of the seriousness of a threat, the reality of the threat, the effectiveness of a coping response, and the ability to engage in a coping response. Finally, if persuasive communicators are confronted with changing receivers' habits, it may be necessary to use fear appeals along with a set of additional messages in order to alter behaviors successfully.

Summary

This chapter has been concerned with message organization and message appeals. In making a list of conclusions, we must caution against hasty acceptance of these conclusions or their application as inviolate laws of human behavior; much scientific study is still needed in this area.

1. There are a number of patterns of organization that seem to be widely used and are thus probably least disturbing to receivers.

2. There seem to be order effects operating in the receipt of persuasive messages, but the choice between climax and anticlimax order must be made after consideration of prior attitudes and the previous commitment of the receiver.

3. Two-sided messages probably are more effective than one-sided messages in the communication situations that the average communicator will encounter, but if the audience is already committed to the communicator's position, strengthening that commitment is best done with a one-sided message.

4. Fear appeals are important in persuasion, although the available research is not definite with respect to whether and under what circumstances high fear appeals are desirable.

5. The use of message appeals is extremely important to persuasive success, although the use of such appeals is highly dependent upon prior attitudes and frames of reference of the receiver.

Footnotes

1. C. Petrie, "Information Speaking: A Summary and Bibliography of Related Research," *Speech Monographs,* vol. 30 (1963), pp. 79–91.
2. K. C. Beighley, "The Effect of Four Speech Variables on Comprehension," *Speech Monographs,* vol. 19 (1952), pp. 249–258.
3. K. C. Beighley, "A Summary of Experimental Studies Dealing with the Effect of Organization and Skill of Speakers on Comprehension," *Journal of Communication,* vol. 2 (1952), pp. 58–65.
4. A. H. Eagly, "Comprehensibility of Persuasive Arguments As a Determinant of Opinion Change," *Journal of Personality and Social Psychology,* vol. 29 (1974), pp. 758–773.
5. E. Thompson, "An Experimental Investigation of the Relative Effectiveness of Organizational Structure in Oral Communication," *Southern Speech Journal,* vol. 26 (1960), pp. 59–69.

6. D. Darnell, "The Relation Between Sentence Order and Comprehension," *Speech Monographs,* vol. 30 (1963), pp. 97–100.

7. G. Kissler and K. Lloyd, "Effect of Sentence Interrelation and Scrambling on the Recall of Factual Information," *Journal of Educational Psychology,* vol. 63 (1973), pp. 187–190.

8. R. Sencer, "The Investigation of the Effects of Incorrect Grammar on Attitude and Comprehension in Written English Message" (Ph.D. dissertation, Michigan State University, 1965).

9. J. McCroskey and S. Mehrley, "The Effects of Disorganization and Nonfluency on Attitude Change and Source Credibility," *Speech Monographs,* vol. 36 (1969), pp. 13–21.

10. M. Burgoon and G. R. Miller, "An Expectancy Theory Interpretation of Language and Persuasion," in H. Giles and R. St. Clair, eds., *The Social and Psychological Contexts of Language* (London: Erlbaum, in press).

11. A. H. Monroe and D. Ehninger, *Principles of Speech Communication,* 7th brief ed. (Glenview, Ill.: Scott, Foresman, 1975), pp. 243–265.

12. S. Toulmin, *The Uses of Argument* (New York: Cambridge University Press, 1958).

13. D. Ehninger and W. Brockriede, *Decision by Debate* (New York: Dodd, Mead, 1963).

14. R. Windes and A. Hastings, *Argumentation and Advocacy* (New York: Random House, 1965).

15. E. Bettinghaus, *The Nature of Proof* (New York: Bobbs-Merrill, 1972), pp. 123–141.

16. H. E. Gulley and D. K. Berlo, "Effects of Intercellular and Intracellular Speech Structure on Attitude Change and Learning," *Speech Monographs,* vol. 23 (1956), pp. 288–297.

17. R. L. Rosnow and E. J. Robinson, *Experiments in Persuasion* (New York: Academic, 1967), pp. 99–104.

18. E. A. Lind, "The Psychology of Courtroom Procedure," in N. L. Kerr and R. M. Bray, eds., *The Psychology of the Courtroom* (New York: Academic, 1982), pp. 13–38.

19. Rosnow and Robinson, *Studies in Persuasion.*

20. Lind, "The Psychology of Courtroom Procedure."

21. C. I. Hovland, A. A. Lumsdaine, and F. D. Sheffield, *Experiments in Mass Communication: Studies in Social Psychology in World War II,* vol. 3 (Princeton, N.J.: Princeton University Press, 1949), pp. 201–227.

22. A. Lumsdaine and I. Janis, "Resistance to 'Counterpropaganda' Produced by One-sided and Two-sided Propaganda Presentations," *Public Opinion Quarterly,* vol. 17 (1953), pp. 311–318.

23. J. R. Weston, "Argumentative Message Structure and Message Sidedness and Prior Familiarity as Predictors of Source Credibility" (Ph.D. dissertation, Michigan State University, 1967).

24. R. R. Harmon, N. Y. Razzouk, and B. L. Stern, "The Information Content of Comparative Magazine Advertisements," *Journal of Advertising,* vol. 12 (1983), pp. 10–19.

25. G. J. Gorn and C. B. Weinberg, "The Impact of Comparative Advertising on Perception and Attitude: Some Positive Findings," *Journal of Consumer Research,* vol. 11 (1984), pp. 719–727; S. Grossbart, D. D. Muehling, and N. Kangun, "Verbal and Visual References to Competition in Comparative Advertising," *Journal of Advertising,* vol. 15 (1986), pp. 10–23.

26. F. H. Knower, "Experimental Studies of Changes in Attitudes: I. A Study of the Effect of Oral Argument," *Journal of Social Psychology,* vol. 6 (1935), pp. 315–347.

27. A. Lefford, "The Influence of Emotional Subject Matter on Logical Reasoning," *Journal of General Psychology,* vol. 34 (1946), pp. 127–151.

28. E. Bettinghaus and J. Swinney (Unpublished study, 1968).

29. N. T. Feather, "Acceptance and Rejection of Arguments in Relation to Attitude Strength, Critical Ability and Intolerance of Inconsistency," *Journal of Abnormal and Social Psychology,* vol. 59 (1964), pp. 127–137.

30. E. Bettinghaus, G. R. Miller, and T. Steinfatt, "Source Evaluation, Syllogistic Content, and Judgment of Logical Validity of High- and Low-Dogmatic Persons," *Journal of Personality and Social Psychology,* vol. 16 (1970), pp. 238–244.

31. T. Steinfatt, G. R. Miller, and E. Bettinghaus, "The Concept of Logical Ambiguity and Judgments of Syllogistic Validity," *Speech Monographs,* vol. 41 (1974), pp. 317–328.

32. G. R. Miller, "Some Factors Influencing Judgments of Logical Validity of Arguments: A Research Review," *Quarterly Journal of Speech,* vol. 55 (1969), pp. 276–286.

33. D. Stewart, "Communication and Logic: Evidence for the Existence of Validity Patterns," *Journal of General Psychology,* vol. 64 (1961), pp. 304–312.

34. V. Cronen and N. Mihevic, "The Evaluation of Deductive Argument: A Process Analysis," *Speech Monographs,* vol. 39 (1972), pp. 124–131.

35. R. Norman, "When What Is Said Is Important: A Comparison of Expert and Attractive Sources," *Journal of Experimental Social Psychology,* vol. 12 (1976), pp. 294–300.

36. H. E. Krugman, "Processes Underlying Exposure to Advertising," *American Psychologist,* vol. 23 (1968), pp. 245–253.

37. R. L. Miller, "Mere Exposure, Psychological Reactance and Attitude Change," *Public Opinion Quarterly,* vol. 40 (1976), pp. 229–233.

38. R. Grass and W. H. Wallace, "Satiation Effects on TV Commercials," *Journal of Advertising Research,* vol. 9 (1969), pp. 3–8.

39. M. L. Ray, A. G. Sawyer, and E. C. Strong, "Frequency Effects Revisited," *Journal of Advertising Research,* vol. 11 (1971), pp. 14–20.

40. M. L. Ray and A. G. Sawyer, "Repetition in Media Models: A Laboratory Technique," *Journal of Marketing Research,* vol. 8 (1971), pp. 20–28.

41. A. Greenberg and C. Suttoni, "Television Commercial Wearout," *Journal of Advertising Research,* vol. 13 (1973), pp. 47–54.

42. G. J. Gorn and M. E. Goldberg, "Children's Responses to Television Commercials," *Journal of Consumer Research,* vol. 6 (1980), pp. 421–424.

43. See Greenberg and Suttoni, "Television Commercial Wearout."

44. See Miller, "Mere Exposure." Also: R. Mayeux, "Repetition Effects: A Proposal" (Unpublished paper, Department of Communication Arts and Sciences, University of Southern California, December, 1984).

45. E. Rogers, "Incentives in the Diffusion of Family Planning Innovations," *Studies in Family Planning,* vol. 2 (1971), pp. 241–248.

46. A. G. Greenwald and C. Leavitt, "Audience Involvement in Advertising: Four Levels," *Journal of Consumer Research,* vol. 11 (1984), pp. 581–592.

47. R. Batra and M. L. Ray, "Advertising Situations: The Implications of Differential Involvement and Accompanying Affect Responses," in R. J. Harris, ed., *Information Processing Research in Advertising* (Hillsdale, N.J.: Erlbaum, 1983), pp. 127–152; M. L. Ray and R. Batra, "Emotion and Persuasion in Advertising: What We Do and Don't Know About Affect," in R. P. Bagozzi and A. M. Tybout, eds., *Advances in Consumer Research,* vol. 10 (1983), pp. 543–548.

48. Ray and Batra, "Emotion and Persuasion in Advertising."

49. T. J. Madden and M. G. Weinberger, "Humor in Advertising: A Practitioner View," *Journal of Advertising Research,* vol. 24 (1984), pp. 23–29.

50. H. B. Lammers, L. Leibowitz, G. E. Seymour, and J. E. Hennessey, "Humor and Cognitive Responses to Advertising Stimuli: A Trace Consolidation Approach," *Journal of Business Research,* vol. 11 (1983), pp. 173–185.

51. P. E. McGhee and J. H. Goldstein, eds., *Handbook of Humor Research* (New York: Springer-Verlag, 1983).

52. D. A. Aaker, D. M. Stayman, and M. R. Hagerty, "Warmth in Advertising: Measurement, Impact, and Sequence Effects," *Journal of Consumer Research,* vol. 12 (1986), pp. 365–381.

53. D. A. Aaker and D. E. Bruzzone, "Viewer Perceptions of Prime-Time Television Advertising," *Journal of Advertising Research,* vol. 21 (1981), pp. 15–23.

54. M. J. Schlinger, "A Profile of Responses to Commercials," *Journal of Advertising Research,* vol. 19 (1979), pp. 37–46.

55. L. A. Alwitt and A. A. Mitchell, eds., *Psychological Processes and Advertising Effects* (Hillsdale,

N.J.: Lawrence Erlbaum, 1985); Aaker, Stayman, and Hagerty, "Warmth in Advertising"; Y. Choi and E. Thorson, "Memory for Factual, Emotional, and Balanced Ads Under Two Instructional Sets," in *Proceedings of the 1983 Conference of the American Academy of Advertising,* ed. A. D. Fletcher (Knoxville, TN: University of Tennessee, 1983).

56. I. Janis and S. Feshback, "Effects of Fear-Arousing Communications," *Journal of Abnormal and Social Psychology,* vol. 47 (1953), pp. 78–92.

57. M. Hewgill and G. R. Miller, "Source Credibility and Response to Fear-Arousing Communications," *Speech Monographs,* vol. 32 (1965), pp. 95–101.

58. C. Colburn, "An Experimental Study of the Relationship Between Fear Appeal and Topic Importance in Persuasion" (Ph.D. dissertation, University of Indiana, 1967).

59. M. Goldstein, "The Relationship Between Coping and Avoiding Behavior and Response to Fear Arousing Propaganda," *Journal of Abnormal and Social Psychology,* vol. 59 (1959), pp. 249–256.

60. F. Boster and P. Mongeau, "Fear-Arousing Persuasive Messages," in R. N. Bostrom, ed., *Communication Yearbook 8* (Beverly Hills: Sage, 1984), pp. 330–375.

61. R. E. Petty and J. T. Caccioppo, *Attitudes and Persuasion: Classic and Contemporary Approaches* (Dubuque, Iowa: Wm. C. Brown Co., 1981).

62. R. W. Rogers, "Cognitive and Psychological Processes in Fear Appeals and Attitude Change: A Revised Theory of Protection Motivation," in J. T. Caccioppo and R. E. Petty, eds., *Social Psychophysiology: A Sourcebook* (New York: The Guildford Press, 1983), pp. 153–176.

63. F. Sternthal and C. Craig, "Fear Appeals: Revisited and Revised," *Journal of Consumer Research,* vol. 7 (1974), pp. 22–34.

64. R. I. Evans, R. M. Rozelle, T. M. Lasater, T. M. Dembroski, and B. P. Allen, "Fear Arousal, Persuasion, and Actual Versus Implied Behavioral Change: New Perspective Utilizing a Real-Life Dental Hygiene Program," *Journal of Personality and Social Psychology,* vol. 16 (1970), pp. 220–227.

65. A. McAlister, "Antismoking Campaigns: Progress in Developing Effective Communications," in R. E. Rice and W. J. Paisley, eds., *Public Communication Campaigns* (Beverly Hills: Sage, 1981), pp. 91–104.

CHAPTER NINE

Using Communication Channels Effectively

We have now looked at sources and receivers of persuasive communication. We have torn apart persuasive messages, and tried to see just what kind of messages will be the most effective. What about the *channels* that must be used if any message is to reach a receiver? Ought we pay the money to get an advertisement placed on television? Or should we just concentrate on getting the receiver in a room where we can communicate face-to-face? These and similar questions are related to the kinds of communication channels that sources can use.

It was not until the invention of radio that a technology existed that could reach literally everyone in the world with a single message. The use of radio began over 60 years ago, and together with

the telephone, it marked the beginning of the communications revolution, and the beginning of a major change in the practice of persuasive communication. Before 1930, a writer on persuasive communication would have been justified in restricting the discussion to platform speaking before relatively large audiences, because that was the best way to reach the largest number of people. Political campaigns were "whistle-stop" campaigns with short messages delivered to audiences gathered to hear the candidate speak from the back of a train. The rest of the country got information about the campaign from newspapers, if they were lucky enough to have access to one.

By 1932 the world had changed forever. President Franklin Delano Roosevelt developed the radio "Fireside Chat," through which he was able to communicate to the entire nation without leaving the White House. Communication channels had changed, and persuasive communication along with it.

During World War II, radio became the most important link between the war and the homefront. No longer did we have to wait for messages to travel by boats and then appear in a newspaper. Edward R. Murrow came into our homes every night direct from London. We bought millions of dollars worth of war bonds when Kate Smith asked Americans to give to the war effort.[1] That war-bond drive was perhaps the first attempt to utilize the electronic media to persuade an entire nation to purchase a product.

Today, the communications revolution continues unabated. The development of mass-marketing techniques for books, magazines, and newspapers; the spread of telephones, radio, television, and movies; the developments in film techniques, sound recording, and transmission facilities; the advent of video-tape and the home video recorder; the use of cable to link homes in a community; the newest technologies of fiber optics, cellular radio, satellite-based programs, and computer-aided transmissions have made us forget the days when a man could expect to influence or be influenced by only those few people with whom he could interact personally.

Today a communicator *must* consider channels in planning persuasive strategies. For many people, the use of a particular channel of communication may be a more important factor in determining whether there will be changes in attitudes, beliefs, or behavior than the actual message being sent or the speaker sending the message. A number of questions are of interest to the persuasive communicator. Are single channels of communication more effective than multiple channels? Under what circumstances is face-to-face communication more effective than communication making use of the mass media? What are the relative roles played in our society by mass media and by face-to-face contact?

Multiple communication channels

Imagine that you are interested in controlling the pollution produced by a local chemical plant. You have been granted a period of time by the city council to present your arguments. What should you do in that period of time? The following are only a few of the possible methods you might consider:

1. A straight persuasive speech to the council members.
2. A speech augmented by slides taken of the smoke pouring from the smokestack of the plant.
3. A speech augmented with short movie scenes of some of the conditions produced by emissions from the plant.
4. A movie with a sound track that would tell the whole story.
5. A speech augmented with charts, diagrams, or models of the plant and surrounding areas showing the effect of the toxic emissions on the area.
6. A video-tape of the plants' operation, shown on a television monitor that you bring to the meeting.
7. A series of tape-recorded interviews that you obtained from people living around the plant who have been affected by the plant.
8. A series of video-taped interviews obtained from people living in the neighborhood of the plant and shown on the evening news before the city-council meeting.

Some of the methods suggested above depend on being able to *see* the major elements of the message while others depend on the receiver's *hearing*. Still others represent a mixture of visual channels *and* aural channels, that is, the use of *multiple channels* of communication. For many years, practitioners of communication have urged the use of multiple channels as being more effective than a single channel. Are they right? Should we immerse an audience in messages for the ear at the same time we send visual messages?

Since people gain all the information they have for making decisions through the senses, it seems reasonable to suggest that the communicator make use of as many senses as possible when transmitting a message. It is this feeling about vision and hearing that produces advice in textbooks on audiovisual education and public speaking to use multiple channels of communication: "It is better to have a movie than just a speech." "It is better to have the speaker present than to have a tape-recorded message from the source." These principles suggest that the straight speech is a less effective method of communication, and any combination making use of both vision and hearing must be ranked as superior to either sight alone, as in a written article, or hearing alone, as in a taped presentation. In general, whenever the persuasive message might be viewed as *highly redundant* or *difficult*, multiple channels are likely to be of some value. Some of the specific types of situations are discussed below:

1. Is the material very complex? Imagine that we wish to argue against a new sewer project on the grounds that it may destroy a natural watershed. The data to be used in this situation are likely to be complex, and not easily understood.

The impact of complexity of material and channel effects in persuasion was most clearly illustrated in a study by Chaiken and Eagly.[2] Students were asked to evaluate a law student's discussion of a dispute between a company and its union laborers. Half the presentations were constructed to be easy to comprehend, the other half were constructed to be difficult to comprehend—more complex sentences were used, along with a more advanced vocabulary. Students exposed to audiotaped messages and to audiovisual presentations rated the difficult messages as less understandable, less pleasant, and were less persuaded than students who were able to read the complex message. On the other hand, easy to comprehend messages resulted in more persuasion when students were exposed to the audiovisual presenta-

tion. Thus, complex messages are best when presented in written form, and communicators should consider using more simple messages when using the audiovisual medium—after all, receivers pay greater attention to cues about the *communicator* when exposed to audiovisual or videotaped speeches than to the *message content*.[3]

Research results indicate that all receivers attend to different areas of the message when given different channels. In the Chaiken and Eagly[4] study, college students paid more attention to the communicator when exposed to the audiovisual message, while others paid more attention to actual message content when exposed to printed messages. The work by Meringoff and her colleagues indicates that similar biases exist among children.[5] Children who are exposed to live presentations of a story learn more about language than children exposed to recorded versions of the same story, and children exposed to television and film remember more visual and behavioral data—such as the characters' actions, gestures, and facial displays. These results indicate a very strong preference for children to pay attention to action and to the characters in the audiovisual channel and suggest that one way to reach children through audiovisual channels is to emphasize the information you want them to retain in the visual area of the message.

2. Is the material likely to be unfamiliar to the receiver? Imagine that the source wishes to use an aerial photograph to illustrate a point. Most receivers would find an aerial photograph quite unfamiliar, and most receivers would have difficulty in identifying objects on the photograph. The use of an oral explanation will help the receiver in understanding the visual presentation.

3. Is the receiver going to be interested in the message? One of the most frequently used ways of attracting attention to a message is by the use of a colorful, multiple-media presentation. A display of flashing lights together with a loudspeaker will attract more attention then either the lights alone or the loudspeaker alone. One study suggests that the use of brightly-colored backgrounds in serial-

learning tasks seems to improve learning.[6] The author also points out, however, that the backgrounds may have produced their effects at the expense of information lost from an auditory signal played at the same time. In other words, while the use of multiple channels did enhance interest, there was some loss in information. The best advice that we can give to a persuasive communicator is that the use of multiple channels to arouse interest is helpful, but that caution should be exercised to ensure that the receiver is also acquiring the *intended message*.

Admittedly, it is sometimes easier to say that one should get the intended message across than it is to create messages that actually ensure that the message gets across. At least two issues must be kept in mind: prompting the receiver to *reflect* on what is being communicated and using multiple channels to *reinforce* the intended message. Scholars have focused attention on how receivers process information and how attention and recall are influenced by any number of message variables. Bryant and Comisky,[7] for example, studied the effects of positioning a commercial during a detective show and found that the commercial received the *lowest* levels of recall when the story reached a climax, but had not reached a resolution phase (climax occurs when a potentially fatal blow might befall the hero, resolution occurs when the hero overcomes the attacker(s)). Recall of the commercial was higher when the content preceding and following the commercial was less involving. Thus, highly involving content may interfere with the content of the commercial surrounding the commercial's airing. According to Bryant and Comisky, receivers need to reflect on (or rehearse mentally) what they are attending to in order to recall the message content, and the greater the involvement with one part of the ongoing presentation may hurt attending to, reflecting on, or rehearsal of, a less involving segment.

A general case can be made in favor of making messages in such a way as to promote reflective thought or rehearsal of material presented in television or in film. Singer and Singer[8] recently summarized work on children's viewing of television

and noted that the vast majority of television viewing involves endlessly changing stimuli that holds the receivers' attention using novelty, fast-paced action, sounds, changes in music and background, and so on. In fact, heavy viewing of fast-paced action is itself sufficient to arousal excitement in children that they will need to dissipate in some manner. In all this blur, what is actually learned and taken away from the television? Children learn from *Sesame Street*,[9] which is relatively fast paced (35 brief segments in 60 minutes), but evidence indicates that after watching *Mister Roger's Neighborhood* children are more likely to engage in spontaneous positive, prosocial behaviors.[9] Why? Mister Rogers "appears on the screen frequently, talks slowly, avoids sudden 'magical' effects, asks children to reflect about issues and encourages them to talk back to the screen"[11] (Can you say _____? Can you do _____?). While children are enthusiastic about both shows, it is likely that the attempts to prompt children to reflect on what is said, to repeat statements, and to participate actively increases the learning of prosocial behaviors as well as influencing the recall of content matter from the television show.

Bryant, Zillmann, and Brown[12] have recently summarized their work on entertainment and education and have concluded that both background music and humor are useful in gaining interest and attention from children, but they also conclude that attention to educational materials is impaired, over time, by continuous presentation of fast and appealing music. Apparently, if appealing music is used constantly throughout a film it becomes the focus of attention and children fail to learn what is on the screen. Also, humor is helpful in education only if the humor is relevant to the concepts being taught. These, and other researchers, find education is improved when visual and audio channels are used to reinforce a message.

4. Is the message a very long one? Receivers have difficulty in attending to long messages and the best advice we give any communicator is, "Keep it short." There are some topics, however,

that simply cannot be covered in a short, simple message. Convincing someone to buy life insurance is not always done in a short five-minute speech. Multiple channels may be helpful in keeping the interest and attention of an audience when long messages are to be presented. Receivers seem to grow fatigued with the presentation of materials through a single channel for long periods of time. The addition of other channels or the switching of sense modalities during a long message may be helpful in reducing this fatigue effect.

5. Is the material highly repetitive? Advertisers frequently have the problem of transmitting a fairly simple message such as "Buy brand X beer" to potential customers. If the advertiser simply repeated that statement over and over again in an advertisement, the chances are that any reader or listener would quickly become bored, and might even refuse to buy the product on the grounds that the company is insulting the intelligence of its potential buyers. Using multiple channels in such situations may help prevent a simple message from being perceived as boring by an audience. The message can be repeated over the air with a voice, shown with pictures, repeated in writing, and the use of a number of channel variations will help fix the attention and interest of the receiver and yet avoid boredom.

The examples we have used illustrate the conclusion that deciding whether or not to use multiple channels for a message is not always simple. The communicator must consider the nature of the situation and the type of materials to be presented before deciding on the presentation to be used. In most cases, using multiple channels to transmit a message *will* enhance the source's chances of obtaining a desired response.

The discussion thus far has been concerned with the use of multiple channels in which the visual mode is going to be used to present charts, graphs, line drawings, or pictures to enhance an oral presentation. The question of the relative effectiveness of written versus oral materials, in situations where the communicator has a choice to make, deserves special attention, because the decision-making process that the source must use is

applicable to many other communication situations.

Imagine that a company has proposed rezoning a tract of land in order to build a new manufacturing plant. A number of people living adjacent to the proposed plant site object to the proposal, because they feel that it will increase pollution and traffic problems, and decrease the value of their own property. What should they do to prevent the plant from being built? Rezoning is the responsibility of the city council. Should they ask for time before the city council? What will be the most effective tactic to use?

1. How difficult is the material that the communicator has to present? We noted above that written communication is better than oral communication for difficult materials. This makes sense, since the reader can set an individual pace, whereas the listener, when listening, is forced to go at the rate of the speaker. Furthermore, the reader can read and reread, while the listener must grasp the message the first time. On the other hand, the communicator who writes a message for the newspaper or who writes a letter to a member of the city council has no chance of obtaining any immediate feedback about the success of the letter. In fact, the source frequently cannot even find out whether a message has been read or not. In a face-to-face situation, where facial expressions can be read and feedback obtained, the communicator has at least some idea that the message is being listened to. The risk is between being sure that one is attended to, although perhaps not understood, and having some confidence that one is understood, even though one is not sure that the message has been read.

2. What are the language skills of the receiver? In the United States less than 6 percent of the population is considered functionally illiterate, and thus unable to read at a high enough level to make use of written materials in everyday life. But for every individual who may be functionally unable to read ordinary adult materials, many more cannot read at a level that would make persuasive written communication an effective form. For such individuals spoken messages are the only re-

alistic message form. In the specific example we have used, however, it is likely that one could expect all members of a city council to be able to read any written messages that might be sent. Since such individuals are generally representative of their communities, some estimate of their ability to understand the message can be made by examining the demographic characteristics of the community.

3. What size audience needs to be reached? As audience size increases, spoken communication in the face-to-face situation becomes expensive and impractical. If the audience is considered to be only the few members of the city council, spoken communication in face-to-face situations is undoubtedly the most effective way to proceed. City-council members, however, frequently make their decisions only after finding out how their constituencies feel about a situation. The *real* audience may be the entire population of the community. It may be necessary to persuade a large segment of the community *before* there is hope of success in approaching the members of the city council. In that case, the persuasive communicator might adopt a strategy of writing letters to the newspaper or asking for editorial space, in order to convince the large body of voters that cannot be reached in face-to-face situations. Following that effort, the city-council members could be approached with face-to-face messages that would have maximum impact.

4. How important is the credibility of the persuasive communicator? City-council members are political beings. They are far more likely to respond to a source that has high source credibility than to one who does not stand out from the crowd. Oral communication bears the stamp of the person delivering the message in an unmistakable fashion. Pick up the newspaper and read all of the editorials and the letters to the editor. Do you get a clear picture of the people who wrote the messages? It is difficult to make an estimate about source credibility from a written message. When a person appears before us, however, we can make far more accurate estimates as to the person's credibility, and thus his or her believability.

5. How much money does the persuasive communicator have to spend? It may seem strange to consider the cost, but the choice of message strategies may hinge on the amount of money that the source has to spend on the message. Preparing high-quality visual aids for a persuasive message takes both time and money. If you are going to appear before the city council to make a presentation in opposition to zoning, it may cost several hundred dollars to collect data, and prepare slides, films, charts, or graphs in order to show the problems that the proposed plant would cause. If it is necessary to have materials printed for distribution to citizens in the community, the cost can escalate quickly to several thousands of dollars. In contrast, driving down to a city-council meeting and asking to appear in the public comment section of the meeting will cost the source some time, but the number of dollars that need to be spent will be relatively small. Even if the personal appearance is not as effective in reaching the required audience, it might be the best choice for a source with limited funds.

Making a decision between an oral message and a written one is not easy. The best advice is to determine what kind of message needs to be delivered to an audience, and then to begin to ask the kind of questions we have discussed in this section. Similarly, there are no easy answers to questions dealing with multiple channels such as "Should I use illustrations in my presentation?," "Should I write out the message?," or "Can I afford movies to illustrate the message?" It *is* possible to improve the chance of success by thinking through some of the problems involved whenever a message is transferred from the idea stage to the presentation stage.

The mass media in society

The communication revolution began to gather a full head of steam with the spread of television following World War II. Now midway through the 1980s, the status of that revolution can be demonstrated in just a few figures. There are over

62,000 different magazines in the United States. You can have a choice of reading some 1,800 daily newspapers or some 7,600 weekly or semiweekly magazines. More than 40,000 new books are published each year in the United States, and there are now more than 400 million radios available to the population. Less than 2 percent of the homes in the country are without television, and the great majority of homes have color television.[13]

From the standpoint of a persuasive communicator, the availability of the mass media is a problem as well as an advantage. Thirty years ago, the average community had a single television station, and the citizen watched that station, or none at all. With the advent of cable television, the citizen in that same community may have a choice of all three major networks as well as independent stations and several educational stations. First-run movies as well as major sporting events are avail-

---

BOX 9.1
THE COMMUNICATION REVOLUTION

Just why do people say that we are in the midst of a communication revolution? After all, newspapers have been around since the early days of the various colonies in America. Why are things different today? The answer to that question lies in the sheer number of ways that people now have to communicate, and the extremely rapid spread of almost every new technological innovation in communication.

Below, we list some of the ways that people have available to assist them in communication. The best thing we can say about these figures is that they will be higher next year, and higher the year after that. We do not discard one innovation when someone comes up with a new idea. In the communication revolution, we simply add the new idea to old, and start looking again.

Technology	*Usage*
Newspapers	60 million copies a day
Daily	Over 1,800
Weekly and semiweekly	Over 7,600
Magazines	More than 62,000 different magazines
Books	More than 40,000 new titles each year
Radio	Over 400 million radios, with an average listening time of almost five hours a day.
Television	163,000,000 with an average viewing time of four hours per day for each adult.
Cable television	More than 12,000,000 homes and growing rapidly.
Satellite antennas	1.8 million
Cellular radio	250,000 cars and growing too fast to have accurate figures.
Computer networks	At least 100,000 paid members in Source and Compuserve, with 1,200 new members per month.

Figures from Donald M. Wood, *Mass Media and the Individual* (Los Angeles: West, 1983), p. 4.

able in the home. Many cable systems provide channels for public use by the city council, the school board, and even local access channels available to the average citizen. Daily and weekly newspapers carry more advertising, and therefore there is a larger amount of space that can be devoted to news, editorials, and other community affairs. The opportunity for an average citizen, in most communities, to be able to get a letter printed in the local newspaper is greater than it was 30 years ago. Where is the problem? It lies in the difficulty of being able to have any assurance that a sizable audience is attending to a message. The persuasive communicator can have less and less control in a society where there are more and more channels open to the populace.

With the increasing availability of mass media, the persuasive communicator needs to have some idea of the functions of the mass media in our society. We would agree with those scholars who argue that there are essentially four major functions fulfilled by mass media:

1. To serve as conveyors of information to the population.
2. To serve as a means of socializing the population in terms of attitudes, values, and behavior.
3. To provide entertainment for the members of the culture.
4. To serve as a forum for those advocating social, political, or economic change.

The last of these functions is most clearly related to persuasion, but each of the others are important to the persuasive communicator.

Information transmission

In their role as conveyors of information to the public, the mass media serve to keep people informed about current events and happenings around the world. Typically, this function is carried out by media personnel who observe and then report on any situations that are *available* to reporters and that are considered *important*

enough to justify either time on the air or space in a newspaper. We have stressed the words "available" and "important" because they illustrate both the strengths of the media as well as the weaknesses.[14]

In a perfect information system, all events would be considered by some unbiased source and rated for their importance to the maximum number of people in the society. We do not have such a perfect information system. The media personnel, that is, the reporters and news gatherers, cannot possibly consider all the millions of events that occur each day in the United States. Further, there are no adequate methods of determining what is important and what is not important in any absolute sense. I may consider a news event to be extremely important, while others may not.

We do not have a perfect information system. What we do have is a system in which the people who work in the media serve as "gatekeepers" for the rest of the society. They determine which events are to be reported and which are not. They determine how important an event is, and thus how much space or time it deserves. In countries where the press is either controlled by the government or is a government monopoly, the decision as to what news will be used and how it will be reported is, of course, subject to the policies of that government.[15] In some countries, news about opposition parties is not allowed in the media. In other countries, stories about government corruption are banned. In the United States, the media are part of the private-enterprise system, owned and operated by individuals who are interested in making a profit on their enterprise. There is government supervision through the Federal Communications Commission over radio and television, and over newspaper advertising by the Federal Trade Commission, but that control is supposed to be exercised to achieve fairness in media operations, and not to ban or to promote certain types of news.

What are some of the criteria used to determine what will be transmitted via the mass media and what will not? The criteria we suggest below may help the persuasive communicator to decide just what events important to a cause are most likely to be disseminated through the mass media.[16]

1. Magnitude. The bigger the event, the more likely it is to be reported. If an event affects many people, or if a large sum of money is involved, the event is more likely to be reported and diffused.

2. Significance. The impact that a problem or an event will have on people is a strong determinant of how likely it is to be reported as news. The passage of a new tax law that will affect large numbers of people is an example of a significant event. In contrast, passage of a resolution of congratulation to an athletic team from the state is likely to receive little attention in the media.

3. Conflict. Any events that cause or could cause conflict between people have a high likelihood of being reported. War news has traditionally had a place of major importance in the news media, even when there is little relation between the conflict and the receivers of the news. For example, in 1979, when the government of Cambodia was ousted in a civil war supported by Vietnamese troops, the news received major treatment in American news media, even though that war did not directly affect the United States.

4. Proximity. How close the event occurred to a particular community is an important determiner of whether the story is going to receive any attention. It is possible that a rezoning issue in East Lansing, Michigan, will receive press coverage in the local newspaper or even on the local television news broadcast. It is doubtful that that story would receive any coverage in the Detroit or Ann Arbor papers.

5. Timeliness. Newspapers are published every day or every week. Normally, a radio station broadcasts news every hour, and a television station broadcasts news twice every day. The closer to the time the story is received, the more likely it is to be used. The news media want to be "first." If an event is several days old, the chances are that it will already have received some attention in another news source, and thus have lost its timeliness for other media. This factor is one frequently forgotten by people who want to get the newspapers to cover some event. If a wedding was a week ago, it has lost most of its news value. If a meeting took place two weeks ago, it has little news value.

6. Prominence. The better known people are, the greater the chance of having their activities reported. The president of the United States has almost every activity reported. The senator from the state in which a newspaper is located (but probably not the senator from a neighboring state) is given news coverage very frequently. The wealthiest person in the community is given coverage. In some cases, the persuasive communicator can obtain news coverage by linking a campaign to someone who is very prominent, and therefore likely to be covered.

7. Unusualness. The news media tend to cover that which is unusual. If an event is very unlikely to occur, it will be covered. Thus we have the stories that are trivial in all other respects, but are complete oddities. The "World's Largest Tomato," or "Woman Is Reunited with Cousin Lost for 50 Years" are examples of stories selected as the result of applying this criterion. In some cases, the persuasive communicator can make use of this criterion to get coverage of an event that might otherwise not be covered.

8. Human interest. There are certain topics that seem to arouse interest whenever they are used. Stories about animals, about small children, and about medical advances are examples of human-interest stories. Editors feel that people are always interested in such stories, and they may be used over stories that might actually have more hard news value. If a desired change can be linked in some way to a human-interest story, it may get more attention than it would ordinarily deserve.

The criteria we suggest above as determinants of what kinds of information will be presented on the mass media are among the most frequently used criteria by local newspapers, television stations, or radio stations in selecting the stories to run. In persuasion, we frequently are interested in making the public aware of an upcoming event, or a situation or condition that we believe needs change or support. If we can find a way to link it to one or more of the criteria we have listed above, we improve the chances that the media will transmit the information to the public.

Socialization

In almost any society, the important values of the culture are transmitted to all citizens via the mass media. This is termed the "socializing" function of the mass media.[17] Obviously, the mass media are not the only institutions in the society that have a socializing role to play. Families serve a role in the process, as do churches, schools, and governments. As societies have grown more complex, however, the mass media have become more and more important in the transmission of societal attitudes and values.

If one thinks just a bit about the questions of socialization, it becomes easy to see the process taking place in our newspapers and magazines, and on our radio and television sets. The media reflect our western-European heritage. Only seldom are there Asian/Pacific music programs, or Asian/Pacific dramas. In recent years, there have been a number of Spanish-language stations and programs but this didn't occur until the Hispanic population of the United States reached a size to make it economically viable.

The mass media do serve as a socializing influence in the society. From "Sesame Street" to "Dallas" to "General Hospital" to "Saturday Night Live," materials appear in the media that tend to reflect the attitudes and values of the society. Many offerings on television are intended for entertainment, but the way in which they are presented makes them excellent vehicles for socialization. Studies made of reactions to prime-time shows and to "soap operas" indicate the extent to which the material viewed is learned and internalized as socializing influences.[18] The persuasive

communicator who can make a message correspond to those attitudes and values will find it easier to obtain media coverage than if the message seems to attack normative values.

Entertainment

It is certainly no secret that one of the major functions of the mass media in our society is to entertain. For television, the entertainment function is a primary one, and large sums of money are spent in trying to find out exactly what will be entertaining to the largest number of people. The same criteria apply to radio, although the pressures are somewhat different, since there are more stations, and appeals can be made to a more limited audience on any specific channel. Many magazines are based on an entertainment function and are successful only to the extent that they succeed in appealing to their audience as entertainment. Newspapers obviously do not have entertainment as a central function, but many of their features, such as the comics, are designed to serve an entertainment function.

The persuasive communicator, of course, is usually interested in topics that are not necessarily oriented to entertainment. Furthermore, to the extent that the media are being used for pure entertainment, they cannot be used for education, for information dissemination, or for persuasion. This suggests that a communicator's strategy ought to:

1. Utilize the nonentertainment functions of the various media. Newspapers and news magazines do have some entertainment functions, but their primary purpose is not entertainment. Readers will be expecting serious messages, and will suffer no violation of expectations when a persuasive message is presented. Even on television, the medium most closely associated with entertainment, there are times when other kinds of materials are presented. The regular newscasts, special documentaries, religious broadcasts, and educational programs are all examples of the regular use of this medium for nonentertainment functions. In many communities, there are cable channels

reserved for education as well as channels reserved for city-council use, or for local-citizen access. While these channels are not heavily watched, the people who do use these channels may be more influential than those who watch only entertainment shows.

2. Approach audiences indirectly when the audience is engaged primarily in using the mass media for entertainment. This can be done through the use of public service announcements (PSAs), or advertisements. Although PSAs tend to be used by stations in non-prime-time slots, they do attract attention, and can be used as persuasive messages. Advertisements cost money, but they can be used during times of high media use, that is, prime time, and more and more people can be made aware of the subject advanced by the communicator.

3. Try tying a cause to an individual associated with entertainment. One of the best examples we have of this strategy is the use of comedians Jerry Lewis and Danny Thomas. Both gained their reputation as entertainers, but both have long been associated with charitable causes, and have raised huge sums of money through their persuasive efforts. This strategy works even at the local level, where local media personnel may carry considerable credibility and may be willing to ally themselves with the communicator's cause. We will discuss this strategy in more detail in considering social action in the final chapter of this book.

4. Attempt to tie a persuasive message to specific entertainment events. It has sometimes been said that the American public prefers their education in small doses, and made as palatable as possible. Persuasive messages can frequently be considered as medicine: necessary but successfully administered only if disguised with a sugar coating. Some radio stations have switched to a format where short news programs, that is, of five minutes' duration, are aired three or four times an hour, rather than for a longer period once an hour. It is sometimes possible to convince local theater associations or local sports associations to tie themselves to your cause, so long as the cause

does not become more important than the entertainment.

Forum

If we think of the primary purpose of *any* communication channel, the forum function of the mass media becomes clear. A channel is used to carry a message from one person to another. By using face-to-face communication we could theoretically eventually reach everyone in the United States, but the spread of our message would be slow, so slow that some people would probably have died before the last person heard the message. If, on the other hand, we use radio, or television, or newspapers, we can reach almost every person in the entire country within a matter of hours. The mass media, then, serve as a means by which the major ideas, problems, and issues in a society can be aired and discussed, solutions proposed, and decisions made and disseminated. That function of the mass media works in the United States as a whole as well as in smaller divisions such as states, cities, towns, and villages.

In an ideal society, one might expect the mass media to serve as the means by which *all* controversial positions are identified and discussed in detail by those concerned, and where the knowledge arrived at serves as the basis for decisions within the society. Ours is not an ideal society. The problem is that there is far more information to be transmitted than there is space in the average newspaper; the electronic media can carry even less information. After considering the huge volume of news that comes into a single Wisconsin newspaper, Cutlip points out that only a small percentage of the information received can possibly be printed.[19] This means that some ideas will not receive attention. Some persuasive messages will never see the light of day. Only a few of the letters to the editor will be printed. As we can see, the mass media *can* serve as a forum for ideas, but not for *all* ideas, not for *all* proposals, and not for *all* potential persuasive messages.

As a result of these limitations the media tend to serve an *agenda-setting* function for dialogue in the society. Those ideas, events, and proposals that receive high exposure in the media tend to be the ones that the public reacts to, and the ones that become discussed and eventually acted upon. The task of the persuasive communicator, therefore, is to first work at getting on that agenda. This has to be done before there can be any expectation that the media can help transmit persuasive messages.

Ordinarily, one assumes that it is the media that influence the general public's interest in a particular topic. That is, the flow of influence is from the media to the public. Roberts and Maccoby suggest that there is also evidence that ". . . public concerns influence the media agenda."[20] They also note that on some issues both the media agenda and the agenda of the general public are determined by external events in the environment. For example, the taking of the United States embassy in Iran in 1979 and the subsequent detainment of hostages drove almost all other items out of the news for several days, and until the hostages were finally released more than a year later, that topic took precedence over other "agenda items." Studies by McCombs[21] and by Sohn[22] show that there is a stronger influence flowing from the media to the public agenda than the reverse.

How can you get your cause on the media and get it on the public agenda? Before looking at strategies for gaining access to the mass media, we should underscore the point that there is no general *right* of access to the media in our society. Even the president of the United States must ask for television time, and the individual networks will judge whether or not they feel the public interest would be served by granting time. Obviously, the president of the United States has a far greater chance of being granted time than the average citizen, but the average citizen can maximize the probability that access to newspapers or radio and television stations will be granted. The persuasive communicator must be able to make a particular cause seem newsworthy or important enough so that the media will devote space or time to the issue. Below are a few suggestions that may help in accomplishing that task:

1. Form a committee or an organization. If the communicator can speak for a committee of people interested in a particular topic, it raises the probability that the media will pay attention. A committee has more weight than a single individual. The Reverend Jerry Falwell is an excellent example of the use of such a committee or organization. Reverend Falwell was simply the pastor of a single church until he formed the organization called "The Moral Majority." The fact that there *was* an organization (regardless of whether it was actually a majority) gave weight to his pronouncements, since he was seen as representing a far larger group of people.

2. Issue a press release. Newspapers just hate the person who calls up and says, "I have something that I want you to put in the paper." They have to take time to take down all the details of the story, and then take further time to write the story. If a story is really newsworthy, calling it in will work, but if the story is borderline in terms of newsworthiness, calling it in is likely to prove a failure. On the other hand, there are almost always "holes" in a paper or on a radio or television news broadcast that need to be filled. An editor is likely to reach for a recent news release when that occurs.

3. Appear before a public body. The media tend to cover the meetings of local city councils, school boards, planning commissions, and other public bodies. At most such meetings, there is a time set for comments from the public. The persuasive communicator who uses that time to make a short, reasoned statement is likely to be covered by whatever reporter is present. Furthermore, the communicator who has a written summary of the remarks available to the press is even more likely to see those remarks in a subsequent story.

4. Write a letter. Newspapers can print only a few letters each day, but there is a good chance that a well-written letter calling attention to a situation that the paper may have overlooked will be chosen for the editorial page. Editors tend to get very few *well-written* letters, and will certainly prefer those over the mass of other mail that comes in. It is important to note that editors tend to reject "form letters" that have obviously been written and sent to a number of different outlets. They far prefer letters that represent an individual's own, well-thought-out viewpoint. Other excellent outlets are television stations. Many television stations have a short editorial space on the evening news and will offer that space to local citizens who write in and make a case.

5. Call in to a talk show. One of the most popular radio formats is the one where the radio host takes calls from listeners who have things they want to discuss. These shows enjoy a large listening audience, and it is quite possible that a question raised during one of these sessions will help the source succeed in transmitting a concern to the intended audience.

The mass media *can* be used even by the average citizen. It does take effort, but it can be done. Few citizens ever go to the trouble of trying to do any of the things we have suggested above. Unless a persuasive communicator has tried some of these methods and still failed, it is unfair to lay the blame on the media for not being responsive to the people. Whether it is in the forum function, or in the information function, the mass media in our society play a major role in determining the outcomes of persuasive campaigns.

The influence of the media

Has a shocking murder been committed? Someone will invariably suggest that the committer of the crime may have gotten the idea from television. Are the media the powerful manipulators of people as they are sometimes portrayed? Or are they simply tools available for message transmission of ideas of all kinds? Two general models of mass communication effects have been postulated. The first can be labeled a "limited-effects model."[23] The basic research for the limited-effects model began with a study by Star and Hughes in 1949.[24] They were interested in the effects of a six-week campaign in Cincinnati to improve attitudes toward the United Nations. Materials were presented on radio, in newspapers, and through other mass-media outlets. Measurements were taken shortly after the campaign was over, and the results showed that relatively little attitude change had occurred. In delayed post-tests the results were quite different. Considerable attitude change had taken place in favor of the United Nations.

Star and Hughes hypothesized that after the presentation of materials through mass-media channels had been made, people in the city turned for confirming evidence to a set of *opinion leaders* and that through interpersonal contact with these opinion leaders, attitudinal changes were finally made.

An extremely simplified version of the original two-stage flow hypothesis is that a communicator has an idea and makes use of the mass media to transmit the idea in a persuasive message to the population of a city or area. All of the people, or at least most of the people, may be exposed to the message, but attitude change after this initial presentation takes place for only a few. Some of the individuals who *are* affected by the message when it is initially presented through the mass media become opinion leaders and proceed to engage in personal persuasive contact with others. If the opinion leaders are successful in their efforts, then, after some time has passed, the message first presented through the media may affect the entire audience, and significant changes will have occurred.

The two-stage flow hypothesis was first fully formulated by Lazarsfeld, Berelson, and Gaudet in *The People's Choice*, a report of an election campaign.[25] Since then, a number of other studies have been performed specifically attempting to test the two-stage flow theory. The studies cover a wide range of topics and audiences. Merton studied the communication patterns and personal-influence patterns in Rovere, New Jersey.[26] Katz and Lazarsfeld[27] made a landmark study in Decatur, Illinois, of the ways in which decisions were made by individuals about marketing, fashions, movies, and public affairs. They confirmed the central notion that there are a small number of individuals who serve as opinion leaders in each of these areas of decision making.

It was the data emerging from these studies that led to the development of the limited-effects model and its full description by Klapper in 1960.[28] The limited-effects model and the two-stage flow hypothesis has been criticized by a number of researchers as being oversimplified.[29] The process of influence is not, they say, a simple two-step process where a single group of opinion givers listens to the media and then feeds its opinions to a less enlightened group of passive receivers. Instead, there seem to be many opinion leaders, operating at several levels. Opinion leaders may have their own opinion leaders. There are different opinion leaders for each topic and group. An individual serving as an opinion leader for one group may not serve the same function in another group. Furthermore, opinion leaders are themselves influenced by other influentials, so that a more accurate portrayal would seem to involve a multistep process.

Recently, this view has received the same kind of criticism as has the two-step flow model. Chaffee,[30] Comstock et al.,[31] and Roberts and Bachen[32] have all pointed to direct and powerful effects of the mass media. Chaffee suggests that direct influence from the media is the rule, and not the exception. In this more current view, the media are posited as having direct influences on the information that people acquire, a direct influence on making people aware of consensus definitions of problems, and as responsible for changing attitudes and opinions under some circumstances.

The opinion leader is still seen as having significant influence in certain kinds of circumstances. There are issues that the media treat in conflicting ways, that one newspaper treats in one fashion and another treats in an opposite fashion. Some issues are reported, but not considered important by a receiver until contact has been made with an opinion leader. Those people who do serve as opinion leaders seem to have a few characteristics that set them apart from the larger mass of receivers:

1. Opinion leaders tend to be greater consumers of the mass media than those who consult the leaders for information. They listen more, read more, and view more television than their followers. Troldahl and VanDam suggest that individuals can be separated into essentially two groups in terms of their mass-media usage.[33] One group consists of individuals with relatively high mass-media usage and also high interpersonal contacts. They ask for information, and they give information. The ranks of the opinion leaders are filled from this set of individuals, and individuals shift from leader to follower status depending on the particular topic under discussion. The second group consists of individuals who are essentially inactive. They do not make extensive use of the mass media, nor do they make many interpersonal contacts. This study is helpful because it separates the active receivers from the inactive receivers, and makes it easier to see the information-receiving characteristics of those who act as opinion leaders.

2. Opinion leaders are centers within a communication net. They are consulted more frequently for information, and they frequently consult the other members of their groups. In other words, there is a constant interactive process through which people give and receive information. A diagram of the process might appear as in Figure 9.1. Mr. A. is clearly an opinion leader. He is talked to by many people, and he talks to many people. Note that Mr. A is the opinion leader for that one group. In another group, Mr. A may seek the advice of another opinion leader, as shown in his relationship with Mr. B. In the Decatur study, there was clear evidence that the flow of information was not always a two-stage process.[34] The authors identified several chains leading from one opinion leader to another, and they pointed out that it may be necessary to trace back through several opinion leaders before finding the primary source of information as it came from the mass media.

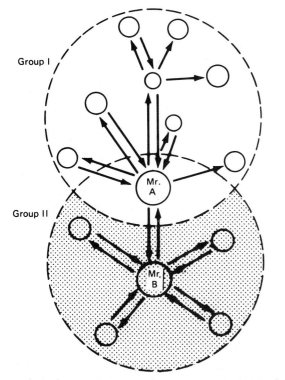

Figure 9.1. Opinion Leaders in Two Groups. Mr. A is an opinion leader for Group I, while Mr. B is an opinion leader for Group II.

Group I

Group II

Mr. A

Mr. B

counteract the influence of the mass media; at other times, a message from the mass media will have the effect of canceling out a message from an interpersonal source. At times, the media may be the only source of information available, and your attitudes may be determined solely by what is shown on the media. At still other times, the media and interpersonal sources will act together to provide a powerful stimulus for attitude change and eventual social action.

Before summarizing our chapter on the mass media channels available to the persuasive communicator, we should give some advice to that communicator wishing to plan a persuasive campaign. Below are some questions that the source ought to ask regarding the use of the mass media as a channel for persuasive messages:

1. Does the communicator merely want to draw the *attention* of an audience to a problem that will be dealt with later in a more extensive manner? The mass media can serve very effectively as an attention-getting, agenda-setting method of reaching an audience.

2. Does the intended audience hold strong or weak attitudes about the proposed topic? The mass media alone may serve to change weakly held attitudes, particularly in the absence of opposing sources, but the mass media alone may not be sufficient to change attitudes or beliefs that are deeply rooted or intensely held.

3. Are receivers in favor of or opposed to the topic being communicated? The mass media are more effective in strengthening attitudes than in changing attitudes. Face-to-face communication may be necessary if strong negative attitudes are held toward a topic.

4. Is there a necessity for personal commitment to a behavior on the part of a receiver? For example, if a persuasive communicator needs to have the personal commitment of a receiver so that the receiver will follow through on a promise, the mass media are a poor channel. Commitment is more easily secured through personal contacts.

3. Opinion leaders themselves are affected more by face-to-face communication than by the media. It is certainly the case that opinion leaders are heavy users of the media and decisions are made on the basis of this contact with the media. But the persuasive communicator cannot expect to place a message on television or an advertisement in the newspaper and then sit back to wait for results. The opinion leader is affected more by people than by the media.

The mass media have a powerful influence to play in our society. They serve as reinforcers of attitudes and opinions, as a determiner of the way in which we view the world around us, and as an important force in shaping behavior. Like many of the other communication variables we have discussed, however, these effects are not simple. At times, interpersonal face-to-face situations will

5. How much money does the source have to work with? Television, on any large scale, requires money in large amounts. A senatorial campaign in a large state might spend more than 2 million dollars for television time alone. A one-minute spot during the Super Bowl may cost over 300 thousand dollars. Personal, face-to-face communication will reach far fewer people than will television or any of the other mass media, but its cost is in terms of the source's time and energy, and thus affordable.

6. Who are the receivers? Many times, a persuasive communicator examines a problem and concludes that all the citizens of a community need to be contacted. A more careful analysis may show that the eventual decision will be made by only a few influentials in the community, and that a face-to-face campaign will be more effective. When only a few must be reached, personal contact may be the most effective method to use. When the audience is large, the mass media may have to be used, even if the message will not be as effective with each receiver.

Questions like these must be answered by the communicator who must choose between a face-to-face presentation of his material and a presentation in which something is interposed between the source and his receivers.

Summary

Communication channels can be viewed by a source in a number of different ways. It is useful first to examine the basic mechanisms that we use to acquire information from the world around us: our eyes and our ears. This examination will assist the persuasive communicator in deciding which is the best channel to use to transmit a particular message. A decision regarding whether the communicator should utilize face-to-face communication or one of the less personal channels will depend on the source's intentions, the nature and size of the audience to be reached, and the type of message to be transmitted.

The mass media are important channels of communication. They allow the persuasive communicator to reach audiences otherwise unavailable, but the source must be aware that the mass media are not a panacea for all problems in reaching an audience. Persuasive communication may depend on a combined use of interpersonal communication and mass communication. The persuasive communicator can maximize efforts by using the mass media to gain attention and to educate, while using face-to-face communication to reach those influentials most important to the persuasive effort.

Footnotes

1. R. K. Merton, *Mass Persuasion: The Social Psychology of a War Bond Drive* (Harper and Brothers, New York, 1946).

2. S. Chaiken and A. H. Eagly, "Communicator Modality As a Determinant of Message Persuasiveness and Message Comprehensibility," *Journal of Personality and Social Psychology*, vol. 34 (1976), pp. 605–614.

3. S. Chaiken and A. H. Eagly, "Communicator Modality As a Determinant of Persuasion: The Role of Communicator Salience," *Journal of Personality and Social Psychology*, vol. 45 (1983), pp. 241–256.

4. Chaiken and Eagly, "Communicator Modality As a Determinant of Persuasion: The Role of Communicator Salience."

5. L. K. Meringoff, M. M. Vibbert, C. A. Char, D. E. Fernie, G. S. Banker, and H. Gardner, "How Is Children's Learning from Television Distinctive? Exploiting the Medium Methodologically," in J. Bryant and D. R. Anderson, eds., *Children's Understanding of Television* (New York: Academic Press, 1983), pp. 151–180.

6. R. N. W. Travers, "The Transmission of Information to Human Receivers," *AV Communication Review,* vol. 12 (1964), pp. 373–385.

7. J. Bryant and P. W. Comisky, "The Effect of Positioning a Message Within Differently Cognitively Involving Portions of a Television Segment on Recall of the Message," *Human Communication Research*, vol. 5 (1978), pp. 63–75.

8. J. L. Singer and D. G. Singer, "Implications of Childhood Television Viewing for Cognition, Imagination and Emotion," in J. Bryant and D. R. Anderson, eds., *Children's Understanding of Television* (New York: Academic Press, 1983), pp. 265–296.

9. See S. Ball and G. Bogatz, *The First Year of Sesame Street: An Evaluation* (Princeton: Educational Testing Service, 1971); G. S. Lesser, *Children and Television: Lessons from Sesame Street* (New York: Vintage, 1974); W. Schramm, *Big Media, Little Media: Tools and Technologies for Instruction* (Beverly Hills: Sage, 1977).

10. Singer and Singer, "Implications of Childhood Television Viewing."

11. Singer and Singer, "Implications of Childhood Television Viewing," p. 274.

12. J. Bryant, D. Zillmann, and D. Brown, "Entertainment Features in Children's Educational Television: Effects on Attention and Information Acquisition," in J. Bryant and D. R. Anderson, eds., *Children's Understanding of Television* (New York: Academic, 1983), pp. 221–240.

13. W. P. Davison, J. Boylan, and F. T. C. Yu, *Mass Media: Systems and Effects* (New York: Praeger, 1976), p. 111.

14. D. F. Roberts and N. Maccoby, "Effects of Mass Communication," in *Handbook of Social Psychology* (Reading, Mass.: Addison-Wesley, 1985), pp. 21–22 of Chapter 23.

15. W. I. Rivers, T. Peterson, and J. Jensen, *The Mass Media and Modern Society* (New York: Holt, Rinehart and Winston, 1971).

16. S. H. Chaffee and M. J. Petrick, *Using the Mass Media: Communication Problems in American Society* (New York: McGraw-Hill, 1975), pp. 34–35.

17. C. R. Wright, *Mass Communication: A Sociological Perspective*, 2nd ed. (New York: Random House, 1975).

18. B. S. Greenberg, *Life on Television: Content Analysis of U.S. TV Drama* (Norwood, N.J.: Ablex, 1980).

19. S. Cutlip, "Content and Flow of AP News—From Trunk to TTS to Reader," *Journalism Quarterly* (Fall 1954), pp. 434–446.

20. Roberts and Maccoby, "Effects of Mass Communication," p. 26.

21. M. E. McCombs, "Newspapers versus Television: Mass Communication Effects Across Time," in D. L. Shaw and M. E. McCombs, eds., *The Emergence of American Political Issues: The Agenda Setting Functions of the Press* (St. Paul, Minn.: West Publishing Co., 1977), pp. 89–105.

22. A. B. Sohn, "A Longitudinal Analysis of Local Nonpolitical Agenda-Setting Effects," *Journalism Quarterly*, vol. 55, pp. 325–333.

23. Roberts and Maccoby, "Effects of Mass Communication," p. 3.

24. S. Star and H. Hughes, "Report of an Educational Campaign: The Cincinnati Plan for the United Nations," *American Journal of Sociology*, vol. 55 (1950), pp. 389–400.

25. P. Lazarsfeld, B. Berelson, and H. Gaudet, *The People's Choice* (New York: Columbia University Press, 1948).

26. R. Merton, *Social Theory and Social Structure* (New York: The Free Press of Glencoe, 1949).

27. E. Katz and P. F. Lazarsfeld, *Personal Influence: The Part Played by People in the Flow of Mass Communications* (New York: The Free Press of Glencoe, 1955).

28. J. Klapper, *The Effects of Mass Communication* (New York: The Free Press, 1960).

29. J. P. Robinson, "Mass Communication and Information Diffusion," in F. G. Kline and P. J. Tichenor, eds., *Current Perspectives in Mass Communication Research* (Beverly Hills: Sage Publications, 1972), pp. 71–94.

30. S. H. Chaffee, "The Interpersonal Context of Mass Communication," in F. G. Kline and P. J. Tichenor, eds., *Current Perspectives in Mass Communication Research* (Beverly Hills: Sage, 1972), pp. 107–137.

31. G. Comstock, S. Chaffee, N. Katzman, M. McCombs, and D. Roberts, *Television and Human Behavior* (New York: Columbia University Press, 1978).

32. D. F. Roberts and C. M. Bachen, "Mass Communication Effects," *Ann. Review of Psychology*, vol. 32, pp. 307–356.

33. V. Troldahl and R. VanDam, "Face-to-Face Communication," pp. 632–634.

34. P. Lazarsfeld and R. Merton, "Mass Communication, Popular Taste and Organized Social Action," in L. Bryson, ed., *The Communication of Ideas* (New York: Harper and Row, 1948).

CHAPTER TEN

Persuasion in Interpersonal Relationships

A good deal of persuasion occurs in interpersonal relationships, and considerable attention has been focused on face-to-face persuasion in the last ten years. In this chapter we will discuss the methods people generally use to effect changes in their daily lives. In the next three chapters, we will explore the effects of messages used during bargaining sessions, in small group settings, and inside the organization. Many of the terms employed in this chapter will be employed in later chapters. For example, in this area of research, the person doing the persuading is called the "agent," and the person who is being persuaded is called the "target."

Social influence

According to Raven and Kruglanski, social influence is defined as a change in one person that has its origin in another person or group.[1] More recently, the term "compliance-gaining" has been used to denote the types of strategies a person uses in order to get another person to comply with a request. There are three issues of interest in the social-influence area: (1) How do people go about influencing each other?, (2) When do people use the strategies, and why?, and (3) How effective are the strategies at influencing others?

Message strategies I: Theoretical sources of influence

Classic work by social psychologists tells us that there are six basic types of social influence: informational, referent, expert, legitimate, reward, and coercive. Each can have a number of effects on a target (receiver)—including whether the target would publicly change a behavior, privately adopt the beliefs of the agent, have more positive interactions with the agent, and increase or decrease identification with the agent. Table 10.1 summarizes, according to Raven and Kruglanski, the relationships between each of these types of influence and these four effects.

Informational influence

An agent may try to persuade another through informational influence—by providing information not previously available to the target. There are many examples of informational influence. Suppose you moved to a new college or started to work for a new company. When people tell you where there are good places to eat, where to park to avoid theft, or how to get off the campus and out of the city easily, they are employing informational influence. Informational influence very of-ten leads to both a change in overt behavior (you park in parking lot X) and in private beliefs (you believe your car is safer there). Simply knowing facts about an area, however, does not necessarily mean people will seek you out as a friend or increase identification with you (see Table 10.1).

Referent influence

Referent influence stems from the fact that the target identifies with the agent, or at least desires identification. Recall from Chapter 4 that the term "reference group" was used to describe the types of groups in which a person desires membership. The term is used here to denote the same kind of desire to be "one" with a source. Often, when people are attracted to each other and perceive similarities between them, they may comply with requests. Married persons, for example, use more referent power than people in other types of relationships.[2] In a strict sense, referent influence is, like source credibility, a quality that is perceived from the target's perspective (he or she would like to grow up to be just like Joe Montana, Jesse Jackson, a Dallas Cowboy cheerleader, and so on). However, we generally call any appeal to similarity or to mutual attraction an instance of referent influence. Referent power leads to a change in both public behaviors and in private

Table 10.1. Effects of Using Different Types of Social Influence in Terms of Moving Closer to the Agent (+), Moving Away from the Agent (0) or Moving Against the Agent (−)

Source of Influence Employed by Agent	Effects on B			
	Public Behavior	Private Beliefs	Interaction with Agent	Identification with Agent
Information	+	+	0(?)	?
Referent	+	+	+	+
Expert	+	+	0	0
Legitimate	+	+	0	0
Reward	+	0	+	0
Coercion	+	−	−	−

Adapted from B. H. Raven and A. W. Kruglanski, "Conflict and Power," in P. Swingle, ed., *The Structure of Conflict* (New York: Academic, 1970), pp. 69–109.

beliefs. It also leads to positive interactions with the agent, and, of course, to increased identification with the agent.

Expert influence

Following from the work on credibility, we say that an agent has expert power over the target if the receiver believes that the source has superior training or ability. Individuals who are gifted at computer work, who have a masterful command of the English language, or who are highly effective are perceived to be experts in these particular domains. As Table 10.1 indicates, expert influence often leads to changes both in public behavior and in private adoption of beliefs.

Legitimate influence

On many occasions, people ask us to do things and we comply because the agents have a *right* to make the request and, thus, we feel *obligated* to comply. In an organization, a supervisor has the right to tell people to work at a particular rate, to be prompt, to be safe, and so on. In our daily lives, we feel that we have a right to peace and quiet in our own homes, and we feel that our rights have been infringed upon by barking dogs, loud stereos, and by phone solicitors who call late at night. However, legitimate influence is the most problematic of all of the theoretical forms of influence because what we see as rights and obligations depends, in part, on how we were socialized. For example, most people would feel that a loud barking dog owned by a neighbor is infringing on their rights, and, therefore, they would try to persuade the person to do something about the dog. There are some people, however, who feel that people have a right to do whatever they desire to do on their own property. Thus, while the barking dog annoys them, they feel it would be infringing upon the neighbor's rights to try to persuade the neighbor ("It's none of my business. I wouldn't want him to come over here and tell me what to do on my property.").

Legitimate influence can be effective in influencing others and in reducing conflict if both par-

ties share the same perspective concerning legitimacy. Legitimate influence can lead to changes in public behavior and in private beliefs.

Reward and coercive influences

If an agent can control the rewards and punishments the target receives, then the agent may use rewards or coercion to effect changes. Rewards and punishments can include physical materials (money, candy) as well as intangible ones (love, affection, disapproval). The use of rewards leads the target to change public behavior. Further, sources who reward their receivers often promote more positive interactions between the target and the agent. However, when we perform a behavior just for the M&M's or bonuses, we do not *necessarily* change our private beliefs. Further, agents who reward targets do not necessarily increase the extent to which the target identifies with them. Coercive power can lead to a change in public behavior. However, we identify less with, avoid interacting with, and learn to dislike the beliefs of, agents who use threats and punishments.

In sum, there are six theoretical methods for influencing others. Each of these may effectively produce a change in public behavior. However, the methods of influence vary considerably in how they affect private beliefs and relational outcomes. We must note that each of these methods of influence differs in the range of contexts to which it may apply.

Message strategies II: Compliance-gaining message strategies

Scholars have employed a myriad of methods and procedures in the analysis of interpersonal persuasion strategies. A partial list would include: Marwell and Schmitt,[3] Falbo,[4] Wiseman and Schenck-Hamlin,[5] Fitzpatrick and Winke,[6] Cody, McLaughlin, and Jordan,[7] Baxter,[8] Kipnis and his colleagues,[9] Clark,[10] and Richmond, Davis, Say-

Table 10.2 A Composite of Typologies of Compliance-Gaining Message Tactics

Type of Tactic	*Explanation/Examples*
I. *Direct request*	The agent simply asks the target to comply to a request. No motivation, inducement, justification, or manipulation accompanies the statement. —Can you give me a ride to the airport tomorrow? —Can you give me a lift to class, if it's not any trouble? —Why don't you think about going to the movies?
II. *Rationality or supporting arguments*	The agent provides one or more reasons why the target should comply—including logic, evidence, data, and so on. —I wrote a detailed plan that justified my ideas. —I diagramed the streets and everything and proved to the judge that it was not possible to leave my house and reach that intersection going 50 mph.
III. *Exchange*	The agent attempts to gain the compliance of the target by proposing an exchange in commodities, services, or favors. —I offered an exchange. —I told him that I'd work his Monday morning shift if he'd do my Sunday afternoon one. —I reminded her of past favors that I did for her.

IV. *Manipulation*	The agent attempts to gain the compliance of the target primarily through emotional means by strategically making the target feel good or bad about him- or herself, or by enhancing the agent's own image.
	I. *Ingratiation*
	  A. *Target enhancement* (flattery, opinion conformity, rendering favors)
	    —I made him feel important.
	    —I put on my happy face and was particularly sweet.
	    —I acted in a friendly manner before asking.
	    —I praised her.
	  B. *Self-enhancement* (agent engages in attractive self-presentations)
	    —I demonstrated my competence before asking.
	    —I performed well, then asked.
	    —I reminded her about my qualifications.
	II. *Negative-identity management*
	  —I showed my disappointment in him.
	  —I acted hurt.
	  —I made her feel guilty.

V. *Coercive*	The agent promises or implies the use of negative sanctions (punishments or loss of rewards) if the target does not comply with a request. —I threatened to give her an unsatisfactory performance evaluation. —I threatened him with loss of promotion. —I simply ordered her to do what I asked.
VI. *Indirect tactics*	The agent attempts to gain compliance to a request by introducing topics during a conversation so that the target will infer or deduce the agent's intended or desired goal. —I'd hint about how boring my weekends have been. —I'd use small talk to see if she was busy that weekend. —I'd beat about the bush about how we loved this new neighborhood, about how quiet it was and everything. I'd never directly mention their barking dog.

Table 10.2 (continued)

Type of Tactic	Explanation/Examples
VII. *Appeals to love, affection; emotional appeals and personal commitments*	The agent appeals to the target's love and affection for agent, or the agent promises to be more loving in the future. —But Dad, if you loved us you wouldn't kill yourself like this. —Please, Mom, for our sake, go to the hospital. —Dad, I want you to take better care of yourself. —I told my son that I really wanted him to study more as a personal favor to me.

lor, and McCroskey.[11] In Table 10.2 we present an overview of the main categories of strategies that individuals use—a compilation of these various studies.

As Table 10.2 indicates, our typology includes seven general ways in which people try to influence each other. When we say "direct request" we mean only that an agent is using a simple statement or a question in order to achieve a goal. The agent employs neither information, reward, coercive power, nor any other type of inducement. Why, then, some readers may ask, would we call a direct request *"persuasive"*? Actually, some research indicates that a direct request is one of the more common methods for getting other people to do things; Kipnis, Schmidt, and Wilkinson, for example, found that 10 percent of the sampled managers employed direct requests.[12] However, what makes a simple direct request persuasive is the context in which it is used. We generally assume that the agent who uses a direct request does so because he or she believes that the request is a reasonable one, and that no further elaboration is necessary. Imagine that you have just started Xeroxing your 29-page persuasion term paper. A person approaches with a single-paged letter and says, "Excuse me, could I Xerox this?" Probably a number of the readers would consider the request a legitimate one—you have many sheets, the other person has only one. No further elaboration or inducement is necessary on the part of the agent. On the other hand, what if the person behind you had a *20*-page paper and *only* said, "Ex-

cuse me, could I Xerox this?" Few people would step aside. The size of the request is now so large that a simple request is not sufficient for us to comply. We would need more reasons for why we ought to comply, such as, "This term paper is late and my professor is leaving for Africa. I've got to get it to her by three o'clock or I'll get an F, and then I'll be put on probation." Direct requests, then, can be effective in influencing others so long as the request appears legitimate, and does not involve much cost.[13]

Rationality (or supporting evidence) includes messages where the agent provides logic, evidence, or data to aid in convincing the target to comply. Rationality serves the function of both legitimizing the request as well as providing an inducement for the target to alter attitudes and behaviors. We should note that it is sometimes useful to specify who benefits from the use of rationality. Sometimes the message claims that the agent benefits, sometimes that the target benefits, and sometimes that both people benefit. Suppose you wanted to persuade your landlord to fix your plumbing promptly. Which of the following messages would you use?

"Listen, the plumbing needs repair soon. It keeps me awake at night and I need to sleep. I'm having people over this weekend, and I can't have the place looking like this."

"Listen, the plumbing needs repair soon. I tried to find the trouble but I don't know what's wrong. But, it does look like the leak's also going down behind the baseboard, which is soaking wet. If you don't repair it soon, it's going to be a pretty expensive repair job for you later."

Exchange compliance-gaining tactics involve an attempt at having the two parties achieve a mutually agreeable compromise. An exchange in commodities, services, or favors is made. Such techniques can simply be one short exchange (two people bargain over materials in Mexico or Jerusalem), an exchange that has been arranged over time ("I'll work your Saturday shift this weekend, if you'll work my Sunday shift on December 1st"), or an elaborate negotiation process.

Manipulation tactics include two general methods of gaining compliance through strategically altering the emotions of the receiver. In one, *ingratiation* is used to enhance the image or self-esteem of the target, or to enhance the image or perceived competence of the agent. In the former, flattery and praise are offered to the target to get him or her in the "right frame of mind"; the agent expresses the same opinions as the target so that the target is led to believe that the agent is likeable. In the second type of ingratiation, the agent demonstrates competence, performs well, reminds others of his or her competence, worth, or training, in order to appear more attractive to others. All of these tactics serve the purpose of getting the target to like the agent.

The second general mode of manipulation is to make the target feel *negative* (hence "*negative identity management*") by displaying disappointment, acting hurt, pouting, and generally making the target feel guilty.

Coercive power was discussed above. Of the examples given in Table 10.2 we should note that some studies have distinguished between two types of "harsh" tactics: negative sanctions and assertiveness.[14] In the former, some economic sanction is used against the target, for example, loss of job or loss of a raise. Assertiveness is used, however, when the coercive influence is directed toward the target personally, as in verbal anger, bawling him or her out, screaming, and similar personal attacks.

In some contexts, we do not want to be bold by directly asking a question or making a direct request (Can you go to a movie Saturday? Can you repay the $20 you borrowed?). We want to know if a person is unattached for the weekend, and likes us; we want to know if the friend has the $20 and doesn't mind our bringing up the topic. In situations such as these we use *indirect tactics* such as hinting and small talk. If the other person gets the hint, he or she may cooperate by providing information we need so that we do not need to ask the question directly.

Finally, a number of studies have suggested a type of strategy called "emotional appeals," "activation of personal commitments," or "appeals to love and affection." In using such tactics the agent displays concern and worry over, or love for, the target. There is an implication that the relational commitment is a compelling reason for the target to comply, and that compliance will either improve the relationship or remove an obstacle to improved relations.

A number of the message strategies identified in the compliance-gaining literature show considerable overlap with the theoretical sources of influence reviewed above. Informational influence directly corresponds to rationality, coercive compliance-gaining techniques directly parallel coercive influence, and personal commitments generally reflect attempts at referent influence. Also, as noted above, agents probably feel that a direct request is legitimate when they use it on others. On the other hand, there are at least two types of compliance-gaining strategies not reflected in the theoretical sources of literature—*manipulation* and *indirectness*.

We have addressed one fundamental issue in social influence: What are the types of messages people use in order to influence each other? Our next issue deals with when and why people use specific messages.

There are three kinds of explanations for strategy selection: (1) People have preferences for certain strategies when trying to influence others; (2) People select strategies based on attributions of causality; and (3) People select strategies based on their knowledge of situations.

Personal preferences

Dogmatic persons, the reader will recall from Chapter 3, have closed minds, and think in black/white, good/bad, dichotomies. Druckman[15] found that highly dogmatic people were less flexible in bargaining situations than low dogmatics, and studies by Boster and his colleagues demonstrate that persons who score high on dogmatism are more verbally aggressive than low dogmatics.[16] Hunter, Gerbing, and Boster[17] recently identified several subcomponents of Machiavellianism (negativism, flattery, rejection of honesty and morality). Boster and his colleagues found that people who score high on negativism (that is, people who feel that others are *not* good, kind, brave, altruistic, dependable, or moral) are more likely to be verbally aggressive than those who score low on negativism.

On the other hand, Pandey and Rastogi[18] found that high Machiavellians were more likely to use ingratiation tactics. In an interview context, higher Machiavellians praised the members of the interview board and expressed agreement with the board members more frequently than low Machiavellians. Christie and Geis[19] and Roloff and Barnicott[20] found Machiavellians more *active* in influencing others by using more tactics than low Machiavellians. These results lead us to conclude that high Machiavellians use more tactics than low Machiavellians and are more willing to use emotion-based tactics (ingratiation, deceit, some forms of assertiveness).

Another personality variable of interest is *internal-external locus of control.*[21] People who are internal in their locus of control believe that their achievements will be rewarded, that they can have an impact on the world and help shape their own destinies, that the future is bright, and that they can prevent war, crime, and poverty. Internals believe that control of their behavior stems from their own internal motivations, abilities, and achievements. Externals, however, have little hope in controlling outcomes, feel that effort is not necessarily rewarded (one has to be in the right place at the right time to get rewards); they believe that their behavior is not motivated internally, but that they are responding to external pressures. Because of their strong achievement needs, internals are more likely to resist pressures to conform or to be influenced by experimenters. They are also more likely to be persistent in influencing others, that is, to try more strategies over time.[22] It is also obvious that the tactics internals and externals use to influence others are affected by their respective philosophies. Goodstadt and Hjelle[23] demonstrated this in the following study.

Goodstadt and Hjelle recruited college students to participate in an industrial simulation. The students were told to be supervisors of three high-school students who were working as clerical assistants. The "supervisors" were told that the workers would report their progress on the clerical work at regular intervals and that their supervisory role required them to keep productivity at a certain level. The supervisors were given a range of tactics they could use to motivate the student workers: *delegated powers*, which included coercive power, reward power, and instruction; and *personal powers*, which included the use of personal encouragements, setting new, personal, achievement schedules for the workers, and personally admonishing the workers.

During the actual study when the workers' progress was reported, Goodstadt and Hjelle manipulated the workers' performances. Each supervisor had three workers. Workers 1 and 3 exceeded the company standards, and tended to improve as time progressed. However, Worker 2 was slower. Half of the supervisors were led to believe that the slow worker was inept—that the worker couldn't understand how to do the clerical task. The other half of the supervisors were led to believe that the slow worker had a poor attitude—that is, the worker claimed that the clerical work was beneath his dignity and intelligence, was ridiculous work, and so on. Goodstadt and Hjelle were interested in what tactics either internal- or external-locus-of-control supervisors would use on inept and poor-attitude workers.

The results of the study indicated that both internal and external supervisors used more "instruction" tactics on inept workers and used more coercive tactics on workers with poor attitudes. The results concerning locus of control were straightforward; internals used more *personal* powers of persuasion than did externals, while externals used more coercive power than did internals.

These results indicate that internals and externals employ tactics compatible with their philosophy of how the world operates—internals perceive themselves to be self-starters and self-motivated and thus use personal tactics that appeal to the same motivations in their subordinates; externals perceive themselves as behaving in accordance with external pressures and thus try to influence others, when given the power, by increasing external pressures on the receivers.

Most of us believe that there are differences between men and women in the types of tactics they use on others. Johnson,[24] for example, argued that the use of power is likely to be affected by sex-role stereotypes, and she demonstrated that women traditionally have less access to concrete resources (thus limiting the use of reward and coercive bases of power), and have less access to resources that facilitate building the impression of competence. As a consequence, Johnson felt that females would be expected to use more indirect, personal, and helpless modes of influence. In her study, she found that coercive, expert, information, legitimate, and "indirect information" tactics were more strongly associated with masculinity while women were expected to use personal rewards and appeals to love and affection. Seven years later, Burgoon, Dillard, and Doran[25] found that these stereotypical expectations still existed: Coercive power was perceived to be masculine and females were expected to use more exchange types of tactics.

These studies indicate that we *expect* males and females to behave in a particular way. Do males and females *actually* differ in the strategies they use? Several studies have in fact documented gender differences, generally indicating that males are more blunt and direct and use more tactics of coercion than do females, who are less direct and,

when employing pressure, are more likely to use some form of emotion-based tactic.[26] However, there is no *consistent* evidence that females select different tactics than males. Instead, it appears that men and women are likely to differ from one another in only a few types of communication situations. For example, Fitzpatrick and Winke[27] conducted a survey on how people handle conflicts and found that there were no significant differences between men and women when they had conflicts with people of the opposite sex. However, sex differences were obtained when males had conflicts with their male best friends and when females had conflicts with their female best friends. Males tended to use abrupt tactics that Fitzpatrick and Winke referred to as "nonnegotiation," such as refusing to talk about the issue, or arguing until the person changes his or her mind, while females tended to talk with the friends, to make their partners feel bad about not complying to the request, or to personally reject the partners.

In a survey conducted in organizational settings, Putnam and Wilson[28] found that females used more indirect tactics than did males—but only during the first year of employment. Putnam and Wilson found that as females became more socialized into the organization, they relied less on avoidance tactics and over a 5-year time span they slightly increased their use of "solution-oriented" tactics. What they called "solution-oriented" tactics included what we have referred to here as exchange and informational influence. Men, however, decreased their reliance on solution-oriented tactics and increased their use of avoidance tactics during the 5-year time span.

Attribution theory and strategy selection

In Chapter 3 we introduced attribution theory, and noted that the central concern of this theory is how people go about making decisions concerning the *cause* of behaviors. Also recall that Kelley[29] suggested that there are three factors we take into consideration when we make attributions of causality: *distinctiveness, consistency, and consensus*. We had concluded that we are likely to make an *internal* attribution when distinctivenesss is low, consistency is high, and consensus is low; for example, when the student drinks beer in many different situations, drinks beer consistently over time, and drinks beer when no one else is drinking beer.

One study that clearly demonstrated the impact of attributions on face-to-face persuasion is a study on roommate conflicts by Alan Sillars.[30] Sillars questioned first-year residents in a dorm at the University of Wisconsin during the eleventh week of the fall semester about conflicts they had with their roommates. He asked them to recall any conflict they might have had, to rate whether they felt that they had caused the conflict or whether their roommate had caused the conflict, whether the conflict was stabilized (that is, whether the conflict was fully resolved or likely to reoccur), and whether they perceived their roommate to be cooperative or resistant to resolving the conflict. Sillars asked how the respondents handled the conflict, and he found that the tactics they reported could be broken down into three categories:

(1) *passive-indirect* (52 percent of all tactics), including letting the issue resolve itself, avoiding the issue, avoiding the person, hinting, joking and setting an example, and submission; (2) *integrative tactics* (19 percent of the tactics), where the agent tries to resolve the conflict to mutual agreement; and (3) *distributive tactics* (29 percent of the tactics), where the agent tries to "win out" over the target, or at least tries to win concessions from the roommate. These latter tactics included "noncoercive compliance gaining" (requests, demanding, and persuading) and "coercive compliance gaining" (aggressive emotion and threats).

Sillars found that respondents used passive-indirect tactics when they felt that the conflict was going to occur again and when they felt that the roommate was not going to be cooperative. Also, they were somewhat less likely to use passive-indirect tactics when they attributed blame for the conflict to themselves. To us, these results generally indicate that when the agents felt that they wouldn't be successful (a difficult roommate and a reoccurring problem—the bathroom has always been left dirty in the morning and it will probably always be left dirty in the morning), then they would use passive-indirect tactics. Second, Sillars found that agents used integrative tactics when the conflict was a one-shot dispute, the roommate was perceived to be cooperative, and the agent felt he or she was the cause of the conflict. For example, if a person, after successfully cleaning up his part of the apartment for ten consecutive Saturdays, fails to clean up his room on the eleventh, he might suspect that his roommate is a little annoyed by it. In such contexts, a person may feel that a resolution can be reached, and thus discloses and/or problem solves. Finally, Sillars found that agents were somewhat more likely to use distributive tactics when they felt that the roommate would not be cooperative and that the roommate was to blame for the conflict.

Obviously, studies in attribution theory indicate that our attributions concerning the cause of behavior do influence how we communicate and behave toward others.

Situational determinants of strategy

For years our students have asked us, "Don't the results of these studies depend on the situation?" Yes, many of our experiences are specific to certain types of situations or events. After being in similar types of situations over the years we learn which types of tactics failed and which succeeded, and we learn which type of tactic is effective and appropriate for particular kinds of events. A number of studies have focused on our preferences for using particular types of strategies, and a number of studies have focused on how we go about persuading others.

As a general rule, studies show that agents first attempt to use direct requests or rational tactics before they use emotionally charged tactics or coercive influence. Table 10.3, for example, presents a summary of results for two of these studies. Rule, Bisanz, and Kohn[31] gave students a list of

Table 10.3. Preference of Using Various Social Influence Tactics

Rule, Bisanz, and Kohn *Rank Ordering of Tactics*	Cody, Canary, and Smith* *First Attempt Tactic*	*Second Attempt Tactic*
Ask	Rationality (52%)	Rationality (31%)
Personal expertise/information	Direct request (47%)	Withdraw (27%)
Personal benefit	Other benefit (28%)	Other benefit (16%)
Invoke role relationship	Appeal to love (14%)	Negative identity (16%)
Bargain favor	Exchange (14%)	Exchange (15%)
Norm	Indirect (12%)	Direct request
Moral principle	Distributive	(wait and ask again)
Altruism	(negative identity	(12%)
Butter up	+ coercive) (12%)	Coercive (9%)
Bargain object		Appeal to love, emotions,
Emotional appeal		and so on (8%)
Personal criticism		
Deceive		
Threaten		
Force		

* Percentages total more than 100% because agents could use more than one tactic at a time.
Adapted from B. G. Rule, G. L. Bisanz, and M. Kohn, "Anatomy of a Persuasion Schema: Targets, Goals, and Strategies," *Journal of Personality and Social Psychology,* vol. 48 (1985), pp. 1127–1140; M. J. Cody, D. Canary, and S. Smith, "Compliance-Gaining Strategy Selection: Episodes and Goals," in J. Daly and J. Wiemann, eds., *Communicating Strategically* (Hillsdale, N.J.: Erlbaum, 1987).

tactics and had the students rank order them from most to least preferred. Rule et al. found that "ask" (what we call direct request) and various rational approaches (personal expertise/gives information, invoke role relationships, norm, moral principle) are the most preferred, followed by exchange tactics (bargain favor and object), and ingratiation tactics (butter up). Next, emotional appeals and altruism, which reflect appeals to love and affection, were ranked over personal criticism and coercive influence (threat and force). Cody, Canary, and Smith[32] used a different approach by having students write essays about how they went about persuading people in various situations. These essays were coded in terms of the "first attempt" message and "second attempt" message (what students did, or what they would have done if they did not succeed with the first attempt message). Cody et al. found, first, that the majority of the first attempt tactics were direct requests or rational tactics. Other benefit tactics was the third

most popular approach, and, paralleling Rule et al.'s results, emotional tactics, exchange, indirect, and distributive tactics followed in descending order of use.

With the exception of exchange (used by 15 percent of the agents as their first message and by 15 percent as the second), agents used very different tactics when overcoming a resistant target (see right column in Table 10.3). Agents used fewer positive tactics and fewer rationality and direct request tactics, and increased reliance on negative tactics. Further, 21 percent of the students withdrew from persuasion if they had not succeeded with the first message. To understand more fully why people use tactics the way they do, we need to talk further about *why* people are trying to persuade others. Several studies indicate that of all the hundreds of events we experience, there are only a small set of reoccuring types of situations we find ourselves in, and we tend to use similar tactics in similar situations. Schank and

Abelson,[33] Rule et al.,[34] and Cody et al. have all discussed different *goals* agents pursue. We will look at the Cody et al. analysis, since they looked at both first and second attempt tactics.

Cody et al. found a number of identifiable goals pursued by persuasive communicators and found that 12 goal-types account for the majority of face-to-face persuasion situations (for college students). These 12 types are presented in Table 10.4).[35] As the results indicate, people use different approaches in each of the different types of goals, and they use different second attempt tactics. A brief characterization follows:

1. *Routine activities* are simply events where you try to persuade others to engage in some common activity—shopping, going out to eat, playing tennis, and so on. Since you expect the friend/roommate to comply, you use a simple direct request. Some agents also include a statement about how the target might benefit from complying (for example, "Let's go shopping. Maybe the alterations on your slacks are done."). If a person failed to gain compliance, a range of second attempt tactics would be used. The typical agent, however, merely withdraws (reason: "It is not a big enough deal to argue over and I'm sure my friend has good reasons for not complying."). Other students would make a statement about how the target might benefit from complying ("Maybe that cute clerk will be there."), while other agents use exchange ("Come on, anyway. I'll help you with that chore later that is keeping you from shopping now."). Our responses to routine activities with parents are different, since we are more dependent upon parents for a number of resources and we make different requests of parents (that is, money, permission to do things, go places, and so on). The typical college student uses a good deal of rationality on parents, along with direct requests. Students also tend to appeal to love, affection, unity, or support, and some use hinting in an attempt, we presume, to see if the parent is open to

persuasion, and so on. If parents refused to comply to the request, students continued to rely on rationality; some, however, would pout or sulk (or otherwise make parents feel guilty for having refused the request). Other students would appeal to love and emotions and others would simply wait until a more opportune time and ask again.

2. *High rights activities* involve trying to get others to engage in an activity that the agent believes others are obligated to perform. That is, a landlord is obligated to make repairs to one's plumbing and one's roommates are obligated to keep phone messages for the student when the student is not home. To gain compliance from others, agents use direct requests (since they do not feel they have to justify their request) and use exchange (appealing to the long-term commitment—"I've paid the rent here . . . ," "I take phone messages for you, you could and should reciprocate."). If they failed to gain compliance, agents use rationality or coercive influence, while some of the agents argue that improved relationships will follow if the target complies (appeal to love and commitment).

3. When we give *advice to others*, we commonly list reasons for how they would benefit from taking our advice, we give general evidence and data to support the advice, we appeal to how our relationship with the advice-receiver might improve (or appeal generally to affection), and we give warnings (we tell advice-receivers what would happen if they didn't take our advice). If peers did not take our advice, we withdraw (since it isn't our business), we list reasons why they'd benefit from taking our advice, and some students would try to make the target feel guilty by not taking the advice (see Table 10.4). Different tactics are used on parents when we give parents advice (for example, "Mom, go ahead and switch jobs if you are so unhappy. . . .") We list reasons that benefit our parents, we use more supporting arguments, and we appeal to emotions (encouraging them, and so on). If our parents

Table 10.4. Use of Tactics in Pursuing Different Types of Goals

Goal-Type	First Attempt* Tactic	Second Attempt Tactic
Routine activities— friends	77% Direct request 41% Other benefit	29% Withdraw 25% Other benefit 18% Exchange
Routine activities— parents	60% Direct request 53% Rationality 16% Appeals to emotions 13% Indirect	47% Rationality 20% Negative identity 13% Appeal to emotions 13% Direct request (wait and ask again)
High rights activities	58% Direct request 21% Exchange	55% Rationality 21% Coercive 16% Appeal to emotions
Advice giving— peers	71% Other benefit 55% Rationality 19% Appeals to emotions 14% Distributive (warnings)	36% Other benefit 38% Withdraw 24% Negative identity
Advice giving— parents	97% Other benefit 67% Rationality 23% Appeals to emotions	51% Other benefit 38% Rationality 15% Appeals to emotions
Relational growth/ initiation	56% Appeals to emotions 26% Indirect	39% Withdraw 16% Direct request (wait and ask again)
Relational escalations	58% Direct requests 34% Other benefit 30% Exchange 16% Appeals to emotions	50% Rationality 25% Withdraw 24% Exchange 17% Negative identity
Normative requests— nonintimates	57% Rationality 25% Exchange 14% Indirectness 14% Distributive	23% Exchange 21% Other benefit 19% Direct request 15% Coercive
Normative requests— professors	77% Rationality 32% Indirect	40% Rationality 26% Negative identity
Bureaucrat/ official	65% Rationality 30% Indirect 20% Distributive	50% Withdraw 20% Negative identity
Selfish requests/ personal benefits	69% Rationality	54% Withdraw
Violation of rights	72% Direct request 17% Exchange	22% Coercive 17% Negative identity 17% Direct request (wait and ask again) 16% Exchange

* More than one tactic can be used at a time. Presented here are only those tactics that were used in each goal-type beyond what you would expect by chance. Adapted from Cody, Canary, and Smith.

didn't take our advice, we tend not to withdraw but to be persistent—offering more reasons why they'd benefit from complying, using rationality, and continuing to appeal to affection, support, and so on.

4. The two most common goals involved in heterosexual relationships for college students involve *relational growth/initiations* and *relational escalations*. Growth/initiation situations include ones where you want to start dating someone, or, during an early phase in dating, persuade the partner to confide more and open up more. In pursuing such goals, an agent appeals to love, affection, and so on. Since the outcome of such situations is sometimes doubtful, some agents use indirect tactics to see how committed the partner might be before trying any tactic. If the agent failed to gain compliance, the typical response is to withdraw (reason: You cannot *make* someone like you), while a small set of agents preferred the tactic of waiting and asking again at some future time. Relational escalations deal with a set of situations where the agent asks the target to comply with a request that, if followed, could mean that the relationship would escalate to a new level of trust and intimacy (for example, go home to visit relatives one weekend, go to a party where there is only your friends, the agent wants to break a date to do something with an old friend, and so on). In events such as these, agents use direct requests, explain a potential benefit to the target, promise to reciprocate in the future or to "make it up to him/her," and appeal to emotions (love, friendship). If the agent failed to gain compliance, the agent uses rationality to support and justify the desired outcome. Virtually a quarter of the students would withdraw from the persuasion (reason: Only harm to the relationship would follow if I persisted), others would try to work out an exchange arrangement, and some would take up the approach of sulking, pouting, and so on (negative identity management).

5. *Normative requests* made of nonintimates involve situations where an agent seeks concessions from, or gains the assistance of, a nonintimate, and where the request may be construed as a type of request one can reasonably make of nonintimates. Situations included in this goal type include asking strangers to help you out by participating as subjects in a class research project, asking a boss to let you go home early, bargaining for an antique chair, and convincing used-car salespersons to give you a good deal on a trade-in. First attempt tactics include rationality, exchange, and indirectness—and some agents try to gain compliance by using distributive types of tactics ("I'll take my business elsewhere."). If they failed to gain compliance, agents would use exchange ("Come on, I'll make it up to you. . . ."), list benefits for the target ("It'll be fun," "I'll recommend your store to my friends."), or wait and ask again; some agents would threaten to take their business elsewhere.

6. *Normative requests* involving professors include those several events where actors propose a grade change, talk about an ambiguous test question, or want to be added into closed sections of classes. Students rely on rationality tactics, but some rely on indirectness apparently to see how resistant the professor might be to the request. If students failed to be persuasive, they would continue to rely on rationality, and a fourth of the students would attempt to make the professor feel badly about refusing the request.

7. *Bureaucrat/official requests* deal with the formal requests made of targets who occupy the position of an official—police officers, bouncers in bars, traffic court judges, and so on. Students rely on rationality; they are sometimes indirect; and some students, in complaining, communicate to the official how they have been treated unfairly, and so on (distributive). If they failed to gain compliance, many students would withdraw, and some would try to make the official feel as if he/she had not treated them fairly, or threaten to go to a supervisor.

8. *Selfish requests/personal benefit requests* include those few requests people make of others where they gain but the target has to give up concessions, and where the nature of the request cannot be considered "normative." Situations included in this goal type include trying to convince your neighbor not to cut down a shade tree that is on the neighbors' property and shades your house—but your neighbor had planned to put up a two-car garage. Other examples include situations where people you know help you with your homework, and so on. In situations such as these, actors use rationality as a first attempt message, and then withdraw if not successful.

9. *Violation of agent's rights* include those events where the target engages in a behavior that annoys the agent, interferes with the agent's activities, and, in the view of the agent, violates the actor's rights. Examples include neighbors with barking dogs or neighbors who play a stereo too loudly at night, people who smoke in your presence constantly, and people who borrow things and fail to return them. As a first attempt tactic, agents rely on direct request, and a few try some form of exchange ("I'll make a deal with you, if you . . ."). If the agent failed to gain compliance, he/she would use coercive influence, attempt to make the target feel guilty, or wait and ask again later. Failure to comply in this situation where the target could be considered blameworthy for the conflict seems to be very similar to the situations Sillars[36] found in which roommates use distributive tactics (in the study discussed above). Also, deTurck[37] recently studied students' responses to a situation like the ones included in this goal-type, and found that students escalated to more punishment-oriented messages if they had to use more than one tactic.

Why are people selecting the tactics the way they do in these studies? One general explanation for much of these results stems from the social exchange theory introduced earlier in this book. A "general hedonistic" principle of human behavior argues that people will attempt to maximize their rewards and outcomes while attempting to minimize costs.[38] This "minimax" principle is important in negotiation research, as we will see in the next chapter. In terms of the results of the studies on interpersonal influence, there can be no doubt that agents generally select tactics that ought to be effective in achieving the agents' goals; they use direct request when they see no reason to use a more elaborate argument, and they rely on more rationality (argument, supporting evidence, reason, and so on) when pursuing other goals. On the other hand, research indicates that people prefer to avoid costs. Sillars[39] found sizable correlations between expected costs associated with tactics and likelihood of use of tactics, and organizational communication scholars argue that coercive influence is used rarely because (a) it is perceived not to be effective in actually changing behavior, and (b) its use is considered costly—resentment, possible retaliation, and so on, might follow from the use of coercive influence (see Chapter 13).[40] Sims,[41] in fact, indicates that coercive influence is not used as a "rational" tactic to shape and mold behavior and direct it toward some productive end—coercive influence is used on subordinates after they have repeatedly performed poorly. Fitzpatrick and Winke[42] also noted that their results could be interpreted as terms of a risk/cost idea, since the couples who appeared to treat each other the nicest were the "engaged couples" (who have more to lose if coercive influence is used) than married couples (it is harder for couples to break off a relationship if they are married and the spouse uses costly tactics).

While agents take into consideration perceived effectiveness of tactics, along with costs and risks associated with the use of tactics, there are clearly other reasons why actors use different tactics when pursuing different goals. Reardon,[43] for instance, argues that actors not only take into consideration perceived *effectiveness* of strategies, but also perceived *appropriateness* and a desire to appear to be *consistent*. Some of the results discussed above take into consideration appropriateness. On the other hand, deTurck[44] interpreted his results dealing with escalation in terms of instrumental learning theory—that is, if an agent uses a tactic on a target and fails to gain compliance, the act of noncompliance is experienced as a punishment that prompts the agent to escalate to another, more punishing tactic. Finally, other scholars argue that a significant motive in social influence processes is the maintenance of fairness or equity.[45] One conclusion is inescapable, however—people do recognize different types of goals they pursue and adapt their choices for tactics to fit what they think will be effective in pursuing the goal in hand.

So far in this chapter we have talked about social influence tactics and why people select them. Now it is time to turn our attention to issues pertaining to the effectiveness of different tactics. In the remainder of this space in this chapter, we will talk about how to make two types of tactics effective, and then take up the issue of effective message strategy use in the next three chapters.

Effectiveness of strategies in fact-to-face contexts: Structuring the direct request and ingratiation

Predicting what strategy is going to lead to successful persuasion in dyadic contexts is not easy. Many factors concerning the source, receiver, and the situation must be taken into consideration. Two issues of effectiveness will be discussed in the present chapter, ones that cut across all types of daily events: (1) structuring the simple and unelaborated direct request in ways to secure increased compliance; and (2) ingratiation.

The foot-in-the door effect

In the mid 1960s, Freedman and Fraser[46] tested the notion that if a person agreed to comply with a small, simple request, then the individual would be more likely to later comply with a larger and more costly second request. Specifically, they had a male experimenter contact housewives in their homes in the Palo Alto area in California, where he introduced himself either as a member of the "Community Committee for Traffic Safety" or the "Keep California Beautiful Committee." Half the women were asked to display a small sign in the front windows of their homes; the other half were asked to sign a petition advocating certain legislation. Both of these requests might be considered "small" since they did not involve much cost or effort on the part of the housewives. After two weeks passed, a different experimenter, representing "Citizens for Safe Driving," asked if the housewives would be willing to place a very large sign reading "Drive Carefully" in their front yards. The experimenter showed each housewife a photograph of the sign—it was so large it appeared to obscure much of the front of the house, and it was poorly lettered. Freedman and Fraser found that only 22 percent of the housewives in a control group (who were never asked a "small" first request) would agree to the sign. However, 55 percent of the housewives who had agreed earlier to putting signs in their windows agreed to have the sign put in their front yard. In this study, Freedman and Fraser introduced the "foot-in-the-door" effect.

Since this first empirical study on the foot-in-the-door tactic, much attention has focused on its value, and two issues are important. First, why does it work? Second, how can we increase the effectiveness of the foot-in-the-door effect? Most theorists believe that the foot-in-the-door effect is mediated by *self-perception processes*. Specifically, Freedman and Fraser noted:

What may occur is a change in the person's feelings about getting involved or about taking action. Once he has agreed to a request, his attitude may change. He may become, in his own eyes, the kind of person who does this sort of thing, who agrees to requests made by strangers, who takes action on things he believes in, who cooperates with good causes. (p. 201)

Several years later, Bem[47] similarly noted that "individuals come to 'know' their own attitudes, emotions, and other internal states partially by inferring them from observations of their own behavior and/or the situation in which this behavior occurs." What does this mean? When the housewives were first approached they may have known in some abstract way that safe driving was important—but they may never have given the issue much thought. When the first request was made, then, they agreed because they had few objections, it didn't cost too much to comply, and they may have been vaguely in agreement with the cause. Later, when asked if they would be willing to put up the large sign, they thought about their behavior and realized that they must have been in favor of good causes (safe driving/keeping California beautiful) since they publicly advertised the fact. Hence, after attributing to themselves the attitude that they favored prosocial issues, it seemed logical to accept the ugly sign.

Two reviews, by DeJong[48] and by Dillard, Hunter, and Burgoon,[49] indicate that the foot-in-the-door tactic does *not always* work. Thus, there are some guidelines that indicate the extent to which it works and indicate how we can increase success:

1. *The first request must be unambiguously smaller than the second request, it must induce compliance, and it must be of sufficient magnitude to commit the individual to future compliance.*

The first guideline argues that the first request must be large enough to get the people to start thinking that they are committed to the cause, but cannot be so large as to be rejected promptly. If self-perception theory explains *why* people comply to the second request, then getting people to agree to a large first request would undoubtedly increase the probability that they would attribute the cause of their accepting the first request to their own attitudes. In fact, Seligman, Bush, and Kirsch[50] documented such a relationship. They contacted four different groups of students by phone, asking the students if they would participate in a survey concerning people's reactions to the energy crisis and to inflation. Each subject was then asked if he or she would help the phone caller by answering a number of questions for the

survey, which would "only take a few minutes." One-fourth of the subjects were asked five yes/no questions (time elapsed: 15 seconds), another one-fourth, 20 yes/no questions (1 minute), another one-fourth were asked 30 yes/no questions (1 minute and 45 seconds), and the final group answered 45 yes/no questions (3 minutes). Two days later, the experimenters called back and said: "We called some of you the other night, but others haven't been called yet. In any case, we would like to complete the survey tonight. Would you be willing to answer 55 questions on the survey?" These researchers found that only 38 percent of the subjects in the first group agreed to the second request; only 35 percent in the second group. However, 74 percent of the subjects in both the latter groups agreed to the second request—*a 15-second or a 1-minute interaction was not sufficiently long to create the foot-in-the-door effect.*

2. *The second request cannot be so large that few would comply; further, the second request cannot be so trivial that all people would comply (otherwise, why bother to use the foot-in-the-door tactic?).*

If the first request is too small, it will not elicit the appropriate self-perceptions. Further, since it is obvious that people take into consideration the costs involved (that is, time, money, physical or mental effort, then the foot-in-the-door tactic would work to increase compliance if the second request wasn't too costly. On the other hand, if the second request involved so little effort that everyone would comply, then there would be no need to use a foot-in-the-door approach.

3. *Different experimenters can be used successfully to elicit the foot-in-the-door effect.*

If subjects in the foot-in-the-door research actually make the self-perception that *they* are generous or charitable persons, then changing experimenters from the first request to the second request should not have any effect on the rates of compliance. Starting with Freedman and Fraser, many studies in fact found that the foot-in-the-door effect does have a good deal of generality in that different persons may make the requests.

4. *If the subjects believed that there were external pressures that led to their compliance on the first request, then they will not perceive their own personal involvement to be the cause of the compliance, and there will be no foot-in-the-door effect.*

For example, Zuckerman, Lazzaro, and Waldgeir[51] called housewives and asked if they would participate in a 5-minute telephone survey. One-half were promised a monetary payment, the other half were not. The housewives were told that if they agreed to participate, an interview would be conducted at a later time. Two or three days later, the housewives were contacted and asked to participate in a 20-minute interview. Forty-five percent of the control group agreed to participate, 33 percent of the individuals who were promised a monetary incentive agreed, and 64 percent of the subjects who agreed to a 5-minute interview out of their own free will, without external pressures or rewards, agreed to participate.

5. *The foot-in-the-door effect works over time—the consequence of committing oneself to the first request slowly declines in impact over time.*

Both the Dillard, Hunter, and Burgoon and the DeJong reviews found that the timing of the two requests was not an important variable in securing compliance. DeJong, in fact, noted that the length of time of the delay may be less important than whether the subject *remembers* his/her behavior (and the apparent cause of it) when asked the second request. Hence, it may prove useful for you to remind the person about the contact they recently had with another member of your organization, group, or church when you make the second request. In this fashion, it appears to matter little if the second request is immediately after the first, delayed for two days, delayed by seven days, or even delayed by up to two weeks.

6. *Compliance can be increased by employing tactics that help to ensure that the subject makes the appropriate self-perception.*

Any methods we might use to help the target attribute the cause of accepting the first request to his or her own attitudes and preferences can then increase the effectiveness of the technique. As noted above, one way to help get a receiver to do this is to remove external pressures or incentives as possible reasons for why the target agreed to the first request. What else can we do? Some theorists have used *labeling* in order to help ensure that the target gets the right attribution. That is, say you just gave $2 to the Heart Fund. The solicitor not only thanks you, but tells you, honestly, "You know, my job would be a lot easier if I met more charitable people like you," and then leaves. Since the solicitor communicated this ready-made attribution *after* you gave him the money, it seems to you that there's no ulterior motive on his part. Therefore, the compliment rings true. Did you not, in fact, behave in a generous manner? You must, therefore, be generous. Two weeks later, when a different solicitor comes to your home collecting for multiple sclerosis, how much do you give him or her?[52]

These guidelines should prove useful for designing methods for increasing commitments to worthy causes. No one, however, can tell you precisely what to do in your own church, recycling group, or charity in order to maximize aid and assistance to the cause. You may need to do some field experiments of your own to see how using foot-in-the-door tactics can be used to increase outcomes. However, one observation should be noted in passing: Most studies involving telephone solicitations rarely link the foot-in-the-door effect to actual physical behaviors; a face-to-face contact in the first request seems useful for increasing *behavioral* compliance to the second request.

A tactic substantively different from the foot-in-the-door tactic has recently been the focus of some research attention, and we will note this tactic in passing. It is called "door-in-the-face." In this tactic, a large first request is made, which is rejected by the targets. Then, the agent makes a smaller request. The targets will feel predisposed to agreeing with the second request because they feel that if they managed to avoid the larger request then they can at least be open to the agent's second request. That is, when we say no and the agent concedes and retreats to a smaller request, we (a) feel that we have won something, and (b) feel that if the agent can concede we should concede. This tactic has been used to increase blood donations and to gain assistance in the fight against traffic violations. Even-Chen, Yinon, and Bizman[53] offered four general rules in the effective use of this tactic:

1. The original request must be rejected by the target person;
2. The original request should be large enough so that its rejection will be perceived by the target person as irrelevant for making self-attribution;
3. The original request should not evoke resentment, anger, or hostility;
4. The second request must be unambiguously smaller than the first.

Ingratiation

Ingratiation tactics, according to Jones and Wortman,[54] are a "class of strategic devices illicitly designed to influence a particular other concerning the attractiveness of one's personality." They are "illicit" because they are manipulative—we may exaggerate how well a supervisor is doing her (or his) job when we talk to her (or him) not because we believe the supervisor is doing such a great job, but because we will ask her (or him) for a letter of recommendation next week. Despite our society's rather negative view of ingratiation, we have all used the technique ourselves with someone at some time. In fact, Jones and Wortman feel that we may not even be consciously aware of the fact that we are ingratiating—we may naturally adopt flirting or self-presentation without giving it much thought.

There are four primary ways of trying to get others to like you: *complimentary other-enhancement* (flattery), *selective self-presentations* (self-bolstering or bragging), *opinion conformity* (you tell the woman you want to date that you, too, are a Republican), and *rendering favors*. Generally, there are three variables that influence how frequently we might engage in ingratiation, and these variables are similar to the ones we discussed above in regard to situational influences. We are

more likely to use an ingratiation tactic if (a) there are rewards for doing so; (b) there is some probability for success; and (c) if the form of ingratiation is perceived to be legitimate for the particular context. The latter variable has received the least amount of research attention, but it is obvious that buying a soda (rendering favors) for a stranger with whom you have *never* talked is too obvious, blunt, and direct. What is perceived as legitimate may also depend upon the beliefs and behaviors of the target. Schneider and Eustis,[55] for example, found that ingratiators match the presentational style of the target—when the target engaged in self-presentations, so did the ingratiator; and when the target was a revealing person, the ingratiator revealed information about him- or herself. The fact that ingratiation tactics are strategically adapted to the audience was most recently demonstrated by Michener, Plazewski, and Vaske,[56] who found that when supervisors valued efficiency, ingratiators bolstered the view of themselves as dedicated workers; and when supervisors valued sociability, ingratiators used flattery that pertained to interpersonal factors.

Thirty years of research has focused on issues involving ingratiation, and we recommend the very readable book by Jones and Wortman for the interested reader who would like more details. We will address two issues: (1) How does ingratiation work? and (2) To what extent does it work? To address the first issue, we will focus attention on one of the four tactics: flattery.

To use flattery and praise successfully, the ingratiator must control the types of attributions the target makes about *why* the praise was given. For example, on their third date Sid praises Sally by saying that she is a great cook or that she is a very sensitive person. As Jones and Wortman point out, there are a number of attributions Sally can make:

1. Sid paid the compliment because he wants something from her; she perceives that there is an ulterior motive. Consequence: Sid is not likely to increase Sally's liking for him. The comment may even hurt.

2. Sid is the kind of person who always makes positive comments to others; Sally does not take the praise personally and does not feel that Sid is discerning. Thus, Sid will not increase Sally's liking for him appreciably.

3. Sid paid the compliment because it was *normative* to do so. Consequence: If the statement is accepted only as a normal type of communication one receives on a date or over dinner, Sid is not likely to increase the amount of liking Sally has for him.

4. Sid did the praising because he was "just being nice to me" or is "trying not to hurt my feelings." Consequence: Since Sid is being such a nice boy, Sally will increase her liking for him, but only modestly.

5. Sally concludes that Sid is sincere. Consequence: Sid will elicit increased liking from Sally.

All ingratiators desire to decrease the likelihood that the first attribution will be made, and desire to increase the chance that Sally will make the last attribution. Here are Jones and Wortman's recommendations:

1. Make the praise credible.
To do so, there are three tactics to employ. First, Sid should try to reduce the perceived dependency on the target person in order to reduce the suspicion that he needs or expects to benefit. The timing of one's praise is obviously important.

Second, Sid can have the praise delivered by a third party. We can avoid the attribution of being manipulative if we can construct the context where someone else tells Sally that we said she was sensitive (or a good cook), and we appear not to know that what we said was repeated.

Third, to make the praise credible, Sid must make the praise plausible. Obviously, Sid must select some topic or issue of praise that Sally is likely to find plausible.

2. Praise an attribute about which the target is insecure.
While this rule may seem simple, an ingratiator must be careful in selecting the topic of his or her praise. Suppose you wanted to persuade a supervisor that he was doing a great job in leading people. If he felt confident that he *was* a good leader, he probably wouldn't question the sincerity of the praise, and he would believe what you said. However, he might also consider the praise to be a normal kind of communication, and he would only moderately or slightly increase his liking for you. On the other hand, if he were insecure about his leadership, and if he believes the praise, then you have helped to bolster his esteem, and he would increase his liking for you significantly. Hence, it pays to offer praise about a topic on which the target is uncertain or insecure.

3. Be discerning.
If an ingratiator avoids complimenting the target person when the benefit desired from him is salient, picks an attribute to admire about which the target person is insecure, but makes sure that his compliment is plausible he should reduce the probability that the target person will attribute ulterior motivations to him. But, in addition to avoiding the conclusion that he is manipulative and self-seeking, the ingratiator should also try to avoid the attribution that he is complimenting the target person because he is the kind of person who always says complimentary things to everyone.[57]

Several tactics are recommended so that the ingratiator appears to be a discerning individual. First, one can employ both positive and negative comments in a message. An ingratiator may acknowledge some negative attributes of the target that are already known to the target and, simultaneously, praise a behavior about which the target feels insecure. Or, an ingratiator may let the target know he has high standards and is thus discerning. Another tactic is to be neutral or even negative toward the target and then, over time, become more and more friendly toward the target. Research indicates that we tend to like people who are pleasant and friendly, but that we like people even more if they were at first cold, distant, and aloof, and later became friendly toward us. There are three main reasons for this: (1) We may feel that something we did or said helped win the negative person over to our side, and we enjoy being successful; (2) their being cold and aloof made us aroused and anxious, and when they started to like us our anxiety was reduced; and (3) while we like being liked by positive people it is even more enjoyable to be liked by a person who we see as having high standards, or who in some way appears to be discerning.

4. Make sure the praise is not seen merely as normative.

Targets are not likely to change their attitudes or focus attention on the agent if any praise is simply seen as that which is due the target. To receive attention, any praise must be different enough to be noticed by a receiver.

5. Avoid the negative effects of praise.

Three negative effects of praise include: Praise may make a person feel awkward by placing him or her in a difficult social situation; praise may imply a low level of expected performance (after all, why did he praise you—did he think you weren't going to do it correctly?); and praise may lead to apprehension over future evaluations, since praise now suggests that you are being attended to and monitored.

Ingratiation involves some risk because people do not like to feel that they have been manipulated. It is very important to hide any ulterior motive if the ingratiation is to be successful. On

Table 10.5. Ingratiation and the Use of Power

Average Performance Evaluations of Workers

Condition	Superior Worker (1)	Average Worker (2)	Ingratiator (3)	Total
Control	28.4	22.9	26.0	26.1
Inept	29.8	27.4	29.1	28.8
Poor attitude	33.0	30.4	32.0	31.8

Number of Promises of Pay Raises to Workers

Condition	Superior Worker	Average Worker	Ingratiator	Total
Control	1.1	.4	.9	2.4
Inept	1.6	.8	1.7	4.1
Poor attitude	1.1	1.4	.9	3.4

Number of Pay Raises Awarded to Workers

Condition	Superior Worker	Average Worker	Ingratiator	Total
Control	1.1	.4	.6	2.1
Inept	1.0	.6	.8	2.4
Poor attitude	1.5	1.1	1.4	4.0

Adapted from David Kipnis and Richard Vanderveer, "Ingratiation and the Use of Power," *Journal of Personality and Social Psychology*, vol. 17 (1971), pp. 280–286. Copyright holder, American Psychological Association.

the other hand, there is no doubt that the use of any of these methods can increase attraction. Can that attraction get us tangible rewards?

Ingratiation can open doors

The classic study by Kipnis and Vanderveer[58] indicates just how helpful ingratiation tactics can be. Four-person work units were created: a superior worker, an average worker, an ingratiator, and a fourth worker who was either a second "average worker" (control group), an inept worker, or a poor-attitude worker. The superior worker worked at a rate faster than the average worker, of course, while the ingratiator worked at an average rate but passed messages along to the supervisor, such as: "Count on me for help—I'll be glad to give it," "I had doubts about having a college student be my supervisor, but you turned out to be real good . . . , and your assistant is nice too." Our interest is in whether ingratiation influenced performance evaluations, promises of pay raises, and actual pay raises. Table 10.5 presents a summary of the results reported by Kipnis and Vanderveer.

The top box summarizes the results concerning performance evaluations. As these numbers indicate, the superior worker received higher performance evaluations than the average worker regardless of whether the fourth worker was a control, an inept worker, or a poor-attitude worker. Further, the ingratiator received significantly higher evaluations than did the average worker—evaluations that were not significantly different from those of the superior worker. Thus, ingratiation can elicit higher performance evaluations. Ingratiation, however, did not automatically result in an increase in pay raises (in fact, superior workers received more pay raises and supervisors "bought off" all workers when the supervisors were confronted with "poor-attitude" workers). However, ingratiators excelled in getting *promises* of pay raises if a co-worker was inept. Ingratiation, then, provides higher performance ratings and can help to open doors.

Summary

In this chapter we have discussed the theoretical bases of power and how their use affects public behavior, private adoption of beliefs, and relationships. We then discussed different compliance-gaining messages, and noted that the messages are used differently by dogmatic, Machiavellian, or internal (versus external) locus-of-control persons, and by females (versus males). We noted that attribution of causality for a behavior has a strong influence on the strategies we select, both inside an organization and in our interpersonal relationships. We also noted that we all possess some knowledge of daily situations, which we use in order to be effective. Finally, we outlined guidelines for the effective use of direct requests, and for the use of ingratiation.

Footnotes

1. B. H. Raven and A. W. Kruglanski, "Conflict and Power," in P. Swingle, ed., *The Structure of Conflict* (New York: Academic, 1970), pp. 69–109.

2. B. H. Raven, R. Centers, and A. Rodrigues, "The Bases of Conjugal Power," in R. E. Cromwell and D. H. Olson, eds., *Power in Families* (New York: Wiley, 1975), pp. 217–231.

3. G. Marwell and D. R. Schmitt, "Dimensions of Compliance-Gaining Behavior: An Empirical Analysis," *Sociometry*, vol. 39 (1967), pp. 350–364.

4. T. Falbo, "A Multidimensional Scaling of Power Strategies," *Journal of Personality and Social Psychology*, vol. 35 (1977), pp. 537–547; T. Falbo and L. A. Peplau, "Power Strategies in Intimate Relationships," *Journal of Personality and Social Psychology*, vol. 38 (1980), pp. 618–628.

5. R. L. Wiseman and W. Schenck-Hamlin, "A Multidimensional Scaling Validation of an Inductively-Derived Set of Compliance-Gaining Strate-

gies," *Communication Monographs*, vol. 48 (1981), pp. 251–270.

6. M. A. Fitzpatrick and J. Winke, "You Always Hurt the One You Love: Strategies and Tactics in Interpersonal Conflict," *Communication Quarterly*, vol. 27 (1979), pp. 3–11.

7. M. J. Cody, M. L. McLaughlin, and W. J. Jordan, "A Multidimensional Scaling of Three Sets of Compliance-Gaining Strategies," *Communication Quarterly*, vol. 28 (1980), pp. 34–46.

8. L. A. Baxter, "An Investigation of Compliance-Gaining as Politeness," *Human Communication Research*, vol. 10 (1984), pp. 427–456.

9. D. Kipnis and S. M. Schmidt, "An Influence Perspective on Bargaining Within Organizations," in M. H. Bazerman and R. J. Lewicki, eds., *Negotiating in Organizations* (Beverly Hills: Sage, 1983), pp. 309–349; D. Kipnis, S. M. Schmidt, and I. Wilkinson, "Intraorganizational Influence Tactics: Explorations in Getting One's Way," *Journal of Applied Psychology*, vol. 65 (1980), pp. 440–452.

10. Ruth Ann Clark, "The Impact of Self-Interest and Desire for Liking on the Selection of Communication Strategies," *Communication Monographs*, vol. 46 (1979), pp. 257–273.

11. Virginia P. Richmond, Leonard M. Davis, Kitty Saylor, and James C. McCroskey, "Power Strategies in Organizations: Communication Techniques and Messages," *Human Communication Research*, vol. 11 (1984), pp. 85–108.

12. Kipnis, Schmidt, and Wilkinson, "Intraorganizational Influence Tactics."

13. See E. J. Langer and R. P. Abelson, "The Semantics of Asking a Favor: How to Succeed Without Really Dying," *Journal of Personality and Social Psychology*, vol. 24 (1972), pp. 26–32; E. J. Langer, A. Blank, and B. Chanowitz, "The Mindlessness of Ostensibly Thoughtful Action: The Role of 'Placebic' Information in Interpersonal Interaction," *Journal of Personality and Social Psychology*, vol. 26 (1973), pp. 635–642.

14. See Kipnis, Schmidt, and Wilkinson, "Intraorganizational Influence Tactics"; see also Chapter 13.

15. Daniel Druckman, "Dogmatism, Prenegotiation Experience, and Simulated Group Representation As Determinants of Dyadic Behavior in Bargaining Situations," *Journal of Personality and Social Psychology*, vol. 6 (1967), pp. 279–290.

16. Frank J. Boster and James B. Stiff, "Compliance-Gaining Message Selection Behavior," *Human Communication Research*, vol. 10 (1984), pp. 539–556; Delann L. Williams and Frank J. Boster, "The Effects of Beneficial Situational Characteristics, Negativism, and Dogmatism on Compliance-Gaining Message Selection," paper presented to the International Communication Association, Minneapolis, Minnesota, 1981.

17. John E. Hunter, David W. Gerbing, and Frank J. Boster, "Machiavellian Beliefs and Personality: Construct Invalidity of the Machiavellian Dimension," *Journal of Personality and Social Psychology*, vol. 43 (1982), pp. 1293–1305.

18. Janak Pandey and Renu Rastogi, "Machiavellianism and Ingratiation," *Journal of Social Psychology*, vol. 108 (1979), pp. 221–225.

19. Richard Christie and Florence Geis, eds., *Studies in Machiavellianism* (New York: Academic, 1970).

20. Michael E. Roloff and Edwin F. Barnicott, "The Situational Use of Pro- and Anti-Social Compliance-Gaining Strategies by High and Low Machiavellians," in Brent D. Ruben, ed., *Communication Yearbook 2* (New Brunswick, N.J.: Transaction Press, 1978), pp. 193–205.

21. For a review of literature concerning internal and external locus of control, consult Michael J. Cody and Margaret L. Mclaughlin, "The Situation As a Construct in Communication Research," in Mark L. Knapp and Gerald R. Miller, eds., *Handbook of Interpersonal Communication* (Beverly Hills: Sage, 1985); Herbert M. Lefcourt, *Locus of Control: Current Trends in Theory and Research*, 2nd ed. (Hillsdale, N.J.: Erlbaum, 1982).

22. For example, see William J. Doherty and Robert G. Ryder, "Locus of Control, Interpersonal Trust, and Assertive Behavior among Newlyweds," *Journal of Personality and Social Psychology*, vol. 37 (1979), pp. 2212–2239.

23. Barry E. Goodstadt and Larry A. Hjelle,

"Power to the Powerless: Locus of Control and the Use of Power," *Journal of Personality and Social Psychology*, vol. 27, pp. 190–196.

24. Paula Johnson, "Women and Power: Toward a Theory of Effectiveness," *Journal of Social Issues*, vol. 32 (1976), pp. 99–110.

25. Michael J. Burgoon, James P. Dillard, and Noel E. Doran, "Friendly or Unfriendly Persuasion: The Effects of Violations of Expectations by Males and Females," *Human Communication Research*, vol. 10 (1983), pp. 283–294.

26. For a review of these studies, consult David R. Seibold, James G. Cantrill, and Renee A. Meyers, "Communication and Interpersonal Influence," in Mark L. Knapp and Gerald R. Miller, eds., *Handbook of Interpersonal Communication* Beverly Hills: Sage, 1985).

27. Fitzpatrick and Winke, "You Always Hurt the One You Love."

28. Linda L. Putnam and Charmaine E. Wilson "Communicative Strategies in Organizational Conflicts: Reliability and Validity of a Measurement Scale," in Michael Burgoon, ed., *Communication Yearbook 6* (Beverly Hills: Sage, 1982), pp. 629–654.

29. Harold H. Kelley, "Attribution Theory in Social Psychology," in D. Levine, ed., *Nebraska Symposium on Motivation* (vol. 15) (Lincoln: University of Nebraska, 1967); also consult Susan T. Fiske and Shelley E. Taylor, *Social Cognition* (Reading, Mass.: Addison-Wesley, 1984).

30. Alan L. Sillars, "Attributions and Communication in Roommate Conflicts," *Communication Monographs*, vol. 47 (1980), pp. 180–200.

31. B. G. Rule, G. L. Bisanz, and M. Kohn, "Anatomy of a Persuasion Schema: Targets, Goals, and Strategies," *Journal of Personality and Social Psychology*, vol. 48 (1985), pp. 1127–1140.

32. M. J. Cody, D. Canary, and S. Smith, "Compliance-Gaining Strategy Selection: Episodes and Goals," in J. Daly and J. Wiemann, eds., *Communicating Strategically* (Hillsdale, N.J.: Erlbaum, 1987).

33. R. Schank and R. Abelson, *Scripts, Plans, Goals, and Understanding* (Hillsdale, N.J.: Erlbaum, 1977).

34. Rule, Bisanz, and Kohn, "Anatomy of a Persuasion Schema."

35. Cody, Canary, and Smith, "Compliance-Gaining Strategy Selection."

36. Sillars, "Attributions and Communication in Roommate Conflicts."

37. M. deTurck, "A Transactional Analysis of Compliance-Gaining Behavior: Effects of Noncompliance, Relational Contexts, and Actors' Gender," *Human Communication Research*, vol. 12 (1985), pp. 54–78.

38. B. R. Schlenker, *Impression Management: The Self-Concept, Social Identity, and Interpersonal Relationships* (Monterey, Calif.: Brooks/Cole, 1980), p. 17.

39. See M. J. Cody and M. L. McLaughlin, "The Situation as a Construct in Interpersonal Communication Research," in M. L. Knapp and G. R. Miller, eds., *Handbook of Interpersonal Communication* (Beverly Hills: Sage, 1985), pp. 263–312; A. Sillars, "The Stranger and the Spouse as Target Persons for Compliance-Gaining Strategies: A Subjective Expected Utility Model," *Human Communication Research*, vol. 6 (1980), pp. 265–279.

40. R. D. Arvey and J. M. Ivancevich, "Punishment in Organizations: A Review, Propositions, and Research Suggestions," *Academy of Management Review,* vol. 5 (1980), pp. 123–132.

41. H. R. Sims, "Further Thoughts of Punishment in Organizations," *Academy of Management Review,* vol. 5 (1980), pp. 133–138.

42. Fitzpatrick and Winke, "You Always Hurt the One You Love."

43. K. K. Reardon, *Persuasion: Theory and Context* (Beverly Hills: Sage, 1981).

44. deTurck, "A Transactional Analysis."

45. F. J. Boster and J. B. Stiff, "Compliance-Gaining Message Selection Behavior."

46. Jonathan L. Freedman and Scott C. Fraser, "Compliance Without Pressure: The Foot-in-the-Door Technique," *Journal of Personality and Social Psychology*, vol. 4 (1966), pp. 195–202.

47. D. J. Bem, "Self-Perception Theory," in Leonard Berkowitz, ed., *Advances in Experimental*

Social Psychology, vol. 6 (New York: Academic, 1972), p. 2.

48. William DeJong, "An Examination of Self-Perception Mediation of the Foot-in-the-Door Effect," *Journal of Personality and Social Psychology*, vol. 37 (1979), pp. 2221–2239.

49. James P Dillard, John E. Hunter, and Michael J. Burgoon, "Sequential-Request Persuasive Strategies: Meta-Analysis of Foot-in-the-Door and Door-in-the-Face," *Human Communication Research*, vol. 10 (1984), pp. 461–488.

50. C. Seligman, M. Bush, and K. Kirsch, "Relationship between Compliance in the Foot-in-the-Door Paradigm and Size of First Request," *Journal of Personality and Social Psychology*, vol. 33 (1976), pp. 517–520.

51. M. Zuckerman, M. M. Lazzaro, and D. Waldgeir, "Undermining Effects of the Foot-in-the-Door Technique with Extrinsic Reward," *Journal of Applied Social Psychology*, vol. 9 (1979), pp. 292–296.

52. See, for instance: R. E. Kraut, "Effects of Social Labeling on Giving to Charity," *Journal of Experimental Social Psychology,* vol. 9 (1973), pp. 551–562.

53. M. Even-Chen, Y. Yinon, and A. Bizman, "The Door-in-the-Face Technique: Effects of the Size of the Initial Request," *European Journal of Psychology*, vol. 8 (1978), pp. 135–140; see also Cialdini and Ascani and reviews by DeJong and by Dillard, Hunter, and Burgoon.

54. E. E. Jones and C. Wortman, *Ingratiation: An Attributional Approach* (Morristown, N.J.: General Learning Press, 1973), p. 2.

55. D. J. Schneider and A. C. Eustis, "Effects of Ingratiation Motivation, Target Positiveness, and Revealingness on Self-Presentation," *Journal of Personality and Social Psychology*, vol. 22 (1972), pp. 149–155.

56. H. A. Michener, J. G. Plazewski, and J. J. Vaske, "Ingratiation Tactics Channeled by Target Values and Threat Capability," *Journal of Personality*, vol. 47 (1979), pp. 35–56.

57. Jones and Wortman, *Ingratiation*, p. 9.

58. David Kipnis and Richard Vanderveer, "Ingratiation and the Use of Power," *Journal of Personality and Social Psychology*, vol. 17 (1971), pp. 280–286.

CHAPTER ELEVEN

Bargaining As Persuasion

You have begun apartment hunting and you are prepared to pay $200 to $300 a month for rent. The exact amount depends upon the condition of the apartment, availability of parking, and distance from campus. You walk into the rental office ready to negotiate for your first apartment.

As the above example indicates, bargaining is not limited to labor-management relations. We bargain when we hunt for an apartment, buy a car, ask parents for an advance on college-support allowance, and so on. Admittedly, bargaining receives more public attention when it is between the big-three auto makers and the UAW. But regardless of who is involved in the bargaining process, bargaining is first and foremost a communication activity that depends upon the use of persuasive messages. As you read this chapter you will find many instances where you could use the

face-to-face persuasive strategies discussed in previous chapters.

In this chapter "bargaining" is used synonymously with "negotiations." While some authors make distinctions between the terms, the distinctions are not consistent.[1] Also, the terms are used interchangeably in everyday conversation and in the media. Therefore, in this chapter bargaining or negotiation is defined as *a process in which there is an exchange of communication between interdependent parties with differing goals in an attempt to produce a joint decision*. Important phrases to note in the definition are: (1) communicative process, (2) interdependent parties, (3) differing goals, and (4) joint decision.

The flow of *communication* in bargaining is a *process* because each message impacts upon the determination of the final decision. Thomas C.

Schelling explains the function of communication in bargaining as follows: "To discover patterns of individual behavior that make each player's actions predictable to the other; they have to test each other for a shared sense of patterns or regularity, and to exploit . . . impromptu codes for signalling intentions and for responding to each other's signals."[2] That is, once it has been delivered, a bargaining message (verbal or nonverbal) has an immediate effect on negotiations by influencing the perceptions and expectations of the involved parties.

The parties are *interdependent* because neither can obtain its desired outcome without the other party. A car salesperson needs a customer and the customer needs the salesperson. If the buyer can achieve his or her goal of having access to a car by borrowing one from a friend then there would be no interdependence between the car dealer and the buyer and consequently, no reason to bargain.

Differing goals means that bargaining occurs in a conflict situation. How the conflict is managed can lead to either cooperative or competitive bargaining. Cooperative bargaining is problem solving. The parties recognize their areas of disagreement and then work for creative solutions to the problem(s). Competitive bargaining is a win-lose situation. What is won by Party A is lost by Party B.[3] Cooperative and competitive bargaining will be discussed in greater detail later in this chapter.

The final component of the definition is *joint decision*. The parties have determined a way to

---

BOX 11.1
STRUCTURE OF BARGAINING

A sale value of $2,000 represents Andy's *resistance point*.	$2,000
	2,100
Betty's *aspiration level* is a realistic desired purchase price of $2,250.	2,200
	2,250
	2,300
	2,400
	2,500
	2,600
Andy's *aspiration level* is $2,750 and is a realistic retail pirce.	2,700
	2,750
	2,800
	2,900
Betty's *resistance point* is $3,000. She will go no higher in purchasing the chair.	3,000

Andy Antique has a rolltop desk to sell. He needs $2,000 to break even and he would like to receive $2,750. Betty Buyer wants to buy a rolltop desk. After inquiring in various shops, she knows $3,000 is the most she should pay. However, she would prefer to pay $2,250. Since the *bargaining range* includes points between Andy's and Betty's resistance points, a negotiated settlement is possible.

manage their differing goals, and have committed themselves and their constituents to act in a prescribed manner. The decision must be of mutual consent so that each party has a stake in the outcome and consequently is dedicated to its fulfillment.

While bargaining situations and research methods can vary, a few common terms are used to describe the structure of bargaining.[4] For simplicity, we will use an example of a buyer and seller in an antique shop. They are negotiating over the price of a rolltop desk. The seller, Andy Antique, needs a minimum of $2,000 to break even on his investment. Betty Buyer is knowledgeable in antiques and knows she can buy a comparable desk for $3,000. The *resistance point* in bargaining is the maximum amount a party will concede. For Andy, $2,000 is his resistance point because any greater concession means an investment loss and he would be better off to wait for another customer. Betty's resistance point is $3,000. At that price she knows she can leave the shop and buy a similar desk at or below her resistance point. The difference between the buyer and seller's resistance points is the *bargaining range*. As long as the bargaining range includes a point at which the parties can agree, then a settlement is possible. However, if Betty's resistance point was $2,000 and Andy's point was $3,000 then no agreement would be possible since there is no common range between resistance points. In cases where parties cannot reach an agreement and cease bargaining, they are said to return to their *status-quo point*.

Even though each bargainer has a resistance point that determines the possible negotiated settlements, the bargainers also have an *aspiration level* that is a realistic preferred outcome. Betty would like to purchase the desk for as little as possible, but realistically she knows $2,250 is about as low as Andy will go. Andy knows that $2,750 is as much as Betty is likely to spend. Because each party has an aspiration level that falls within the bargaining range, a settlement that approximates the aspiration levels but does not violate either resistance point is possible. The resistance point, status-quo point, and aspiration level comprise a bargainer's *utility schedule*. An example of this structure is provided in Box 11.1.

It is important to be familiar with these terms as they are used throughout this chapter. The next section of the chapter will highlight some of the theoretical perspectives of bargaining research. The third section will discuss the role of persuasive strategies and tactics in bargaining. Skills for successful bargaining are presented in the fourth section.

Theoretical perspectives

Game theory: determinate solutions

Game theory is a mathematical, economics-based model for explaining strategic behavior. The theory is prescriptive in that it predicts how a rational person will act in a bargaining situation.

To understand this perspective we must first define several terms. *Determinant solution* is a single, predictable settlement upon which the bargainers will agree. *Variable-sum* refers to a situation when the parties' payoffs vary with the outcome. For example, if nonagreement leaves both parties with poorer outcomes than another solution, there is a variable-sum element in the bargaining problem. A *zero-sum game* refers to a situation where what is won by Party A is lost by Party B. Finally, the "minimax" principle states people will try to minimize losses while maximizing gains.

Samuel B. Bacharach and Edward J. Lawler present a thorough review and critique of various game-theory perspectives. They highlight the work of John Nash as providing the foundation of determinant-solution, game-theoretical models. Nash rejected the premise that variable-sum bargaining could not have determinate solutions. In explaining how a determinant solution was possible, Nash outlined nine assumptions about the nature of the bargaining relationship. These are listed in Figure 11.1. Nash concludes that the

1. **Bargainers are rational and expect others to be rational. People are logical, rather than emotional, in their strategic choice.**

2. **Bargainers attempt to maximize their gains and minimize losses.** This is often referred to as the "minimax" principle. Bargaining decisions are made for immediate rewards. The strategy of early concessions to gain later benefits is excluded from the decision-making process.

3. **Bargainers have complete information on the utility of alternative settlements for both parties.** This assumption greatly restricts the role of communication in bargaining. If both parties have complete information, then bluffs, threats, promises, and so on, are irrelevant.

4. **Neither party will accept an agreement that is not a mutually-satisfactory solution.** For example, neither the antique dealer nor buyer will agree to a settlement that does not give them at least as much as they would get from no settlement. Nor will a party accept an agreement if another agreement will give the party a greater payoff without causing the opponent to accept a lower payoff.

5. **Once a party makes an offer it cannot be retracted, and once an agreement is reached it is enforceable.** The problem of wildcat strikes does not exist.

6. **If the last demands and offers are incompatible, the parties receive the utility accorded a failure to reach an agreement, 0.0 payoffs.** This assumption ignores the possibility that no agreement may be a net gain for one party and a loss for the opponent. For example, no agreement in the air-traffic-controllers' strike meant a loss for the union (members lost their jobs) and a gain for the government (the union's bargaining power was lost). In some cases, the bargaining parties may have had a positive experience even though no agreement was reached. The "good will" that can be developed through sincere and open negotiations can have positive payoffs for the dealer's reputation.

7. **If the set of possible settlements is smaller than the bargaining range, the determinate solution remains as long as the original solution based upon the entire bargaining range is included in the smaller set.** This assumption is complex and needs an example. A tourist and vendor are bargaining over the price of a vase. The tourist will pay no more than $100, the vendor will sell for no less than $50. The determinate solution is $75. However, if the tourist makes a large initial offer of $80 and the vendor asks for $60, the determinant solution now becomes $70.

8. **The only significant differences between the bargainers are those reflected in their "utility schedules."** Also referred to as the symmetry assumption, this assumption says that each party's "relative preference" for different outcomes are reflected in the party's utility schedule. Relative preferences reflect whatever influence contextual factors have upon the bargainer's choice.

9. **A constant value added to the utilities will not affect the solution.** This assumption allows symmetry to be imposed upon the solution, allows no agreement to be assigned zero utility, and gives the same utility score for each party's maximum payoff even if the party's satisfaction with the payoff differs.

Figure 11.1. Game-Theory Assumptions

only solution that can satisfy the nine assumptions is one in which a party can gain half of its desired outcome. In other words, the parties will split-the-difference between desired bargaining outcomes.[5]

There are three problems with applying determinant-solution game theory to actual negotiations. Assumptions such as perfect information do not reflect most bargaining situations, and later we will discuss how bargainers intentionally withhold or surrender data in order to build their bargaining position. A second problem is that Nash's determinant solution predicts negotiators will "split-the-difference" between solutions. However, this does not always happen and the theory offers no explanation why. Thomas C. Schelling explains the third problem. He notes the flaw in the zero-sum game is that the analysis is really of only one decision. While there may be two people bargaining, the minimax strategy predicts two unilateral decisions that converge at the center payoff. Consequently, there is no need for shared meaning or understanding; neither communication nor interpersonal relations are important. As Schelling states, the minimax solution in game theory "is a means of expunging from the game all details except the mathematical structure of the payoff, and from the players all communicative relations."[6] In other words, the real failure of game theory is its contempt for the ability of communication to affect outcomes.

Game theory: mixed motive

Schelling and other bargaining researchers modified the assumptions of game theory to create *mixed-motive* bargaining.[7] Mixed-motive bargaining allows the parties to compete and/or cooperate. The most frequently used matrix game to study mixed-motive bargaining is Prisoner's Dilemma (PD). The game situation is presented below.[8]

Two suspects are taken into custody and separated. The district attorney is certain that they are guilty of a specific crime, but (s)he does not have adequate evidence to convict them at a trial. (S)he points out to each prisoner that each has two alternatives: to confess to the crime the police are sure they have done, or not to confess. If they both do not confess, then the district attorney states (s)he will book them on some minor trumped-up charge such as petty larceny and illegal possession of a weapon, and they will both receive minor punishment; if they both confess they will be prosecuted, but (s)he will recommend less than the most severe sentence; but if one confesses and the other does not, then the confessor will receive lenient treatment for turning state's evidence whereas the latter will get "the book" slapped at him/her. In terms of years in a penitentiary, the strategic problem might reduce to:

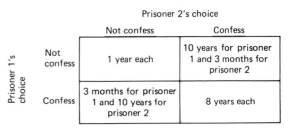

Figure 11.2. Prisoner's Dilemma Matrix

As stated earlier, this game is called mixed motive because the bargainers have the option to cooperate or compete. The cooperative choice is the "not confess" because it has the minimum sentence for opponent, either one year or three months depending upon opponent's move. The "confess" move is competitive since it gives the opponent either ten or eight years in prison. Also, exploitation of the other prisoner occurs if prisoner 1 confesses and prisoner 2 does not confess.

One reason for the extensive use of the PD game is that it provides researchers a clear and concise bargaining situation from which they can go on to test various bargaining conditions and influences. A very abbreviated list of the topics that have been investigated using the PD game includes: the availability of communication channels; the amount of trust between opponents; demographic characteristics; personality traits; the number of issues to be bargained; and power differences.[9] As previously stated, prisoner's dilemma and other game-theoretical models of bargaining have lost their early prominence in bargaining research for most disciplines, especially communication, labor relations, and international relations. Issues such as personality traits of bargainers, negotiator accountability and constituent pressure, and external influences have contributed to the development of alternative perspectives on bargaining. Each of these will be discussed in the social-psychological perspective.

Social-psychological perspective

Bargaining studies that fall into the social-psychological perspective look at both motivational and cognitive processes that operate during negotiations. The motivational issues are taken from game theory and are the player's interest in the outcomes. It still is assumed, for example, that bargainers will try to maximize gains and minimize losses. The cognitive processes explain how negotiators' ideological orientations influence their moves. The combination of these two areas of research has caused social psychological research to be interdisciplinary in nature. The main concern of these researchers is how the *person*, *role*, and *situation* determine bargaining behavior.[10]

The "person" variable is the individual who acts as the negotiator. The studies examine how personality characteristics, communication style, bargaining experience, and so on, affect the negotiation process. For example, Bertram I. Spector used a simulated business bargaining scenario to investigate how different personality profiles affect the choice of bargaining strategies. Spector reports four findings.[11]

1. Highly cooperative bargainers who agreed to *share their payoff* with the other side were motivated by self-oriented needs for social approval and emotional support rather than outgoing needs for cooperation and friendship.
2. Altruistic bargainers who *transferred payoff* that could have been theirs to the opposing side were motivated by defeatist and harm-approaching needs.
3. Bargainers who *bluffed and deceived* were motivated by needs for play, seduction, cleverness, and exhibitionism.
4. Hostile bargainers who employed elements of *coercion* were motivated by the mirror-image hostility of their opponents.

"Role" refers to either the negotiator or the constituents. A bargainer selected to represent the interests of other people has a constituency. The constituents' role may be very minor or great. If the bargainer must bring back all offers to the constituency, then the bargainer has no decision-making power and the constituents are in control. In cases where the bargainer is able to negotiate and commit to a final settlement without conferring with the constituents, then the bargainer has the power. R. J. Klimoski[12] studied the effects of intragroup forces on intergroup conflict resolution in simulated labor-management negotiations. Accountability was defined as the potential for evaluation by the group. The accountability was manipulated in the following ways. In the *no-evaluation* condition, participants were told that because of time restrictions they would not meet with their bargaining team again. In the *evaluation* condition, the participants were told they would report the bargaining results to their teams, and then the team members would vote as to whether they would ever want this bargaining representative again. Klimoski found negotiators in the evaluation condition were more resistant to compromise than those in the no-evaluation condition. In other words, negotiator accountability and constituent pressure led to fewer concessions by the negotiator.

Finally, "situation" includes all contextual influences upon the bargaining process. These influences include bargaining history, economic conditions, political climate, and so on. Richard E. Walton and Robert B. McKensie's *A Behavioral Theory of Labor Negotiations* is drawn from studies in economics, psychology, and sociology. This interdisciplinary orientation is reflected in their conception of "labor negotiations as an example of social negotiations, by which we mean the deliberate interaction of two or more complex social units which are attempting to define or redefine the terms of their interdependence."[13] Persuasion is a key element in this theory because it is the means through which the defining and redefining of the bargaining relationship occurs. This definition process operates through four subprocesses: distributive bargaining, integrative bargaining, attitudinal structuring, and intraorganizational bargaining.

Distributive bargaining is competitive in nature and occurs when the parties' interests are in conflict. It also represents a fixed-sum, win-lose situation. Competition is communicated by withholding information about one's own preferences while attempting to persuade the opponent to modify his or her preferences. Thus, the bargaining messages operate as offensive or defensive strategies designed to secure outcomes.

Integrative bargaining "refers to a system of activities which is instrumental to the attainment of objectives which are not in fundamental conflict with those of the other party."[14] The bargaining situation can be dealt with through cooperative tactics that facilitate problem solving such as the promotion of information exchange and brainstorming for alternative solutions. More specific tactics for competitive and cooperative bargaining are discussed in the next section. These two first subprocesses reflect the influence of game theory in Walton and McKersie's theory; the next subprocess includes all three social-psychological variables.

Attitudinal structuring is the subprocess that recognizes the interplay of person, role, and situation upon bargaining communication. The theoretical basis of attitudinal structuring are cognitive-balance theory and reinforcement theory. These theories were discussed in Chapter 2. Attitudinal structuring represents the maintenance or restructuring of the attitudes each bargainer (person) has taken toward the other party. Role becomes important because the attitude of an organizational member can differ substantively from

the institution's attitudes. The situational factors that influence the relationship include such things as the technological market, and power levels of the bargainers and their shared bargaining experiences.

Intraorganizational bargaining is the final subprocess and it concentrates upon the roles of negotiator and constituents. In addition to bargaining with the opponent, a negotiator must deal with the expectations of constituents. Thus, intraorganizational bargaining represents strategies and tactics a negotiator uses to bring the expectations of the constituents into alignment with those of the negotiator.

Communication perspectives

Linda L. Putnam and Tricia S. Jones cite three theoretical perspectives of communication in bargaining: mechanistic, psychological, and pragmatic. The *mechanistic view* treats communication as "the act of transmitting a message through a designated channel; thus, communication resides in the channel or in the transmission."[15] Bargaining research conducted within the mechanistic perspective examines the availability and method of communication between parties. This research found that face-to-face interactions prompted more cooperative moves than audio, written, or video messages. Bargainers felt face-to-face communication was more spontaneous, informal, and reciprocal, whereas audio interactions were described as impersonal and task oriented.[16]

The *psychological perspective* looks at communication as information processing. That is, researchers vary the bargaining message as to its accuracy, completeness, ambiguity, and so on, and then interpret the results for effects upon the orientation and expectations of bargainers.

Finally, the *pragmatic perspective* examines bargaining messages as communicative acts with both relational and content dimensions. Content refers to the information contained in the message. What does the message say? The relational

---

BOX 11.2
CUE-RESPONSE NEGOTIATION CODING SYSTEM[a]

Category Name	*Category Definition*
Responding Tactics: *Attacking*	
Deny fault with personal rejection	Challenging, disagreeing, or rejecting the immediately preceding utterance accompanied with a rationale and personal affront.
Topic change	Introduction of a new idea changing the direction of the interaction.
Assert rights/needs	Statement that addresses requirements/expectations consistent with prior subject area, clearly arguing for compliance.
Responding Tactics: *Defending*	
Reject proposal	Challenging, disagreeing, or rejecting any part of the other's proposal.
Reject rationale/utterance	Challenging, disagreeing, or rejecting the immediately preceding utterance that is not related to the proposal per se.
Extension	Extending or continuing the topic in the immediately preceding utterance.
Responding Tactics: *Integrating*	
Proposal other support	Giving agreement, assistance, acceptance, or approval to any part of the other's offer or proposal.
Rationale/utterance other support	Giving agreement, assistance, acceptance, or approval to the immediately preceding utterance that is not related to the proposal, per se.
Extension question	An extension of the prior utterance's topic phrased in the interrogative form.
Other	Any response not conforming to these category types.
Cueing Tactics: Attacking	
Assert proposal/offer	Asking the other to accept specific modifications in the proposal under discussion.
Change fault/responsibility	Attributing lack of good faith, incompetence, negligence; derogating something about the other.
Decision	Positive structuring of the procedures for discussion.
Cueing Tactics: Defending	
Substantiation	Providing information or evidence supporting the speaker's own position.
Clarification request	Asking for additional information.

Box 11.2 (*continued*)

Category Name	Category Definition
Deny relevance	Reject suggested structuring of the procedures suggested and/or assert the relevance of the issue/information raised by the other.
Cueing Tactics: Integrating	
Offer concession	An offer that is less than the speaker's immediately prior offer.
Information concession	Offering less information than is requested.
Conciliation/flexibility	Proposing flexibility in the speaker's position.
Other	Any cue not conforming to these category specifications.

[a] William A. Donohue, Mary E. Diez, and Mark Hamilton, "Coding Naturalistic Negotiation Interaction," *Human Communication Research,* 10, no. 3 (1984), pp. 403–425.

aspect considers how messages are connected to one another. Studies that code messages and then try to identify regularities of behavior exemplify the pragmatic view.

Recently, Donohue, Diez, and Hamilton developed the Cue-Response Negotiation Coding System to code naturally occurring negotiations[17] (see box 11.2). This system is representative of the pragmatic perspective. The content dimensions of the coding system classify messages as attacking, defending, and integrative. For example, the content may attack the opponent's position, defend one's own position, or support some or all of the opponent's proposal. More specifically, attacking tactics are used to take the offensive by proposing discrediting changes in the opponent's position or by proposing changes in the negotiator's own position to undermine the opponent's level of aspiration. The defensive tactics are used to stabilize one's own expected outcomes by either rejecting the opponent's proposal or supporting one's own position without referring to any proposal of the opponent. Finally, integrating tactics accept the opponent's modifications of the negotiator's position. They can reveal weakness or lack of faith in the negotiator's own position as well as a willingness to concede in order to improve the proposed solution.

The relational dimension consists of cue and response tactics (hence the name of the system). Each bargaining utterance is analyzed as a response to the opponent's prior utterance and as a cue to subsequent utterances. Consequently, the relational dimension focuses upon the impact of Party A's utterance on Party B's response, while taking into consideration the fact that Party A is responding to B's previous response.

Let's take a look at a few exchanges in a hypothetical bargaining encounter and see how they would be coded as cue responses.

BETTY. (*looking at the price tag on the desk*) Considering the great number of desks in area antique shops, $3,000 is a lot of money for this desk.
[*DEFENDING CUE; SUBSTANTIATION*]
ANDY. Other antique dealers may have desks, but this one is in much better condition and is worth $3,000.
[*ATTACKING RESPONSE; ASSERT RIGHTS/NEEDS*]
[*ATTACKING CUE; ASSERT PROPOSAL/OFFER*]
BETTY. Some of the other desks may be in poor condition. . . .
[*INTEGRATING RESPONSE; PROPOSAL OTHER SUPPORT*]

however, this one is not perfect and is not worth
$3,000.
> [*DEFENDING CUE: SUBSTANTIATION*]

ANDY. What flaws do you see?
> [*INTEGRATING RESPONSE; EXTENSION QUES-*
> *TION*]
>> [*DEFENDING CUE; CLARIFICATION RE-*
>> *QUEST*]

Donohue, Diez, and Hamilton used the Cue-Response Negotiation Coding System to analyze labor-management contract negotiations in a major American communications company. They found union bargainers used an attacking strategy to respond to management attacks. Managers used integrating tactics in responding to labor attacks and then managers gave defending cues.[18] These results do reflect the bargaining process in a natural setting. Generally, it is the union that is making demands for a change, hence, attacking the status quo. Management responds by either integrating desired changes with the status quo or by defending the system as it currently operates.

Bargaining strategies and tactics

Message strategies and tactics can be thought of as a bargainer's game plan and plays, respectively. Each strategy is made up of specific communicative acts called tactics. The tactics examined below are: threats, promises, commitments, initial bids, and size of concession rates. The importance of knowing the effects of various bargaining messages is two-fold. First, bargaining messages reveal the attitude of the parties toward the bargaining. Second, the information exchanged through bargaining tactics discloses a party's utility schedule. But before discussing the research on message strategies and tactics, we need to become familiar with two forms of bargaining tactics, *explicit* and *tacit*.

As the name implies, explicit bargaining messages are those in which the bargainer's intent is stated unequivocally. The message contains no "hidden" meanings. For example, "The rank and file will not ratify a contract without a cost of living clause" is an explicit message. Tacit bargaining messages use subtle nonverbal cues and other behaviors to communicate a bargainer's intentions without explicitly stating them. That is, a bargainer can use vocal intonations or strategic word choice to send a message with an implied meaning. To illustrate this point, consider the following sentence: "We could live with that arrangement." Using the word "could" rather than "will" implies a commitment without explicitly stating one. Thus, the message is tacit. Tacit bargaining messages are often used between chief negotiators when they are being observed by their constituents. The use of these messages allows the bargainers to communicate with each at one level, but have the message interpreted differently by the constituents. The benefit to the bargainers is that they can be moving toward a settlement while not appearing to be making many concessions, thus enabling them to appear "tough" to the constituents.

Threats, promises, and commitments

Before discussing how these bargaining tactics operate in formulating an overall bargaining strategy and in affecting negotiated settlements, some definitions are necessary. A *threat* communicates one's intent to punish the target if the target fails to concede. A *promise* is a pledge to do, or not to do, something for the target. Most often a promise is thought of as a type of reward. A *commitment* tells the opponent that a bargainer will not move from a stated position so it is up to the opponent to make a move. Threats and commitments are tactics generally used in competitive bargaining strategies, whereas promises can be used in either cooperative or competitive strategies.

The effectiveness of these tactics is influenced by the bargainer's *credibility* and *believability*. Tedeschi and Rosenfeld define these terms as follows: "Credibility refers to the truthfulness of the source over the occasions when his or her communications can be checked for accuracy. . . . Believability is the target's assessment of how likely it is that the source's present communication is true."[19] Credibility and believability research has focused primarily on the credibility of threats and promises. Three findings are noted below.

First, a person who consistently carries through on his or her threats gains more compliance from the opponent than a bargainer who fails to enforce threats. Consistent performance of promises increases the effectiveness of *both* promises and threats in gaining compliance. However, the consistent enforcement of threats does not have the same effect on promises. In other words, a person who fulfills promises establishes a level of credibility for delivering threats as well as promises. But a person who establishes credibility for the execution of threats does not gain "carry-over credibility" for promises.

Second, the credibility of threats and promises is affected by the status of the source. High-status individuals are perceived to be more credible. Finally, the "cost factor" of a threat or promise impacts upon its credibility. Credibility decreases when a threat or promise is perceived by the opponent (target) to be too costly to the bargainer (source). But when a threat can be enforced with little cost to the source, an opponent is likely to comply.[20]

When threats are used in bargaining they may gain compliance, but generally they increase conflict and tension (see Chapter 10). Once a threat is made, the opponent must either counter the threat, which exacerbates the conflict, or concede, which signals weakness. Therefore, a threat should be thought of as a "tactic of last resort." In addition to whether or not a threat gains a concession is the issue of how large a concession the threat gains. In other words, the strength of the threatened punishment also must be considered. Tedeschi and Rosenfeld argue that threats will be related to compliance when the threatened punishment is significantly greater to the target than the loss the target will suffer if he or she concedes.[21]

For example, nation A threatens to withhold aid of $300 million to nation B unless nation B concedes its plan to sell weapons to nation C. Excluding all contextual and interpersonal considerations, B will comply because the cost of the enforced threat is greater than the benefits of sales to C. That is, enforcement of the threat means B loses $300 million and gains $100 million for a net cost of $200 million. Conceeding to the threat means B only loses the $100 million in weapons sales, but it retains the $300 million in aid for a net gain of $200 million.

While it is easy to see how threats communicate a competitive strategy, it is not as easy to tell what strategy is communicated through promises. Promises can be viewed as revealing a cooperative strategy when a concession gains the opponent a reward. However, failure to make the necessary concession to gain the promised reward turns the promise into a threat, which is competitive. To illustrate, student A promises to do a study guide for the final if student B prepares a study guide for the midterm. But if student B does not cooperate, then A is implying a threat not to do a final-exam study guide.

To determine if a tactic is a threat or a promise, Pruitt[22] suggests one should take the receiver's point of view. If the receiver believes noncompliance will result in a loss, then the bargaining message is a threat. But if compliance yields a gain, then the tactic is a promise. Pruitt also notes a special factor unique to promise credibility. The greater the influence of the party receiving the promise over the party making the promise, the greater the likelihood the receiver will make the concession to gain the reward. This is the opposite of threat credibility where greater source influence yields increased opponent compliance.

The way promise credibility operates in this situation is interesting. Once the necessary concession is made, the receiving party has a legitimate right to the promised reward. If the receiver of the promise has access to legal recourse, public pressure, and so on, then he or she has some influence over the source that will help ensure reward fulfillment. For an example let us refer back to Andy

Antique and Betty Buyer. Andy promises that he will repair a broken drawer handle and fill in some nicks in the wood if Betty will pay $2,500 for the rolltop desk. If Andy agrees to put the promised repairs in the sales agreement, Betty will be more likely to accept this offer. With this written agreement, Betty has legal recourse, that is, legitimate power, over Andy. Consequently, his promise is more credible.

Commitments are statements that communicate how firmly a party is taking a certain position. Once a commitment is made, then the opponent must act. However, the opponent's reactions to a commitment is dependent upon what type of commitment is made. Walton and McKersie identify three language factors that signal the "firmness" of a commitment. These factors are communicated through language that is *final*, *specific*, and *states explicit consequences*.[23] The following explicit bargaining message leaves little room for reinterpretation: "We must have a $4-per-hour increase or we will strike." Finality is expressed through "must have." The "$4-per-hour increase" is a specific demand. The explicit consequence is a strike.

When firm commitments are made, conflict escalation is possible because the opponent must either counterattack or concede the point. The firm commitment represents a win-lose issue. Thus, there is no room left for integrative, win-win bargaining.

Flexible commitments employ ambiguous messages and lead to more accommodations and reciprocal concessions. The ambiguity in the message allows the parties to explore different implications of the commitment. A flexible commitment can be contingent upon future concession by the opponent so that the bargainer can concede in the future without losing face. Or if a strike occurs, the bargainer can *increase* his or her demands to adjust for the new costs.

Demands and concession rates

"What do I offer?" "What do I accept?" These are two of the most frightening questions facing a bargainer. The opening offer/demand is a difficult decision to make. Not only is the uncertainty in the bargaining situation unnerving, but you realize that this initial bid is a tacit bargaining message that reveals some of your utility schedule. Also, the level of your initial bid and your subsequent concession rate affects the likelihood of reaching a negotiated settlement as well as the size of the agreement.

One determinant of an opening bid is the bargainer's utility schedule. As discussed earlier in this chapter, the utility schedule defines the resistance points and aspiration level of a bargainer. One reason for making an initial demand that is higher than your aspiration level and then offering concessions is to encourage negotiations that will result in a negotiated agreement that approximates your aspiration level. By making this level of demand and giving subsequent concessions, the bargainer is protecting his or her aspirations and alternatives. When a bargainer concedes something that had been considered a desirable alternative he or she suffers a *position loss*.

A second determinant of demand and concession rate is *image loss*. A bargainer suffers image loss when some *other* person feels the bargainer lacks firmness. The other person can be either the opponent or the bargainer's own constituents. A bargainer who is concerned about image loss is likely to exhibit face-saving behaviors such as making higher demands and giving lower concessions to the point of reaching no agreement. This same behavior is found in bargainers who must account for the negotiated outcome to their constituents.

Another example of image loss deals with the level of familiarity between the bargainers. How well you know the other bargainer is the third determinant of demands and concessions. Studies comparing bargaining between strangers and between married couples found strangers had higher demands, conceded more slowly, and broke off negotiations more frequently than married couples. It is believed that people involved in intimate relationships are less concerned about either position or image loss and more likely to try and find a mutually-beneficial solution.

Fourth, time pressure and amount of elapsed bargaining time affect demand and concession rate. It is common to read of contracts being settled just minutes before the start of a strike. Time pressures act to spur negotiators to a settlement because of the costs associated with continued negotiations or an impasse. The increase in likelihood of a settlement is because bargainers may begin to make lower demands and increase concessions. In light of the costs associated with continued negotiations or an impasse, bargainers will modify their aspiration levels and utility schedules to take account of these new variables.

A final determinant is the opponent's reaction to a party's demand and concessions. This determinant involves the issue of reciprocity of moves. Putnam and Jones found that reciprocity in integrative bargaining resulted in cooperative moves that facilitated agreement. However, when distributive strategies were reciprocated, in the form of one-upmanship, the dyads were caught in a conflict spiral and no agreement was reached. Specifically, a conflict spiral occurs when an attack is followed by an attack and also when defensive behavior is followed by defensive behavior.

After a bargainer has decided what his or her demand will be and what concessions may be necessary, he or she needs to be aware of the probable effects of these decisions. While the research on the effect of demands and concession rates is not as definitive as other types of bargaining research, three general conclusions are presented.[24] Any special conditions to these conclusions are noted.

First, *lower initial demands and faster concession rates by one or both parties will increase the likelihood that an agreement will be reached and will decrease the time needed to reach the agreement.* This finding is not surprising since the low demands put the bargainers closer to agreement and fast concessions will move them to a mutually acceptable outcome. This is especially true when both parties reciprocate the opponent's move. However, when reciprocity does *not* occur, an interesting deviation results. If one bargainer makes a low initial demand and concedes rapidly, there is a *decrease* in the likelihood of reaching an agreement and an increase in time used if a settlement is reached. The reason for this occurrence is that after the opponent receives a low demand and gets some fast concessions, the opponent will exploit the situation. That is, the opponent has been given some concessions, expects more may be forthcoming, and is going to hold out for that possibility.

A second general conclusion is that *large initial demands and smaller concessions will give the bargainer a larger outcome and the opponent a small outcome as long as an agreement is reached.* In the cases where agreement is reached it is thought that the large initial demand affected the opponent's impression of the other party's utility schedule and consequently the opponent modified his or her level of aspiration to accept a smaller gain. A person is likely to modify his or her aspiration level if the negotiations are over an item or issue with which he or she is not familiar.

The third conclusion is drawn from the previous two findings. There is *an inverted U-shaped relationship between* a *party's initial demand and the average outcomes.* Box 11.3 illustrates this relationship. Too low a demand and either too slow or too fast a concession rate yields low profits since there is little for the party to win. Large demands with slow concessions also will yield low average profits because frequent failures to reach agreements will mitigate the times when a large outcome is won. This is similar to playing the slot machines in Las Vegas. Even though someone occasionally will win a jackpot, most people win little or nothing; therefore, the average payoff is small. A bargainer's "best bet" is with moderate demands and concessions.

Exact quantification of a "high" versus "low" demand or concession rate is impossible. The amount is specific to each bargaining encounter. An opening demand of $75 is very low for a new ten-speed bicycle, very high for a child's second-hand tricycle, but about right for a child's second-hand bicycle.

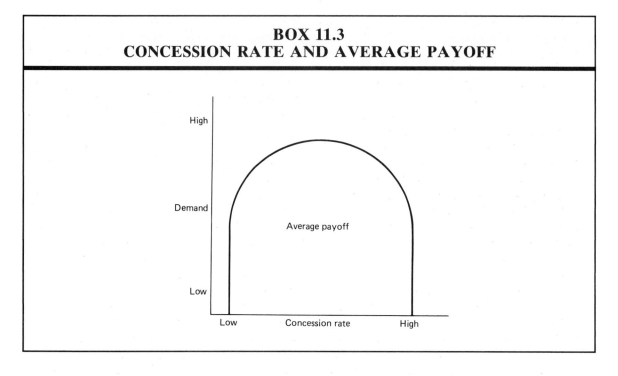

BOX 11.3
CONCESSION RATE AND AVERAGE PAYOFF

Skills for successful bargaining

Successful bargaining should not be interpreted to mean you win everything and your opponent receives nothing. In many cases, the parties will be involved in future negotiations so they need to develop and maintain a good working relationship. Consequently, parties make concessions in order to establish that relationship. What this section discusses are methods for improving the bargaining situation for both parties. Specifically, this section discusses the skills for bargaining in competitive and cooperative situations.

Before discussing the bargaining skills, one point needs to be made. Not all negotiations produce settlements. Sometimes the parties fail to maintain an adequate level of information exchange or they become involved in a conflict spiral and negotiations end in an impasse. At this point, a neutral third party may be brought in to either mediate or arbitrate the dispute. A mediator helps to guide the parties through the bargain-

ing process, so the parties may decide their own settlement. If the dispute goes to arbitration, it is the arbitrator who decides how the conflict will be settled. Mediation and arbitration are extensive topics and a discussion of these procedures is beyond the scope of this chapter. But students should be aware that negotiations do not always produce settlements and mediation and arbitration are means of dealing with bargaining impasses.

Competitive bargaining

Earlier sections have discussed how competitive behaviors may yield higher profits for one party, but at the expense of the bargaining relationship. Yet some issues are inherently distributive and must be dealt with competitively. Thus, the question becomes one of balance. How do negotiators bargain competitively without damaging the relationship? The following suggestions are designed to gain the advantages of competitive bargaining without incurring the disadvantages:[25]

1. *Use competitive tactics to defend basic interests rather than a particular solution.* For example, Andy Antique could use competitive tactics to defend his basic interest not to lose money on the desk and to make a reasonable profit.

2. *Send signals of flexibility and concern about the other party's interests in conjunction with competitive displays.* Such maneuvers are designed to make the integrative potential seem large enough to the other party that further attempts at bargaining seem justified. Andy Antique could acknowledge that Betty Buyer does not want to overspend on the desk and he believes that his interest in a fair profit and her interest of a "good buy" can be met.

3. *Insulate competitive behavior from cooperative behavior so that neither undermines the other.* This can be accomplished with the "white hat/ black hat" approach. One team member bargains competitively and another team member bargains cooperatively. This strategy functions in the following manner. After black hat has given a series of threats, white hat's cooperative messages are more likely to be reciprocated. The strategy is used also to persuade the opponent to give in *now* because the party's superior will not be so sympathetic in his or her approach to the negotiations.

4. *Employ deterrent threats rather than compellent threats.* Deterrent threats indicate the party is opposed to the opponent's favored option, but it does not address other options. Compellent threats require that a particular option be adopted. To illustrate, labor uses a deterrent threat when it rejects management's last wage package and waits to get a better offer in order to avert a strike. But labor uses a compellent threat when it tells management that labor's proposed wage package must be adopted in order to avert a strike.

Cooperative bargaining

In the early 1980s, Professor Roger Fisher and William Ury of the Harvard Negotiation Project published a national bestseller, *Getting to Yes: Negotiating Agreement Without Giving In.*[26] The book focuses upon methods of making bargaining situations cooperative rather than competitive in order to achieve mutually-satisfying results. The first four suggestions presented by Fisher and Ury are most appropriate for bargaining situations between parties of relatively equal power. The fifth suggestion is for bargaining with someone with greater power.

First, *separate the people from the problem.* The bargaining process demands a great deal of psychological and emotional energy. Thus a good interpersonal relationship is important, especially if this is an ongoing bargaining relationship. Fisher and Ury note three communication barriers to effective negotiations. First, the negotiator may fail to address the opponent and instead is talking to impress himself or herself or the constituents: "Effective communication is all but impossible if each plays to the gallery," says Fisher and Ury.[27] Second is poor listening skills. A poor negotiator is mentally preparing the next argument rather than attending to the opponent's current message. The final communication problem is misunderstanding or misinterpretations. This is likely when the parties have different native languages as in international bargaining situations, or if there are many technical terms with which one party is unfamiliar.

Fisher and Ury's second guideline to effective negotiations is to *focus on interests rather than positions.* To discover each party's underlying interests is a step toward finding creative solutions. Their example of the 1978 Camp David talks between Israel and Egypt illustrates this point well. Israel had occupied the Egyptian Sinai Peninsula since the 1967 Six Day War. Egypt wanted to regain sovereignty over this land. Restated, Egypt's interest was to control this land that had been a part of Egypt for centuries. Israel's interest was in secured borders. They did not want Egypt to be able to invade at a moment's notice. The agreement worked out at Camp David was for Israel to return the Sinai to Egypt, but a large portion of the peninsula was to be demilitarized. Thus, Israel's interest of security was met as was Egypt's interest in regaining sovereignty over the Sinai.

Invent options for mutual gain is another guideline. This can be accomplished by employing creative problem-solving techniques, searching for many possible solutions, avoiding premature judgments or "fixed-pie" assumptions, and working to solve the opponent's problems as well as yours. The fourth guideline is to *establish objective criteria* to judge possible solutions. Items to be considered in developing these criteria include: precedent, equality, equity, scientific judgment, market value, and professional standards, and so on. The use of these standards allows the parties to reach an agreement based upon principle rather than pressure.

In situations when you are negotiating with a more powerful opponent, Fisher and Ury suggest you develop a BATNA, *best alternative to a negotiated agreement*. Your BATNA is determined by analyzing what is in your best interest and what alternatives you have outside of the negotiation process. The BATNA then becomes the standard against which every proposal is compared. By comparing a proposal with your BATNA, you can determine if the opponent is offering something that meets enough of your interests and should be accepted, or if you are better off to leave the bargaining relationship. In summary, the BATNA protects the less-powerful party from accepting an unfavorable proposal or rejecting a proposal that has potential benefits.

Summary

This chapter has shown how bargaining is a communicative process that relies heavily upon the use of face-to-face persuasive messages. These messages can take many forms and can result in many different types of negotiated settlements. While bargaining situations vary greatly, they have similar bargaining structure. That is, the bargainers have aspiration levels, resistance points, and a status-quo point contained in their utility schedules.

The theoretical foundation of bargaining is moving away from mathematical, static models such as game theory and is going toward social-psychological models that incorporate person, role, and situation. Skills for successful bargaining should be understood as guidelines rather than absolute rules. But by understanding the structure of bargaining situations and the interplay of bargaining messages, these guidelines should enable people to have more productive bargaining encounters. A final point of emphasis is that successful bargaining is dependent upon a sufficient flow of information between the parties. If that flow is cut off or if the parties become too competitive to negotiate, then a mediator can help the parties to reach a negotiated settlement or an arbitrator can decide the issue for them.

Footnotes

1. Linda L. Putnam and Tricia S. Jones discuss the interchangeability of "bargaining" and "negotiations" in "Reciprocity in Negotiations: An Analysis of Bargaining Interactions," *Communication Monographs*, vol. 49 (1982), p. 171.

2. Thomas C. Schelling, *The Strategy of Conflict* (Cambridge: Harvard University Press, 1981), p. 85.

3. Richard E. Walton and Robert B. McKensie, *A Behaviorial Theory of Labor Negotiations* (New York: McGraw-Hill, 1965), pp. 13–17.

4. James T. Tedeschi and Paul Rosenfeld, "Communication in Bargaining and Negotiations," in Michael E. Roloff and Gerald R. Miller, eds., *Persuasion: New Directions in Theory and Research* (Beverly Hills, Ca.: Sage, 1980), pp. 227–228.

5. Samuel B. Bacharach and Edward J. Lawler, *Bargaining: Power, Tactics, and Outcomes* (San Francisco: Josey-Bass, 1981), pp. 6–13.

6. Schelling, *The Strategy of Conflict,* p. 105.

7. Schelling, *The Strategy of Conflict,* p. 89, and Walton and McKersie, *A Behavioral Theory,* pp. 161–169.

8. Jeffrey Z. Rubin and Bert R. Brown, *The Social Psychology of Bargaining and Negotiations* (New York: Academic, 1975), p. 20.

9. Rubin and Brown, *The Social Psychology of Bargaining,* pp. 20–32.

10. Daniel Druckman, *Negotiations: Social-Psychological Perspectives* (Beverly Hills, Ca.: Sage, 1977), pp. 28–37.

11. Bertram I. Spector, "Negotiation As a Psychological Process," in I. William Zartman, ed., *The Negotiation Process: Theories and Applications* (Beverly Hills, Ca.: Sage, 1978), pp. 55–56.

12. R. J. Klimoski, "The Effects of Intragroup Forces on Intergroup Conflict Resolution," *Organizational Behavior and Human Performance,* vol. 8 (1972), pp. 363–383.

13. Walton and McKersie, *A Behavioral Theory,* p. 3.

14. Walton and McKersie, *A Behavioral Theory,* p. 5.

15. Linda L. Putnam and Tricia S. Jones, "The Role of Communication in Bargaining," *Human Communication Research,* vol. 8, no. 3 (1982), p. 265.

16. Putnam and Jones, "The Role of Communication," pp. 265–266.

17. William A. Donohue, Mary E. Diez, and Mark Hamilton, "Coding Naturalistic Negotiation Interaction," *Human Communication Research,* vol. 10, no. 3 (1984), pp. 403–425.

18. Donohue, Diez, and Hamilton, "Coding Naturalistic Negotiation Interaction," p. 234.

19. Tedeschi and Rosenfeld, "Communication in Bargaining," p. 234.

20. D. G. Pruitt, *Negotiation Behavior* (New York: Academic, 1981), p. 72.

21. Tedeschi and Rosenfeld, "Communication in Bargaining," p. 236.

22. Pruitt, *Negotiation Behavior,* p. 79.

23. Walton and McKersie, *A Behavioral Theory,* pp. 93–98.

24. Rubin and Brown, *The Social Psychology of Bargaining,* pp. 262–269, and Pruitt, *Negotiation Behavior,* pp. 20–21.

25. D. G. Pruitt, "Strategic Choice in Negotiation," *American Behavioral Scientist,* vol. 27, no. 2 (1983), p. 190.

26. Roger Fisher and William Ury, *Getting to Yes: Negotiating Agreement Without Giving In* (Boston: Houghton Mifflin, 1981).

27. Fisher and Ury, *Getting to Yes,* p. 33.

CHAPTER TWELVE

Persuasion in Small-Group and Legal Settings

Millions of decisions are made each day in small-group contexts—in business, government, juries, and so on. It is therefore important for the versatile persuader to understand how groups function, and how influence is exerted in small groups. In this chapter, we will be concerned primarily with answering questions about how groups operate. In doing so, we will also discuss how principles of small-group processes are relevant to juries. Why juries? First, the jury is one type of small-group experience that is fundamental to our system of justice, and it is one important type of small-group encounter that *all* readers of this book may experience. Also, there has been a tremendous amount of research on juries—and all things legal—in the last several years. Further, many of our readers probably entertain the idea of entering the legal profession, and so some atten-

tion given to this topic would be worthwhile. Those readers interested in communication or persuasion inside the courtroom will first note that much of what we have already said in this book is applicable, and are further referred to Fontes and Bundens,[1] Miller and Bundens,[2] Kerr and Bray,[3] and Kassin and Wrightsman.[4] Our main topic in this chapter is small-group processes, and what happens when a jury leaves the courtroom to deliberate.

Persuasion in the small group

Considerable communication, pressure, and persuasion occur when people meet to sort through data, debate evidence and testimony, offer solutions, evaluate solutions, and arrive at decisions. Our attention for the remainder of this chapter will be devoted to persuasion in such a group context. We will focus on six fundamental topics: group size, spatial arrangement, emerging leaders, feedback and process, influence in the group, and group composition.

Group size

Much persuasion occurs in face-to-face situations in which the source must conduct a give-and-take session with receivers. The most obvious effect of an increase in group size is to decrease the amount of time any person in the group has for interaction with the source or for interaction with other group members. Thus, as a group's size increases, any effects of persuasion that might be caused simply by the amount of personal communication from a source will be diminished. Furthermore, as the number of different people increases, the potential number of positions on an issue will also increase. This can mean that a compromise position may be reached by the group that does not represent the views of any one member of the group.

Studies by Hare[5] and by Slater[6] indicate that as group size increases, member satisfaction decreases. Slater's groups seemed to prefer five members as the optimum size when they were working on a solution to a human-relations problem. Both of these studies were concerned with task-oriented groups, that is, groups actively dealing with various problems. These, and similar studies, suggest that when the persuasive task is the defense of a proposed solution or the proposal of an alternative solution, a small-group situation in which considerable interaction is possible produces a higher degree of group satisfaction. In fact, Pervin argues that satisfaction is always the result of the interaction of an individual with a particular situation and a given task.[7] The amount of group satisfaction may turn out to be an important factor in the acceptance of any message upon which the group finally agrees. Groups in which the members become individually dissat-

isfied with their participation are not as likely to be willing to change attitudes and behavior as a result of messages presented within the group.

In some persuasive-communication situations the source will be faced with opposition, opposition that is also engaged in persuasion. Sometimes these are formal groups that will give equal time to all sides. In most situations, however, the source will have to get a message across in spite of an opposing member. As the size of the group increases, however, the total amount of communication per unit of time does not increase to a significant degree. Instead, the relative amount of participation by each member of the group decreases. Thus, any individual member of the group may be involved less and less as the group gets larger and larger.[8] In such a situation, a source is faced with several alternatives. It may be possible to increase the *quality* of a message, so that it stands out from the background of all other messages, and people will pay more attention to it. This is the method followed by an advertiser who hopes that the advertisement for a company's product can be made more distinctive than that for any other product.

A second method that frequently works is to divide the group into smaller groups. Sometimes it is possible to have subgroups working on a topic, thus increasing the time proponents of a measure will have available to them to advocate a particular stand. Sometimes, it is even possible to structure the small subgroups in such a way that much of the opposition is concentrated in a single group, while the support is distributed among several groups.

A recommendation sometimes made is for the persuasive communicator to attempt to be appointed as the leader of a group, thus obtaining more time and prestige with the group members. The prestige factor is clearly important in very large groups, where the leader may be able to control the agenda, and have a prominent place on that agenda. In smaller informal groups, the leader of the group doesn't necessarily have that same set of advantages. In smaller groups, there is a greater expectation that the amount of time available will be shared, and the individual attempting to dominate such a group may encounter hostility.

Studies by Bales and Borgatta[9] of communication behavior in groups ranging from two to seven members provide at least some tentative hypotheses for the persuasive communicator to consider. Their conclusions suggest that smaller groups inhibit overt disagreements and expressions of dissatisfaction from group members more than do larger groups. The persuasive communicator who leaves a small group feeling that there is agreement in the group may be misled because of the reluctance of the group to engage in active disagreements. On the other hand, it would also seem to follow that the communicator will have more trouble in controlling larger groups in which dissatisfactions are more openly expressed.

The Bales and Borgatta findings also suggest that when people communicate in small groups, they are reluctant to express negative feelings about the other members of the group. Larger groups tend to have subgroups, and these subgroups provide *support* for diverse opinions, and therefore, support for more open expressions of dissatisfaction. For example, if I am a source talking to a group of five people, it may be that one person doesn't agree with me. He or she says nothing, however, because he or she may think that everyone else agrees with me. If I am talking to a group of 25 people, however, there may be several who do not agree with me. Those individuals may form a subgroup, and thus feel less constrained about openly disagreeing with me, since they receive support from other members of the subgroup.

Thus far, our discussion has been limited to groups of two to nine members and to groups in which there is ample opportunity for interaction with the communicator. As groups become even larger than nine members, several things happen. First, the probability that there will be a formal leader increases. When there are 20 people in a room, bedlam will result unless there is someone charged with the responsibility of conducting the session. When there is a leader, social power (the ability to achieve compliance from group members) tends to accrue to that leader. In such a situation, it becomes imperative that the outside communicator or the individual group member work with the leader in the presentation of messages. In many situations, the presence of a formal leader other than the persuasive communicator may reduce the work that the communicator has to do. Rather than concentrating on reaching every member of a group, it may be enough to persuade the formal leader, and then to depend on that leader to do the persuading with the rest of the group, or at least to smooth the way for access to the rest of the group. When a persuasive communicator shares a message with a group leader, there is a distinct risk of having the message distorted by the group leader, as well as having much of the credit for any persuasive success be given to the leader and not to the originator of the idea. Thus, there are advantages and disadvantages in approaching larger groups where there is a leader already designated.

Second, larger groups are more likely to have cliques and splinter groups. In small groups, social pressures operate to prevent cliques and splinter groups that deviate from the beliefs of the majority. In larger groups, the pressures to prevent deviance are harder to apply, and deviant groups are more likely to form. For the persuasive communicator, the danger is that the probability of overt, organized opposition to a message will increase. The increase may not occur because of any fault in the message, but merely because a large group has permitted the formation of a splinter group in opposition to any policy advocated by the leadership. It should be noted, however, that the clique or splinter group may also serve as a wedge into a group that would normally oppose the communicator's message. The persuasive source may be able to use the splinter group to gain entry to the larger group. If the splinter group can be convinced of the desirability of some goal, it may carry the message to the larger group despite the opposition of the formal leaders of the group.

Third, as groups become very large, the entire mode of group operation changes, and the presentation of messages to the group will change.

That is true in all persuasive situations, whether the goal is an eventual change in attitude or in behavior. Typically, large groups develop *rules* for monitoring the flow of communication within the group. These may be extremely formal sets of rules, such as the rules developed by legislatures and formal organizations. Perhaps the best known example of such rules are those codified in *Robert's Rules of Order*.[10] Even in less formal groups, rules of conduct will develop. Students learn in the first grade to raise their hand when they want to talk. The formality of the rules is almost always directly proportional to the number of people involved. An instructor can conduct a class for college students with complete freedom on the part of the student to ask questions, interrupt, and make comments when there are five or ten members of the class. When there are 25, such freedom becomes more difficult, and when the group size reaches 100, the constraints on both the teacher and the student force changes in the way in which materials are prepared, in the way in which they are presented, and in the amount of interaction that any one class member may have with fellow students or with the instructor. In general, the mode of presentation becomes more formal.

We should note that there are both advantages and disadvantages to the formality attached to large groups. The disadvantages lie in the lower satisfaction levels found in such large audiences and in the difficulties of gaining entry to large groups. But there are some advantages for the persuasive communicator who does gain an audience with a large group. Usually, the source will have more time to present a message, and will not have to face severe questioning by other group members. There may be opposition, but the opposition will have the same time constraints, and the merits of the proposal can be argued equally.

Thomas and Fink[11] have reviewed a number of studies in the small-group area concerned with group size. They suggest that group size has a significant effect on both individual and group performance, on the nature and kind of interaction that will occur, on the type of group organization that will emerge, and on several psychological variables. The persuasive communicator must be concerned with all of these factors in planning for the presentation of messages to groups of receivers.

In legal research, the size of the jury has pronounced effect on participation patterns, among other variables. Kessler,[12] for example, had six-person juries and 12-person juries deliberate an automobile negligence suit. Only two of the 48 members of the various six-person juries failed to participate verbally in deliberations, compared to 24 percent of the 96 members of the various 12-person juries. Saks[13] similarly found that communication rates were more varied in the 12-person jury than in the six-person jury for criminal cases. Further, there is evidence that the size of the majority faction and the size of the minority faction also influence the group process:[14] (1) the larger faction produces more verbal messages than the minority and, over the length of the deliberations, this imbalance increases as the majority increases in membership; (2) discussion is terminated, typically, when the majority faction reaches a size required to form a verdict.

Since the early 1970s, a debate has focused on whether to retain the 12-person jury with a required unanimity rule or to switch to a six-person jury requiring a majority rule.[15] If it can be demonstrated that the two groups (12- and six-person) do not differ in verdicts, then considerable expense for the state can be saved by adopting the smaller jury. Bermant and Cappock,[16] among others, found that verdicts are identical in six-person and 12-person juries. However, not all studies have found this to be the case, and a number of studies indicate that group size influences group decision-making processes. For example, Valenti and Downing[17] varied six-person and 12-person juries in mock trials involving an assault and battery case. In one version of the testimony it appeared quite likely that the defendant was guilty (high apparent guilt), while in the other half of the cases it appeared that the defendant was not guilty (the "strong evidence" for the prosecution was deleted from the case).

Valenti and Downing found that when apparent guilt was low, both the six-person and 12-person juries were identical in verdicts (only two out of ten juries of each size reached a guilty verdict). However, when apparent guilt was high two out of the ten 12-person juries convicted the defendant while nine out of the ten six-person juries convicted the defendant. Further, the six-person jury who heard the high-guilt testimony: (a) required less time (12.3 minutes) to reach a verdict than did other groups (18 minutes to 38 minutes); (b) felt they had less of an opportunity to express opinions freely (compared to other groups); and (c) felt they had not thoroughly discussed the facts presented in the case. Apparently, when persons in the six-member juries started to deliberate and realized that there was initially high agreement, dissent was suppressed and the group simply made a decision without discussing the case completely.

The most thorough analysis of group processes of six- and 12-person juries was done by Saks.[18] Saks presented a video-tape of a trial simulation of a burglary case to jurors in Ohio. His observations are summarized as follows:[19]

Large juries, compared to small juries, spend more time deliberating, engage in more communication per unit time, manifest better recall of testimony, induce less disparity between minority and majority factions in their ratings of perceived jury performance and in sociometric ratings, and less disparity between convicting and acquitting juries in number of arguments generated, facilitate markedly better community representation, and, though not achieving statistical significance, tend to produce more consistent verdicts. Small juries allow jurors to initiate more communication per member (although the total group communication was less than in twelve-person juries), share more equally in the communication, better recall arguments as a percentage of total arguments, obtained higher sociometric ratings of reasonableness and contributions to the jury's task, and although no significant differences occurred in the distribution of verdicts, the tendency of large juries to produce more consistent (or more "correct") verdicts means that small juries would produce more acquittals (as long as trials usually end in convictions).

Saks felt that both the six- and 12-person jury had advantages and disadvantages and argued that one way to resolve the debate is to implement an innovation where one 12-person jury (to ensure better community representation) would split itself into two juries of six each, be required to achieve a 4/6 consensus, and where both twin juries would have to agree on a guilty verdict in order to find the defendant guilty. However, this innovation does not offer the advantage of increased recall of testimony offered by the 12-person group, nor does it reduce costs for the state. Nonetheless, while we are sure to see additional research on the issue of jury size, recent studies indicate clearly that group size influences communication processes in predictable ways.

Spatial arrangement

Figure 12.1 shows how the variable of spatial arrangement might operate in a persuasive-communication situation. When people are seated so that interaction between each member is as easy as interaction with the communicator (type B), the nature of the communication in the group will obviously be different from the communication occurring when people are seated so as to reduce communication between group members and increase communication with the speaker (type A).

In the situation illustrated in A, the communicator will have maximum control over communication in the group. Messages will tend to originate with the source, and flow to the receivers. It is difficult for private conversations to take place between the receivers. In the type B situation, the source will have much less control over the receivers. Two receivers can sit and talk to one another, with relatively little risk that the source can control their discussion. In type A, the source can monopolize the communication more effectively than in B. On the other hand, in A, the source will find it far more difficult to obtain feedback from the members of the group. The situation is so formal that receivers may be reluctant to volunteer comments to the source. In B, feedback is much easier to obtain; the situation is less formal.

The best-known study of the effects of organization patterns on group performance is that by Harold J. Leavitt.[20] Figure 12.2 illustrates the

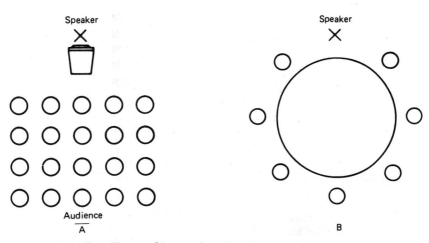

Figure 12.1. Two Types of Interaction Situations

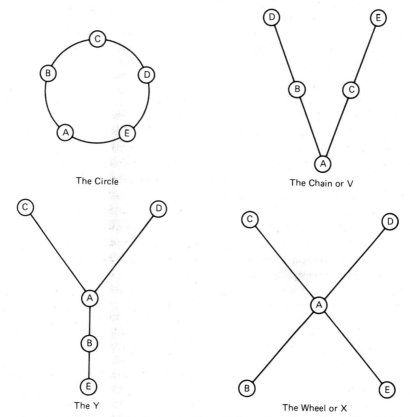

Figure 12.2. Patterns of Group Organization. Reprinted from Harold J. Leavitt, "Some Effects of Certain Communication Patterns on Group Performance," *Journal of Abnormal and Social Psychology,* vol. 46 (1951), with permission of the author and the American Psychological Association.

four types of spatial arrangements with which he was concerned. With the circle type of arrangement, each member could talk to any other member. In the wheel arrangement, the members forming the spokes could not communicate with each other, but only with the person in the center. In the chain, or V, arrangement, individual A could communicate only with B who could communicate only with C, and so on. In the Y type, however, A and B could communicate with C, who could work with D, who could communicate with E. Leavitt was interested both in group satisfaction and group productivity. The major interest we have in this study lies with the group-satisfaction variable, since it may be directly related to persuasion. Leavitt found that the circle arrangement seemed to produce the greatest amount of group satisfaction. On the other hand, the wheel pattern was the most effective pattern when the variable was productivity. It is easy to see what happened in the Leavitt studies. In the circle arrangement, everyone was allowed to talk to everyone else. The members of the group did talk to everyone else to set up the production system. That took time, and the extra time caused productivity to fall off. In the wheel arrangement, no extra time was needed, because the person in the middle simply issued orders, and did not worry about whether other members of the group agreed or were satisfied with the arrangement. Other research studies have tended to support the Leavitt findings, but offer more detail about predictions of morale level for other kinds of communication situations.[21]

Perhaps the most important finding in these studies as far as persuasion is concerned is related to the concept of "centrality." Centrality is the relationship of the individual to communication receiving and sending. Individual A, in Leavitt's wheel arrangement (Figure 12.2), is more central than any of the other group members, while in the circle arrangement, all group members are equally central to the group. Centrality, therefore, is concerned with the amount of communication *control* an individual can exercise over other members of the group. Control obviously depends on whether an individual is dependent on others for the ability to communicate, or is independent of others. The more control, the more independent an individual is, and thus the higher the centrality of the individual. The research shows that the more central an individual is, the higher the satisfaction with being in the group.

The patterns of spatial arrangement and communication studied by Leavitt and those additional patterns reported in a review of Glanzer and Glaser[22] are for small groups of five to seven. There are no studies of the most satisfactory spatial arrangements of group members in situations involving large groups. Given that the intent of all persuasive communicators is to effect some change in the attitudes, emotions, or behavior of a receiver or set of receivers, perhaps the best advice we can offer the source is that an arrangement in which the source has the ability to direct the flow of communication ought to be more effective than one in which there is the opportunity for cliques to form, for private discussions to start, or for leadership to be shifted to someone else in the room. It is certainly true that when members are allowed free interaction with everyone else in the group, more satisfaction with the situation and with any decision ought to result. But the danger is that with increased interaction, the communicator may lose control over the group, and the idea that satisfies the group may not represent the persuasive communicator's ideas, but some modification of those ideas. Thus, an arrangement such as illustrated in B of Figure 12.1, with people sitting in a large circle, might not be as satisfactory as the other arrangement in the A of Figure 12.1, with receivers facing the source. Hare and Bales[23] have done some preliminary work that indicates that cliques will form and leadership will vary as a function of seating position. Spatial arrangement, then, is an important part of the communicator's concern in planning for persuasive communication.

Not surprisingly, physical arrangements play an important role in jury research. A foreman, for example, is more likely to be selected from an end position of a rectangular table than from other positions.[24] Generally speaking, 46 percent to 56 percent of the time a foreman will be selected if *he* (78 percent of foremen are, in fact, *men*) is sitting in a more visible, central, and traditional seat of authority. Further, classic work by Strodtbeck and Hook[25] indicates that jurors in more visible or central positions talk more than do others, and additional research indicates that foremen are responsible for one-fourth to one-third of all verbal messages.[26]

Emerging leaders

Groups meeting over long periods of time with relative frequency are very likely to have a leader. Groups that come together for short periods of time, have no social structure, or in which no social structure has developed are likely to have no designated or discernible leader. The group coming together for a dormitory "bull session," the neighborhood "coffee klatch," the informal political meeting, the meeting of individuals in a student-union building, are all examples of situations in which leaders may not be easy to identify.

Social psychologists tell us that in any group that has been together for any length of time, leadership will emerge. It may be a shifting leadership, there may be more than one leader, people in the group may not always agree on who the leader is, but there *will* be individuals who exercise leadership functions. This suggests that many groups will have *emerging leaders*, that is, individuals who exercise leadership functions but have not been designated or recognized as formal leaders. The persuasive communicator improves chances of success by being identified as an emerging leader or by prior interaction with a potential leader.

The importance of locating an emerging leader within a small group lies in the boost that might be given to a persuasive message because of the leader's support, and in the diminished probability of success if a leader emerges who opposes the goal of the persuasive communicator. Furthermore, since emerging leaders have the best chance of becoming permanent, formal leaders, an early

convert to the communicator's position may become an even greater asset at a later time. Thus sources who are going to be working with groups should spend time to locate leaders and emergent leaders and to direct communication carefully to them in the hope of adding influential supporters.

It is easy to say, "Look for an emerging leader," but what do we look for? How can we identify those people who will eventually become the leaders in small group settings? One way of going about the task is to look at the functions that leaders perform. Our list is not complete. Burgoon, Huston, and McCroskey[27] provide a rather complete list of leadership functions. Here, however, are five general functions relevant to any small group context:

1. Initiation. Leaders tend to speak more than other people in the group. New ideas come from leaders more than from other members of the group. Thus we can look for people in our groups who are verbal, always beginning a conversation, throwing out new ideas, or buttonholing different members of the group. Such an individual is likely either to be a leader or to be in the process of getting accepted as a leader.

2. Organizational efforts. Informal groups usually do not exist for long without some structure. They may begin as entities with an informal structure, but their continued existence usually depends on eventually having some formal type of organization. Emerging leaders are usually involved in attempts to formalize the group structure. This may mean attempting to get the group to set an agenda, or proposing systematic meetings, or suggesting tasks the group could do. The point is that individuals who try to get groups to organize themselves are likely to be emerging leaders.

3. Integration efforts. One of the major problems with informal groups is that they tend to break up as easily as they form. If people are relatively happy with their experiences in the group, however, they tend to want to continue with the group. Emerging leaders frequently attempt to create the kind of conditions that will make group members want to stay in the group. If you find people in the group talking about being satisfied, trying to resolve conflicts among group members, or trying to set up pleasant experiences, it is likely that those individuals will be group leaders in the future.

4. Information management. One of the more important characteristics of the group leader is the amount of communication transmitted relative to the rest of the group members. In general, leaders speak more often, issue more statements, have fewer questions than others, interrupt more frequently, and try to manage the nature of the communication that flows between members of the group. A potential leader may often be spotted by the attempts made to manage information to the group.

5. Gatekeeping function. In a small-group situation, someone has to manage the way communication is handled. Not everyone can speak at the same time, although when a group has just formed it may seem as if everyone is speaking at once. Eventually, someone will suggest rules (usually informal in nature) to straighten out the maintenance of communication within the group. Eventually, if the group ever becomes a formal, stable group, someone will arise as a leader to function as a manager of information within the group. Potential leaders may frequently be spotted by their beginning attempts to get a group to work together.

In the legal setting, a foreman is often selected in the first two minutes of jury work[28] (although Wanamaker[29] reported an instance where foreman selection required over an hour). Foremen are typically men, are selected because of their centrality (as noted above), and are likely to have had previous jury experience—experienced jurors were selected as foreman in 51 percent of the cases studied in one article, while the chance level for comparison was 40 percent.[30] Individuals with higher-status occupations are also likely to become foremen. Strodtbeck's research[31] indicated that in one-third of juries studied, the first person who spoke became the foreman.

In their role as leader and coordinator, foremen talk more and are spoken to more often than are any single individuals. Foremen are also more likely to discuss deliberation procedures and the judge's instructions than are nonforemen, and are more likely to give information, give opinions, and seek opinions than are nonforemen. Unfortunately, we must caution against making too many generalizations about the actual behaviors of foremen, because only one in 12 or one in six jurors is a foreman, and sample sizes for any systematic study of foreman behavior are small. Nonetheless, one important aspect of the role of foreman deals with when and how the foreman polls the jury. Hawkins[32] observed that four different polling methods can be used by foremen: (1) the *go-around* (where each juror announces his or her verdict preference with or without comment), (2) the *secret ballot*, (3) the *show of hands*, and (4) the *verbal dissent* (where only those opposing a proposition registered a verbal comment). Hawkins found that the first two methods were used the most, while the last two were used relatively infrequently. After analyzing 46 mock-jury cases, Hawkins offered two conclusions relevant to our discussion: (1) hung juries had relied more on secret balloting than juries that did not get hung; and (2) the sooner juries took the first poll, the sooner they had finished the deliberation. Hawkins argued that early polling lets jurors know who stands where quickly, and this facilitates a movement into majority and minority factions. Secret balloting, however, makes it difficult for jurors to know who belongs in what camp and to identify whom one should talk to in order to influence dissenters. Not surprisingly, Hawkins noted that majority factions preferred frequent and public polling. Thus, not only can foremen lead and direct jury discussion, but by polling early and in public, the foreman can help gauge and structure the group process.

Feedback and process

Feedback is any information that the source gains from receivers about the probable reception of the message. In small-group encounters, feedback is immediate—people nod or verbalize agreement or disagreement as a person speaks. In other contexts, such as in advertising and political campaigns, feedback is delayed, since the communication adviser may not truly know the results of an advertisement until surveys are conducted, the quarterly sales figures are tabulated, or the election is held. In small-group encounters, then, one often adjusts messages on the spur of the moment as individuals attempt to influence one another. What can be said about the process of group work, especially as it pertains to jury deliberations? Relying on the Stasser, Kerr, and Bray[33] thorough review, we can talk about who speaks, who is spoken to, and what is said.

Who speaks

We have noted that foremen participate more than the average juror. There is evidence that conversation in most juries is uneven—three or four jurors talk more than do the remaining group members. One study found that in 82 percent of juries surveyed the three most active participants produced one-half of the total verbal acts.[34] Further, classic work in jury research indicates that males participate more than do women, and that males are more likely to be perceived as helpful in achieving a decision than are women.[35] Also, individuals who have higher-status jobs participated more and were perceived as more helpful than jurors of lower status. Similarly, better-educated jurors participated more than less-educated jurors. Finally, there is some weak evidence that black jurors participated less than white jurors (when not foremen), but this result should be viewed skeptically since blacks have been underrepresented in jury panels, especially in the 1950s and 1960s.[36] Nonetheless, what individual is more likely to participate in jury deliberations? A well-educated, high-status male who sits in a more visible or central location is more likely to participate than other jurors.

Who speaks to whom

People who speak the most are more likely to be spoken to the most. For example, foremen not only initiate more comments, but also receive the most comments,[37] and, as evidenced recently in Nemeth, Endicott, and Wachtler,[38] men talk more than women and also receive more communications than women.

However, since small groups include many people, it is sometimes more convenient to discuss general communication principles than discuss which specific person talks to which other specific person. Two features of interaction patterns are of interest to the communication scholar who desires to understand group work: There exist *sequential stages* in group discussions, and there are *characteristic ways* in which majority and minority factions communicate.

Work by small-group researchers[39] indicates that communication progresses through stages during discussion. First, during an *orientation phase* members define issues, discuss initial ideas, and state personal preferences. If differences of opinion are identified, an *open conflict phase* occurs in which group members take different sides of issues, become committed to different factions, actively defend one position, and attack the opposing position. Next the group emerges into a *conflict-resolution phase,* where members seek solutions acceptable to the group. Ultimately, an outcome appears probable to the group and the conflict-resolution phase is followed by the *reconciliation phase.* In this final phase, members attempt to heal wounds, reestablish rapport, express support for one another, and so on.

As Stasser, Kerr, and Bray have noted,[40] these phases commonly occur in jury deliberations. First, members express their opinions to the group as a whole. Then, as factions are identified, more and more messages are directed toward the opposing faction. Members of one faction continue to direct comments to the opposing one until either enough members are swayed to the majority side or until it becomes apparent that the jury is hopelessly hung. Hawkins[41] found that communication directed toward the opposing faction increased clearly from phase one (53 percent of comments) to phase two (60 percent) to phase three (67 percent), while communication directed toward the juror's own faction (and to the group as a whole) decreased. In the final, fourth, phase, Hawkins found that jurors decreased the number of messages directed toward opposite factions (to 46 percent of all messages during the phase), and resumed communication that was directed toward the whole group.

What is said

Surprisingly little research effort has been expended in coding all the statements made by jurors during deliberations. A classic in this area is the work by Simon.[42] Deliberations of ten mock juries discussing a burglary case were coded into five types of statements: *references to testimony, opinions on facts of the case, references to court's instructions, comments on deliberation procedures*, and *experiences from personal and daily life*. Simon[43] found that 44 percent of the comments made during the deliberations focused on the evidence of the case (15 percent "references to testimony" and 29 percent "opinions on facts of the case"). Eight percent of the comments dealt with court's instructions (which may be a high number considering the case involved an insanity plea), 26 percent of the communication dealt with "comments on deliberation procedures," and 22 percent with "experiences from personal and daily life." As these figures suggest, jurors appear to be particularly involved in sticking to the issue at hand—the issue of guilt versus innocence, and how the jury deliberations ought to proceed.

Further, Simon and other researchers[44] had statements coded in terms of relevance or lack of relevance to the case. It is comforting to note that the vast majority of the issues discussed (82 per-

cent) were considered legally relevant.[45] In terms of the five categories noted above, jurors stuck to discussing issues relevant to the deliberation in regards to opinions of the facts, references to testimony, and to comments on deliberation procedures. However, the percentage of relevant statements was lower for references to court's instructions (62 percent of the messages were considered relevant to the legal process—indicating that clarity of instructions is an important concern for legal professionals), and for personal and daily experiences (only 57 percent of the comments were relevant to the case—indicating that many jurors get sidetracked into discussing personal experiences that are irrelevant to the legal matter at hand).

What is said is also affected by who is saying it. Women accept the role of "socioemotional" leader more than men by making more statements of agreement, and of showing solidarity to other members, by displaying positive reactions, and by helping to reduce tension.[46] Men are typically more task oriented, and tend to "give opinions" and "give information" more than women. Further, persons who are less educated have less to say about the judge's instructions and the deliberation procedures than do the better-educated jurors, and are often inaccurate about their responses on these topics. Clearly, these results indicate that a lawyer must adapt his or her messages to make instructions and messages more comprehensible to less-educated jurors when complex cases are being decided.

So far, we have primarily *described* what goes on in the small-group situation, and have not discussed how or why people influence one another. Let's now look at how individuals, and factions, influence and persuade one another in small-group situations.

Influence in the group

Individuals in juries have initial ideas on how they would vote after hearing testimony and before actually deliberating. Once the deliberation starts, the jury's purpose is to sort through data, testimony, and evidence in order to decide the defendant's innocence or guilt ("beyond reasonable doubt"). Once the jury begins their task, two general types of effects may be observed.[47] A *majority effect* occurs when juries move toward the side initially favored by the majority of members. That is, suppose eight of 12 jurors favored the not-guilty verdict on the first ballot that is taken. After deliberations, the probability is high that the jury will vote "not guilty" as the final verdict. In fact, Kalven and Zeisel[48] found that in 215 juries that contained an initial majority, only six reached a verdict that did not have a majority support on the first ballot. The idea that a lone, yet determined, juror can influence all other jurors (for example, *Twelve Angry Men*) is more movie material than a reality.

On the other hand, a *leniency effect* is the tendency for jurors to move from the majority to acquitting the defendant (also see below). That is, as jurors deliberate the guilt of a defendant "beyond reasonable doubt" there is a shift toward letting the accused go free—a "risky shift." Nemeth,[49] for example, constructed various four-to-two combinations of jurors (four for acquittal with two for guilty verdicts or four for guilty verdicts with two for acquittal), and found that when four people initially favored acquittal they persuaded the remaining two toward acquittal votes 89 percent of the time. However, in 19 juries studied where four persons favored guilt (and the remaining two favored acquittal), seven juries reached a guilty verdict, seven reached a not-guilty verdict, and five were hung. The results reflect a leniency effect. Finding a person guilty "beyond reasonable doubt" is a difficult assignment.

How can you tell what will be the outcome of a small-group discussion? According to Stasser, Kerr, and Bray[50] two observations can be used to identify what may be a probable outcome of the discussion. Once a person shifts a position (after the initial public balloting), the person is unlikely to shift back (in public balloting), and the first shift in voting is a good predictor of which side will lose support. However, these observations do not tell us *why* a group will proceed to its final verdict. We need to discuss the underlying reasons for both the majority and the leniency effect.

Majority effects: Types of influences

The small-group literature[51] indicates that there are two forms of influence operating in a small-group task. *Informational influence* (see Chapter 10) occurs when facts, logical arguments, common sense, or data concerning one's personal experience is used to influence other members of the group. *Normative influence* occurs when members feel obligated to change in order to comply with other members' expectations. Stasser, Kerr, and Bray[52] note that the strength by which these influences exert pressure on a member is directly related to the size of the faction. Stasser, Kerr, and Bray argue that the persuasive potential of a faction to employ informational influence rests on the faction's ability to supply supporting evidence during the discussion. Thus, if each person in a faction can supply some minimal number of arguments for his or her position, then the larger faction ought to be able to exert stronger informational influence. Also, recall from Chapter 3 that involved receivers are more likely to be persuaded if they hear multiple arguments from multiple sources. Finally, some studies have explored group outcomes using a "valence" model.[53] In this approach, the "valence" or attractiveness of a particular stand is related directly to the total number of arguments made in support of the position. Thus, once a valence for one alternative begins to exceed the valence of another alternative, it will emerge as the chosen alternative.

Further, the size of the majority faction affects the amount of normative pressure in several ways. First, the more people adopt a particular stand, the more that position is seen as being legitimate, fair, and reasonable. Second, the more support a faction receives, the greater the pressure minority members will feel to conform to the majority position. Avoiding disapproval from ten people and gaining their approval is more important than keeping the approval of only one person. Minority members do not automatically give in to the majority; rather, support for the minority position is eroded during the course of the deliberations, sometimes slowly, after the first balloting.

Leniency effects: Causes

"All things being equal, jurors acting individually are more likely to convict than are juries, and jurors are more likely to favor conviction before than after deliberations."[54] Both of these trends are true, of course, when individual jurors lean toward acquittal before actually deliberating, but lenience effects can also occur when a large number of jurors initially leaned toward a guilty verdict. On occasion this "group shift" toward lenience can also result in a shift toward guilt (a "group polarization" in the opposite direction), if testimony suggests, reliably, that the defendant is likely to be guilty.

There are many possible reasons for why shifts occur. We will note three here. It may be argued, first, that a not-guilty position is more easily defended in deliberations. Juries are charged with the duty of finding a defendant guilty only if no reasonable doubt remains, and jurors know that the prosecution is charged with the burden of proof. Thus, the prosecution must, first, establish guilt and must, second, discredit alternatives, and if it fails to do so, it may be possible for a relatively small number of minority members to find one weak argument in the prosecution's case to hang the jury, or find for acquittal.

A second reason for lenience bias, or any group shift, has to do with the number of and the persuasiveness of the arguments presented.[55] We have already commented on the fact that many more arguments might be presented by a majority faction; however, arguments can also vary in terms of strength. Thus, as we noted in Chapter 1, the observation by a sole juror that a woman with an allegedly injured back would not wear high-heeled shoes is a critically important piece of evidence. Similarly, the argument that a woman is unlikely to reach over across the bed to get her glasses, put them on, and move to a window to identify an assailant through the El-train—or the realization that an assailant would not stab a victim with a switchblade knife by using a downward motion—were convincing pieces of evidence in *Twelve Angry Men*. The uniqueness and persuasiveness of arguments, along with the number of arguments, may help explain group shifts.

A third reason why information influence results in lenience shifts is that jurors begin to reevaluate the risk associated with guilty or not-guilty verdicts once they are involved in deliberations. That is, when a juror, as an individual, hears the testimony and evidence, he or she may feel that the defendant is likely to be guilty. After the closing comments and instructions to the jury, the juror proceeds to the deliberation room where two concerns become important when minority members (who vote for acquittal) present arguments. First, the juror understands that it causes risks and costs for society if he errs and allows a guilty person to go free. Second, it goes clearly against democratic and libertarian principles to find an innocent person guilty, or to punish an innocent person. It is possible that as jurors deliberate and a juror hears more arguments presented by the proacquittal faction he or she decides not to be linked to the second potential type of error—that it is better to let a guilty person go free than to incarcerate an innocent person. Thus, the desire not to punish the innocent, along with persuasive arguments and with the defensibility of the not-guilty verdict, leads the juror to switch to a different verdict.

Group composition: Bias?

A variety of studies suggest that the people who make up the group influence group processes and outcomes. For example, textbooks in small-group communication suggest that authoritarians, or dogmatics, are firm, demanding, directive, and adhere strictly to norms and roles when they are leaders. When such personalities are in subordinate positions, they tend to be submissive and compliant. In jury settings, the question of whether juror characteristics affect processes and outcomes is a critically important one, since defendants are presumably judged *fairly* by a panel of peers. Are there strong possibilities of bias, and, if so, what can be done about it?

Trial lawyers develop ideas as to what to expect from particular types of (potential) jurors. Simon[56] has explored the trial-procedure literature and identified this rather extensive list of possible biases that (some) lawyers may have adopted:

Age and sex

1. A young juror is more likely to return a verdict favorable to the plaintiff than to the defendant.

2. An older juror is more likely to be sympathetic to the plaintiff than to the defendant in civil, personal injury cases.

3. A juror whose age closely approximates the age of the client, lawyer, or witness is more likely to give a favorable verdict.

4. A woman juror is more likely to be emotional and sympathetic and to return a verdict favorable to the plaintiff.

5. A male juror is more likely to return a verdict favorable to the plaintiff if she is an attractive female.

6. A female juror is more likely to return a verdict favorable to the plaintiff if he is an attractive male.

7. A woman juror is more likely to be intolerant to the complaints of her own sex and thus return a verdict unfavorable to a party of her own sex.

Socioeconomic characteristics

1. A juror belonging to the same fraternal organizations, union, or political party as the client or witness is more likely to return a verdict favorable to that party.

2. A juror belonging to the same occupation or profession as the client will be more likely to give a favorable verdict. Exception: If a person of the same occupation (car salesperson) is in close proximity "jealousy" may influence a juror toward an unfavorable vote.

3. A juror belonging to an occupation or profession traditionally antagonistic to the occupation or profession of the client or witness is more likely to return an unfavorable verdict.

4. A juror who has or had extensive dealings with the public in matters of law enforcement and investigation is more likely to give a decision favorable to the defendant.

5. A juror whose occupation is that of a bellboy or taxi driver is more likely to be defendant-prone in a criminal case. They see so much of the frailties of human nature that they are not easily shocked.

6. A juror with a small income is more likely to be sympathetic with the poorer party.

Personality types

1. An intelligent, courageous juror is more desired by parties who feel they have a good case while a weak-minded juror is more desired by parties who feel they have a doubtful case and are dependent upon emotional, sympathetic appeals.

2. A juror who adheres to defiant political or moral values is more likely to use nonlegal sources as his or her basis for arriving at a verdict. Hence, such people are less predictable, among other things.

3. A juror who claims strong opinions on any topic is more likely to be dogmatic and less able to bring various facts together for comparison purposes.

Many of these specific beliefs can be grouped into a small set of biases: *social class*, with older or richer jurors seen as being more conservative than younger and poorer ones; *similarity*, with jurors who are similar to either the plaintiff or defendant seen as being more lenient toward the similar other; *sex roles*, with women seen as being more emotional, socially oriented, and as displaying, in some situations, greater sympathy than men; *susceptibility to stereotypes* (for instance, the idea that men are suckers for good-looking women, women are saps for good-looking men, and so on); and *personalities* (for instance, the idea that dogmatic, authoritarian, or "harsh" persons convict more frequently than equalitarians, liberals, or independent-minded persons.

Do these biases actually operate in real juries? In reality, little *consistent* evidence indicates that these biases influence jurors' decisions. For example, Simon[57] found that trial manuals asserted that a juror's occupation was a very important piece of evidence for predicting bias; yet surveys of jury work have failed to conclude that higher-status occupations lead to more conservative judgments. However, bias is sometimes evident—one study (cited in Simon) found that higher-status jurors were more likely to convict than were lower-status jurors (thus protecting society and property). Another study found that Democrats awarded more money (8 percent above average) in personal-injury cases than Republicans (2 percent below the average), thus indicating that Democrats are more willing to protect the victim and help the "little guy" than Republicans.[58]

Hastie, Penrod, and Pennington,[59] in a study of jury work in felony cases, found that juror characteristics such as demographics, personality, and general attitudes are only *weakly* related to verdict preferences. In their view, some jurors' world knowledge concerning events and individuals involved in the facts of the case *may* affect verdict decisions. An upper-American, for example, may not have a framework for evaluating what are normal weekend activities in an urban ghetto, or possess only stereotypes of such events and activities. To the lower-class juror the fact that the defendant kept a weapon in his car may seem normal, while to the upper-American the fact that a person kept a weapon in his car may be construed as supporting the idea that the defendant was looking for trouble. A number of inferences and judgments such as these may cumulatively result in upper-American and working-class jurors reaching different conclusions, in some cases. As a general rule, the individual characteristics of jurors are weakly related to verdicts. Instead, juror characteristics are more strongly related to participation in deliberations—since jurors with higher in-

comes, better jobs, and longer years of education will participate more in jury deliberations and will be more persuasive.[60]

While juror bias is not consistently evidenced, the fact that bias is occasionally observed should prompt people to consider ways in which to reduce possible bias. In fact, there is some evidence that the reliability of the evidence presented as well as the amount of evidence presented helps to reduce bias. There are at least three areas where this has been demonstrated: physical attractiveness, authoritarian influences, and racial prejudices.

Considerable evidence accumulated over the years indicates that we have positive attitudes toward attractive people (see Chapter 5), and there is solid evidence that indicates that both male and female jurors are more lenient toward good-looking defendants (of both sexes) than toward unattractive defendants. The one exception to this trend is when the beautiful defendant uses good looks in her or his line of crime. Sigall and Ostrove,[61] for example, manipulated a number of versions of a courtroom situation where a female defendant was charged with either burglary or with swindling a 50-year-old male. In half the versions, she was portrayed as beautiful—in the other half, she was unattractive. In the burglary case, she was sentenced to only 2.80 years of prison when attractive, but received 5.20 years when she was unattractive. However, in the swindle case, she was assigned 5.45 years of prison when she was good looking, and 4.35 years if she was unattractive. In the burglary case, attractiveness is not related to the crime per se, and jurors were more lenient toward the attractive defendant. In the swindle case, the jury realized that the defendant was using her good looks to her advantage in her crime and realized that she may use her good looks again to transgress against society. Hence, they were harsher on her.

Despite this exception, Baumesiter and Darley[62] found that leniency toward the beautiful may be reduced by emphasizing the quality of the evidence presented in the trial. Baumesiter and Darley constructed different versions of a drunk-driving case where the defendant was either a good-looking male or an unattractive male. In "vague" versions of the testimony, witnesses reported that the defendant, Mr. Sanders, had "several drinks" or had "a couple" and witnesses reported that he had been "speeding a little more than other cars." In the "strong" versions, Sanders was described as having exactly six drinks, that the police medical examiner had found a specific amount of alcohol in his blood, and that an analysis of the skid marks indicated that Sanders had exceeded the speed limit by 14 mph. Baumesiter and Darley found that when testimony was vague (but mildly incriminating), Mr. Sanders was denied fewer months of driving suspension when he was attractive (21.1 months) than when he was unattractive (43.8 months). However, when the case was clear cut, Sanders received the same sentence when he was attractive (48.3 months) than when he was unattractive (48.2 months).

Kaplan and Miller[63] similarly found that by manipulating the reliability of evidence one can increase or decrease the amount of bias displayed by "harsh" or lenient jurors. These authors studied a number of traffic-related trials and characterized the source of the evidence in the trials as either reliable or unreliable. A third group of jurors was not told anything about the source of the evidence. They found that harsh jurors were more harsh and lenient jurors were more lenient when no description of the source was provided. However, when the source of the evidence was described as reliable, there were no differences between the verdicts given by lenient-prone or harsh jurors.

Finally, Ugwuegbu[64] reviewed literature on racial factors and juror decisions, and argued that there was a trend for jurors to find defendants of another race to be guilty of rape charges. However, the full level of guilt assigned depended upon the race of the rapist, the race of the victim, race of the juror, and the level of incrimination of the evidence. Ugwuegbu constructed three versions of testimony: near-zero incriminating evidence, marginal evidence, and strong evidence. When the level of evidence was near-zero, little

room for racial prejudice was evident since jurors found it difficult to prosecute the defendant "beyond reasonable doubt." Further, there was little room for bias when there was strong evidence against the accused rapist (except Ugwuegbu found that black jurors were slightly more lenient toward own-race defendants when the evidence was strong). However, when evidence was marginal, there was a tendency for jurors to judge other-race defendants more harshly than same-race defendants. Strong evidence, then, reduces bias.

Summary

In this chapter we have overviewed some of the main communication variables relevant to courtroom contexts, and we have introduced the types of messages people use when attempting to neutralize "offenses." Secondly, we discussed six fundamental topics in small-group communication and have related these topics to the jury context. These topics were group size, spatial arrangement, emerging leadership, feedback and process, influence in the group, and group composition. Finally, we examined that literature that looks at bias in group processes, and tried to isolate the effects of bias.

Footnotes

1. N. E. Fontes and R. W. Bundens, "Persuasion During the Trial Process," in M. E. Roloff and G. R. Miller, eds., *Persuasion: New Directions in Theory and Research* (Beverly Hills: Sage, 1980), pp. 249–266.

2. G. R. Miller and R. W. Bundens, "Juries and Communication," in B. Dervin and M. J. Voight, eds., *Progress in Communication Sciences*, vol. 3 (Norwood, N.J.: Ablex), pp. 127–162.

3. N. L. Kerr and R. M. Bray, eds., *The Psychology of the Courtroom* (New York: Academic), pp. 119–168.

4. S. M. Kassin and L. S. Wrightsman, eds., *The Psychology of Evidence and Trial Procedure* (Beverly Hills: Sage, 1985).

5. A. P. Hare, "Interaction and Consensus in Different-Sized Groups," *American Sociological Review*, vol. 17 (1952), pp. 261–267.

6. P. E. Slater, "Contrasting Correlates of Group Size," *Sociometry*, vol. 21 (1958), pp. 129–139.

7. L. A. Pervin, "Performance and Satisfaction As a Function of Individual-Environment Fit," in N. S. Endler and D. Magnusson, eds., *Interactional Psychology and Personality* (Washington, D.C.: Hemisphere, 1976), pp. 73–74.

8. R. F. Bales, *Personality and Interpersonal Behavior* (New York: Holt, Rinehart and Winston, 1970), pp. 467–470.

9. R. F. Bales and E. F. Borgatta, "Size of Group As a Factor in the Interaction Profile," in A. P. Hare, E. G. Borgatta, and R. F. Bales, eds., *Small Groups: Studies in Social Interaction* (New York: Knopf, 1965), pp. 495–512.

10. H. M. Robert, *Robert's Rules of Order Revised* (New York: Scott, Foresman, 1951).

11. E. J. Thomas and C. F. Fink, "Effects of Group Size," in A. P. Hare, E. F. Borgatta, and R. F. Bales, eds., *Small Groups: Studies in Social Interaction* (New York: Knopf, 1965), pp. 525–536.

12. J. Kessler, "An Empirical Study of Six- and Twelve-Member Jury Decision-Making Processes," *University of Michigan Journal of Law Reform*, vol. 6 (1973), pp. 712–734. See also G. Stasser, N. L. Kerr, and R. M. Bray, "The Social Psychology of Jury Deliberations: Structure, Process, and Product," in N. L. Kerr and R. M. Bray, eds., *The Psychology of the Courtroom* (New York: Academic, 1982), pp. 221–256.

13. M. Saks, *Jury Verdicts: The Role of Group Size and Social Decision Rule* (Lexington, Mass.: Lexington, 1977).

14. See Stasser, Kerr, and Bray, "The Social Psychology of Jury Deliberations."

15. See Saks, *Jury Verdicts;* M. Saks, "Innovation and Change in the Courtroom," in N. L. Kerr and R. M. Bray, eds., *The Psychology of the Courtroom* (New York: Academic, 1982), pp. 325–352.

16. G. Bermant and R. Cappock, "Outcomes of Six- and Twelve-Member Jury Trials: An Analysis of 128 Civil Cases in the State of Washington," *Washington Law Review*, vol. 48 (1973), pp. 593–596. See G. R. Miller and R. W. Bundens.

17. A. C. Valenti and L. L. Downing, "Differential Effects of Jury Size on Verdicts Following Deliberation As a Function of the Apparent Guilt of the Defendant," *Journal of Personality and Social Psychology*, vol. 32 (1975), pp. 655–664.

18. Saks, *Jury Verdicts.*

19. Saks, *Jury Verdicts,* p. 105.

20. H. J. Leavitt, "Some Effects of Certain Communications Patterns on Group Performance," *Journal of Abnormal and Social Psychology*, vol. 46 (1951), pp. 38–50.

21. For a discussion of these studies, see R. T. Golembiewski, *The Small Group: An Analysis of Research Concepts and Operations* (Chicago: University of Chicago Press, 1962), pp. 93–97.

22. M. Glanzer and R. Glaser, "Techniques for the Study of Group Structure in Small Groups," in A. P. Hare, E. F. Borgatta, and R. F. Bales, eds., *Small Groups: Studies in Social Interaction* (New York: Knopf, 1965), pp. 400–426.

23. A. P. Hare and R. F. Bales, "Seating Position and Small Group Interaction," in A. P. Hare, E. F. Borgatta, and R. F. Bales, eds., *Small Groups: Studies in Social Interaction* (New York: Knopf, 1965), pp. 427–433.

24. See Stasser, Kerr, and Bray, "The Social Psychology of Jury Deliberations," pp. 223–224.

25. F. Strodtbeck and L. Hook, "The Social Dimensions of a Twelve-Man Jury Table," *Sociometry*, vol. 24 (1961), pp. 397–415.

26. Stasser, Kerr, and Bray, "The Social Psychology of Jury Deliberations," p. 226.

27. M. Burgoon, J. Huston, and J. McCroskey, *Small Group Communication: A Functional Approach* (New York: Holt, Rinehart and Winston, 1974), pp. 147–148.

28. See Stasser, Kerr, and Bray, "The Social Psychology of Jury Deliberations," p. 223.

29. W. B. Wanamaker, "Trial by Jury," *University of Cincinnati Law Review*, vol. 46 (1977), pp. 191–200.

30. N. L. Kerr, D. Harmon, and J. Graves, "Independence of Verdicts by Jurors and Juries," *Journal of Applied Social Psychology*, vol. 12 (1982), pp. 12–29.

31. F. L. Strodtbeck, R. James, and C. Hawkins, "Social Status in Jury Deliberations," *American Sociological Review*, vol. 22 (1957), pp. 713–719.

32. C. Hawkins, "Interaction and Coalition Realignments in Consensus Seeking Groups: A Study of Experimental Jury Deliberations" (unpublished doctoral dissertation, University of Chicago, Chicago, Illinois, 1960); C. Hawkins, "Interaction Rates of Jurors Aligned in Factions," *American Sociological Review*, vol. 27 (1962), pp. 689–691; see also Stasser, Kerr, and Bray, "The Social Psychology of Jury Deliberations," p. 228.

33. Stasser, Kerr, and Bray, "The Social Psychology of Jury Deliberations."

34. F. Strodtbeck, R. James, and C. Hawkins, "Social Status in Jury Deliberations," *American Sociological Review*, vol. 22 (1957), pp. 713–719.

35. Stasser, Kerr, and Bray, "The Social Psychology of Jury Deliberations," p. 227; Miller and Bundens, "Persuasion," pp. 155–157.

36. See Stasser, Kerr, and Bray, "The Social Psychology of Jury Deliberations," p. 227.

37. Stasser, Kerr, and Bray, "The Social Psychology of Jury Deliberations," p. 229.

38. C. Nemeth, J. Endicott, and J. Wachtler, "From the '50s to the '70s: Women in Jury Deliberations," *Sociometry*, vol. 39 (1976), pp. 293–304.

39. R. F. Bales and F. Strodtbeck, "Phases in Group Problem-Solving," *Journal of Abnormal and Social Psychology,* vol. 46 (1951), pp. 485–495; B. Fisher, "Decision Emergence: Phases in Group Decision Making," *Speech Monographs*, vol. 37 (1970), pp. 53–66; T. Scheidel and L. Crowell, "Idea Development in Small Discussion Groups," *Quarterly Journal of Speech,* vol. 50 (1964), pp. 140–145.

40. Stasser, Kerr, and Bray, "The Social Psychology of Jury Deliberations," pp. 228–229.

41. Hawkins, "Interaction and Coalition Realignments."

42. R. J. Simon, *The Jury and the Defense of Insanity* (Boston, Mass.: Little, Brown, 1967). See also R. James, "Status and Competence of Jurors," *The American Journal of Sociology*, vol. 64 (1959), pp. 563–570.

43. See also Stasser, Kerr, and Bray, "The Social Psychology of Jury Deliberations," pp. 229–230.

44. Kessler, "An Empirical Study."

45. Stasser, Kerr, and Bray, "The Social Psychology of Jury Deliberations," p. 230.

46. See Miller and Bundens, "Juries and Communication," pp. 155–157; Stasser, Kerr, and Bray, "The Social Psychology of Jury Deliberations," pp. 230–233.

47. Stasser, Kerr, and Bray, "The Social Psychology of Jury Deliberations," p. 236.

48. H. Kalven and H. Zeisel, *The American Jury* (Boston, Mass.: Little, Brown, 1966). Also see Stasser, Kerr, and Bray, "The Social Psychology of Jury Deliberations," p. 236.

49. C. Nemeth, "Interactions between Jurors As a Function of Majority vs. Unanimity Decision Rules," *Journal of Applied Social Psychology*, vol. 7 (1977), pp. 38–56.

50. Stasser, Kerr, and Bray, "The Social Psychology of Jury Deliberations."

51. For instance, see M. Deutsch and H. Gerard, "A Study of Normative and Social Influences Upon Individual Judgment," *Journal of Abnormal and Social Psychology* vol. 51 (1955), pp. 629–633.

52. Stasser, Kerr, and Bray, "The Social Psychology of Jury Deliberations," p. 241.

53. L. R. Hoffman, *The Group Problem Solving Process: Studies of a Valence Model* (New York: Praeger, 1979).

54. Stasser, Kerr, and Bray, "The Social Psychology of Jury Deliberations," p. 247.

55. See, for instance, A. Vinokur and E. Burstein, "The Effects of Partially Shared Persuasive Arguments on Group Induced Shifts: A Group Problem Solving Approach," *Journal of Personality*

and Social Psychology, vol. 29 (1974), pp. 303–315.

56. Simon, *The Jury*, pp. 33–35.

57. Simon, *The Jury*.

58. Simon, *The Jury*.

59. R. Hastie, S. D. Penrod, and N. Pennington, *Inside the Jury* (Cambridge, Mass.: Harvard University Press, 1983).

60. Hastie, Penrod, and Pennington, *Inside the Jury*.

61. H. Sigall and N. Ostrove, "Beautiful but Dangerous: Effects of Offender Attractiveness and Nature of the Crime on Juridic Judgment," *Journal of Personality and Social Psychology*, vol. 31 (1975), pp. 410–414.

62. R. F. Baumesiter and J. M. Darley, "Reducing the Biasing Effect of Perpetrator Attractiveness in Jury Simulation," *Personality and Social Psychology Bulletin*, vol. 8 (1982), pp. 286–292.

63. M. F. Kaplan and L. E. Miller, "Reducing the Effects of Juror Bias," *Journal of Personality and Social Psychology*, vol. 36 (1978), pp. 1443–1455.

64. D. C. E. Ugwuegbu, "Racial and Evidential Factors in Juror Attribution of Legal Responsibility," *Journal of Experimental Social Psychology*, vol. 15 (1979), pp. 133–146.

CHAPTER THIRTEEN

Persuasion in the Formal Organization

This chapter analyzes formal organizations, their nature and structure, and discusses some of the tactics that persuasive communicators must use when working within such organizations. Two major variables are of importance to persuasive communication as it occurs in formal organizations. First, interpersonal relationships and interpersonal influence are the fundamental building blocks of organizations—a superior spends between one-third to two-thirds of his or her time in communication with subordinates, usually in face-to-face activities. Hence, we will closely examine the *superior-subordinate link*. Second, we shall discuss the various *roles* individuals have in the *informal flow of information* in the organization, and discuss the characteristics of individuals who occupy these roles.

The superior-subordinate link

Every formal organization has an organizational structure that specifies roles and rules—including who talks to whom, who "takes orders" from whom, and who "is responsible for" which worker(s). We refer to an organization as exhibiting minimal flexibility if the organization adheres to strict rules and limits the flow of communication, while an organization is considered flexible if informal channels of communication are open and few restrictions on communication are imposed. In this section we are interested in examining the characteristics that describe communication between two individuals in the formal, hierarchical structure of the organization: the superior and the subordinate. Research in this area will be presented under four topic headings: (1) Managerial influence; (2) Superior characteristics and effectiveness; (3) Upward influence and upward distortion; and (4) Feedback.

Managerial influence: Persuasive strategies used by superiors

The work on strategy selection discussed in Chapter 10 directly applies to organizational settings. Further, for those who are interested in why people use the tactics they do, two additional issues are important. First, power and status are emphasized in some organizations, and the differences in power influence the tactics the agent employs, the target's promptness of complying, and the superior-subordinate relationship. For example, Kipnis, Schmidt, and Wilkinson[1] found that in organizations that were unionized (thereby giving more power to workers), superiors used more ingratiation tactics and workers used less rationality (supporting evidence) and workers used more blocking (work slowdowns, forming coalitions) in order to influence superiors. Similarly, Wilkinson and Kipnis[2] found that more powerful organizational units used stronger and more controlling tactics on less powerful units (especially when overcoming resistance). Power differences can, in fact, corrupt the "powerholder," making her or him feel more distant from the people who are influenced, and prompting him or her to devalue those who are controlled.[3]

The second issue is that a good deal of the influence between superior and subordinates is *reciprocal* in nature—not only do leader behaviors produce changes in subordinate satisfaction and performance, subordinate behaviors cause changes in the supervisor's mode of behavior. Studies by Farris and Lim, by Greene, by Herold, by Lowin and Craig, and by Sims and Manz demonstrate the reciprocal nature of influence processes.[4] For many years leader behaviors have been classified as "considerate" (in which case the relationship is characterized by friendship and warmth, mutual trust, rapport, and tolerance) and

as "initiating structure" (in which case the supervisor makes overt attempts to organize, define, direct, structure, and lead his or her work unit). Greene studied these types of leader behaviors in an organization and found that leader consideration *caused* greater worker satisfaction and that workers' high productivity rates *caused* leaders to be more considerate. Obviously, when workers' efforts can reflect positively on the supervisor, she or he will behave differently toward the workers than when their performance constitutes a negative reflection on the superior.

While the *selection* of strategies is an extremely interesting issue, our main purpose in this chapter deals with *effectiveness*—when are various influence attempts effective either in influencing worker performance or worker satisfaction? In 1968, Bachman and his colleagues[5] reported a summary of their findings:

1. When asked to list reasons for complying with a superior, subordinates listed legitimate power and expert power as the most important. Of lesser importance were referent power and reward power. Across all organizational units studied, coercive power was rated as the least likely reason for complying with a request;

2. Expert and referent power provided the strongest positive correlation with job satisfaction (or with satisfaction with one's supervisor), and did so with a great deal of consistency across organizations. Coercive power was associated with low job satisfaction. Superior's use of legitimate power and reward power were positively correlated with job satisfaction among insurance agents and production workers (but not among sales personnel and college faculty—for whom knowledge of legitimate rights and obligations and knowledge of rewards may stem from many sources *outside* one's own immediate supervisor);

3. Expert power showed the most consistent relationship with high performance. Referent power was associated with enhanced productivity in branch offices (which included

sales and personnel who gave out information to clients) and in production work units (routine production of electrical appliances). However, referent power was unrelated to performance in insurance agencies (when an agent's superior may be a regional manager and with whom contact may be infrequent). Further, the correlation between reward power and performance were predominately positive. Finally, legitimate and coercive power did not have a consistent influence on productivity. Legitimate power was slightly related to increased productivity for insurance salespersons, but had no impact on other types of organizational units. Coercive power was associated with low productivity, or was unrelated to performance.

There are undoubtedly some types of jobs where the worker has considerable autonomy in selecting what to do and in selecting ways in which to achieve goals; jobs where one's success is not related to the behavior of the immediate supervisor (for example, insurance salespersons or industrial salespersons). When workers are less dependent upon the input of the immediate supervisor, the effects of strategies will be reduced. For example, Richmond, Davis, Saylor, and McCroskey surveyed school teachers and found that a supervisor's use of compliance-gaining tactics was either *negatively* related to teacher satisfaction or was unrelated to teacher satisfaction—*no* influence tactic was positively related to teacher satisfaction. On the other hand, when teachers attempted to influence students (a context where there is considerable daily interaction and involvement), Richmond and McCroskey[6] found that referent and expert power were related to increased learning, that reward power was unrelated to learning, and that coercive power (and to a lesser extent legitimate power) corresponded to poorer learning outcomes—results similar to the results discussed above.

The results of the above studies indicate that the role of legitimate influence must be clarified. On one hand, workers rank legitimate influence as the most important reason for complying with a request by a supervisor. On the other hand, legitimate influence is not related to productivity. Part of this discrepancy may rest in the fact that when workers rank legitimate influence as important, they have in mind compliance to specific and single requests that the superior makes, such as taking an immediate dictation, rushing an order to the airport, reducing the number of personal phone calls, and so on. Insofar as the superior and the subordinate share the same perception on rights and obligations, then subordinates ought to comply with these requests. However, increased *productivity* reflects a cumulative amount of work produced over a span of time, and many factors influence such a rate—factors well beyond a superior's right to make a specific request. If this reasoning is correct, then legitimate influence ought to be important when specific decisions are made. Patchen[7] found that informational influences were extremely important when major corporations were making decisions, as were expert and legitimate influences. Referent, reward, and coercive influences were rarely mentioned as reasons for making decisions. Thus, when a specific decision was to be made, legitimate authority was taken into consideration, along with expertise and information.

The finding that reward power does not have a consistent impact on performance may, at first, appear to be surprising to some readers. However, keep in mind that rewards (and promises of rewards) are given for many reasons. Rewards are not only given to superior workers for high productivity, but also as a means to reward ingratiators, and to buy the support of people in the work unit when an insecure supervisor is confronted by a hostile worker (recall Chapter 10). Obviously, then, not all reward influence would be related to productivity. Recently, increased attention has focused on how to make rewards and punishments effective. Padsakoff,[8] for example, argued that leaders who administer rewards *appropriately* (that is, contingent upon performance) "cause increases in performance and satisfaction. Superiors who administer rewards inappropriately (that is, noncontingently) or not at all are likely to produce many dysfunctional effects, including declining productivity, feelings of inequity, and expressions of negative affects and dissatisfaction among their subordinates." In fact, House[9] argued that superiors' behavior can lead to increased productivity when (a) the rewards under a supervisor's control are, in fact, valued by subordinates, (b) allocation of the rewards are contingent upon performance, and (c) the contingency rules for receiving rewards are clearly and accurately understood by the subordinates. We would add (d), that the organization's rules for allocating rewards must be adhered to consistently over time.

Designing programs that would make coercive power effective in increasing productivity is a different matter. Since coercive influence involves so many costs, it is rarely used, and when it is used it is typically used as a "last resort" tactic. Arvey and Ivancevich[10] list three beliefs about punishments that help explain why they are used rarely: The use of punishments by an employer will result in undesirable emotional effects, the use of punishments is thought to be unethical and nonhumanitarian, and people believe that punishments never really eliminate undesirable behaviors. Certainly, much of the literature we have selected to overview supports the belief that coercive influence often leads to dissatisfaction and that it is not related to productivity. However, Arvey and Ivancevich provide six propositions concerning how to make punishments effective:

1. Punishment is more effective in organizational contexts if the punishment is delivered immediately after the undesirable response occurs than if the delivery is delayed.

2. Moderate levels of punishment are more effective than low or high intensity levels. (Punishments that are too low in intensity may be ineffective, and punishments too high in severity may cause anxiety, which would inhibit learning, and create high levels of job dissatisfaction.)

3. Punishment procedures are more effective where the agent administering the punishment has relatively close and friendly relationships with the employee being punished.

4. Punishment of undesirable behavior is more effective within organizations if: (a) punishment consistently occurs after *every* undesirable response; (b) punishment is administered consistently across different employees by the same managers; and (c) different managers are consistent in their applications of punishment for the same undesirable response.

5. Punishment is more effective when clear reasons are communicated to employees concerning why the punishment occurred, what the contingency is, and what the consequences of the behavior are in the future.

6. To the extent that alternative desirable responses are available to employees and these responses are reinforced, punishment is enhanced.

The studies reviewed here demonstrate that influence tactics have a significant impact on satisfaction and performance. However, they represent only part of the process of social influence in the organization. Hence, a more expansive look at the communication patterns of superiors and their relationship to subordinate behaviors is required. This is the next topic for discussion.

Supervisor characteristics and supervisor effectiveness

For many years organizational communication experts have tried to identify and describe the characteristics of effective supervisors. Redding[11] provided one of the first thorough treatments of the topic, and more recently Jablin[12] has reviewed the area in depth. Here are the major reasons why some supervisors are more effective than others:

1. The better supervisors tend to be more "communication minded": they enjoy talking and speaking up in meetings; they are able to explain instructions and policies; they enjoy conversing with subordinates;

2. The better supervisors tend to be willing, empathic listeners; they respond understandingly to so-called silly questions from employees; they are approachable; they will listen to

suggestions and complaints with an attitude of fair consideration and willingness to take appropriate action;

3. The better supervisors tend (with some notable exceptions) to "ask" or "persuade" instead of "telling" or "demanding";

4. The better supervisors tend to be sensitive to the feelings and ego-defense needs of their subordinates; they are careful to reprimand in private rather than in public;

5. The better supervisors tend to be more open in their passing along of information; they are in favor of giving advance notice of impending changes, and of examining and explaining the "reasons why" behind policies and regulations;

6. The better supervisors score high in both "consideration" and in "initiation structure" (see above). Further, some studies indicate that high consideration is related to job satisfaction and may be inversely related to performance, since little pressure, motivation, or structure exists if *only* consideration is high.

These conclusions are offered as general guidelines for effective supervisory behavior. While they are *generally* true, any particular style of communication or leadership will be more effective in some types of organizations and with some types of workers.

For example, Klauss and Bass[13] conducted a thorough analysis of job satisfaction, satisfaction with one's communication partners, and so on, in three types of organizations. They found that increased openness consistently led to increased job satisfaction, and found that both openness and specific communication variables led to increased satisfaction with one's communication partner. They also found that the specific variables that were associated with satisfaction varied from one type of organization to the next, depending upon their importance in the work environment. People were more satisfied with a superior if he or she were *open, informal, frank*, a *careful listener*, and a *careful transmitter* of information. In a Navy civilian agency, where rigidity and inflexibility may be typical, workers preferred an *informal* and *open*

communicator who *accurately transmitted* messages. In a social-service agency, workers need to solve problems and, hence, a person who is a *careful listener* was rated as a preferable colleague.

Other studies on organizational openness have focused on two critical aspects in the formal organization: (1) perceptions of organizational climate; and (2) the effects climate has on satisfaction and performance. An organizational climate is the state of the organization's internal nature, as perceived by its members.[14] According to Redding,[15] "the climate of the organization is more crucial than are the communication skills or techniques (taken by themselves) in creating an effective organization." Redding characterized climates as being composed of varying degrees of openness and candor, along with supportiveness; participative decision making; trust, confidence, and credibility; and emphasis on high-performance goals. Openness, and hence climate, has a strong impact on a number of organizational variables, as the reviews by Falcione and Kaplan, by Hellriegel and Slocum, by Jablin, and by James and Jones indicate.[16]

Hellriegel and Slocum summarized 31 studies that indicated that organizational climate is related to job satisfaction in terms of interpersonal relations, group cohesiveness, task involvement, and the like. However, the climate-satisfaction relationship was more consistently observed than a climate–job performance relationship. Why? First, people apparently can adapt to the internal workings of an organization in order to perform effectively in it. Frederickson,[17] for example, found that workers performed better when they perceived the climate *consistently* as either "rules oriented" (less flexible) or "innovative" (very flexible, emphasizing freedom) than when the climate was perceived to be inconsistent. Workers do not function well if supervisors are sometimes open, sometimes closed; sometimes rule conscious, sometimes ignoring rules. There is also evidence that inconsistency in the internal workings of an organization leads to increased job stress,[18] and that impoverished climates are linked to higher rates of employee turnover.[19] Thus, open superior-subordinate relationships and supportive climates led to increases in job satisfaction and, usually, to increases in performance; however, the lowest levels of job performance occur in organizations with inconsistent climates.

Also important to the relationships between climate and either satisfaction or performance is the personality of either the supervisor or the subordinate. Downey, Hellriegel, and Slocum[20] explored the way in which climate interacts with individual personality in influencing job satisfaction and performance. Climate was measured as "decision-making" capabilities, warmth, risk, openness, rewards, and structure, and three important relationships were tested and supported: (1) individuals needing social contact and interdependence who perceived the climate as open and empathic and as encouraging high standards for achievement were more satisfied with their supervision than those who perceived a closed, bureaucratic, and impersonal climate; (2) individuals who were self-confident and who perceived clearly-assigned responsibilities and clear-cut policies were more satisfied with their coworkers than those who perceived the organization as unstructured; and (3) highly-sociable managers who perceived their climate as encouraging, as lacking in threats, and as humanitarian performed better than less sociable managers.

Jablin[21] summarized the research results for internal- versus external-locus-of-control supervisors: (a) internal-locus-of-control subordinates are most satisfied with participative decision-making superiors, whereas externals are most satisfied with directive supervisors; (b) internal subordinates see their supervisors as more considerate than do externals; (c) internal superiors tend to use persuasion to obtain subordinate cooperation, whereas externals rely more on coercive power. Compatible with these conclusions are the results of Pritchard and Karasick:[22] a highly-supportive climate leads to high job satisfaction for all types of managers; however, managers with a high need for order performed more effectively in a more structured climate, while managers with a high need for autonomy were more satisfied in a climate that was low in decision centralization than were managers who were low in autonomy needs.

Several studies, reviewed by Jablin,[23] explored subordinates' perceptions of superiors' communication behavior and personality. These studies indicate:

1. Superiors who are apprehensive communicators are not particularly liked by subordinates;

2. Subordinates' satisfaction with superiors can be predicted from several dimensions of homophily-heterophily;

3. Authoritarian subordinates are most satisfied when they work for directive superiors;

4. Subordinates' satisfaction with immediate supervision is related to subordinates' perception of superiors' credibility;

5. Confirmation of subordinates' needs for affection and dominance results in greater perceived frequency of interaction between superiors and subordinates;

6. Subordinates in small groups, who require high interaction with coworkers and superiors and high interdependence, have negative attitudes toward authoritarian supervisors, whereas subordinates in large work groups, with restricted interaction and highly independent work, have more positive attitudes toward authoritarian supervision; and,

7. Subordinates, regardless of their personality, tend to be most satisfied with superiors high in human-relations orientation.

To this last list of results, we will add Goldhaber's[24] conclusion. Goldhaber believes that "the most important contributor to job satisfaction is the quality of the relationship employees have with their supervisors," and that the most important characteristics are (1) a boss who praises subordinates; (2) a boss who understands a subordinate's job; (3) a boss who can be trusted; (4) a boss who is warm and friendly; (5) a boss who is honest; and (6) a boss with whom subordinates are free to disagree.

In sum, persuaders who are managers will find their jobs easier in the organization if they do not have to overcome resistance on the part of the subordinates, if they do not have to deal with suspicion when sending messages down the hierarchy, and if the superior and subordinates have a trusting, cooperative relationship. Hence, it is important for the persuader to (a) create the ideal image of being a communication-minded individual who is open, frank, honest, a careful listener, and a careful, articulate communicator; and (b) create an open, supportive, trusting, and consistent climate. However, while general openness is highly valued in some organizations, different communication abilities are valued in different types of organizations. In organizations that have to adapt quickly to changes all communication variables are important in creating satisfaction; in organizations where workers have to solve problems, they will be more influenced by the perception that the superior is carefully listening to them.

Upward communication and upward distortion

According to Goldhaber, upward communication refers to "messages which flow from subordinate to superior. It is usually for the purpose of asking questions, providing feedback, and making suggestions. Upward communication has the effect of improving morale and employee attitude, and therefore upward-directed messages are usually integrative ('pro-social') and innovative." There are a number of reasons why superiors should value and encourage upward communication: (1) It indicates the receptivity of the environment for downward communication; (2) it facilitates acceptance of decisions by encouraging subordinate participation in the decision-making process; (3) it provides feedback about subordinate understanding of downward communication; and (4) it encourages submission of valuable ideas. Further, the most effective way to reinforce upward communication is to listen sympathetically during the many day-to-day informal contacts both in and outside the department.

While considerable work has been directed toward studying downward communications and messages, very little research has focused on how subordinates persuade or influence their superi-

ors. Most organizational communication research has focused on ways in which one can make the *organization* more effective, for example, what makes for effective supervision, for reducing job stress and job turnover, while issues concerning what is effective for the typical worker on the production line are understudied. In fact, it is interesting to note that the major area of research that examines message *production* from the subordinate looks at an organizational communication problem: *distortion*.

Only since the late 1970s and the early 1980s have specialists explored influence attempts on the part of subordinates. Kipnis and his colleagues, Wortman and Linsenmeier, Porter, Allen and Angle, and Schilit and Locke[25] provide the most relevant literature on upward influence. Wortman and Linsenmeier provide a thorough review of literature on ingratiation, and discuss the possible effects of ingratiation in organizational settings, and Porter, Allen and Angle offer a number of propositions concerning what types of influence methods different subordinates might use. Wortman and Linsenmeier come to this conclusion about how one might impress a superior:[26]

An ingratiator trying to impress a more powerful other should probably avoid the more obvious tactics. Most types of other-enhancement fall into this category. Directly praising the target person should be avoided, both because it is such an obvious tactic and because it may seem presumptuous. The tactic implies that the subordinate has the capacity to evaluate his superior, that he knows how his superior should behave and how his job can best be done. Other-enhancement of a superior may be effective, however, if the subordinate compliments the superior on job areas in which the subordinate is recognized as knowledgeable, or on personal qualities that are unrelated to job performance. More subtle other-enhancing strategies, such as positive nonverbal gestures, may also be quite effective, as may other-enhancement if the compliment is conveyed by a third party.

Rendering favors may not be an especially good tactic, since it so often gives rise to the feeling that something is expected in return. Opinion conformity is also risky. . . . [Two studies] . . . have found that when a person's dependence upon another is obvious, he is liked better when he avoids lavish agreement with that person. Strategies such as anticipating the target person's views and expressing them before he has had a chance to do so, or mixing agreement on major issues with disagreement on minor ones would also seem prudent.

Ingratiation, however, is only one of many tactics subordinates may use in the organization. The work by Kipnis and others indicates that superiors have a considerably wider range of tactics to select from than do subordinates, and that subordinates primarily rely on rationality, self-presentation, and forming coalitions in order to influence superiors. The Schilit and Locke study is the only survey to date that asked for both the subordinate's perspective and the superior's perspective on upward influence, and examined the effects of influence attempts. They found:

1. The typical employee, attempting to have influence on the organization, communicates directly with the superior;

2. Both subordinates and superiors thought that the more common method of influence was to present ideas logically ("rationality"). Rationality was more commonly mentioned in successful situations than in unsuccessful influence attempts;

3. Superiors and subordinates typically recall the same tactics as being used, and, after rationality, listed *persistence*, using *organizational rules*, *trading job-related benefits* (exchange), and *going over the supervisor's head* as the more common methods. However, although 19 types of tactics were studied, none of these tactics was, for subordinates, *strongly* related to success. The tactic, "threatening to resign," however, was significantly related to *failing* to gain compliance. From the superior's perspective, trading job-related benefits (exchange) was a significant way to influence them. Also, superiors claimed to be influenced when the subordinate "used them as a platform for presenting ideas." On the other hand, superiors claimed to be resistant to influence when (a) the subordinate challenged the authority of the supervisor, (b) the subordinate threatened

to go over the head of the supervisor, and (c) the subordinate used external pressure.

4. The causes of successful and unsuccessful influence attempts were attributed differently by both superiors and subordinates. The cause of successful influence attempts were attributed to personal qualities by both the superior and the subordinate. Subordinates who were successful felt they were successful either because (a) they were competent, (b) they made a positive presentation, (c) the influence attempt contained favorable information and, finally, (d) they had the support of the organization. When superiors claimed to have been influenced, they felt they were influenced because (a) they had favorable relations with the subordinate, or, (b) they were open-minded. Both superior and subordinate attributed failure to reasons external to themselves; when they failed, subordinates felt they failed either because the boss was closed-minded or because the organization's budget did not permit success. Superiors felt that the main reason subordinates failed to influence them involved the budgetary problems of complying.

The results of this study are clear: Subordinates fail to gain compliance when using ultimatums, or when challenging the authority of the superior. However, they can increase the chance of being successful if they can convince the superior that he or she will benefit in some important way by complying, and if they can emphasize gains over costs for the organization.

Work in the area of *upward distortion* is important for at least two reasons. First, to function effectively, an organization needs accurate information in order to reduce uncertainty and to make appropriate decisions. The more an executive is removed from the operational level, the more messages concerning the status of operations must go through a number of superior-subordinate links. If subordinates want to "look good" to their immediate supervisor, then the information the executive receives may be simply wrong. Thus, if the executive made a decision to increase sales believing that production is high, problems will emerge. Second, understanding upward distortion is important because a communicator/persuader (in middle management or higher) may think that workers below him or her are more supportive and less resistant to persuasion than is actually the case.

It is important, then, to identify sources of either distortion (the transforming of the meaning of a message) or omission (deletion of all or part of the message), and to identify methods for reducing the effects of such problems.[27] In dysfunctional circumstances, people of lower rank will omit critical comments in their communications with higher-ranking personnel who have power over the subordinates' advancement, resulting in a distinct lack of negative feedback at the higher levels of the hierarchy that may further result in incorrect decisions being made by upper management. According to Krivonos,[28] subordinates tend to: (a) distort information upward in a manner that pleases their superiors; (b) tell their superiors what they want them to know; (c) tell their superiors what they think they want to hear; and (d) tell their superiors information that reflects favorably on themselves.

Traditional organizational communication literature indicates that three variables have a strong impact on upward distortion: *trust* in the supervisor, the subordinate's *perception of how his or her future is controlled* by the supervisor, and the subordinate's *mobility aspirations*. Of these three variables, trust appears to be the more important variable and is most consistently related to upward distortion.[29] Each of these variables is related to the subordinate's motivations to distort upward messages. If trust is low, you may feel that information may be used against you. Obviously, the other variables reflect the need to maintain a good image with someone who controls your fate when you are ambitious.

In the last ten years, some attention has focused on identifying additional variables that influence upward distortion. Athanassiadas,[30] for example, found that less upward distortion was likely to occur in "autonomous" organizations (ones that

give the worker considerable freedom) and more likely to occur in "heteronomous" organizational climates (more restrictive climates). Later, Young[31] found that less distortion occurs if the superior and subordinate are dependent upon each other, rather than when the subordinate is dependent upon the superior.

Level and Johnson[32] noted two factors relevant to reducing the subordinate's use of upward distortion—increasing the trust and openness between superior and subordinate, and increasing the accuracy of downward information. However, if there has not been much openness or trust in the organizational climate in the recent past, it is not simple to build trust quickly. Rogers and Agarwala-Rogers[33] offered three ways for dealing with problems of omission and distortion:

1. *Redundancy* is the repeating of a message in different forms, over different channels, or over time. For example, if an official has any reason to doubt the accuracy with which messages are relayed, she or he may create two or more channels to report to him or her.

2. *Verification* is ensuring the accuracy of a previous message. When distortion or omission is suspected in a message, an individual may try to use "counterbias" as a means to reduce the effects of distortion. In this case, a superior discounts some of what she or he hears as good or positive information and pays closer attention to (or emphasizes) negative information.

3. *Bypassing* is elimination of intermediaries in a communication flow. According to Rogers and Agarwala-Rogers, bypassing may be accomplished in one of three ways:

a. By creating "flat" organizations by reducing the number of hierarchical levels through which messages flow. Here the age-old communication principle that the more links a message must pass through increases the message distortion is applied.

b. By having high officials directly inspect the operational level.

c. By using such devices as suggestion boxes

or other intermediaries as the bearers of ill tidings.

Unfortunately, all of these methods for dealing with distortion increase the number of messages that are in circulation, and some organizations may already be overloaded with messages and information.

Effectively changing behavior through feedback

A common complaint by both supervisors and subordinates is that they do not receive sufficient or relevant feedback. This is obviously unfortunate, since feedback, according to Jablin,[34] "provides information that denotes the success or failure of policies and objectives, that suggests the need for corrective actions and controlling mechanisms, and that provides the members of the dyad with knowledge of the other party's sentiments about formal and informal organizational activities." Two issues are of interest: (1) the positive and negative *relational* consequences of feedback; and (2) how feedback is used to increase performance.

Not surprisingly, research has demonstrated that negative feedback has detrimental consequences on the superior-subordinate relationship. As Jablin noted, studies demonstrate that positive feedback transmitted to a leader makes him or her more task oriented, while negative feedback increases negative social-emotional behavior—*negativity is reciprocated*. Further, negative feedback may not have an effect on performance if there are no specific suggestions concerning how the target of the feedback can improve.

More recently, Jablin[35] conducted a number of studies on the impact of communicative responses on the superior-subordinate dyad. He distinguished between five types of messages:

1. *Confirmation* (a response that provides a speaker with both positive content and positive relational feedback);
2. *Disagreement* (a response that provides a

speaker with negative content feedback and positive relational feedback);
3. *Accedence* (a response that provides a speaker with positive content feedback and with negative relational feedback);
4. *Repudiation* (a response that provides a speaker with both negative content feedback and negative relational feedback); and,
5. *Disconfirmation* (a response that provides a speaker with irrelevant content feedback and irrelevant relational feedback).

The results of his studies indicated the following:

1. Disconfirming messages were not acceptable in superior-subordinate relationships.
2. Subordinates preferred message responses from superiors that provided positive relational feedback.
3. A substantial degree of reciprocity existed for confirming messages, regardless of the openness or the closedness of the superior-subordinate relationship.
4. Regardless of perceived openness or closedness of the communication relationship with the superior, subordinates expected the same types of responses from a superior but evaluated the *appropriateness* of the responses differently. Subordinates in open climates felt that repudiating or disconfirming responses were not appropriate responses. However, appropriateness in closed climates was also influenced by whom the message was about. Subordinates in closed climates felt that it was appropriate for a superior to reciprocate a negative relational feedback, but that it was not appropriate for a superior to use negative relational tactics if the subordinate had already sent an unfavorable message about himself (herself) to the boss. That is, subordinates in closed climates were more likely to be defensive than subordinates in open climates, and both superiors and subordinates experience greater freedom to communicate in open climates.
5. Subordinates who perceived a closed relationship with their superior were prepared to

respond to a superior's message that contained negative relational feedback with a response transmitting negative relational feedback toward the superior; however, this was not true for subordinates who perceived an open climate. That is, subordinates in closed climates were more likely to retort, or reciprocate, if they received negative information from the superior. Subordinates in open climates, however, would find that the use of negative relational feedback would prove costly by potentially ruining a positive and open relationship with their superiors.

Jablin lists a number of additional conclusions concerning the effects of superior's feedback or rewards/reinforcements on subordinate's performance and/or satisfaction:

1. Superior's feedback to a subordinate that shows a lack of trust in the subordinate results in subordinate dissatisfaction and aggressive feelings.

2. Superiors perceived as expressive are more likely to provide subordinates with social approval than those superiors perceived as instrumental (task oriented or directive).

3. In conflict situations supervisory responses that relate acceptance and encouragement of subordinate disagreement were associated with high subordinate satisfaction.

4. Under low surveillance (infrequent need to report to superior) positive feedback from superior to subordinate leads to greater subordinate compliance than when the subordinate receives no direct feedback, whereas under high surveillance conditions subordinates who receive positive feedback from their superiors comply less than when they receive no direct feedback from their superiors.

5. Positive rewards from a leader are generally associated with subordinate satisfaction, but the relationship between leader punitive actions and subordinate satisfaction varies as a function of the nature of the task performed by each work group.

6. Supervisors who frequently criticize their subordinates for poor work are generally rated as less effective than those who criticize less frequently.

7. A supervisor provides positive reinforcement to a subordinate when he or she is positively reinforced by the subordinate's performance and negatively reinforces a subordinate when he or she is negatively reinforced as a result of the subordinate's performance.

These conclusions, based on years of research, provide some rules that should be followed in order to make feedback more useful and effective.

Beyond these conclusions, Locke[36] has proposed a theory of "goal-setting" where productivity can be increased if a manager or persuader follows several rules: Set specific and sufficiently challenging goals, select a performance level within the workers' range of abilities, use feedback ("knowledge of results") on a frequent basis to keep workers on track, offer rewards to attain the goal, be a supportive manager, and assign goals that the workers find acceptable. Several studies also demonstrate that the type of feedback given to workers has a major impact on performance. A study by Kim and Hamner[37] is one of our favorites.

Kim and Hamner went into four separate production plants of a telephone company and employed a different feedback system in each plant. Hence, there were four groups:

1. Workers in one plant received goal-setting instructions and informal feedback. That is, each Monday morning, each foreman would meet with his workers and reemphasize goals that had not changed, and explain any new goal. There was no formal feedback, but workers could receive informal feedback. (Control group.)

2. Workers at another plant received superior's feedback and praise. Workers received from their foreman on Mondays the number of workers who had met the weekly goal. Also,

the goals for the current week were set or re-emphasized at the meeting. Then, some time during the week, the foreman would visit each employee and praise him on the performance categories on which he had exceeded his past week's performance and/or exceeded the company's performance goals. These sessions were informal and of short duration. The foremen were not allowed to give negative feedback during this session with the employee. (This group represented the goals and superior's feedback and praise group.)

3. Workers at a third plant received "formal self-feedback." That is, each Monday morning the foreman would meet with his employees to set goals or reemphasize goals for the current work week. On Friday of each week, the workers would rate themselves on a set of forms provided (the same forms the superior filled out), in terms of safety, number of days absent, and so on. These workers received "formal self-feedback." No feedback from the superior was given.

4. The fourth and last plant received all of the above types of feedback—goals + formal self-feedback + superior's feedback + praise.

Kim and Hamner studied the effects of goal setting and feedback on cost performance (efficiency of production), the supervisor's ratings of the quality of performance, safety, and job satisfaction. They found that, first, the goals + self-feedback + superior's feedback + praise group improved dramatically in cost efficiency over the 90 days, and was safer during the last 30-day trial than the control group. Finally, the self-feedback group expressed less satisfaction with their present work assignment than did all other groups. Two conclusions: (1) While it is possible to improve performance merely by implementing a goal-setting program, performance was generally enhanced even more when combined with self-feedback, superior's feedback, and praise; and (2) "formal self-feedback" was occasionally not sufficient to provide optimum results.

Communication networks and roles

The first section of this chapter discussed details of communication between two individuals who are placed in a hierarchical structure. However, much communication relevant to persuasion occurs in informal channels. People "shoot the breeze" discussing politics, satisfactions, dissatisfactions, innovations, and so on, while eating lunch, at the water cooler or on the golf course, and so on. To study the informal channels of communication, scholars study *networks*—how are people interconnected with one another through communication? These informal communication patterns are, typically, more likely to emerge spontaneously, and be less structured and less predictable than communication in formal channels. An understanding of the flow of information in the organization is important for any persuader; since we can only briefly present the ideas here, the reader will find the best discussions of network analysis in Farace, Monge, and Russell, in Goldhaber, in Rogers and Agarwala-Rogers, and in Rogers and Kincaid.[38]

Networks and network roles

When you were in high school you probably observed that the members of the varsity football team tended to "hang out" together. Also, certain members of the team tended to eat together and do things together after school. The members of the team formed a looser knit subgroup of the high school. Further, it is possible that the quarterback may have been popular enough to be elected student-body president. This individual may, over time, be a part-time member of a number of groups, but not a routine or typical member of any one group. If you have made observations such as these, then you have already experienced the dynamics and consequences of networks.

We study networks in order to compare the organizational structure (formal channel) with the actual flow of communication (informal channel), to identify specialized roles in the flow of information, and to study how the flow of communication impedes or enhances the communication of the organization. We will discuss both network *roles* and *information flow*.

Figure 13.1 presents an example of an organizational network pattern. By observation or by use of questionnaires, we identify who speaks to whom. A *communication group* is a set of individuals who routinely communicate with one another. There are three groups (or cliques) in Figure 13.1. There are several characteristics about communication groups persuaders need to note. First, a group may be highly *interconnected* if all members in the group talk to all other members of the group. Groups 1 and 3 in our figure are highly

interconnected. On the other hand, a *radial* network is one in which an individual interacts directly with others who do not interact with each other. Rather, they interact with others outside the first small clique. For example, a person is a quarterback, member of the Model U.S. Club, student-body president, cocaptain of the basketball team, and is an active member of a Christian youth club. This person's personal network extends out to many more people and is called "radial."

Considerable research demonstrates that the distinction between radial and interconnected networks is important. Members of groups that are highly interconnected tend to be similar to one another, have the same knowledge and opin-

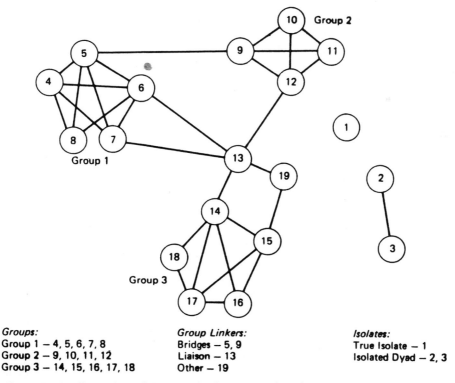

Groups:	Group Linkers:	Isolates:
Group 1 — 4, 5, 6, 7, 8	Bridges — 5, 9	True Isolate — 1
Group 2 — 9, 10, 11, 12	Liaison — 13	Isolated Dyad — 2, 3
Group 3 — 14, 15, 16, 17, 18	Other — 19	

Figure 13.1. Illustration of Communication Network Roles

From R. V. Farace, P. R. Monge, and H. M. Russell, *Communicating and Organizing* (Reading, Mass.: Addison-Wesley, 1977).

ions, and are, as a consequence, less likely to be innovative. Individuals in radial networks, however, have access to more different types of information; they are more likely to be well informed and generate more innovative ideas.

. A second important characteristic of groups is the degree to which they are interconnected with the rest of the organization. All three of the groups in our figure are equally interconnected with other organizational members. However, suppose person 12 left the organization; group 2 would be poorly connected. Further, if a message were transmitted out to organizational members from person number 16, the message may not accurately reach group 2 (that is, the more links a message goes through, the more likely it will be distorted).

Bridges are those individuals who help link or "bridge" one group to another. Obviously, a moderately high number of bridges is desirable if one wants a flexible and unrestricted flow of information in the organization. However, little research has been done on the characteristics of bridges. Research does, however, indicate that between 45 percent to 75 percent of the members of any organization will be group members and bridges.[39] Persons 5 and 9 are bridges in Figure 13.1.

Isolates are individuals who choose not to talk to others and who are not chosen by others as communication partners. These individuals often become "information sinks" (when they hear something they fail to pass it along), they are less satisfied, they inhibit the flow of information, they are less secure, they are younger, they have fewer years of experience in the organization, and they perceive the organization as less open. Surprisingly, some research indicates that in some organizations the frequency of isolates may range from 27 to 50 percent. Generally speaking, the fewer the isolates, the better the functioning of the organization.

Of the roles depicted in Figure 13.1, the *liaison* role is clearly the most important for our purpose. Liaisons interact with two or more groups, but

are not members of any group themselves. Roughly 5 to 15 percent of members of any organization are liaisons (and as many as 40 percent of the faculty at a university are identified as liaisons). Since the role played by liaisons is so important, considerable research has focused on identifying the characteristics of liaisons. There are three types of conclusions.[40]

I. Actual differences between liaisons and nonliaisons include:
   A. liaisons have higher agreement between themselves and others they talk to about the identity of their contacts than do nonliaisons;
   B. liaisons are more likely than others in the organization to serve as first sources of information;
   C. liaisons have higher formal status in the organization than do nonliaisons;
   D. liaisons have been organizational members for longer periods of time than have nonliaisons;
   E. the levels of formal education and the ages of liaisons are similar to those of nonliaisons;
II. Liaisons' perception of themselves versus nonliaisons' perceptions of themselves:
   A. liaisons perceive themselves to have greater numbers of communication contacts in the organization;
   B. liaisons perceive themselves to have greater amounts of information with respect to the content dimensions upon which their role is defined;
   C. liaisons perceive the communication system as more "open"—information is seen as more timely, more believable, and more useful;
   D. liaisons perceive themselves to have greater influence in the organization;
III. Others' perceptions of liaisons:
   A. liaisons are perceived by others to have greater numbers of communication contacts in the organization;

B. liaisons' communication contacts are seen as having a wider range throughout the organization structure;

C. liaisons are perceived as having more information about the content dimensions on which the network is defined;

D. liaisons are perceived as having more control over the flow of information in the organization;

E. liaisons are perceived to have more influence over the "power structure" of the organization;

F. liaisons are perceived to be more competent at their organizational activities.

Goldhaber[41] adds, from his own research, that liaisons are more gregarious, influential, and satisfied than are isolates and that liaisons hold higher official positions in the organization, and are integrated with diverse groups that enhance their power.

To the persuader who is inside or outside the organization, knowledge of who are "linkers" (liaisons and bridges) is going to be important in influencing others. First, if you can persuade the liaisons early in the process, they will help spread the word, help persuade others because they have the contacts and because they influence others, and they will help diffuse resistance. One of the worst things that could happen to a persuader is to find that the liaisons in the organization are resistant to his or her proposed changes, because the liaisons have an automatic coalition already formed. Second, the potential persuader would find it useful to have access to liaisons because they can provide the persuader with more information about the internal workings of the organization that would help the persuader to better adapt messages to different audiences in the organization.

Information flow

Nearly all organizations will develop both formal and informal channels of communication. In a *flexible* organization, there will be considerable freedom to communicate. There are several consequences that follow from allowing increased freedom, and there are several issues persuaders will want to keep in mind. There are five issues of importance we will discuss here:

First, organizations that exhibit high degrees of flexibility or that have well-developed grapevines tend to have high levels of knowledge among members. Such flexibility allows for the transmission of information to every member of an organization, rather than only to those people in authority positions. The communicator can often use such channels to avoid material being buried at any given level. There are two disadvantages in working with such an organization. First, there are times when a persuasive communicator might not want information to reach all members of the organization, and that is difficult to prevent when there is high flexibility. Second, the likelihood that an unapproved, unofficial message is circulated is greater when there is a strong grapevine operating. Because the message has not been authorized for transmission, the people who pass it along are frequently not accurate in transmitting the message.

Second, grapevines can frequently be used to sound out the members of an organization. Frequently, individuals in positions of authority will leak information into an informal network as a test. If there seems to be general acceptance of an idea, the message is then placed within the formal system as policy. If the message provokes significant objections while it is in the informal network, the individual releasing the information can deny making the proposal, and thus, avoid losing credibility or authority. Sometimes, the communicator can reach an individual who is not willing to commit to a proposal, but is willing to leak the proposal.

We should note that this suggestion of "floating a trial balloon" works best in those organizations in which there is a grapevine. In those situations where there is high flexibility, the trial balloon idea does not always work. When everyone in the organization has easy access to everyone else, it is easy to check on the accuracy of any new idea with other people in the organization. (Rogers and Agarwala-Rogers had this in mind when they suggested bypassing earlier.)

Goldhaber[42] makes several points concerning the grapevine. The grapevine is fast, it carries much information, the grapevine travels by cluster (that is, information does not spread out in a chain-like fashion; information spreads in leaps and bounds), and the grapevine can be very accurate. In fact, Goldhaber argues that the grapevine can be accurate 78 to 90 percent of the time (for noncontroversial topics). However, rumors can also spread falsehoods and rumors spread more quickly based on the importance and the ambiguity of the information. Obviously, once a *rumor* begins, it is critically important to convey accurate information to all relevant and affected parties.

Third, organizational flexibility is closely related to the accuracy with which a message is received within an organization. An organization that has high flexibility is one that encourages feedback, and individuals within the organization are thus able to check the accuracy of any persuasive messages that have been transmitted within the organization. On the other hand, an organization that has relatively low flexibility but a well-developed grapevine may have a tendency to distort any persuasive messages transmitted within the organization. Feedback is more difficult when a grapevine is being used, since accuracy checking is not sanctioned in any official manner. The informal channel is more likely to make use of oral communication, and thus increase the possibility that a message will be distorted as it passes from person to person. This is a disadvantage because a persuasive message placed by an outside communicator into a channel may become completely distorted and yet the source will have no opportunity to correct the message.

Fourth, there are few checks on the operation of compliance in an informal channel. When a message ordering some action, or even suggesting some action, is transmitted within a formal network, the individual occupying a higher position has the power to urge compliance on those in lower positions. For the message that passes through the informal network, however, no such compliance mechanism is present. The message will have to succeed or fail on its own merits.

Finally, there is no way to determine just how a grapevine is likely to be organized or how it will operate. For example, there may be a grapevine composed of all members of the organization who attend the same church, or who went to school together, or who are in the same car pool. An individual who is in one informal net as a member of a car pool may be in another as a member of the company bowling team. One network may overlap with another solely as a result of this one individual. Predicting exactly who will be in a particular network is difficult, and this may result in the failure of a message to pass through the network. Most organizations include both formal and informal networks. Which can be used with the most effectiveness is a decision that the communicator will make after careful analysis of the situation.

Buyer-seller interactions

No matter what the relative importance organizations assign to production, innovation, or maintenance functions, one aspect of the formal organization will never change in terms of its importance: sales. Effective sales is fundamental to all organizations—both in terms of sales to clients, and in terms of industrial sales.

Sales effectiveness

To date, the model proposed by Barton Weitz[43] is probably the most complete model of sales effectiveness. In Chapter 5 we argued that not all factors of credibility were equally important in persuading others—sometimes expertise was important, and sometimes source-receiver similarity was important. When we say that the effectiveness of a credibility factor *depends* on (that is, is *contingent* upon) the type of situation involved, we are proposing a "contingency framework." Weitz also argues that no single approach will always be successful in sales. He argues that the salesperson's level of expertise and the level of similarity in the salesperson-customer relationship are both effective, but in different situations. He offers a *contingency* approach to sales interactions.

Weitz offers one basic postulate and several propositions relevant to our discussion of effectiveness. First, the basic postulate, and a definition of terms, is in order:

Basic postulate: The effectiveness of sales behaviors across customer interactions is contingent upon or influenced by (a) the salesperson's resources; (b) the nature of the customer's buying task; (c) the customer-salesperson relationship, and the interactions among (a), (b), and (c).

By "salesperson's resources" we mean two types of resources: (a) *personal resources* include, most importantly, a salesperson's level of expertise—the salesperson's actual skills or abilities, knowledge of the products and the customer—and a range of the alternatives that can be offered to prospective clients; and (b) *company resources*, including the company reputation, range of alternatives the company can offer to the client, and the flexibility the company offers to its sales personnel. Obviously, it doesn't do a salesperson any good to be competent and to know exactly what his or her clients' needs are if he or she cannot provide them with the appropriate package of materials, products, or services that fulfills the customer's needs.

Second, by "nature of the customer's buying task" Weitz argued that the customer's buying tasks can vary from the *complex* to the *simple*.

Finally, Weitz argues that three characteristics of the customer-salesperson relationship are important in determining sales effectiveness: *similarity*, *relative power*, and *conflict* (which reflect the quality of the customer-salesperson relationship). Other customer-salesperson characteristics potentially relevant to the effectiveness of sales are the salesperson's anticipation of future interactions with the customer and whether the salesperson is

the "in" (or current) supplier of the product or the "out" supplier (who is trying to make a first sale). With this arsenal of variables in mind, Weitz made five specific propositions concerning the effectiveness of sales interactions.

a. Proposition concerning adaptive behavior. According to Weitz:

Proposition 1. Engaging in adaptive sales behaviors across interactions is positively related to effectiveness in the following circumstances:

(a) salesperson resources—the salesperson has the resources, both personal abilities and product alternatives, to engage in adaptive sales behaviors;

(b) customer buying tasks—the salesperson's customers typically are engaged in complex buying tasks that could result in large orders;

(c) customer-salesperson relationship—the salesperson has a good relationship with the customer characterized by a low level of conflict, and the salesperson anticipates future relationships with the customer.

This "contingency" proposition tells us several things we should keep in mind. First, a salesperson is most likely to be adaptive to the needs of his or her customers when he or she is high in expertise and when the company allows for flexibility. Second, adaptive behaviors are most likely to be effective in achieving sales when the customer is involved in a complex task—in fact, offering a package of materials or products tailor-made to the client's problem is critical to sales in these circumstances. We are more likely to be influenced by an expert when we want to know more about the external environment (versus issues involving personal preference), and hence expertise is important when the purchasing task increases in complexity. As these propositions also indicate, adaptive sales behaviors lead to success when there exists a good relationship between salespersons and customers, there is low conflict, and when the salesperson anticipates future interactions with the customer. Why? In part, these relationships are true because of the salesperson's motivation to work hard and adapt a quality solution to a client who has a complex purchasing task. Weitz argues that adaptive sales behavior is positively related to sales performance when the benefits outweigh the costs of adaptive strategies. Since adapting a sales package to a complex task is time-consuming and costly, a salesperson is unlikely to commit too much time or energy into designing a flexible or adaptive program for a customer whom she or he will never see again and from whom only a small order will come.

b. Proposition concerning the establishing of an influence base.

Proposition 2. Attempting to establish an expertise base of influence is positively related to effectiveness in the following circumstances:

(a) salesperson resources—the salesperson has a high level of expertise and a high level of knowledge of the customer's needs;

(b) customer buying tasks—the salesperson's customers are engaged typically in high-risk, complex, buying tasks;

(c) customer-salesperson relationship—the salesperson typically is an out supplier.

This proposition states that as the customer's task becomes more difficult, effective sales require increased salesperson expertise. This point follows directly from our discussion in Chapter 5 as well as from Wilson,[44] who argued that salespersons must expend effort during initial stages of customer encounters establishing "credibility and legitimization." Further, while expertise is important whenever the customer has to overcome obstacles, it is especially important when the salesperson is selling to the client for the first time (an out supplier).

Proposition 3. Attempting to establish similarities with a customer as a base of influence is positively related to effectiveness in the following circumstances:

(a) salesperson resources—the salesperson is actually similar to the customer in terms of characteristics related to the purchase decision;

(b) customer-buying task—the salesperson's customers are engaged, typically, in simple, low-risk purchase decisions;

(c) customer-salesperson relationship—the salesperson typically is an in-supplier.

As Weitz[45] notes:

> One method for establishing rapport is for the salesperson to create a link with the customer by identifying similarities—characteristics they have in common. Establishing similarities may increase the trustworthiness of salespeople, facilitate the exchange of information about salespeople and customers, and lead customers to feel their needs and problems are well understood. Salespeople who actually are similar to the customer will be in a better position to establish this base of influence. When customers are making simple purchase decisions, their information needs are not great. In these situations, an influence base associated with getting the customers to identify with the salesperson will be more effective than an expertise base of influence.

Thus, for simple decisions that require little cost, the salesperson is advised to create an image of similarity and work on maintaining rapport with the customer; in other contexts the salesperson needs to establish an image of expertise.

c. Proposition concerning the use of influence techniques.

Proposition 4: The use of closed as opposed to open influence techniques is more effective under the following circumstances:

(a) Customer-salesperson relationships—

1. the salesperson typically is more powerful than his or her customers;

2. the level of conflict between the customers and the salesperson is high;

3. the salesperson typically does not anticipate future interactions with the customer.

Weitz argues that open influence tactics are probably more effective when both the customer and supplier are highly involved in the sell, and when the buyer-seller relationship is positive. On the other hand, salespersons have to resort to closed, manipulative tactics when relations involve some element of conflict—as when the salesperson desires to win out over the customer. In such contexts, the salesperson desires to make a profit from the one sale and forgo future potential sales. The stereotypical "used-car salesperson" is a good example of this type of context.

d. Proposition concerning control of the sales interactions.

Proposition 5. Attempting to exert control over the sales interaction is related to effectiveness in the following circumstances:

(a) customer's buying task—customers are engaged in ambiguous purchase decisions;

(b) customer-salesperson relationship—

1. future interactions between customers and the salespersons are not anticipated;

2. the salesperson typically is more powerful than the customer.

There is considerable evidence that high-pressure selling fails to sell because buyers experience psychological reactance,[46] and it is recommended that low-pressure selling related to increased sales when the customer is informed and knowledgeable, and when continued goodwill is important. Thus, salespersons may run the risk of attempting to control the interaction when they believe that the customer may be an easier "mark" who is uncertain, less powerful, and who is not likely to come back again. Again, sales of automobiles may be used as an example. If we take the opening bid offered by automobile salespersons as one of several ways in which to control the interaction, it is interesting to note that black females, as a demographic group, receive the highest price quotation when they bid on a new car.[47] Why? While several interpretations are available, one interpretation is that females know less about cars than do males, and that black females may have less access to blue-book figures on cars and are less likely to argue strongly for the car. Thus, in a 1974 study, a black female was quoted, on the average, the price of $4459.15 for a car, a white female $4330.90, a black male $4348.00, and a white male $4368.10. Bargaining "tough" may counterbalance or offset such a bias.[48]

In Weitz's model, if one works for a reputable company, has a well defined product with no competition, and has positive relations with a client, sales are relatively straightforward and easy; one needs to emphasize expertise if the buyer has a difficult task and the client is a first-time client, and one needs to emphasize similarity when the purchasing decision is simple and one is involved with (or intends to recruit) a steady customer. Finally, when poor relations exist and sales are "competitive" (what one wins the other loses), the use of manipulation and control will be used and perhaps be successful—contexts where the buyer should beware.

Summary

In this chapter we have focused on persuasion topics relevant to the organization. In regard to managerial influence, we noted that persuaders should strive to achieve expertise and referent influence. To be effective, a number of guidelines must be followed when using rewards and punishments. We've also seen that personality differences play a strong role in responses in the organization—differences a careful communicator would keep in mind when trying to effect changes. However, there is little doubt that communication abilities, along with openness, trust, and supportive and consistent climates, are related to satisfaction, and are typically related to performance. Also, we noted that to persuade up the organization, one must take the superior's perspective—try to make the superior look good, be careful about the costs of the proposed change, and never use ultimatums or challenges. Further, we discussed causes and cures to upward distortion, discussed how to make feedback useful, and noted the features of informal networks that are relevant to persuaders, or general change agents. Finally, we outlined some of the more important concerns in buyer-seller interactions.

Footnotes

1. D. Kipnis, S. M. Schmidt, and I. Wilkinson, "Intraorganizational Influence Tactics: Explorations in Getting One's Way," *Journal of Applied Psychology,* vol. 65 (1980), pp. 444–452.

2. I. Wilkinson and D. Kipnis, "Interfirm Use of Power," *Journal of Applied Psychology,* vol. 53 (1978), pp. 315–320.

3. D. Kipnis, *The Powerholders* (Chicago: University of Chicago Press, 1976); D. Kipnis, P. J. Castell, M. Gergen, and D. Mauch, "Metamorphic Effects of Power," *Journal of Applied Psychology,* vol. 61 (1976), pp. 127–135.

4. G. F. Farris and F. G. Lim, "Effects of Performance on Leadership, Cohesiveness, Influence, Satisfaction and Subsequent Performance," *Journal of Applied Psychology,* vol. 53 (1969), pp. 490–497; C. N. Greene, "The Reciprocal Nature of Influence Between Leader and Subordinate," *Journal of Applied Psychology,* vol. 60 (1975), pp. 187–193; D. M. Herold, "Two-Way Influence Processes in Leader-Follower Dyads," *Academy of Management Journal,* vol. 20 (1977), pp. 224–237; A. Lowin and J. R. Craig, "The Influence of Level of Performance on Managerial Style: An Experimental Object-Lesson in the Ambiguity of Correlational Data," *Organizational Behavior and Human Performance,* vol. 3 (1968), pp. 440–458; H. P. Sims and C. C. Manz, "Observing Leader Verbal Behavior: Toward Reciprocal Determinism in Leadership Theory," *Journal of Applied Psychology,* vol. 69 (1984), pp. 222–232.

5. J. G. Bachman, D. G. Bowers, and P. M. Marcus, "Bases of Supervisory Power: A Comparative Study in Five Organizational Settings," in A. S. Tannenbaum, ed., *Control in Organizations* (New York: McGraw-Hill, 1968), pp. 229–238.

6. V. P. Richmond and J. C. McCroskey, "Power in Classroom II: Power and Learning," in *Communication Education* (in press); see also P. Kearney, T. G. Plax, V. P. Richmond, and J. C. McCroskey, "Power in Classroom IV: Alternatives to Discipline," in R. Bostrom, ed., *Communication Yearbook 8* (Beverly Hills: Sage, 1984), pp. 724–746.

7. M. Patchen, "The Locus and Basis of Influence on Organizational Decisions," *Organizational Behavior and Human Performance,* vol. 11 (1974), pp. 195–221.

8. P. M. Padsakoff, "Determinants of a Supervisor's Use of Rewards and Punishments: A Literature Review and Suggestions for Further Research," *Organizational Behavior and Human Performance,* vol. 29 (1982), p. 58; see also C. N. Greene and P. M. Podsakoff, "Effects of Withdrawal of a Performance-Contingent Reward on Supervisory Influence and Power," *Academy of Management Journal,* vol. 19 (1976), pp. 514–542.

9. J. J. House, "A Path-Goal Theory of Leader Effectiveness," *Administrative Science Quarterly,* vol. 16 (1971), pp. 19–30; see also R. T. Keller and A. D. Szilagyi, "Employee Reactions to Leader Reward Behavior," *Academy of Management Journal,* vol. 19 (1976), pp. 619–627.

10. R. D. Arvey and J. M. Ivancevich, "Punishment in Organizations: A Review, Propositions, and Research Suggestions," *Academy of Management Review,* vol. 5 (1980), pp. 123–132; see also H. P. Sims, "Further Thoughts on Punishment in Organizations," *Academy of Management Review,* vol. 5 (1980), pp. 133–138.

11. W. C. Redding, *Communication within the Organization* (New York: Industrial Communications Council, 1972).

12. F. M. Jablin, "Superior-Subordinate Communication: The State of the Art," *Psychological Bulletin,* vol. 86 (1979), pp. 1201–1222.

13. R. Klauss and B. M. Bass, *Interpersonal Communication in Organizations* (New York: Academic, 1982).

14. E. M. Rogers and R. Agarwala-Rogers, *Communication in Organizations* (New York: Free Press, 1976), p. 73.

15. C. Redding, *Communication within the Organization* (New York: Industrial Communications Council, 1972), cited in G. M. Goldhaber, *Organizational Communication,* 3rd ed. (Dubuque, Iowa: William C. Brown, 1983), p. 222.

16. R. L. Falcione and E. A. Kaplan, "Organizational Climate, Communication and Culture," in R. Bostrom, ed., *Communication Yearbook 8* (Beverly Hills: Sage, 1984), pp. 285–309; D. Hellriegel and J. W. Slocum, "Organizational Cli-

mate: Measures, Research, and Contingencies," *Academy of Management Journal,* vol. 17 (1974), pp. 255–280; F. Jablin, "Organizational Communication Theory and Research: An Overview of Communication Climate and Network Research," in D. Nimmo, ed., *Communication Yearbook 4* (New Brunswick, N.J.: Transaction, 1980), pp. 327–347; L. R. James and A. P. Jones, "Psychological Climate: Dimensions and Relationships of Individual and Aggregated Work Environment Perceptions," *Organizational Behavior and Group Performance,* vol. 23 (1976), pp. 95–103.

17. N. Frederickson, "Administrative Performance in Relation to Organizational Climate" (paper presented at the American Psychological Association Convention, San Francisco, September 1968); N. Frederickson, "Some Effects of Organizational Climates on Administrative Performance," Research Memorandum RM–66–21, Educational Testing Service, 1966; cited in Hellriegel and Slocum, "Organizational Climate."

18. C. L. Cooper and J. Marshall, "Occupational Sources of Stress: A Review of the Literature Relating to Coronary Heart Disease and Mental Ill Health," *Occupational Psychology,* vol. 49 (1976), pp. 11–48; D. F. Parker, "Organizational Determinants of Job Stress," *Organizational Behavior and Human Performance*, vol. 32 (1983), pp. 160–177; L. R. Smeltzer, "The Relationship of Communication to Work Stress" (paper presented to the International Communication Association Convention, Boston, Mass., 1982).

19. R. E. Kushell, "How to Reduce Turnover by Creating a Positive Work Climate," *Personnel Journal,* vol. 58 (1979), pp. 551–552.

20. J. K. Downey, D. Hellriegel, and J. W. Slocum, "Congruence Between Individual Needs, Organizational Climate, Job Satisfaction and Performance," *Academy of Management Journal,* vol. 18 (1975), pp. 149–155.

21. Jablin, "Superior-Subordinate Communication," *Psychological Bulletin,* vol. 86 (1979), pp. 1201–1222.

22. R. Pritchard and B. Karasick, "The Effects of Organizational Climate and Managerial Job Performance and Job Satisfaction," *Organizational Behavior and Human Performance,* vol. 9 (1973), pp. 110–119.

23. Jablin, "Superior-Subordinate Communication," *Psychological Bulletin,* vol. 86 (1979), pp. 1201–1222.

24. G. M. Goldhaber, *Organizational Communication,* 3rd ed. (Dubuque, Iowa: William C. Brown, 1983), p. 226.

25. C. B. Wortman and J. A. W. Linsenmeier, "Interpersonal Attraction and Techniques of Ingratiation in Organizational Settings," in B. M. Staw and G. R. Salancik, eds., *New Directions in Organizational Behavior* (Chicago, Ill.: St. Clair Press, 1977), pp. 133–178; L. Porter, R. Allen, and H. Angle, "The Politics of Upward Influence in Organizations," in L. L. Cummings and B. M. Staw, eds., *Research in Organizational Behavior,* vol. 3 (Greenwich, Conn.: Aijai Press, 1981), pp. 109–149); W. K. Schilit and E. A. Locke, "A Study of Upward Influence in Organizations," *Administrative Science Quarterly,* vol. 27 (1982), pp. 304–316.

26. Wortman and Linsenmeier, "Interpersonal Attraction and Techniques of Ingratiation in Organizational Settings," in B. M. Staw and G. R. Salancik, eds., *New Directions in Organizational Behavior* (Chicago: St. Clair Press, 1977), pp. 161–162.

27. Rogers and Agarwala-Rogers, *Communication in Organizations,* p. 93.

28. P. Krivonos, "Distortion of Subordinate to Superior Communication" (paper presented to the International Communication Association Convention, Boston, 1982); see also Goldhaber, *Organizational Communication.*

29. See, for instance, K. H. Roberts and C. A. O'Reilly, "Failures in Upward Communication in Organizations: Three Possible Culprits," *Academy of Management Journal,* vol. 17 (1974), pp. 205–215.

30. J. Athanassiadas, "The Distortion of Upward Communication in Hierarchical Organizations," *Academy of Management Journal,* vol. 16 (1973),

pp. 207–226; J. Athanassiadas, "An Investigation of Some Communication Patterns of Female Subordinates in Hierarchical Organizations," *Human Relations,* vol. 27 (1974), pp. 195–209.

31. J. W. Young, "The Subordinate's Exposure of Organizational Vulnerability to the Superior: Sex and Organizational Effects," *Academy of Management Journal,* vol. 21 (1978), pp. 113–122.

32. D. A. Level and L. Johnson, "Accuracy of Information Flows Within the Superior/Subordinate Relationship," *Journal of Business Communication,* vol. 15 (1978), pp. 13–22.

33. Rogers and Agarwala-Rogers, *Communication in Organizations,* pp. 93–94.

34. Jablin, "Superior-Subordinate Communication: The State of the Art," *Psychological Bulletin,* vol. 86 (1979), p. 1212.

35. F. M. Jablin, "Message-Response and Openness in Superior-Subordinate Communication," in B. D. Ruben, ed., *Communication Yearbook 2* (New Brunswick, N.J.: Transaction, 1978), pp. 293–309.

36. E. A. Locke, K. N. Shaw, L. M. Saari, and G. P. Latham, "Goal Setting and Task Performance: 1969–1980," *Psychological Bulletin,* vol. 90 (1981), pp. 125–152. Also consult D. R. Ilgen, C. D. Fisher, and M. S. Taylor, "Consequences of Individual Feedback on Behavior in Organizations," *Journal of Applied Psychology,* vol. 64 (1979), pp. 349–371. The reader interested in feedback should consult S. J. A. Ashford and L. L. Cummings, "Feedback As an Individual Resource: Personal Strategies at Creating Information," *Organizational Behavior and Human Performance,* vol. 32 (1983), pp. 370–398.

37. J. S. Kim and W. C. Hamner, "Effect of Performance Feedback and Goal Setting on Productivity and Satisfaction in an Organizational Setting," *Journal of Applied Psychology,* vol. 61 (1976), pp. 48–57.

38. R. V. Farace, P. R. Monge, and M. H. Russell, *Communicating and Organizing* (Reading, Mass.: Addison-Wesley, 1977); Goldhaber, *Organizational Communication;* Rogers and Agarwala-Rogers, *Communication in Organizations;* E. Rogers and D. L. Kincaid, *Communication Networks: Toward a New Paradigm for Research* (New York: Free Press, 1981).

39. Concerning statistics, see Goldhaber, *Organizational Communication.*

40. Farace, Monge, and Russell, *Communicating and Organizing.*

41. Goldhaber, *Organizational Communication.*

42. Goldhaber, *Organizational Communication.*

43. B. A. Weitz, "Effectiveness in Sales Interactions: A Contingency Framework," *Journal of Marketing,* vol. 45 (1981), pp. 85–103.

44. D. T. Wilson, "Dyadic Interaction: An Exchange Process," in B. Anderson, ed., *Advances in Consumer Research* (Cincinnati, Ohio: Association for Consumer Research, 1975), pp. 394–397.

45. Weitz, "Effectiveness in Sales Interactions."

46. See S. S. Brehm and J. W. Brehm, *Psychological Reactance: A Theory of Freedom and Control* (New York: Academic, 1981).

47. See G. L. Wise, "The Effect of Customer Demographics on Initial Price Quotation by New Car Salesmen," in P. H. Reingen and A. G. Woodside, eds., *Buyer-Seller Interactions: Empirical Research and Normative Issues* (Chicago: American Marketing Association (Proceedings series), 1981), pp. 63–74.

48. R. B. Cialdini, L. Brickman, and J. T. Cacioppo, "An Example of Consumeristic Social Psychology: Bargaining Tough in the New Car Showroom," *Journal of Applied Social Psychology,* vol. 9 (1979), pp. 115–126.

CHAPTER FOURTEEN

Social Action

The United States has always been characterized by social action. We have struggled and fought to preserve the right to make changes in our government and in our institutions. At any given time in a typical community in the United States, one group will be organizing a petition drive to put a school-millage proposal on the next ballot, and another group will be organizing to defeat any new millage. While some people in the community may be working to organize a civic club, others a student social club, a third group is working to secure a tax abatement for a new industry, and others are spending their time working for a political candidate. In each case, they are engaged in *social action, the process by which decisions are made and actions taken in communities, institutions, organizations, and countries.* In this chapter, we shall look first at some of the tactics that people have

used to achieve social changes, and we shall examine a model of social action that attempts to identify a set of strategies that seem to accompany successful social-action campaigns.

Tactics for change

The past two decades have seen the full development of strategies for changing society. Some of the tactics have been highly successful. Others seem to have produced few real social changes. In this section, we shall analyze some of the methods used, and the results secured by those methods. The reader who wishes to obtain an analysis of various tactics is referred to Saul Alinsky's book *Rules for Radicals,*[1] which presents a careful philosophical analysis of the success that varying groups have had in achieving change. Here, we look at some of the more common techniques, techniques that are not beyond the scope of the average persuasive communicator. These techniques include (a) opinion letter-writing campaigns, (b) petition drives, (c) mass demonstrations or marches, (d) mass strikes, slowdown activities, or economic boycotts, and (e) the use of the mass media.

Opinion letter-writing campaigns

In the past several decades, a number of groups have organized mass letter-writing campaigns in which each member of the organization was urged to write a letter to a congressman, a state senator, a governor, or the president of a national corporation urging some action that the group was in favor of. The tactic has been used by conservative groups, liberal groups, business groups, religious groups, community groups, and political groups. Such groups not only write themselves, but they are also urged to get their friends and neighbors to do likewise. The obvious belief is that a vote can be swayed or a decision changed if people of influence believe that a majority of their constituents favor or oppose some proposed social change.

What effect does writing a persuasive letter have on its receivers? John Bear[2] reports mixed results regarding the effects of opinion letter writing. For example, the Pillsbury Company, makers of Funny Face powdered drink mixes, originally had two flavors labeled "Chinese Cherry" and "Injun Orange." Letters to the company from a relatively small number of people protesting the perceived racial slurs in these names were apparently responsible for the company's changing the names to "Choo Choo Cherry" and "Jolly Olly Orange."

If we look at more serious questions, however, the success of mass letter-writing campaigns is less assured. Bear examined 44 separate letter-writing campaigns conducted by the John Birch Society over a five-year span. The society suffered 34 total failures, eight partial successes, and two total successes. Of these ten successes, however, no more than five could have been influenced by the efforts of the society. They just happened to be cases in which the letter-writing campaign of the society corresponded with changes that the organizations concerned had already decided to make. Thus, the society was perhaps responsible for changes in only five of 44 campaigns.

Other organizations, however, claim to have had real success with this tactic. The National Rifle Association points to its ability to organize massive letter-writing campaigns as one of the reasons for the association's success in preventing the passage of any meaningful handgun legislation. What are the characteristics that might lead to more successful opinion letter-writing campaigns? The one pointed to most often by legislators, corporation executives, and other influential people is the characteristic of *quality*. The letters written by members of the John Birch Society were relatively "low-quality" letters. Each letter was approximately the same. Each letter contained many of the same phrases that had been originally suggested by the society's publication. The recipients of such letters apparently did not pay much attention to them, regardless of the number.

On the other hand, testimony from many politicians, senators, and congressmen would indicate that individual letters, containing the writer's own language and thoughts, can be of real importance in changing attitudes and votes on crucial issues. It is not so easy to generate letters of high quality, original in nature, and stating the writer's opinions in words that are not echoed by every other writer. Without originality, the letters are not likely to be of much importance in changing the opinions or behavior of an individual or a corporation.

Petition drives

One of the most popular persuasive techniques is that of the petition drive. Petitions can be loosely divided into two types. The first is the petition attempting to *influence* potential legislation or policies. Groups have collected signatures in favor of abortion reform, for capital punishment, in favor of nuclear disarmament, and many other topics of interest. In general, petitions that merely indicate that a group of people favor or do not favor a current policy seem to have relatively little effect, except on the people who work at collecting signatures.

The second type of petition drive is more important. This is the drive to collect signatures to place an item on the ballot of a state or community. This type of drive *can* materially affect behavior. Drives have been successful in reducing the income tax, defeating additional property taxes, recalling politicians, and placing abortion reform on the ballot. Here, the persuasive communicator is working for a specific end. Success depends on whether the issue can legitimately be placed on a ballot, and whether the number of signatures collected is the right percentage. In some cases, 10 percent of the voters must sign, in others a larger percentage is required. There may be restrictions as to the wording of the petition, and restrictions on the number of signatures per page, so the reader should study his or her local and state laws.

It may be possible for a single person to successfully conduct a petition drive, but it would be exceedingly difficult to do so. Thus, it becomes imperative that a persuasive communicator first convince a number of other people of the desirability of the proposed action in order to be able to have others help with the collection of signatures. If the drive is to involve more than a single neighborhood, the necessity of careful organization becomes more important. Those people who are to collect signatures have to be provided with copies of the petition, assigned to neighborhoods, and encouraged to make sure signatures are correctly collected. Major campaigns fail because signatures were not collected with enough care, and the certifying bodies had to throw out enough signatures to invalidate the entire drive. Appropriate publicity must appear in the mass media of the community or the state during the time the drive is being conducted. Drives fail because people are suspicious about signing "just anything." Success is greater if there is appropriate publicity accompanying the petition drive.

The petition drive to advance a ballot proposal has proven to be an extremely useful weapon in the persuasive communicator's arsenal of tactics. However, it is typically only a first step. After signatures have been gathered in sufficient numbers, the group advocating a change will still be faced with the necessity of conducting a campaign to assure that an eventual ballot proposal will be successful. That subsequent campaign will involve persuasion in the same way that the original drive did, but it will be directed toward all of the voters of a state.

Mass demonstrations or marches

The mass demonstration, or march, probably saw its finest day during the late 1960s. Many antiwar demonstrations and marches were undoubtedly successful in maintaining a constant spotlight on the war in Vietnam. Although we have no way of adequately documenting the fact, they may also have been important in changing official policy toward the war (even though there was little apparent change in the conduct of the war). They were also an important weapon used by minority groups in their struggle to secure equal rights. In recent years, however, mass demonstrations have fallen off in number and in effect. The public may have become tired of demonstrations and may no longer support such persuasive tactics. For example, the farmers who drove tractors to Washington during the winter of 1979 to protest farm policies were greeted with jeers in the press and massive indifference by the rest of the population.

There is one major benefit to be derived from the involvement of masses of people in a demonstration or march. Even if the march is not successful in achieving its immediate objective, the people involved in the march usually have been convinced as to the justice or merits of the cause. They may be individuals upon whom the communicator can call for further efforts. Their behavior shows that they have become committed to the cause, and are likely to vote, or to take further actions favoring the cause.

Strikes, slowdowns, and boycotts

The strike is a time-honored method of persuasion in the United States. From the time of the great Pullman strike of 1898 through the Ford sitdown strikes of the 1930s, to the many strikes we experience today, striking has been an effective weapon. In general, it has been used to advance the economic status or improve the working conditions of workers in specific plants or industries. In similar fashion, the work slowdown or the boycott of a particular industry or product has been used to draw attention to a problem and to change the attitude of an industry or a particular corporation.

In general, strikes, slowdowns, and boycotts have been successful only when performed by the employees of a particular company, who have had the time and the motivation to carry on the strike until management is forced either to close the organization or to bargain effectively with the workers. There are only a few cases of community groups being able to successfully carry out such tactics. One notable exception came with the great "Grape Boycott" of the late 1960s when millions of people refused to buy table grapes until the grape growers in California acceded to union demands. There is no direct evidence that the boycott was actually responsible for the growers' recognizing the union, but they eventually did so, and the boycott may have been at least partly responsible.

The effectiveness of strikes, slowdowns, and boycotts as instruments for social change seems to have decreased in recent years. In 1984, for example, the same groups that organized the great "Grape Boycott" decided to organize a similar effort in protest against the California growers. The effort has proven almost a total failure. With the possible exception of a few cooperating unions,

there has been no compliance and even no attention paid to the call for a boycott.

Many people have tried to organize tax boycotts, in which they attempt to get large numbers of people to refuse to pay their taxes until a particular policy has been changed. In general, these attempts have been unsuccessful. Some publicity has been gained, but few people actually have refused to pay their taxes.

While boycotts and slowdowns depend on getting large numbers of people involved, strikes may be carried out by relatively few people. The teachers who strike a public school system may be few in number, but their actions may affect thousands of schoolchildren and a similar number of families. A strike of that kind puts real pressure on administrators, city officials, and school-board members to settle the dispute and get children back to school. The major problem with a strike today is that it depends on having significant time in which hardship can be demonstrated, and the pressures for settlement build to the point where the strikers' demands are met. Such pressures and demands are not met in a short period of time, and if the strike "drags on" for a long period of time, the public may lose interest and patience and simply demand that the strike be settled on any terms at all.

Strikes in some cases can be effective. The strike of a garbage-handlers' union, for example, is felt within the first week. Although most states and communities outlaw strikes by state and municipal employees, strikes do occur, and have been relatively successful. The secret, of course, is that the service being performed has to be one that is not easily replaced, and that is considered vital by the public.

Organization of a strike, slowdown, or boycott is difficult. It takes careful organization to get large numbers of people to engage in such activities. If the communicator has an organization that can make a strike meaningful, it may be worthwhile exploring this tactic. Ordinarily, however, only the well-organized labor organization can expect to carry out such a strategy successfully.

The mass media

As we discussed in Chapter 9, the media, particularly television, *can* be used to impart new information. The media *are* important tools for socialization. News travels fast when placed on the network evening news show. The question we raise in this chapter is not whether the media are effective in imparting information, but whether social change is likely to occur as the result of the use of mass media alone.

Atkin[3] reviews a series of "information" campaigns that were conducted primarily by use of the mass media. They were all labeled as information campaigns, although there was in each case an underlying desire to have receivers eventually change their behavior in some way. Some of the information campaigns listed by Atkin as "ineffective" included the classic Cincinnati campaign to increase knowledge about the United Nations,[4] an automobile seatbelt campaign,[5] a family-planning campaign,[6] a program on public television aimed at increasing awareness about health,[7] and a series of antidrug campaigns.[8] Each of these campaigns was conducted using public service announcements (PSA's) as the primary vehicle by which to reach the public. Some of the campaigns may have been unsuccessful because they were conducted largely on public television, and there were few viewers.

Perhaps the most successful of all campaigns utilizing the mass media has been the Stanford Heart Disease project, a multiyear study designed to get people in the California counties surrounding Stanford University to take measures to improve their health.[9] This project, still ongoing, used heavy amounts of media time to raise information levels about heart disease and potential prevention behaviors. While the Stanford study is perhaps the best example of a successful and major mass media campaign, there are other examples. A program on venereal disease was reported by Greenberg and Gantz to have increased information levels, and resulted in thousands of people visiting VD clinics.[10] Back in 1973, a mass-media campaign designed to have the entire country watch a program on driver education and take a National Driving Test was deemed highly successful. Ratings showed that over 30 million people watched the show, and over a million actually sent letters to the network.[11]

There are a number of reasons that explain the different kind of results that have been obtained. In some cases, the campaigns seemed poorly conducted, with few messages being used, and a television or radio channel that reached a small percentage of the audience. Some researchers claim success when a relatively small number of people respond to the campaign, while others hold out for larger numbers. Perhaps the most important point to be made is that the most successful campaigns were ones like the Stanford Heart Project that built follow-up into the campaign as an integral part. Individuals were urged to call in to their doctors, or take action to get additional materials, to talk to health workers, and in general to have further contacts after attending to the mass-media campaign. Alfred McAlister emphasizes the importance of follow-up efforts in his review of antismoking campaigns when he notes that having "... *interpersonal support for mediated communications*" is extremely important to mass-media efforts.[12] He points out that lasting change needs a supportive social environment. The mass media *may* be used alone to transmit information and induce behavior changes, but it is far more successful if the mass media are used in conjunction with other tactics. These combined tactics form the basis for the rest of this chapter, in our attempt to build a model for social action.

A model for social action

Social scientists such as Paul Miller,[13] Charles Loomis,[14] Harold Kaufman,[15] Charles Hoffer,[16] and Christopher Sower,[17] have all presented models attempting to delineate the stages of a successful social-action campaign. Paul Miller, for example, analyzed community health campaigns and suggested that they seem to require four stages in their development:

1. Recognition of some prior social situation.
2. Some initial activity on the part of individuals.
3. The beginning of organized sponsorship of the proposed campaign.
4. The organization of the entire community toward the mobilization of resources.[18]

Other descriptions have been suggested on the basis of investigation of social-action campaigns. Rogers and Shoemaker[19] suggest a model attempting to account for the adoption of new ideas in communities all over the world. Their model is concerned with the diffusion of innovations within social systems. Recently McGuire examined a number of theories related to conducting social-action campaigns, and suggests that attention must be paid to seven phases of such campaigns.[20] These include:

1. Reviewing the realities. McGuire suggests that some objectives just cannot be met, and that adjustments in objectives to meet the realities of the situation are necessary.

2. Examining the ethics. Any social campaign will have consequences that may be unfortunate. For example, reducing smoking will reduce the sale of tobacco. That may place hardships on those who grow tobacco, and McGuire suggests that attention to possible consequences may allow early planning to reduce negative consequences.

3. Surveying the sociocultural situation. One may aid the development of the campaign by looking for unique characteristics of the environment that might assist in message development.

4. Mapping the mental matrix. McGuire suggests that analysis of the mental states of re-

ceivers may lead to useful techniques to get people to change behavior.

5. Teasing out the target themes. In this phase, the persuasive communicator attempts to isolate the most promising themes to be used in messages.

6. Constructing the communication. This phase is the one that would make use of all of the ideas and suggestions we have advanced in our chapters on message design and construction.

7. Evaluating the effectiveness. McGuire suggests that any public-communication campaign should have evaluation built into the process. It is the only way in which to assess the effectiveness of the campaign or to be able to usefully design subsequent campaigns.

The model of social action presented here builds on the work by McGuire and by Miller, and was first used in the National Project on Agricultural Communication training workshops on communication. Since its original publication, Beal has suggested a number of changes in the construct.[21] For our discussion, we have retained the general framework suggested by Beal and his associates, but made a number of modifications based on the analyses of McGuire and others in order to generalize the model to more situations.

Stages in social action

Below, we take up the stages in social-change programs that have bean identified by a number of researchers. We first describe each stage in the process, and then examine the role that persuasive communication plays within each stage.

Stage I: The prior social situation

Some social-action campaigns fail because those interested in advocating a particular social change have forgotten to make a careful analysis of the prior social situation existing in the group or community. Consider the case of the student group that wants to introduce a new student government organization on campus. If there has recently been such a reorganization, the new proposal, no matter how meritorious, may fail until the student body has had an opportunity to ascertain the results of the recent changes.

If we consider some of the more recent social changes, it is easy to see that there had to be a set of prior conditions that facilitated the change. In Uganda, in Nicaragua, and in the Philippines, the lot of the average person had not improved, although the countries had large increases in their revenues. The perception that the revenues were going to only a few privileged people led to the revolutionary movements in those countries. The addition of information about conditions in other countries further fed the fires of revolution within each country.

Not only were there economic and political events that shaped the prior social situation in these countries, there were also communication events that played major roles. It was not the case that a single persuasive communicator, wishing to overthrow the government, began a campaign. Many people made persuasive speeches calling for change. Many people called attention to problems within those countries. If a communicator has made no analysis of prior communication and prior decisions, there can be no effective use of past experiences.

Stage 2: Defining the underlying problem

The social situation at any given time may be seen as undesirable by many residents of a community or citizens of a state. Yet simply feeling that something is wrong is only the first step in attempting to provide a remedy. At some stage, for every social-action situation in which someone seeks to induce social change into a society, a problem is responsible for the suggested change. It is important to recognize precisely what the problem is, what the dimensions are, how it may be best de-

fined, and the relationship between the underlying problem and the suggested solution.

Defining the problem is not always easy. Just what is the underlying problem that causes an extremely high rate of unemployment for black teenagers in Detroit? Is the problem caused by the lack of training of these youths, or by inflation, or the school system, or an economic recession? There are a number of different causes for the underlying problem, but if any solution is to be proposed, the different causes must be identified and clearly defined.

Frequently, groups, institutions, and communities cannot recognize their own problems. It may be necessary for someone from outside the particular social system to define the nature of the problem. Companies hire outside experts, groups bring in consultants, and communities invite government teams or citizen panels to inspect their operations and define the nature of the problems the community faces.

This stage in social action usually involves some definition of the nature of the problem, some indication of the seriousness of the problem for the group, some tentative selection of desired goals, and at least some decisions as to the appropriate lines of action to be taken. This does not mean that further changes will not be made as time goes on. This early recognition of a problem, however, is usually responsible for the suggestions advanced.

Stage 3: Locating relevant groups and institutions

For every problem that may be identified within a community, there will be some people who are directly affected by the problem, others who are less affected, and still others that seem not at all affected. A careful campaign will attempt to identify all the groups that will be affected by a proposed change, and the ways in which they might be affected. If groups are overlooked, or bypassed, the communicator may find at a later stage that these same groups are in active opposition to the project. Overlooking relevant groups has occurred frequently in situations involving new housing developments or rezoning problems. A developer will make plans for a large, new housing project, and take the plans directly to the planning commission or the city council for approval. Neighbors hear about the proposal, and immediately oppose the proposal on the grounds that it might affect their own property. If the developer had involved the neighbors from the beginning, the opposition might have been avoided. Care taken in the beginning of the campaign may prevent this later opposition, and help solidify the entire community behind the proposed change.

Stage 3 is not a stage in which much active, overt persuasion is going on. It is primarily an information-gathering phase in which the communicator prepares for the future. There may be some minor need for interpersonal persuasion while locating relevant people and groups, but there will be little need to engage in mass persuasive efforts. The groups located in stage 3 are those that will eventually become the groups to which later persuasive efforts are going to be addressed.

Stage 4: Using initiating sets

Very few social changes are begun and carried through to completion by a single individual. Generally, an idea must be accepted by many other people before the social change can be expected to take place. In looking at examples of induced social change, researchers have noted that the early period is characterized by the formation of a number of small groups of individuals who are in agreement with the aims of the proposed change and who can be used to contact other individuals and groups. These small groups have been called "initiating sets," and their role is to instigate communication with other relevant individuals.

There may be only a single group of people serving as an initiating set, or the proposal may require several groups of people who can be persuaded to serve as initiating sets. These groups may have different reasons for joining the first group, and there may be varying numbers within

each group. In all likelihood, the individuals with whom the idea originated will be part of one of the initiating groups. Each of these groups will fulfill *consultations*, *problem definition*, and *contact* functions within the campaign.

The role of the persuasive communicator in the initiation stage is easy to see. Persuasive communication is necessary in order to reach the prospective members of the initiating sets. The communicator will engage in what McGuire referred to as "Mapping the Mental Matrix." The communicator will contact members of the community that seem likely to be supporters of the project, and then engage in persuasion to convince them to become active members of the program or project. It is essential that the source engage in careful analysis of the individuals selected in order to attempt to ascertain just what messages might be persuasive to them.

It is necessary to emphasize personal contact because forming the initiating set is so important that the change agent will wish to select set members carefully. The communicator may have to approach a number of community groups either through persuasive speeches made to members of the groups, or through written or televised messages designed to elicit support. The communicator will want to approach groups that seem relevant to the situation, since the chances of attracting interested members from relevant groups is high.

One might think that finding interested people to help solve social problems is easy, but evidence suggests that this task is usually one of the hardest ones. There may indeed be a number of people interested in a set of ideas, but moving those people from the interest stage to an involvement stage is not easy. Most people do not want to get involved until they see everyone else involved. Leaders in a community frequently do not want to get involved because they are afraid of losing credibility if the idea proves to be a poor one. Persuasive communicators may feel inclined to "go it alone," but experience suggests that this is usually impossible. There are few situations where a single person has been able to accomplish meaningful social change within an organization or society.

Stage 5: Using the power base

Within every community, within every organization, company, or institution, there are certain individuals who hold authority over new ideas. If they reject an idea, the probability is that the idea will fail. If they are willing to give their blessing to the proposal, the probability of acceptance by the rest of the community increases.

We can refer to these key people as *legitimizers*. One of their major functions is to improve or disapprove of proposals for social change. Paul Miller studied a group of these legitimizers in Lansing, Michigan.[22] There were 40 members from a number of different groups, but they had many attributes in common. All of the 40 knew that they were influential persons. The majority were over 50 years of age. They tended to belong to many different organizations, an average of over 13 organizations each. The influential person either was active or had been active in each of the organizations, active in the sense that he was responsible for major policy decisions within the organization. Over 80 percent had attended college. Each of them held or had held a position in a company or a governmental body that could be described as having high prestige. The characteristics we have cited might change slightly from community to community, but these are the kinds of individuals who form the power base in a community.

The role of legitimizers is a peculiar one. They are seldom active in the early stages of a social action campaign. They do not make speeches in favor of the proposal. They do not write letters to the newspaper, and they frequently ask that their name not be associated with the new idea. They may not want to give a formal approval to a new proposal. Yet they can effectively block the adoption of a new idea by saying "No." If legitimizers do come to agree that the proposal is a desirable one, the way may seem miraculously cleared for the future operations of the change agent.

A power base depends on two kinds of people. The first type is the *formal* legitimizer. This is an individual with the legal or appointed power of decision making. The mayor, chief of police, and president of a university are all individuals who may be formal legitimizers. Their role is to examine new proposals and lend the weight of their office to their acceptance or rejection. For example, a group of students in one midwestern university town wanted to organize a fireworks display for a Fourth-of-July celebration. The proposal seemed to receive general acceptance from various city and university officials. When the plan was submitted to the chief of police, however, he said "No." He pointed out the difficulties of controlling traffic and the possibility of fire. A proposal may die because of a single negative statement from a formal legitimizer with specialized authority within the group to be affected by a proposed idea.

The second type is the *informal* legitimizer. Informal legitimizers are much like opinion leaders. They may not hold any office that would give them control over a proposal, they might not even be extremely well known, but if such informal legitimizers are not consulted in some way and their acquiescence secured, the proposal is likely to fail. In a university, the president and other top officials are the formal legitimizers, but there may be several long-term faculty members who serve as informal legitimizers. Without consultation and agreement from those faculty members, the proposal is likely to fail.

Regardless of whether we are talking about formal or informal authority figures, the process of legitimization is perhaps the most important in social action. The legitimization stage can seldom be bypassed successfully. In recent years, many groups have sought to bypass formal authority and take their message directly to "the people." At first, it may appear that such tactics have been successful. But if you look at what happens after the people have been stirred up, too frequently it is the case that the actual program is worked out by the normal people in authority, and the end result is a bypassing of the change agent, not the authority figures. Thus changes are minimal, and made within the original groups and institutions. People interested in change must learn that legitimizers, both formal and informal, are where they are because they have their finger on the public pulse and are able to predict and act in ways the rest of the public will accept and emulate.

Before we move on to the next stage, we should note that initiating-set members may also be formal or informal legitimizers. This is not always the case since the functions are different. In situations where the social institutions involved in the proposed change are hierarchically arranged, some individuals within the organization may be members of an initiating set as well as being legitimizers whose formal approval is sought. This situation illustrates the difficulties of making clear distinctions between various parts of the social-action process. We emphasize the *functions* that need to be performed, and these will always remain.

Stage 6: Getting the word out

In order to induce social change within a community or institution, knowledge about the problem must move at some time from the stage of being known to only a small group or groups to a stage where the project becomes known to all the people who will be affected by it. This is particularly true in situations where there has to be an eventual vote on the proposal. This means that at some point, information about the proposal will have to be *diffused* to that portion of the population or group that previously has not heard about it. Those groups of individuals who engage in diffusion of information can be referred to as *diffusion sets*. As in the case of initiating sets, there may be one or several diffusion sets.

Members of a diffusion set are characterized by:

1. The access they have to many people or groups of people;
2. The abilities they have in persuading and transmitting information;
3. The amount of time they have to engage in diffusion activities;
4. The organizational abilities they possess that can be directed toward diffusion.

Members of a diffusion set might include local ministers, newspaper and broadcast personnel, the secretary of the chamber of commerce, and officers in local civic organizations. Each of these individuals, by virtue of the position they hold and the skills that they have developed, may be qualified to become a member of a diffusion set.

The role of the persuasive communicator in the diffusion stage is analogous to the role in forming initiating sets. Diffusion-set members are people who have agreed to the principles behind the proposed change, and are willing to talk to others about it. The change agent will have to first persuade the potential diffusers of the merits of the proposal. It may be that people who have already been convinced, and are initiators, will be willing to work extensively to accomplish the diffusion task. In addition to convincing potential members of the necessity for the proposed change, the change agent will have to supply them with information about the proposal.

We should note that many diffusion programs fail because the persuasive communicator may have selected an appropriate diffusion set, but then failed to follow up on the even more important task of making sure that all members of the set are informed about the problem, its definition and dimensions. Diffusion cannot be accomplished with willing but uninformed people.

Stage 7: Defining the need for a change

Defining the need begins when the process of social action is first started. As the initiating sets are formed, the legitimizers contacted, and the diffusion sets made, the persuader will have to explain through persuasion why the change is desirable. Change almost never occurs in the absence of a feeling that there is a need for the change. Why should I vote for increased taxes, if I do not understand what the additional money is going to be spent for?

Defining need must go beyond convincing the key members of a campaign. Eventually everyone who will have to vote on the issue, or decide on the issue, will have to be convinced of the merits of the proposal. This means that at some time it will be necessary to convince the general public of the necessity for the change. This is one of the functions to be assumed by the diffusion sets, or you may find that you can work with subgroups of the general public but that others can be reached only through the mass media.

Basic education. For social changes that are new or that might be considered "far out," a campaign to educate the public up to the point where it can accept the new idea may be necessary. For example, in underdeveloped countries, we know that spraying puddles of water to eliminate mosquitoes will help to eradicate malaria, but if villagers do not know that mosquitoes carry malaria, or even know that germs and viruses cause disease, it may be difficult to obtain cooperation in a spraying program.

Demonstration or trials. Nothing is quite as persuasive as seeing a successful demonstration of a new idea. Obviously, a city cannot build a trial civic center in order to see whether it is a good idea, but it can put on a series of teenage dances in an unused building in order to show that there are uses for a civic center. It can also send groups of citizens and officials to other communities that have such facilities in order to report on their success. Of course, a demonstration must be successful if it is to prove persuasive.

Questionnaires or surveys. We tend to think of ourselves as a nation of people who will always side with the underdog. Actually, there is more evidence to suggest that the majority of the public waits until a trend seems to appear before agreeing with a proposition. The use of a well-designed

questionnaire and adequate survey techniques may produce results that can be used to persuade "fence sitters" to accept the proposed change.

The spirit of competition. The spirit of competition is a strong motivating force for many groups in the United States. We frequently talk about "keeping up with the Joneses" when describing the motivations of an individual. On a community or institutional level, the competition motive can be evoked by pointing to a similar community or institution that has adopted a particular change as a valid reason for your community to do the same. Institutions in our society seem to have a drive to have everything that the next institution has. Almost all cities have Little League baseball diamonds and programs. Many of these programs have been established at the instigation of leaders who did not wish "Othertown" to be better than "Ourtown."

Part of this strategy is to suggest that a change must be made in order to provide parity with another institution. Faculty argue for raises on the basis of comparisons of their salaries with the salaries of others. Students argue for higher grades by comparing average grades in one school to those in another. In order to be persuasive, however, comparisons must be meaningful. To argue that a city of 25,000 inhabitants needs the same budget as a town of 100,000 is not very persuasive. Comparison among comparable entities, however, is an effective technique.

Development committees. Many communities have citizens who form groups known as "program-development committees," or "planning boards," or "citizens' advisory boards." Frequently, the function of such groups is to diffuse information, with a formal seal of approval, to the remainder of the community. The change agent can go to such groups with proposed changes and use the group as a diffusion set. When the community does not have such a group, the change agent may find it helpful to organize one.

There is some risk in using an already established program-development committee as a diffusion set charged with defining the need of programs for a community. The risk arises from the fact that a committee already given some formal authority may decide to make major changes or modifications in the ideas advanced by the change agent. Such changes might work in the direction of improving the proposal, but they might also result in changes not desired by the change agent. Once given to such a committee, however, the change agent is bound to accept the results as they emerge from the committee. In 1983, the newly-elected governor of Michigan, James Blanchard, appointed such a "Blue-Ribbon" committee to study the higher education system in Michigan and make a report to him regarding that system. The committee had hearings for a year, and finally issued a report calling for larger expenditures for higher education in general, and specifically recommended that the four research-oriented universities be given a differential amount of the increases. The Blue-Ribbon commission's report received wide publicity, and millions of people in the state were made aware of the serious problems facing higher education in the state. It is probably also the case that the steps recommended by the commission are steps similar to those that the newly elected administration would approve of. But recommending more government spending is never popular. Being able to point to the commission of respected community and state leaders and say, "See what these fine people say about our higher-education system," takes political pressure from the governor and the legislature, and allows them to vote for more money in what is now a popular cause.

Channeling complaints. This technique has been widely used in social-action campaigns. Within any community there are always individuals who voice some dissatisfaction with the current state of affairs. They may object to current school programs, the lack of intramural facilities on a college campus, or the lack of a lunch counter in a factory. Complaints seem to be a natural part of society, and complaints can frequently be *chan-*

neled to suit the desires of the persuasive communicator. An example will help clarify this technique. Imagine that you are the president of a local theater group. Although you have an active group, the facilities that you use for your productions are totally inadequate. They are small, cramped, and not always available. After surveying the situation, you decide that the best solution is to build a new civic center that will have facilities for theatrical productions. In order to obtain the necessary funds, you will need the help of a large segment of the population who will have to support a bond issue. At this point, you are going to be able to start "channeling gripes." You find that there are some citizens who are complaining that teenagers have nothing to do in the town, and are getting into trouble. You point out to those people that the new civic center can be used for teenage dances and other activities. You go to the conductor of the local symphony, who has been complaining that there is not a decent place to perform, and suggest that your proposal will help meet the needs of the symphony. You go to the local chamber of commerce, whose members have been complaining about the lack of business, and talk about the number of jobs that will be created by the building of a new civic center.

To each of these people or groups, the persuasive communicator has indicated that a prior problem or complaint may be alleviated by adopting the social change desired by the communicator. This technique has proven to be a valuable one.

Use of past programs. We indicated earlier that social change takes place against a backdrop of prior social situations. The past social situations will undoubtedly have produced a number of programs designed to solve past problems. Frequently, the persuasive communicator can use past actions as a framework for future actions. In fact, sometimes the actual organizations developed in the past can be used as the framework for new programs. For example: A group of students wish to have students participate in evaluating faculty performance. They might point to the prior addition of students to faculty committees on an ad hoc basis as a justification for their ideas, suggesting that the proposed change is not a far-out proposal, but simply an extension of past policies.

This technique works because many people are afraid of the new and the novel. They worry about radical social change, and attempt to resist it. If a proposal can be attached to an old, established institution or program, however, the potentially radical nature of the proposal is diffused, and the proposal becomes "progress" and not "revolution."

Readiness to exploit a crisis. Social action is not an automatic process through which any new idea is easily introduced into an institution, community, state, or nation. Frequently, a change agent *will* get the most influential people in agreement. Initiating sets and diffusion sets *will* be established and be working. A number of people *will* become interested in the idea, and the appropriate legitimizers will have indicated support for the proposal, but the bulk of the population simply remains uninterested, and the proposal languishes as a result of massive disinterest.

This situation should not mean a complete abandonment of the idea. Rather, a waiting game may have to be played in this situation, with the people advocating change ready to move when conditions change. Sometimes, the occurrence of a crisis within the community or society will make it possible to introduce a new idea successfully. In Indiana, for example, a group of people had been suggesting changed safety regulations for a number of years. Their proposals included suggested changes in the location of fire exits and in the regulations regarding the ways in which doors should open in public buildings. The group had been unsuccessful in getting the changes adopted by city officials or the state legislature. Then a theater fire occurred in which a number of people lost their lives. The group was ready. They immediately reintroduced their proposals and were successful in getting them adopted almost immediately. They had taken advantage of a crisis.

No one should wait for a theater fire in order to introduce some new legislation. Nor does anyone wish to manufacture a crisis in order to get ideas across, but the good change agent is always ready to exploit a crisis when it occurs and to make a persuasive link between the crisis and a proposed program. The motivating principle behind this stage in the social-action process is that people who feel something is needed to make life better are more willing to take some action or agree to a new idea. The person who sees no need for a change is a contented person and very difficult to reach through persuasion.

Stage 8: Obtaining a commitment to action

In earlier chapters, we pointed out the strong link between an individual's public commitment to an action and his eventually taking that action. Persuasion is far more likely to be successful if the individual has been asked to make a public commitment to some action. There is ample evidence, from research and past social-action campaigns, to demonstrate the necessity of obtaining public commitments from those individuals who are going to be needed to make any program a success. Commitment may take several forms. It may be merely an agreement in support of the change agent. It may be an agreement to vote for a bond issue, or it may involve a pledge of money or a promise to work in the campaign. Churches planning a building program usually collect pledges from their members ahead of time. They have learned the hard way that mere agreement on the need for a new church is not sufficient to justify breaking ground.

It is certainly the case that individuals may fail to live up to even those promises to which they have publicly committed themselves. In the previously cited research studies there were significant numbers of people who did not live up to their commitments, but the research also shows dramatic differences between those who had committed themselves and those who had not. (See Chapter 10.)

Stage 9: Defining goals

For many reasons, it is a bit unfair to place this stage so late in our analysis of social action. Identifying and defining goals is something that occurs throughout the social-action process. The originator of an idea has goals in mind when the idea first occurs. The members of the initiating sets and the diffusion sets have goals when they agree to join the campaign. Legitimizers have goals when they agree to a project. We discuss it here because of its importance when considering the larger public that will be affected by a proposed change. When a proposal cannot be placed in operation without the cooperation of large sections of the public, it is essential that those goals relevant to that public be identified and defined.

It may seem unnecessary to discuss this function separately, since varying goals will have been set by those interested during the process. Nevertheless, studies of successful social-action campaigns seem to indicate that if future success is to be secured, the various social systems that will be affected by a change must undertake the process of developing a set of goals for themselves, or must accept a set of goals offered to them by the change agent. It is important to note that various groups may agree to quite different sets of goals that can be accomplished by a particular proposal. For example, consider the case of the community contemplating the development of a mass transportation system. Members of the city department concerned about street maintenance may find the proposal desirable since it contributes to the elimination of heavy traffic from automobiles, and thus to cheaper maintenance activities. Members of a model-cities board in the same city probably are not much concerned about street maintenance. They see the transportation system as an effective way of allowing their constituents to get to jobs in the suburbs, thus raising the quality of life for the citizens in the neighborhoods with which they are concerned. Local labor unions see the system as a source for new jobs, and that fits in with their overall goals. The change agent must be able to analyze the relevant groups in the larger community and show them that the proposals will help meet some of their goals.

Goals may be explicitly stated in a step separate from the definition of a need, or they may be more effectively included as a portion of the persuasive messages that help to define the need. Regardless of how such an identification and definition occurs, social-action campaigns show that this function is an important one.

Stage 10: Agreeing on the methods

Many social-action situations involve the possibility of using more than one solution to the original problem. Consider the situation in which a college campus is faced with a sudden increase in vandalism and theft from dormitories. Once the decision has been made that a problem exists, and that some steps must be taken to alleviate the situation, there will remain the problem of deciding exactly how the problem is best solved. Additional police could be hired. The campus could be closed to all outsiders. A system of self-locking doors could be installed so that rooms would be automatically locked when the student leaves the room. Any of these methods could possibly serve as a deterrent to additional theft, but from the standpoint of the students who are to be served, each of them is not equally desirable. And from the standpoint of the administration that has to administer and fund any solution, not all solutions are equally desirable. At some point in the social-action process, the relevant groups will have to make decisions regarding the methods to be used to solve the problem.

In actual campaigns, there frequently seems to be a blurring of the stages from defining a need through securing commitment and the formation of goals and methods to be used. The persuasive communicator can sometimes accomplish several of these tasks in the same message or in only a few messages. Individuals who agree with the message received from a diffusion set suggesting the need for some action are also likely to agree that a specific set of methods is the best way to accomplish those goals. The fact that these steps are not easily separated in practice should not lead us to ignore any of the functions. It has happened in many campaigns that the people responsible for the idea do obtain general agreement from a group of receivers, and then think that the work is done. The result is that the community fails to implement the idea while arguing over the methods to be used, and the problem is never solved.

Stage 11: Constructing a formal plan of work

Whenever someone gets an idea for a change in an institution, community, or society, there are going to be steps that will be necessary for implementing the idea. Perhaps a law will need to be changed, a zoning change made, money raised, or land bought. In most cases, the persuasive communicator, however, will be spending much of the time in the early parts of a campaign in securing the necessary cooperation from those groups and individuals who will be involved in the initiation, diffusion, and legitimization phases of the campaign. There is typically little time devoted to the details of a plan of action. Nevertheless, when the larger public has finally committed itself to the idea, when a vote has been taken, there does have to be a formal *plan of work* detailing the steps that have to be followed if the idea is finally to be implemented.

In Michigan, a group was successful in getting an issue on the ballot to raise the drinking age from 18 to 21 years of age. The ballot proposal passed by a comfortable margin. After the election, however, it was discovered that the petitioners had failed to specify any penalties for the possession or use of alcohol by minors. Thus, there was no formal plan of work to implement the new constitutional provision. As a result, some communities passed ordinances that treated possession of alcohol by a minor much like a parking violation, with minimal fines of $5 or less. Clearly, this is not what the originators of the petition drive had in mind when they started their campaign. If a plan of action had been decided upon

before the vote, and included in the petition, there might have been some opportunity to have the action steps closer to the wishes of the original change agents.

The formal plan of work will include decisions about financing, operational steps to be taken in implementation, the time sequence that has to be followed, and most important, the specific tasks that each individual or group associated with the implementation will have to perform.

Stage 12: Formally launching the program

If all has gone well in a social-action campaign, it will eventually be introduced and started. Many social-action programs will include a formal *launching* ceremony as a part of the project. A bottle of champagne is broken over the hull of a new ship, the mayor and the city council dig the first shovels of dirt for the new civic center, and the hospital has an open house to show off its new X-ray facilities. There will be some formal, public recognition of the beginning of a proposed social change.

Stage 13: Action steps

For minor social changes, the actual steps to be taken will have been carefully described in the formal plan of work, and the change agent need only follow the plan of work that has been developed. For major social-action programs, however, it may be that the plan of work merely cites a sequence of programs to be followed rather than a set of details for each separate action step necessary. In such a complex system, one action step will be followed by an evaluation and then by a series of decisions concerning the next step to be undertaken. It may also happen that in a complex set of programs, completing one step will lead to radical changes in future plans, and the entire social-action process will have to be started all over again.

The number and complexity of the actions that might be involved in complex kinds of social-change projects require detailed kinds of plans and the flexibility to make changes in those plans. The model we have outlined is appropriate to large-scale social-action projects, but everyone should realize that all progress, no matter how small, is made through the efforts of people working together to make the world a better place in which to live. Our own efforts and our own ideas may be small, but if we do become better communicators, our ideas will broaden and our efforts will have to be increased. In complex social-action situations, the change agent and the persuasive communicator play a special role. They must take care to keep all the relevant social systems informed of the progress of the campaign. Failure to keep up the interest of the public in a complex campaign may result in disinterest that can prevent the rest of the plan from being adopted.

Stage 14: Evaluation

The evaluation stage has been placed last, but evaluation is not really a single stage. Evaluation will occur at frequent intervals during the entire social-action process. Decisions are made, and changes are suggested. An idea is proposed, and it is evaluated by everyone who comes into contact with the idea. Evaluation is not always formal in nature. Any of the individuals involved in social action, whether it is the person who originated the idea, those involved in legitimizing the proposal, or the people charged with diffusion, will be making evaluations. Any individual who decides that the campaign is not progressing well, or that it is not accomplishing what it should accomplish, may withdraw support or suggest modifications.

In addition to these informal evaluations, however, there is a definite place for formal evaluation of the effects of a campaign. A formal evaluation is one way of finding out whether a change that has been introduced is actually accomplishing what it was intended to accomplish. Such an evaluation may also indicate the next steps to be taken in a complex series of social changes. Evaluation ought to be built into any proposal for planned social change.

The functions to be completed for any evaluation of a social-action campaign include:

1. Obtaining an agreement on campaign goals;
2. Evaluating the degree to which goals were accomplished;
3. Evaluating the adequacy of the planning that went into the campaign, with particular attention to the adequacy of the plan of work;
4. Evaluating the efficiency of the groups involved in the campaign, with particular attention paid to the talents that might have been uncovered during the campaign;
5. Assessing the adequacy of the communication structure and methods used during the campaign; and
6. Measuring the degree to which the change actually met the needs that were established at the beginning of the campaign.

Evaluation efforts can be complex, and consume thousands of dollars, as when the federal government wants to test a new drug that has been proposed. But evaluation can be simple in most cases, and consist of one or more people attempting to answer the kinds of questions posed above.

While evaluation concentrates on the proposed change, a successful project tends to bring credit to the change agent. It may increase credibility for future ideas. An evaluation will frequently identify and credit the persuasive communicator in ways that would not occur if an evaluation had not been done. Evaluation, then, helps in planning for future efforts, identifies the strong and weak elements of a program, and allows us to give credit, or blame, where credit or blame is due. It is an essential part of the social-action process.

Summary

The social-action model that has been described here is obviously only a construct. It cannot be followed blindly. It is not a foolproof scheme for changing the hearts and minds of men. In actual practice, the change agent will have to take into account local conditions, and adapt the model to those conditions. Nevertheless, use of this model has resulted in a number of highly-successful, social-action campaigns. Several years ago, a small group of students, townspeople, and local ministers established an organization to aid the victims of a war in Bangladesh. Their goal was to conduct a national drive to collect millions of dollars for the victims of the war. The plan they eventually evolved was based largely on the social-action construct we have discussed at length. And the program was a success. They eventually had workers all over the United States volunteering their efforts, and millions of Americans contributing funds for their project. This was *planned* social change, change that could not have come about without the efforts of persuasive speakers, campaign workers, and all of the other people and resources that a major campaign takes.

Footnotes

1. S. D. Alinsky, *Rules for Radicals* (New York: Random House, 1971).

2. John (Klempner) Bear, "People Who Write In: Communication Aspects of Opinion-Letter Writing" (Ph.D. dissertation, Michigan State University, 1966).

3. C. K. Atkin, "Mass Media Information Campaign Effectiveness," in R. E. Rice and W. J. Paisley, eds., *Public Communication Campaigns* (Beverly Hills: Sage, 1981), pp. 266–279.

4. S. Star and H. Hughes, "A Report on an Educational Campaign: The Cincinnati Plan for the United Nations," *American Journal of Sociology,* vol. 55 (1950), pp. 389–400.

5. L. S. Robertson, "The Great Seat Belt Campaign Flop," *Journal of Communication,* vol. 26 (1976), pp. 41–45.

6. J. R. Udry, *The Media and Family Planning* (Chapel Hill: University of North Carolina Press, 1974).

7. A. McAlister, "Antismoking Campaigns: Progress in Developing Effective Communica-

tions," in R. E. Rice and W. J. Paisley, eds., *Public Communication Campaigns* (Beverly Hills: Sage, 1981), pp. 91–104; N. Maccoby and D. S. Solomon, "Heart Disease Prevention: Community Studies," in R. E. Rice and W. J. Paisley, eds., *Public Communication Campaigns* (Beverly Hills: Sage, 1981), pp. 105–125.

8. G. Hanneman, "The Medicine Man Message" (Los Angeles: University of Southern California, Annenberg School of Communication, 1977); F. R. Smart and D. Fejer, "The Effects of High and Low Fear Messages about Drugs," *Journal of Drug Education,* vol. 4 (1974), pp. 225–235; D. Schmeling and E. Wotring, "Agenda Setting Effects of Drug Abuse Public Service Ads," *Journalism Quarterly,* vol. 53 (1976), pp. 743–746.

9. N. Maccoby and D. S. Solomon, "Heart Disease Prevention: Community Studies," in R. E. Rice and W. J. Paisley, eds., *Public Communication Campaigns* (Beverly Hills: Sage, 1981), pp. 105–126.

10. B. S. Greenberg and W. Gantz, "Public Television and Taboo Topics: The Impact of VD Blues," *Public Telecommunications Review,* vol. 4 (1976), pp. 59–64.

11. H. Mendelsohn, "Some Reasons Why Information Campaigns Can Succeed," *Public Opinion Quarterly,* vol. 37 (1973), pp. 50–61.

12. A. McAlister, "Antismoking Campaigns."

13. P. A. Miller, "The Process of Decision Making Within the Context of Community Organization," *Rural Sociology,* vol. 17 (1952), pp. 153–161.

14. C. P. Loomis, "Toward a Theory of Systemic Social Change," in *Rural Sociology in a Changing Society.* Proceedings of the North Central Rural Sociology Committee Seminar (Columbus, Ohio: Ohio Agricultural Extension Service, Ohio State University, 1959), pp. 12–48.

15. H. F. Kaufman, "Health Programs and Community Action," Mississippi Agricultural Experiment Station, Preliminary Reports in Community Organization, no. 1, 1954.

16. C. R. Hoffer, "Social Action in Community Development," *Rural Sociology,* vol. 23 (1958), pp. 43–51.

17. C. Sower, J. Holland, K. Tiedke, and W. Freeman, *Community Involvement* (New York: Free Press of Glencoe, 1957).

18. P. A. Miller, "Process of Decision Making," pp. 153–161.

19. E. M. Rogers and F. Floyd Shoemaker, *Communication of Innovations: A Cross-Cultural Approach* (New York: Free Press, 1971).

20. W. J. McGuire, "Theoretical Foundations of Campaigns," in R. E. Rice and W. J. Paisley, eds., *Public Communication Campaigns* (Beverly Hills: Sage, 1981), pp. 66–69.

21. G. M. Beal, "Social Action: Instigated Social Change in Large Social Systems," in J. H. Copp, ed., *Our Changing Rural Society: Perspectives and Trends* (Ames, Iowa: Iowa State University Press, 1964), pp. 233–264.

22. P. A. Miller, "Process of Decision Making," pp. 153–161.

Index